"*Tiger & Phil* is the wonderfu[...] [...]e remembered for their contributio[...] [...]okreporter

"The only thing I enjoyed more than broadcasting the Tiger-Phil rivalry for over twenty years was reading all the juicy tidbits from behind the scenes by the amazing Bob Harig. Every golf enthusiast will want to dive into this."
—Jim Nantz, CBS-TV

"Bob Harig was born to write this brilliant and definitive historical document on the Tiger-Phil rivalry. After walking step for step with these two titans for decades, Harig delivers fascinating, previously untold stories about the battles that defined them. This is the ultimate insider's look at the real Tiger-Phil relationship, and at the high-stakes pursuit of golf immortality."
—Ian O'Connor, three-time *New York Times*
bestselling author of *Arnie & Jack*

"In many ways golf has never had a rivalry to match Tiger and Phil's. Tiger was a perfectionist and an icy star much like Ted Williams, and he always had that hard cold stare of high purpose. Phil was golf's version of the Leaning Tower of Pisa, creating awe from error, and he always had that paw-in-the-cookie-jar smile. They weren't so much oil and water as they were thesis and antithesis. Bob Harig writes a book we all want to read as much as we all wanted to watch them play."
—Brandel Chamblee, Golf Channel analyst,
former PGA Tour player, and author of *The Anatomy of Greatness:
Lessons from the Best Golf Swings in History*

"Tiger vs. Phil is the most delicious rivalry in sports, and Harig has been there for all of it. There's so much good stuff in here, somebody should make a movie."
—Rick Reilly, former *Sports Illustrated*
and ESPN writer and author of *So Help Me Golf*
and *Who's Your Caddy?*

"There is no one more qualified to write a book on Tiger and Phil than Bob Harig. He's probably walked more holes with them than anyone—with the *possible* exception of their caddies—and been around

for every important moment in their careers—both with one another and separately."
—John Feinstein, author of *A Good Walk Spoiled,*
The Majors, and *Raise a Fist, Take a Knee*

"The narrative is enlivened with interesting quotes from players and caddies, much golf lore, and up-close descriptions of tournaments and the players' games in action. Insider portraits tailor-made for golf enthusiasts."
—*Kirkus Reviews*

TIGER
& PHIL

GOLF'S MOST FASCINATING RIVALRY

BOB HARIG

ST. MARTIN'S GRIFFIN
NEW YORK

Published in the United States by St. Martin's Griffin, an imprint of St. Martin's Publishing Group

www.stmartins.com

Designed by Kelly S. Too

The Library of Congress has cataloged the hardcover edition as follows:

Names: Harig, Bob, author.
Title: Tiger & Phil : golf's most fascinating rivalry / Bob Harig.
Other titles: Tiger and Phil
Description: First edition. | New York : St. Martin's Press, 2022. | Includes index.
Identifiers: LCCN 2021060599 | ISBN 9781250274465 (hardcover) |
    ISBN 9781250274472 (ebook)
Subjects: LCSH: Woods, Tiger. | Mickelson, Phil, 1970– | Golfers—United
    States—Biography.
Classification: LCC GV964.W66 H368 2022 | DDC 796.352092/2 [B]—dc23/eng/20211222
LC record available at https://lccn.loc.gov/2021060599

ISBN 978-1-250-83021-0 (trade paperback)

Our books may be purchased in bulk for promotional, educational, or business use. Please contact your local bookseller or the Macmillan Corporate and Premium Sales Department at 1-800-221-7945, extension 5442, or by email at MacmillanSpecialMarkets@macmillan.com.

First St. Martin's Griffin Edition: 2023

10 9 8 7 6 5 4 3 2 1

For Jackie and Jack,
who became quite the experts
in all things Tiger and Phil

CONTENTS

· · · · · · · · · · · · · · ·

TIGER
& PHIL

INTRODUCTION

Thirty years removed from his first PGA Tour victory, Phil Mickelson returned to the scene of one of his most underrated triumphs, the Omni Tucson Resort, where in 1991, he defied history to become the last player on the PGA Tour to win as an amateur.

Mickelson was just 20 years old at the time, a burgeoning career already in the works, possessing plenty of the moxie for which he grew famous but still a junior in college at Arizona State and with more amateur glory to attain. The following year, he went on to win his third National Collegiate Athletic Association (NCAA) individual title. He had already won the U.S. Amateur. His first years as a professional were set up handsomely, due to the exemption he received for winning what was then called the Northern Telecom Tucson Open.

And yet even with such a glitzy résumé, there was no way to have any realistic expectation that he would go on to win dozens of tournaments, including six major championships, and become one of the game's greatest icons. There have been plenty of hotshot amateurs; Phil was among the rare ones to deliver on such promise.

Who could know that someone just as good—someone, as it turns out, who was better—was coming along a few years behind Mickelson?

Tiger Woods was 15 then, cleaning up against the old guys at the Navy Golf Course in Cypress, California, playing off a +2.3 handicap or thereabouts and still a few months away from winning the first of six consecutive United States Golf Association (USGA) titles, an unprecedented feat that not even the great amateur Bobby Jones accomplished. But Tiger had nothing on Phil, who prior to Tiger's emergence was a local legend in San Diego as a junior player and dusted all manner of opponents.

Like Mickelson, Woods possessed more golf trophies than he could stuff into his bedroom, and college recruiters were already knocking at his door. And he added a few more before signing multimillion-dollar endorsement deals that made him set for life before ever putting a tee in the ground as a professional.

Tiger and Phil didn't know each other then, but that would soon change. The trajectory of their careers would be intertwined for the better part of three decades with Tiger, a prolific winner not seen since the days of Jack Nicklaus, and Phil holding his own and hauling in a significant share of hardware himself, despite the presence of Woods. If Tiger was Jack in terms of victories, then Phil was Arnold Palmer in the way he won and lost dramatically, while also endearing himself to the masses.

Woods challenged the all-time PGA Tour victory record set by Sam Snead and made it his mission to haul down Nicklaus' major mark, with combatants such as Mickelson treated as debris along the path to glory. While there was respect, at times there was also pettiness and standoff-ishness; their rivalry came in and out of focus as their careers endured various peaks and valleys.

Now, all these years later, things were different.

Mickelson was 50, playing in a PGA Tour Champions event at the same course where he won as an amateur, enjoying the memories, still as popular as ever—but with a cloud hovering over the proceedings.

Woods was in a Southern California hospital, recovering from surgery performed earlier in the week after a horrific one-vehicle crash that could have claimed his life. That he was reported to be alert and capable of answering texts from some of his closer golf friends was encouraging yet somber news. The accident was severe enough to put in doubt the kind of qualify of life, at age 45, Woods might have going forward. Thinking about resuming his golf career was far too distant a thought to even consider under such troubling circumstances.

The Woods-Mickelson battles of bygone days—when they often didn't get along, with Tiger many times lording over Phil—seemed inconsequential, unimportant.

At times, their rivalry was bitter, other times just banter. They needled each other and took some pointed shots, too. For a while, they never spoke, and later on, they collaborated on pay-for-play television matches, including a $9 million "winner take all" contest in Las Vegas.

Whether they were truly rivals—or even friends—might be debated on barstools until closing time and beyond. Tiger stood above the rest, his 82 victories and 15 major titles part of a résumé that elicits talk of "the best ever." Phil's 45 wins and six majors look scrawny by comparison—but of course, such a comparison is unfair. Nobody has come close to Tiger. And yet, in their era, no one else has come close to Phil. It is nearly inconceivable that anyone today could match Phil's record, let alone Tiger's.

There is no question they were two of the most popular players the game saw since the days of Greg Norman and Nick Faldo, since Tom Watson and Johnny Miller, since Nicklaus and Palmer and Gary Player, since Ben Hogan and Sam Snead and Byron Nelson.

Mickelson got fired up to play against Tiger, knowing full well the difficulty and frustration in trying to beat him. And Woods wanted to defeat no one more than Phil, knowing full well that keeping any rival beyond a flagstick length only enhanced his ability to keep dominating the game.

All of that was in the background on February 28, 2021. Surely the memories might have flooded back for Phil. If he wanted to reflect, he could look back on any number of times that the names "Woods and Mickelson" were in the golf headlines.

Maybe it was when neither could quite overcome Payne Stewart at the 1999 U.S. Open—the first time both players were in contention at the same major championship.

Maybe it was in the final round of the 2001 Masters, when Phil played his way into an opportunity to knock the Tiger Slam sideways—with Woods instead winning a fourth straight major championship.

Maybe it was the 2004 Masters, when Phil finally won his first major championship while Tiger was a rare bit player in the drama.

Take your pick: perhaps later that year when Tiger and Phil were disastrously paired as Ryder Cup partners? Or when Phil seemingly had the 2006 U.S. Open in his grasp while Tiger missed the cut for the first time in a major? Or how about in 2010 when Tiger returned to competitive golf for the first time since his own personal travails only to have Phil block his path to a green jacket?

There were other showdowns, dustups, and eyebrow-raising moments, to be sure.

Nobody ever said they needed to be buddies, and even in their late Tour years, despite appearances, they were not really close. Respect grudgingly grew between them. Appreciation for each other's accomplishments undoubtedly came into focus more as they grew older. But when they were younger? No chance. Both were striving for the same things, and Woods became known as someone who was not going to let his rivals get too close.

"When Tiger burst onto the scene so quickly and wins so much and then Phil wins 45 times, I definitely think there was a rivalry," said Mark O'Meara, who befriended Woods when he moved to his Orlando, Florida, neighborhood despite an 18-year age difference. "I can't speak to what Tiger was thinking. He was a smart kid, a smart guy. He didn't let many people into his inner circle. He wouldn't get too close to other players. He was close to me because I was like his big brother, but I wasn't really a threat—although I did beat him down the stretch a few times. But during Tiger's prime, there weren't many guys who took him down, whether it was Phil or Ernie Els or David Duval. It's not easy."

Mickelson always played nice, often complimenting Woods for what he meant to the game in general and his competitive influence on Phil in particular. He appreciated how Tiger's presence helped indirectly pad his bank account while also forcing him to get better as a golfer.

There were times when Mickelson wondered if things might have been different if there had been no Woods blocking his path. And yet, he humbly admitted that, without Tiger, perhaps Phil might not have put in the work he felt necessary to be a worthy challenger.

Although Phil had a five-year head start as a pro on Woods and won nine times on the PGA Tour by the time Tiger arrived in 1996, it didn't take long for the younger star to catch up. And, of course, there was that matter of Woods rattling off eight major championships while Mickelson was stuck on zero.

Grudgingly, there was acceptance from Woods, who acknowledged that Phil was due his level of reverence, although he never let on much publicly, always trying to keep that edge.

"Way back, Tiger was single and living in Florida; Phil was living in California with kids," said Rick Smith, who coached Mickelson for more than 10 years. "Was there a rivalry? They were living totally different lives. Everybody thought that was part of the ice between them. They didn't hardly see each other until they played. There wasn't that 'in your face' stuff going on at the time.

"I think people misunderstood it. And I think the media looked at it a little different. When Tiger worked with [coach] Butch [Harmon], we had been friends well before that. I worked for his brother Dick [Harmon] at one time. It was a good competition. A great energy. And it was very driving. I think it drove Phil. He realized, seeing Tiger, how important it was to get into shape, and Tiger was very instrumental in that."

None of that mattered following the final round of the 2021 Cologuard Classic in Arizona. In headier times, Tiger might have playfully—or perhaps behind the scenes, not so playfully—mocked Phil for the senior event and its title sponsor. (In serious times, Tiger was far more pragmatic. His father, Earl, was diagnosed with prostate cancer in 1998; and when Phil's wife, Amy, was diagnosed with breast cancer in 2009, Tiger was among those who quickly reached out.) Now, that kind of teasing would have been more than welcome, given the severity of the situation.

Mickelson explained why he was wearing red and black to show appreciation for Woods while he dealt with such serious injuries.

"Two things happened today," said Mickelson, the ASU grad in UA land. "I wore red on Sunday in honor of Tiger to let him know that the players support him and appreciate all that he's done, and I had to buy a red shirt, and of course every red shirt here has a big 'A' [for the University of Arizona] on it. I hope he knows that we're supporting him. Because that was a lot for me to do that."

Self-deprecating to a fault, Mickelson's gesture was appreciated nonetheless. Like others across the golf world on that Sunday, Mickelson was wearing red and black as a nod to Tiger. Players on the PGA Tour and LPGA Tour did as well. Tony Finau, who played in the final group with Woods as he won the 2019 Masters, even arrived at the golf course in

Bradenton, Florida, wearing his Nike cap backward—in the way that Woods often did when he entered a course. It was a gesture of respect and appreciation—and to let Tiger know they were thinking about him.

Red, of course, long ago became Woods' signature color, and he almost always wore it for final rounds or big tournaments. It dated to his junior days, and he credited his mother, Kultida, because she believed "it was my power color." Woods later cited superstition for keeping with the tradition that exists today, through his last Masters victory and when he played in a Father-Son tournament with his son, Charlie, in December of 2020.

Injuries, specifically a herniated disk, plagued Woods as he approached his forties. That allowed his own mood and temperament to soften. The struggles gave him a new gratefulness for what he accomplished and the awareness that it could soon be over. He saw himself taking a stately role, a ceremonial role, and yearned to stay close to the game through an association with the various national teams.

And after taking on duties alongside Mickelson in 2014 as part of the U.S. Ryder Cup effort, he became a vice captain in 2016 when he missed the entire year due to those back problems. He was also an assistant for the 2017 U.S. Presidents Cup team.

"Our relationship turned around 2016 when we were working together for the Ryder Cup," Mickelson said. "He was an assistant captain. We spent a lot of time on the phone. When we worked together for a common goal, it brought us closer."

It took until the 2018 Masters for the two golf legends to play a practice round together—some 20 years after they had last done so at the 1998 Los Angeles Open, where Phil rubbed it in without mercy after extracting $500 from Woods in what became more than a friendly match. Mickelson made photocopies of Woods' five $100 bills and put them in his rival's locker along with a note: "Just wanted you to know Benji and his friends are very happy in their new home."

Mickelson relished telling that story; Woods seethed. And their practice round days were done for two decades.

For much of that time, they barely played together in tournament rounds, especially in the early stages. The PGA Tour purposely kept them on opposite sides of the tee-time pairings draw, mostly for the purposes of the television window that would allow them equal airtime. That, unfortunately, kept them from playing together more often.

So of course it was a shock when they were grouped for the first two rounds of the 2018 Players Championship just a month after that practice round at Augusta National. As were Woods' words on the eve of that tournament.

"When I was trying to deal with the nerve [pain] in my back, trying to come back and trying to play, and I wasn't very good, [Phil] always texted me some very encouraging words," Woods said of the time he was away from the game in 2016–17. "On top of that, when you guys all saw how I was chipping so poorly [in 2015], my nerve and my back was not doing very good, and I was flinching a lot, he offered numerous times to help. He's one hell of a competitor and it's always a challenge to try to beat him."

Woods won more majors (15 to 6) and more PGA Tour events (82 to 45) than Mickelson. And while Mickelson never got to No. 1 in the world, he was a constant in Woods' career. On the very day Woods won the third of three straight U.S. Amateur titles in August of 1996—and just hours ahead of announcing he would be turning professional—Mickelson, then 25, moved to ninth in the world with his fourth victory of that season, his first time cracking the top 10 and securing a space atop the game he occupied for most of the next 15 years.

Tiger won early and won big as a pro and was No. 1 in the world less than a year into his career, but much of the time the guy right behind him was Mickelson, who spent eight different periods at No. 2 for a total of 270 weeks—all with Woods in the top position.

While Woods won more, one could imagine Mickelson becoming a Hall of Famer anyway. Woods was winning everything, everywhere, but in his professional era, Mickelson managed 36 PGA Tour victories, including six major championships. Mickelson is tied for eighth all-time on the PGA Tour with his 45 victories, but the 36 he captured in the Tiger era is bettered by just 11 others in the entirety of their careers.

Grouped together over the years in PGA Tour events, Woods and Mickelson were amazingly close, with Tiger holding a 19–15–4 edge in their rounds while taking 2,653 strokes to Phil's 2,677—just a 24-stroke difference over 38 rounds.

They each come from Southern California, but their backgrounds and influences are starkly different. Tiger was the son of an Army man and got his start playing on hardscrabble public courses, some of which he was denied access to due to his race; Phil was a country club kid (although he did work for his playing privileges), the son of an airline pilot whose schedule allowed him to play golf with his son. Woods' father, Earl, was a huge influence on Tiger's golf career; Mickelson's dad, Phil Sr., played a big part but was far more in the background.

This goes beyond the obvious, clichéd reasons: that Tiger is of mixed race and Phil isn't . . . that Tiger is right-handed and Phil left-handed . . . that Tiger was detached and standoffish while Phil would sign autographs until his pen ran out of ink . . . that Tiger impacted society, but Phil was often the people's choice . . . that they were teammates on Ryder Cups teams but only in two instances paired (calamitously) together.

Theirs isn't a rivalry in the classic sense. Golf doesn't really work that way. But Woods has always been aware of Mickelson, and Mickelson has certainly always been aware of Woods.

"It's been an incredible opportunity for me to play my career against him, but also been incredibly difficult," Mickelson said. "I oftentimes wonder what my career would be had he not come along, and I think it could go either way. He's brought out the best of me at times, and it's also been very intimidating and difficult to compete against his level of play."

Their relationship has run the gamut from frigid to friendly, with some epic moments along the way: that ill-fated Ryder Cup pairing; a highly publicized spat between Woods' caddie, Steve Williams, and Mickelson; Phil's deriding of Tiger's equipment; and an underlying racial bias that seemed to shift some popularity toward Mickelson despite Woods' better record.

Less than a year after their Ryder Cup debacle, Woods and Mickelson battled in what could quite easily be described as their greatest duel, an epic final round at the Doral tournament in Miami, where they were paired together in the last group, nobody caring that the first major championship of the year was still a month away.

Woods was without a major championship victory since the 2002 U.S. Open and was still in the midst of a swing change while Mickelson's game jelled when he first won the Masters a year earlier and then won twice in three starts leading into the Florida tournament.

It was setting up to be a big year in the major championships but often the showdowns on golf's smaller stages are just as compelling, and this was the tussle of all tussles, a back-nine battle that ultimately saw Woods prevail but not before watching in awe as Mickelson made a late charge at him. Spectators were in full throat, and the players reveled in the hair-raising atmosphere. "When we got to the tee boxes, my ears were ringing," Woods said.

The scene was as good as any major championship Sunday, and the raucous nature of the inspired South Florida overflow gathering rivaled any Ryder Cup. For drama, for entertainment, for highs and lows and joy and heartbreak, it was nearly impossible to beat.

Finally getting from Mickelson what he'd long expected—and perhaps wanted—even Woods could not help himself when Phil stuffed an approach shot on the back nine, setting up a birdie putt that could tie him, the crowd in full frenzy. "Great fucking shot, Phil!" Woods screamed, his words drowned out by all the cheering.

Woods won, but not before Mickelson narrowly missed holing a greenside chip for a birdie on the 18th that would have tied. "I enjoyed and loved playing against Tiger at his best," Mickelson said. "It was fun. Just don't like the result. The result sucks."

Woods won the Masters five weeks later, and thus continued the peak of their rivalry as Mickelson won the PGA Championship a few months after that. When Mickelson captured the Masters in 2006, the duo traded green jackets just as Palmer and Nicklaus did from 1962 to 1965, their rivalry seeing them dominate with championship hardware and headlines.

Much like Arnie and Jack, Phil and Tiger typically had their "sides." To many, you were a "Phil fan" or a "Tiger fan" and rarely both. That meant rooting for one at the expense of the other, not unlike Magic and Bird or the Yankees and the Red Sox or Ohio State and Michigan.

And while they might not have always gone head-to-head, they were always there, competing in the biggest tournaments, especially the major championships. In fact, it took until the 2019 Open for a remarkable statistic to emerge: for the first time in 83 major championships in which they both competed, they each missed the 36-hole cut.

Time passed, but Woods slowly developed more admiration for Mickelson as Mickelson won majors and became a competitive force. Both employed noted coach and instructor Harmon at critical points in their careers: Woods early (from 1993 through 2002) and Mickelson late (from 2007 to 2016). It was Harmon who helped Woods win eight majors. And it was also Harmon who presided when Phil upstaged Tiger at Pebble Beach in another final-round duel and again when Mickelson claimed his biggest victory at the 2013 Open at Muirfield.

Both of their caddies were iconic figures in their own right: Williams, who steadfastly protected Tiger without a care as to whom he might have offended, and Jim "Bones" Mackay, who spent more than 25 years by Mickelson's side. Later, Tiger employed Joe LaCava, who put together his own Hall of Fame career that has lasted more than 30 years.

Year after year, decade after decade, Woods had Mickelson, and Mickelson had Woods. They pursued championships and No. 1 rankings, but they also pursued each other. Their battles have had an iconic quality to them. Their respective defining shots take up much of the room on any top 10 list. And few players could verbally spar with one another like Woods and Mickelson or compete for the same endorsement real estate, which led to lucrative business holdings for both.

And what a history they produced, combining for 21 major championships and 127 PGA Tour victories, and a dozen more around the world. They were the closest thing the sport had to a rivalry in an era of dominance produced by Woods that has been nearly unprecedented.

And the hope is that it is not complete. Both will captain future U.S. Ryder Cup teams—and might even serve as underlings for each other, as they came together several years ago to serve as the backbone for a U.S. Ryder Cup committee that exists to nurture future captains and assistants. Woods has already served as a winning U.S. Presidents Cup captain—and he played on his own team, going 3–0 at Royal Melbourne in December of 2019, the best player on either side. That happened to be the first time Mickelson was not on a U.S. Ryder Cup or Presidents Cup team dating to 1993.

The assumption had always been that they would continue to play in major championships, especially the Masters, as their bodies, their skills, and their egos allowed. Woods' crash put that all in doubt, a troubling and somber thought.

For those of us who followed his career up close and walked mile after mile inside the ropes to get an incredible view of history, the speculation over whether he might recover from his latest back surgery in time to play in the 2021 Masters all of a sudden became so trivial. Questions about clubs and balls and practice routines and rivals and schedules were no longer in play. It was medical terms, police reports, and a realization that for all of Woods' accomplishments, his greatest challenge awaited.

Meanwhile, it was Mickelson who just a few months later pulled off the unthinkable, becoming the oldest major champion in the history of the game by winning the PGA Championship at age 50. It was almost as if Mickelson was going to not only enhance his legacy but also prolong the Tiger-Phil rivalry with a bit of one-upmanship that few saw coming. Even Tiger, from afar, had to tip his cap, acknowledging the remarkable accomplishment via social media.

It took until September for there to be even a glimmer of hope as it related to Woods' future, when U.S. Ryder Cup captain Steve Stricker said, "I've talked to Tiger a lot because of his ongoing rehabilitation to try to get better and to try to play golf again and this is going well. He's progressing, he's doing well, things are moving in the right direction."

Woods would not be joining the team in Wisconsin as a vice captain, and yet those words from Stricker produced the best news relayed about Woods since the day he went into the hospital.

If Tiger is to come back and take a final walk across the Swilcan Bridge on the Old Course at St. Andrews or wave to the masses on the 18th at Augusta National as so many legends of the past have done, Phil will undoubtedly be there cheering him on, too, while maybe even holding back a tear.

There was a time that such a gesture might not have seemed possible—and it is but one example of their complicated, fascinating relationship.

1

OAKLAND HILLS

Tiger Woods squinted, incredulous. He was unable to determine the exact landing point but too furious to care as his gaze quickly turned into a sharp dagger aimed squarely at Phil Mickelson.

Woods did all he could to maintain complete ambivalence about Mickelson's poorly hit shot as he stood on the back of the 18th tee, but his eyes betrayed him. "What the hell are you doing?" might have been an appropriate thought bubble, although the actual language a bit saltier.

The two most talented players in golf whose indifference toward each other was not lost on anyone in the game were paired together at the 2004 Ryder Cup, with the hope that differences would be put aside for the good of team U.S.A. in its biennial competition against Europe. It was a surprising and controversial pairing, given their uneasy relationship, the fact that they rarely, if ever, played casual golf together—not to mention the huge bull's-eye placed on the backs of the two biggest names in American golf.

It wasn't like Tiger and Phil were exchanging Christmas cards and getting together for weekend barbecues or even offering up the most benign of golf advice to one another.

And so their day as Ryder Cup teammates could not have been a bigger disaster, with the look on Woods' face portraying a venom no words could describe, their struggles in two matches together at Michigan's Oakland Hills Country Club epitomizing American incompetence that week. They were about to lose for the second time in a span of 10 hours, setting the tone for a European rout, with Tiger and Phil the biggest scapegoats, deserved or not.

Hal Sutton, the U.S. captain, was a no-nonsense former major champion who, in his own playing career, stood up to both Jack Nicklaus and Woods in capturing prestigious titles. Given the honor of leading his own U.S. Ryder Cup team, Sutton saw no reason why Tiger and Phil should not only get along but also prosper. Beating Jack at the 1983 PGA Championship gave Hal a certain gravitas, as would his showdown 17 years later when he held off Tiger to win the 2000 Players Championship. "Be the right club today!" is a phrase still uttered in celebration of his clinching approach shot to the final hole at TPC Sawgrass that held off Woods—who would go on to win three major championships that year. Sutton certainly wasn't worried about hurting anybody's feelings or how they might have viewed each other.

"When I announced they were going to be partners, the crowd roared," Sutton said in an interview 16 years later. "Everyone loved it. That is what people wanted to see."

And yet . . .

"I thought it was a very poor idea," recalled Steve Williams, who caddied for Woods for 13 of his major championships, including five Ryder Cups, and was on the bag from 1999 through 2011. "It was just bizarre. Earlier that week, Phil was practicing at another golf course, and you can imagine what Tiger thought of that.

"Whilst I get what Hal was trying to accomplish by putting two of golf's universal superstars in the same group, I don't think he consulted enough people to know whether he thought that pairing was going to be good that day. And you saw it immediately. When they went to the first tee, Phil, being a left-hander, went to the left side of the tee. Tiger was on the right. But when it comes to the Ryder Cup, guys should be standing together. Right from the first tee, you could see that wasn't going to happen."

WOODS SPENT THE MAJORITY OF HIS WILDLY SUCCESSFUL PRO career to that point swatting away any runs made at him by Mickelson, who forged his own level of brilliance and popularity while left in Tiger's immense shadow. Only a few months prior, at the Masters, Mickelson finally won his first major championship at age 33, a mystifying omission on a résumé that would grow to Hall of Fame stature. But his career achievements to that point were lacking to a level that Woods could not comprehend.

At 28, Woods had already captured eight major championships and dominated the sport unlike any other player. He wasn't keen on allowing anyone to get too close, certainly not a player he deemed to be among his major competitors. Mickelson, five years older and with more than a four-year head start in the professional game, was a huge fan favorite who signed autographs for hours on end, posed for photographs, smiled, made small talk, and generally endeared himself to the masses. There are those who believe it was done purposely to counter Woods, always the cold-blooded competitor, who typically had blinders on when navigating a crowd, a stark difference from the more accommodating Mickelson. And while he was well aware of Mickelson's talent, Woods thought "Lefty" came across soft as a golfer, his career record disappointing. Mickelson's victory earlier that year at Augusta National only put a small dent in the imposing wall Woods erected between the two golf titans.

It also left Woods quietly seething. While he grudgingly respected Mickelson's game, he didn't much like Lefty stepping up to take the hardware he wanted to horde. They were about to embark on the greatest, most intense portion of their rivalry, when they would trade green jackets, and yet both experience the highs and lows that go with the pursuit of the biggest titles.

Not helping Woods was the still-lingering taste of a poor 2004 by his standards. He won just once on the PGA Tour and was not a threat at any of the four major championships as he endured the process of retooling his swing under a new coach, Hank Haney, a relationship that would not become public for months. At the Masters, where Phil prevailed with a dramatic 18th-hole birdie to edge Ernie Els by a stroke for a gratifying and electrifying first major title, Tiger finished tied for 22nd, a third-round 75 knocking him out of any chance to contend.

And now here they were, expected to get along for this lone week, work together, put any differences aside. They might have put up a good front, especially before the cameras and even to the 10 other teammates.

But it was a big ask of Tiger and Phil. Especially Tiger, who was not close to his peers back then. That was part of his aura: keeping everyone at a rigid arm's length while letting the legend build.

OAKLAND HILLS COUNTRY CLUB HAS A LONG, STORIED HISTORY in American golf, although neither Tiger nor Phil can count much success at the venue located in Bloomfield Hills, Michigan, a suburb of Detroit.

When the 2004 Ryder Cup commenced, it had been eight years since the last big professional tournament, the 1996 U.S. Open, won by Steve Jones. Mickelson won eight PGA Tour events to that point and was competing in his sixth U.S. Open, fourth as a pro. But Mickelson was not a factor, finishing in a tie for 94th after 108 players made the cut. Woods, still an amateur and playing his second U.S. Open and just months from turning pro, wasn't much better, finishing in a tie for 82nd.

So while the venue might not have lent much in the way of positive vibes for Tiger and Phil, it certainly did for the Americans. And it was the first Ryder Cup to be played in the United States since the stirring yet controversial American victory at The Country Club in Brookline, Massachusetts, in 1999, where there was considerable unruly fan behavior, the bulk of it directed at European star Colin Montgomerie. The U.S. team overcame a 10–6 final-day deficit to post a rousing victory—and that turned out to be the only time that Woods and Mickelson played on the same winning Ryder Cup team.

In 2002, after the matches had been postponed a year due to the September 11, 2001, terrorist attacks, both sides vowed to tone down the rhetoric and have a more civil competition at the upcoming Ryder Cup being played at The Belfry in England. Europe prevailed for the third time in four Ryder Cups, with both Tiger and Phil having their moments of frustration.

Mickelson was a respectable 2–2–1 but suffered a huge upset at the hands of Welshman Phillip Price in Sunday singles, losing 3 and 2. Price, who made the 2001 team, which was locked after the Ryder Cup was postponed, was in poor form.

European captain Sam Torrance showed little faith in Price, as he sat him the first day then played him in just one of the team matches, a second-day foursome in which he and partner Pierre Fulke lost to Mickelson and David Toms 2 and 1.

With the teams tied at 8 entering the final day, the vibe was intense. European golf fans smelled opportunity, every match crucial. Noise echoed throughout the American-style course and U.S. captain Curtis Strange would have expected a victory out of Mickelson, the No. 2 ranked player in the world. Price was ranked 119th and was "thrown to the wolves," he said. But Price quickly got up three holes over Mickelson, who missed an 18-inch putt early on and never got closer than two holes, losing in a shocker that sent the English midlands into hysterics.

At a celebratory gathering among European players later that night, Englishman Lee Westwood toasted Price for his victory while standing atop a barroom table. Price, in all his glee, tugged at Westwood's pants and said, "Tell 'em who I beat, Lee! Tell 'em who I beat!"

Yeah, taking down Mickelson was akin to Buster Douglas defeating Mike Tyson. It was the 11th of the 12 matches (the eighth decided) and put the Europeans in position to secure a victory two matches later when Paul McGinley halved his match against Jim Furyk in what eventually became a 15½ to 12½ win.

Like Mickelson, Woods also went 2–2–1, his singles match in the last position against Jesper Parnevik rendered meaningless with the Cup already decided, thus ending in a tie.

WOODS AND MICKELSON EVENTUALLY WENT ON TO POST TWO OF the worst overall records in U.S. Ryder Cup history, but in 2004 their standing was such that they were still expected to dominate. It was a mistake American teams and captains often made, relying too much on their big stars. Although Woods was just 5–8–2 in his three appearances to that point, well, he was still Tiger, an intimidating presence on the golf course who possessed that remarkable history of match play success going back to his junior and amateur days. And Mickelson headed to Oakland Hills with an 8–5–3 mark but having been part of three losing teams out of four.

Nobody gave much thought to the idea of putting Woods and

Mickelson together as partners. The conventional wisdom was you'd prefer to spread their strengths among other partners and give other players a boost. The theory went that you gave yourself two strong teams instead of one, although it never seemed to work out that way.

Strange, the 2002 captain, said he did ponder the idea for "about 60 seconds" before thinking better of it.

"What I saw were two type A personalities, highly motivated, competitive individuals who came from two completely different backgrounds," Strange said. "Two individuals who looked at things differently, reacted differently. Different personalities. Other than golf, what did they have in common?"

And yet, if Sutton was looking for some sort of precedent, all he needed to do was go back to the days of American Ryder Cup glory, when the competition was more of an afterthought, a U.S. squad taking care of what was then a team comprised of players from Great Britain and Ireland.

Three times, Nicklaus played Ryder Cup matches with Palmer: once in 1971 and twice in 1973. For the early part of their careers, the golf legends were not exactly buddies. The combo went 2–1 in lopsided outcomes for the U.S. team.

In 1977, Nicklaus lost his famous "Duel in the Sun" with Tom Watson at Turnberry, shooting 65–66 to Watson's 65–65 in one of the game's most epic encounters. Afterward, Nicklaus walked off the green with his arm around Watson, congratulating him on his victory. It's a scene that few could ever envision with Tiger and Phil.

The Nicklaus-Watson rivalry was intense, but it didn't stop them from playing a match together that fall at the Ryder Cup played at Royal Lytham & St. Annes and prevailing easily. There was no talk of frostiness between them.

In fact, Nicklaus and Watson combined to go 4–0 in Ryder Cup play, winning three times during the 1981 matches played at Walton Heath—after the competition was expanded to include all of Europe.

It was a different time, and the Ryder Cup was then considered a foregone conclusion for the Americans. Still, what's the big deal about rivals playing together in the Ryder Cup?

———

AS IS CUSTOM, EACH CAPTAIN PUTS HIS FIRST-DAY LINEUP AND order together without knowing what the other captain will do. There is some maneuvering to get a strong team out first, and consideration is given to who might also be asked to play in the afternoon session.

At Oakland Hills, the order saw four four-ball matches (best ball) followed by four foursomes (alternate shot) on the first two days for a total of 16 points. The final day consisted of 12 singles matches, meaning every player on both teams would compete.

Only the first morning session results were to be announced on Thursday afternoon, and there were some rumblings that a Tiger-Phil pairing could be in the works. There was a collective tremble throughout Michigan when Tiger and Phil were presented as teammates to take on the European pair of Scotland's Montgomerie and Ireland's Pàdraig Harrington.

"We came here to win," Sutton said. "I don't know that we could pair two guys together that were more matched for one another than those two guys."

Sutton was determined to sell the idea of a Tiger-Phil Ryder Cup pairing, and much of the attention centered on that despite the fact that theirs would be just 1 point out of 4 in the morning session—with the afternoon matches to be determined later.

The first four questions Sutton received in the Thursday news conference after the pairings were unveiled were about Tiger and Phil. In all, there were 31 queries, with 19 of them dealing with Woods and Mickelson in some form, ranging from how he told the two superstars about his decision to who they'd be playing to why Mickelson was practicing on another course.

"I wasn't really concerned with if they were bosom buddies or anything," said Sutton, who years later confirmed that neither player objected when told. "They know what the job is and they are going to go out there and they are going to get it done."

"I thought it was super cool," said Chris Riley, a member of the U.S. team that year who would play a match with Woods on Saturday. "They were the two best players in the world, and Hal was going out to get that point for sure."

But Riley's caddie at the time, John Wood, remembers feeling differently about it, despite the excitement.

"They had kind of a contentious relationship," Wood said. "I don't think they enjoyed each other. They did things very opposite from each other. Phil was struggling with his game a little bit at that point, too, going through an equipment change. I don't think Tiger was thrilled with that."

Sutton told Woods and Mickelson of his decision on Wednesday night and later notified the entire team of his plan. He reported no pushback, no resistance.

Woods and Mickelson said what you would expect them to say in such circumstances.

Tiger: "We're totally excited about it, we're geared up. Can't wait to get out there and play."

Phil: "I love the pairing of Tiger and myself. It's been put up to us to get the U.S. side off to a good start."

Of course, there was a downside that Woods fully acknowledged when asked. What if the two top players (Mickelson was ranked fourth in the world at the time) failed in such a setting?

"Obviously it has its pros and cons," Woods said. "Throwing the top two guys out there, but if you lose, yeah it's kind of tough."

Mickelson spent Wednesday and most of Thursday practicing by himself on the North course, leading to speculation that he might be ill.

He was not physically sick, but Phil was certainly uneasy about the prospect of playing with Woods, for among other reasons the golf ball they would be using in the alternate shot part of the competition. Tiger's ball was unlike anything Phil was used to hitting.

WHEN IT WAS LEARNED THE DAY BEFORE THE START OF THE RY-der Cup that Mickelson was practicing on the North course and not with his teammates, foreheads ached across Oakland Hills due to pronounced eye rolls.

What the hell was he doing? Many thought it was simply Phil being

Phil. Mickelson frequently would play a practice round off-site at another course leading into tournaments. Not a major championship, but perhaps the Players Championship or someplace where he felt it better to get away from the crowds and simply enjoy the golf leading into an event.

It wasn't the typical way of doing things, but then again, Mickelson has never gone about his business in a conventional fashion.

But that wasn't the reason.

Nor was it because Mickelson was trying to get used to the new Callaway clubs he put in play.

A few weeks earlier, Lefty signed a lucrative endorsement deal with Callaway to use the company's clubs. This typically means a player is under contract to have a certain number of the company's clubs in his bag. Mickelson would be paid millions per year—quite likely eight figures; if not, then very close—and Callaway would reap the marketing benefit of one of the game's top players using its equipment.

This was great for Callaway—but not necessarily so great for Phil in this moment. Getting used to new equipment can take time. There are examples galore of players cashing in on their success, only to struggle while making the adjustment to new equipment. (It should be noted that Mickelson maintained a long-standing relationship with Callaway into his fifties.) Such changes are usually made when there is significant downtime. All players have to weigh this decision and how best to navigate it. Phil doing so in September right before the Ryder Cup was a curious move to say the least, and when Sutton heard about it in the weeks leading up to the event, he was furious.

Making Sutton stew even more was the fact that Mickelson needed to get used to not only his new equipment but also his own new Callaway golf ball. The clubs were one thing. But a new ball—and knowing there might be another ball to play in alternate shot—simply complicated matters even more.

"I never talked about that publicly," Sutton said in a 2021 interview. "But [Phil] had to get used to the Callaway ball he had just switched to."

Mickelson caught considerable heat before and after the Ryder Cup for that decision. He was called greedy, among other things. But Mickelson is an equipment geek. He first got interested in Callaway's golf ball in January of that year. And living not far from the company's Carlsbad, California, headquarters, Mickelson was a frequent visitor, testing and tweaking. Phil, much like Tiger, would work to gets his clubs exactly to the specifications he wanted.

And yet . . . not even that was the reason Mickelson ventured out alone the day prior.

It was because of Tiger's golf ball. Not only was he still uncomfortable with the one he'd been planning to use, but he was also uncomfortable with the ball his partner used. This presented a big problem for Phil.

And it suggested that Sutton already made the decision to have Woods and Mickelson play together in the afternoon foursomes, the formal name for the format known as alternate shot, where having to play with Tiger's golf ball would become an issue. It would have no impact if they simply played a morning four-ball match together, where they essentially could play by themselves and take the best score. And thus, another questionable decision.

In alternate shot, only one ball is used. And in the Rules of Golf, you must play the same ball for the entire hole. At the time, the Ryder Cup required that the same golf ball be used throughout the round (now you are allowed to change the ball on each tee), so even the idea of switching balls to one more of Phil's liking on alternate holes was not going to fly.

Woods plays a ball that produces a lot of spin. That is a choice that works for him. Not so much for Phil. In fact, Mickelson found that hitting Woods' ball into the wind presented a huge problem: it simply did not go as far for him. That's what he was trying to work out the day prior to the matches. And there was no chance anything other than Tiger's ball would be put into play. Everyone knew, including Phil, that when it came to that kind of decision, Tiger would prevail. That only added to the dynamic of what would be a failed team.

"They're a terrible partnership," said Harrington, who 17 years later was the European captain at the 2021 Ryder Cup. "Back in the day, you chose guys based on their personality, whether they are friends or not. Now it's all about do they jell together as golfers? That was not a good pick. Who's the captain [of their pairing]? Phil has to be the captain in every match he plays, but how can he be the captain when he's playing with someone who is a better player than him?

"Phil and Tiger have great respect for each other's game and understand who each one is. That doesn't mean they make a good partnership on the golf course. We all know Phil is special. But it takes an individual to play from where Phil plays golf. And Phil knows that."

That was Harrington's nice way of saying that Mickelson's reputation was as a player who sprayed the ball over the landscape.

IF THERE WAS ANY APPREHENSION ON SUTTON'S PART, HE CERTAINLY wasn't letting on. He showed up on the first tee early Friday morning wearing a Texas-sized cowboy hat, one the U.S. caddies gave him as a gift—and one they also suggested he not wear at that time.

By the end of the day, Sutton would want to cover his eyes with that big lid, as bad as things played out. All hat, no cattle, as they say—not that there was anything he could do about it once he sent his players out to take on the Europeans.

And the signs were there as the first tee shots pierced the air—none finding the fairway among Woods, Mickelson, Harrington, and Montgomerie. Tiger went right, Phil went left and, symbolically, they were never together again.

"Tiger pushes his way right of the bunker I was in," Montgomerie said. "Phil pushes his the other way. One way right. One left-hand rough. And they marched off. Now Pàdraig and I walked down the meter-wide path together with our caddies behind us. It's interesting, isn't it?"

Montgomerie never won a major championship, but he captured the European Tour's Order of Merit eight times. He was also money in the Ryder Cup, never losing a singles match and going 20-9-7 over eight consecutive competitions from 1991 through 2006. As much as he struggled in the biggest events—and he never did win an official tournament title in the United States—the Scotsman was a rock for Europe, also captaining the team to victory in 2010. At the Ryder Cup, Monty walked with a swagger that was all too often missing in the major championships. But these were his majors, and he treated them as such.

Nobody bothered him, not even big, bad Tiger Woods. Monty also had experience playing against Woods in the Ryder Cup, having done so in 1997 and 2002. And the prospect of going up against Woods produced inspiration rather than dread.

Harrington would go on to win three major championships, including the PGA Championship that was played at Oakland Hills four years later. He also loved the Ryder Cup experience and relished the challenge.

"It was a no-lose situation for us, wasn't it?" Montgomerie said. "We're playing away from home. So it was game on. We're underdogs. Hal Sutton has put them out first to get American momentum out there, to get a point on the board, to get the crowd going. And it was loud, boisterous.

"I'm not being derogatory in any way; it was all to lose for America. Nothing to gain. Expecting to win is never good in golf. It's the hardest thing to achieve. Look at how many underdogs have won. It happens a lot. It was strange. We play as a team; Europe is very much a team. We're probably one of the greatest team units that's been brought together in international sport. We're very proud of it. A tight group."

Monty was describing this scene years later, when he was well into his senior career, and you could hear the passion in his voice. Like many of his European teammates, he loved the Ryder Cup, loved the camaraderie, loved being underappreciated, and loved taking down the Americans. European unity became the mantra over the years, whether you believe that has anything to do with playing good golf or not. Oftentimes, that's all it is—just play better. But throughout a stretch of Ryder Cup dominance, European players bought into that idea with all of their souls.

For Monty, much of his Hall of Fame résumé was compiled from his Ryder Cup brilliance, and it was clear, even now, that talking about the competition still stirred his competitive instincts.

"But we felt we had an opportunity if we played together," he said. "We weren't going to beat them on the length off the tee. Or our ability with iron play. Not with chipping or putting, my God. Probably weren't going to beat them with mind games. The only way to beat them that day was to score lower."

And they did.

"Tiger was always an opportunity to go up against because Tiger was meant to win his match," Harrington said. "You always felt good going out there. Everybody expects him to win, so it was a shot to nothing. And ever so more with the Tiger-Phil situation. We were both experienced at doing our own thing. You didn't want to send someone out there who would try and not play their own game. We were older at that stage, we're going to do our thing and play our game. They lost the shock value by saying they were going to play together. If they're going to do it maybe they should have not told anyone and that would have produced some shock value."

Monty set the tone when he knocked his approach from the bunker to 10 feet to set up a birdie and a 1-up lead. In fact, Montgomerie and Harrington combined to birdie the first four holes and never were less than 1-up the rest of the way.

That is not to say Tiger and Phil were terrible. They each won two holes in the match and combined to make five birdies. Many times, such a performance would win a match, which shines a light on the crapshoot that match play can foist on a player. In fact, none of the other three European teams made more than five birdies in that morning session. But Monty and Harrington combined to make eight birdies. Montgomerie also won two holes, and Harrington won four, including three between the 8th and 14th holes.

When Harrington birdied the 14th, the Europeans enjoyed a 3-up lead with four holes to play, all but clinching the match. And with all the blue on the scoreboard, it was a boost to the other European players on the course, who saw their teammates taking care of the American superstar team, to the shock of those lining the fairway ropes and packed into grandstands. Mickelson kept the match alive with a birdie at the 16th hole, but Montgomerie's par at the 17th closed it out, with the Europeans winning 2 and 1.

The idea of Tiger and Phil leading the Americans on some dramatic charge to an overall team victory was gone.

ALTHOUGH THEY DID NOT PLAY PARTICULARLY POORLY, WOODS and Mickelson lost that morning encounter, part of an overall U.S. drubbing that saw the Americans fail to win a single match, falling behind 3½ to ½. And it seemed an appropriate time to cut the losses and move on and try to salvage the afternoon session.

Instead, Tiger and Phil paired in the tricky alternate shot format against Northern Ireland's Darren Clarke—who defeated Woods in the final of the WGC Match Play Championship in 2000—and England's Westwood.

Was Sutton being stubborn? Perhaps. But captains are often in no-win situations. They're criticized for changing their minds and not sticking to the plan, while also taking heat for sticking to the plan and not changing their minds. Sutton didn't waver.

In the afternoon, Woods and Mickelson got off to a fast start, winning the second, third, and fourth holes to take a 3-up lead. They combined to make two birdies and a par and were 3-up through five holes. But a bogey at the relatively simple sixth changed momentum—and the Tiger-and-Phil combo would not make another birdie the rest of the way. In fact, they won just a single hole, earning a par at the 17th to square the match after having fallen behind after a bogey at the 11th hole.

That set up the drama at the 18th, where winning the hole would give the Americans a much-needed victory.

"The United States needed to win that point or at least get a half," said Williams, Woods' caddie. "It was a big swing there. It's a two-point swing as opposed to losing a point. It was pivotal."

It was Mickelson's tee shot and Williams could see that Mickelson and Mackay were taking some time to discuss the shot. He wondered if Woods might intervene. "You can imagine what he said to that. 'Why don't you say something?'" Williams said.

Mickelson chose a 3-wood—one of the new clubs he recently put in his bag—and sent the ball nowhere near intended, the expression on his face upon impact and body language as he leaned right an indication it was sailing wide left. The ball didn't go out of bounds, but it came to rest against a mesh boundary fence.

Woods, arms crossed and watching from behind the tee, tried to follow the flight of the ball without making it look obvious, unable to see exactly where it was headed beyond a group of trees. The ball was unplayable, meaning Woods needed to take a penalty drop. The duo lost the hole to a Westwood-Clarke bogey and lost the match 1-up.

Those who were not playing in the afternoon session went to watch and cheer on the others, and since Riley was not playing, Wood, his caddie, decided to follow Tiger and Phil.

"You didn't see them say a word to each other," Wood said. "If it weren't for the uniform, you wouldn't even know they were teammates. Everybody was kind of excited to see what would happen, but there was also some trepidation. They are the biggest names in the world of golf. But to put them back out in the afternoon . . . everyone just kind of rolled their eyes. It didn't work."

Years later, at the 2016 Ryder Cup, Mickelson said that a lack of communication in his earlier Ryder Cups led to decisions like the one Sutton made. He suggested the pairing might have worked if he and Woods had been given notice weeks ahead of time, so Phil could work with Tiger's ball. Mickelson later apologized to Sutton for the remarks and, to this day, laments what he said. "I overreacted, and I've done that several times in my career and I regret it," Mickelson said.

But Sutton remained wounded by the entire episode—a decade and a half later. In discussing his tenure as captain, Sutton moved between anger, disappointment, even despair.

"He could have hit a square ball straighter than he hit the ball on 18 in that second match," Sutton said. "Excuse after excuse after excuse. Give me a break. He was the fourth-best player in the world at the time. I don't care what Tiger's ball was made out of; he could have played it better than he did. He didn't care what he said about me. It was made up stuff, almost. It was a half-truth."

It is often said in sports that decisions are simply judged by their outcomes. Sutton looks like a genius if Woods and Mickelson win; he's the goat if they don't. Never mind that the players hit the shots. And never mind that, to some, the idea to put them together was perfectly understandable.

"I know what I thought when I first heard it," said Davis Love III, who was scheduled to play in the second match behind Woods and Mickelson with Chad Campbell. "We're going to send Tiger and Phil out and Davis and Chad and we're going to win those first two matches. And I was like, 'Let's go get them.' Nobody thought it was a bad idea. Nobody thought we could lose. We're going to be 2-up [in matches]. We're going to load the boat. That's Hal being aggressive.

"Nobody in that team room late at night said that's a bad idea. Now I don't know what Tiger and Phil were saying."

They weren't saying much when it was over.

To put an exclamation point on a horrendous day for the Americans, Tiger and Phil went 0–2. And the U.S. team trailed 6½ to 1½ on their way to a record margin of defeat 18½ to 9½.

Mickelson's final-hole drive is what is most remembered, and he took the brunt of the heat, whether it be for his decision to change clubs on the eve of the Ryder Cup or practice at another course, or simply because he didn't get the job done along with Woods.

Sutton piled on—both then and now.

"We'll all be scratching our heads on that," Sutton said. "But the most important person that's going to have to wonder about that is going to be Phil Mickelson. It's not going to cause us any grief in the morning because he's going to be cheering instead of playing."

Mickelson was benched in the following morning session while Woods partnered with Riley in a 4 and 3 victory over Clarke and Ian Poulter. And their partnership underscored what had long been a simple strategy of captains: put players together who get along.

"It was the highlight of my professional career," Riley said. "Just being on that team meant so much to me. And playing with Tiger solidified it. It was like the World Series to me. I know a lot of people made a lot out of Tiger and Phil playing, but I can tell you, Tiger was so competitive. He was super mad that we were losing and it showed."

Woods was comfortable playing with Riley, a friend and player he never viewed as a threat.

Mickelson, meanwhile, carried the anger of how that all came about for years, pushing for changes to how the Ryder Cup captain is selected following another loss in 2014. Then, on the eve of the 2016 matches, he explained to a massive media throng why he objected to Sutton's decision.

"We were told two days before that we were playing together," Mickelson said. "And that gave us no time to work together and prepare."

According to Sutton, Mickelson never mentioned that he was trying to get used to his own golf ball, too. But he stressed needing time prior to the event to test Tiger's golf ball.

"It doesn't allow me to play my best," he said. "What allows me to play my best is to learn the course, sharpen my touch on the greens, sharpen my chipping of the rough and ball striking, and so forth.

"Instead I'm taking four or five hours, and I'm out trying to learn another ball to allow us to play our best. Had we known a month in advance, we might have been able to make it work. I think we probably would have made it work. But we didn't know until two days prior."

The bottom line is, the United States lost another Ryder Cup. The Sunday singles played out like a funeral, as the Americans began the day trailing 11–6, a huge deficit that would have required them to earn 8½ points out of 12; it was nearly impossible.

Woods and Mickelson were the first two players out for the United States, with the hope of gaining some early momentum. That worked with Tiger, who defeated Paul Casey 4 and 3. But Phil couldn't deliver, getting 2-up over Sergio García through eight holes but failing to make another birdie and losing 3 and 2.

Halfway through the singles matches, the Europeans clinched the Ryder Cup.

And Tiger and Phil were part of the problem. Woods went 2–3, Phil 1–3. It was a humiliating defeat, the fourth in five Cups.

And it did nothing to solidify a relationship that Sutton seemingly wanted to force.

"I'm looking at them, and they look like they don't care for one another," Sutton said in 2021. "But I left every Ryder Cup and everybody I ever played with as a closer friend to them win or lose. So I said to myself, if something I did, a decision I made, to make them closer, then everybody wins. Golf wins. Everybody wins. So that was the thinking behind it. I didn't think that two of the best players in the world could run afoul that far. I don't think anybody saw that."

In the aftermath of the Ryder Cup, Sutton said, "You know, Arnold and Jack didn't start out to be the best of friends. There was a kind of dethroning going on there. They ended up being great friends. I felt the world of golf would be better off if Tiger Woods and Phil Mickelson became friends, and I felt like if they played together, had fun and beat somebody, they would end up being friends.

"They didn't beat anybody. It couldn't be their fault. It had to be my fault. It had to be."

If Sutton was bitter, well, it was understandable. He was vilified, and he felt the sting. During an interview more than 16 years later, the disappointment was clear in his voice. Emotional, Sutton said the criticism was so severe it caused him to leave the game. Sutton, who won 14 times and went 7–5–4 in four Ryder Cup appearances, never played a regular event on the PGA Tour after his first tournament of 2006. To think that the honor of being a captain in an event that is supposed to be an exhibition could lead to that outcome is both shocking and sad.

Woods and Mickelson had their individual careers to get back to, but neither was pleased. At the time, they combined to win nine major championships. None of the players they faced in that Ryder Cup managed a single major victory to that point.

"The two best players in America are supposed to win most of the time," Sutton said. "It should have worked, but they will never have another chance."

This was but one example of the Tiger-Phil dynamic. It was never simple. It was often explosive. And it rarely disappointed. This time, the circumstances didn't produce the intended result, and it only heighted the friction between two of the game's most famous combatants.

And it came at a crucial juncture in their careers, with a trail of history in their past and plenty more to come.

2

SoCal

Earl Woods provided his son with an abundance of guidance. He all but nurtured him from the crib to be a golfer and wasn't surprised in the least when Eldrick Tont "Tiger" Woods went on to stardom.

But Earl didn't think of everything. A Screen Actor's Guild membership might have been appropriate for young Tiger, so much was his television airtime. By the time the kid was 13, he had already appeared on *Today, Good Morning America,* ESPN, and each of the major networks' evening news shows.

Jim Hill, a former NFL defensive back and longtime Los Angeles sports anchor, got a call from Tiger's mom, Tida, and conducted an "interview" with Woods when he was barely out of diapers. Getting Woods to say anything became a big challenge—and foreshadowed the accomplished, famous Tiger. Among the never-aired responses to Hill, but saved for the archives, was "I have to go poo-poo," which a cynic might suggest was simply the start of Woods giving crappy interviews.

And yet, over the years, whenever Woods would run into Hill, he would give the television reporter a big hug. Hill was still conducting interviews with him some 40 years later when the global iconic figure had won 15 major championships.

Just before his third birthday, Tiger made his debut on national television with Bob Hope and Jimmy Stewart on *The Mike Douglas Show.* Douglas proposed a putting contest with Hope, which led to Tiger picking up his ball, setting it next to the cup, and tapping it in. The audience roared.

Stewart was not as impressed. Author Tom Callahan said he spoke to Douglas. "Bob Hope and I loved the kid, but Jimmy Stewart hated that," Douglas said. "He said, 'I've seen too many sweet little kids like this and too many starry-eyed fathers.'"

On another show called *That's Incredible!* cohosted by former NFL quarterback Fran Tarkenton and Cathy Lee Crosby, Tiger looked into the camera and declared, "When I get big, I'm going to beat Jack Nicklaus and Tom Watson." Of course, Woods would go on to play in several tournaments against those legends when they were well past their prime.

Philip Alfred Mickelson didn't get that kind of television exposure and opportunity to hone his interview skills at an early age like Tiger. But he was racking up trophies just the same. And he would come to like the microphone and an audience far more than Tiger.

Tiger's early prowess as a golfer, and the influence his dad, Earl, had on his development, is legendary, the stuff of books and movies. Woods cited his dad's impact for years after Earl's 2006 death.

But Phil was no slouch. Quite the contrary, Lefty was every bit the child prodigy that Tiger was, and in some ways, his record might be viewed as better for that period of their lives.

It didn't take long before Phil was piling up platitudes, hauling in trophies, and making a name for himself.

Mickelson was born on June 16, 1970. He has an older sister, Tina, and a younger brother, Tim, who in 2017 became Phil's full-time caddie.

Phil Mickelson Sr., a former navy pilot and commercial airline pilot, started Phil early with a cut-down club that he swung left-handed to mirror his dad hitting from the right side. Mickelson is right-handed in just about everything else he does, including writing and throwing. The older Mickelson would take baby Phil to a backyard playpen of sorts—a small area he fashioned to look like a tee box where Phil could watch his dad chip golf balls.

Young Phil, soon after he started walking, would grip the cut-down club left-handed, much to the chagrin of his father.

Dad tried to coax him to swing right-handed, but Phil kept going to the other side of the ball and rearranging his grip. Dad let that ride, allowing his son to mirror him, thus leading to the best left-handed golfer of all time.

Phil's dad, once a 4-handicap golfer, taught his kids the game but kept them at arm's length so that they would enjoy golf on their own without pushing too hard.

Before Phil was 10, a bunker and flagstick were added to the backyard playpen, as was a mounded area so he could hit all manner of pitch and chip shots. Beyond the green was a large canyon, into which Phil would hit full shots with discarded range balls. Meanwhile, he would make up shots in the backyard, experiment, play games—and get extremely good at chipping, one of the hallmarks of his career.

"I appreciate that he never pushed me," Mickelson said. "He never said, 'You need to go practice, you need to do this, you have to do that.' Yet the opportunity was always there for me to play and practice. If I needed to go to the golf course, my mom or dad would always be there to take me.

"What turned me onto the game was how much I enjoyed playing in the afternoons with my father. We would go out to a lot of the local public courses and we would play together. I loved that so much that it kept my interest and drive for the game high and I always wanted to practice, whether it was to beat him or just to play with him."

It was clear pretty early that young Philip—that is how his mom and dad refer to him—enjoyed an affinity for the game, with the hand-eye coordination and necessary motivation to excel.

"He won the junior world in the 10-year-and-under division," Phil Sr. said, referring to the Junior Worlds Championship that attracts players from around the world and dates to 1968. "At that point, he told me he wanted to be a professional golfer. I remember thinking, you can look at the people you know who play golf. Of the people you are personally acquainted with, what number of people at one time in their life thought they wanted to be a professional golfer?

"Of all those people, when you look at the percentage of success, you think, 'My son wants to be a professional golfer? One out of how many would succeed at that?'

"Instead of pushing him, I told him, 'You know some people already who wanted to be professional golfers and now they're instructors or working at a club or in a pro shop. You need to realize how difficult that would be.' The more I would tell him how difficult it was, the more convinced he was what he wanted to be; he would try harder. I never had to say that if there was a tournament coming up, that this might be something he ought to work on. He would do it on his own. We would just try to support him."

It didn't take long before Phil was piling up platitudes, hauling in trophies, and making a name for himself.

"I was in awe of Phil," said Chris Riley, a former PGA Tour pro and Ryder Cup teammate of both Tiger and Phil, who now coaches golf at the University of San Diego. "He was three and a half years older than me, my idol growing up.

"He is an entertainer. I remember, in junior golf, he was always a showman. As a young man, he was always going to do great things. You didn't know how good he was going to be, but you knew he was definitely more talented than anyone else and he had that competitiveness. He won junior golfer of the year in San Diego like every year."

Given what we already know about Phil, it comes as no surprise that he owned a mischievous side that dates to the days long before he became famous. His sister, Tina, has no issue with dishing some of that dirt.

On a Thanksgiving Day in their youth, she said Phil snuck out of the house with his clubs and paid a neighbor to take him to Stardust Country Club, the local course he worked at near downtown San Diego (now Riverwalk Golf Club). He managed to play his way around to the back nine before his mom and dad arrived on a golf cart, knowing exactly where to find him.

Phil started working at the semiprivate course, driving the picker on the range and gathering up the balls, and in return received practice privileges.

"My parents were hosting Thanksgiving dinner and told him he couldn't play golf," Tina Mickelson-Topacio recalled. "They made him get in the car, and as they drove home, Phil knew he was in trouble. But he said, 'Good golfers are a dime a dozen. I'm good now. But if I don't practice today, there are other people who are practicing. They're getting better while I'm not.'

"That was his mentality. My parents had a hard time disagreeing with that. It made them look at the situation in a different way."

Even as Phil turned 50, some of those qualities were still apparent to his dad. "He's a young guy at heart," Phil Sr. said. "He's always a lot of fun to be around and do things with. And if you are playing some sort of game with him, you don't want to lose because you'll hear about it."

Yes, the chirping that Phil made famous with practice round partners, competitors, media, Twitter followers, even Tiger extends to his own family, including Tim (a former golf coach at Arizona State), and Tina, who is a PGA of America professional and has been teaching since 1994.

"We were playing against each other from six years old, every single tournament," said Harry Rudolph, who competed with Mickelson in high school, college, and briefly as a pro. "Every tournament you could have played in we were there. Back and forth as much as it could be from that age until he started beating everyone. We were always friends, but there was a rivalry there. It was good for both of us. It pushed us to levels we might not have gotten to otherwise.

"You just knew that your competition was working hard. And he worked hard. People don't realize how much Phil has practiced and dedicated in his life to golf. He loves playing. And he's done that for a long time. People think it comes easy or that it comes natural. He works his butt off and has his whole career."

It highlights something that is easily blurred by the 45 PGA Tour victories, the six major championships, the 12 consecutive U.S. Ryder Cup teams, the 25-plus years of being ranked among the top 50 in the world, the Hall of Fame induction: Mickelson has been good at golf for as long as anyone can remember.

"Everyone knew who he was," said another junior rival, Kevin Riley—older brother to Chris Riley. "Phil was really involved with San Diego junior golf and that was right before the AJGA [American Junior Golf Association] started taking off. Every time they sent your tee times for a tournament in the mail, the No. 1 player was always in the first group and that was always Phil. He led off every tournament."

Mickelson won 12 AJGA individual events from 1985 to 1988, a career record that still stands and is four better than the next two: Woods and Bob May. He also had five runner-up finishes and was out of the top 10 just five times. In two seasons, he won four times each, tied with Woods for second in AJGA history.

So accomplished was Mickelson that college golf recruiters were poking around before he was in high school.

"His family was very supportive," said Dean Reinmuth, Mickelson's first coach. "They were a very close family. A strong family. And played a lot of golf. They practiced together and did a lot of stuff in the early days. They had a backyard chipping green. And they were involved in the sense that they wanted to see him have the best chance and career that he could. You couldn't ask for much more."

Unlike Woods, who worked with his first coach at age four, the Mickelsons didn't seek a coach like Reinmuth for Phil until he was a teenager. To Phil Sr., it just seemed like time that he did all he could do. His son could routinely beat him now, a humbling and proud thought rolled into one.

"He was about 10 years old," Phil Sr. said of their round at Mission Trails. "I played a routine round, nothing great, nothing bad but it was 82. And he beat me by seven shots. I was excited about what he had done." It was the first time Phil scored better than his father, even though, as Phil recalls, it was 81 to 73.

And so in time, it seemed best to get somebody else with a professional bent to look after Phil's game when appropriate. Mickelson met Reinmuth at a *Golf Digest* instruction school and their relationship lasted well into Mickelson's pro career.

"We didn't talk too much about instructional stuff at all," Reinmuth said. "Phil and I would get together and work. His parents were always welcome to come by and watch and tell me anything. It was a group thing. I ask parents to be involved because they might see them practice or play more than I do, and they might see something that is helpful.

"He was the type of player who really liked to hone a skill. That's different than a lot of players. A lot of players are looking for something that works instantaneously. Phil was more pragmatic in that he understood a skill and then really worked on it."

———

TIGER WOODS DID NOT HAVE A PRACTICE GREEN IN HIS BACK-yard. Nor a bunker. Nor a canyon where he could hit full shots. But his father, Earl, and mother, Tida, made sure he received plenty of opportunities.

Earl, an Army veteran, had access to the Navy Golf Course near the family home in Cypress, California, and that is where the two forged their bond and where Tiger played a good bit of his early golf. It wasn't luxury, nor did it matter. And Tiger didn't know any better.

He'd put three cherries in his Coke and enjoy the place, oblivious to the fact that there were none of the luxuries of country club life, such as showers in the locker room or even air-conditioning in the pro shop.

Owned by the Naval Weapons Station at Seal Beach, the Orange County course sat at the end of a regular street behind a sign that read "U.S. Military Reservation, Naval Golf Course, Authorized Personnel Only."

It is where Tiger shot 48 for nine holes—at age three. It is where he learned to play with the noise of fighter planes taking off and landing from the adjacent Joint Forces Training Base in Los Alamitos. It is where there was a tall elm tree on the sixth hole known as "The Tiger Tree," which stood more than 300 yards from the tee. Tiger hit it as a teenager. His dad would say he'd be ready for tournaments once he got his tee shots to roll past it. Woods considered Navy his home course until he went to college.

Much like Phil Mickelson Sr. and Phil, Earl had Tiger copying his swing, but in the garage where the older Woods would hit practice balls. The kid was a natural, as many have pointed out over the years, and the legend grew from there.

Earl was far more gregarious than Tiger ever became, a larger-than-life character who loved the microphone and had no problem touting his son's ability to any reporter asking him questions. In that way, he was the complete opposite of Tiger. At an early age, Tiger grew weary of the probing questions and wondered as a young man why he needed to deal with them. That carried over into his pro career. Earl always told him to not give any more than necessary.

That wasn't Earl, however. He once boasted that Tiger would "do more than any man in history to change the course of humanity," in a 1996 *Sports Illustrated* story. "He is the Chosen One. He'll have the power to impact nations. Not people. Nations. The world is just getting a taste of his power."

For all his bluster, Earl was not the type to push too hard, as has often been the unfortunate characterization. Sure, Earl Woods rattled coins in his pocket to try and throw a young Tiger off his game. He called his son names and tried to make him uncomfortable. He pointed out the racial epithets he might hear. He warned him about out-of-bounds stakes, hit the brakes really hard on a golf cart, and coughed on demand to distract him.

While this might have annoyed Tiger, it was meant to embolden him, to strengthen him. Earl knew exactly what he was doing. And while he endured criticism from all corners for his methods, it is Tiger, himself, who years later responded to a question about what would be his ultimate foursome by saying it would be just two: "Me and my pops."

More than anything, Earl gave his son the opportunity then stepped aside, with Tida there for support, always taking her son to the various tournaments and rooting him on from afar.

"The notion that he was a product of overbearing parents who orchestrated his life is a fallacy," wrote John Strege in his 1997 biography of Woods. "They never told him that he had to practice. Often, they had to rein him in and were concerned that golf was too much of an obsession."

Consider for a moment that Tiger had a biography written about him when he was barely 21—before he'd won his first major championship.

Strege was a reporter for the *Orange County Register* and saw Woods from his earliest days. He got to know both of his parents and wrote his book as Tiger's amazing amateur career was climaxing, with a promising pro career looming. All these years later, it is remarkable to think how good and transcendent Woods was that a 200-page book could be written about him when he was barely out of college.

His youthful greatness cannot be overstated; Earl recognized it so quickly that he had Tiger working with a coach at a young age.

"That was a wonderful time in my life, being able to see that up close and in person," said Rudy Duran, who now teaches golf in Arizona. "I remember one time he hit this shot. We were over at the Navy course. He kind of had a sparse lie, a winter lie. His ball was on partial grass and partial mud. He had a bunker in the way, and the hole was cut close. Sand wedge.

"And he picks that ball almost like it was off concrete, way up in the air, and it lands like a butterfly with sore feet. Rolls to a few feet [from the pin]. I think that's the best shot I've ever seen. And I'm the only one to see it.

"You remember that chip at the Masters [in 2005] at the 16th? " Duran asked, referring to a shot Woods holed from the back of the green that he played away from the pin, off a bank, then watched it trickle ever so slowly toward the cup and then drop in. "That was special and probably better. But this one was really amazing."

Early on, Earl developed the concept of Team Tiger. In addition to Duran, he enlisted Jay Brunza, a Navy captain and clinical psychologist to help his son, often as his caddie but also to help him with the mental side of the game, perhaps making Tiger the youngest player ever to have a sports psychologist at his side.

In 1982, Tiger was invited to partake in an exhibition with Sam Snead, the Hall of Famer who held the record for most PGA Tour victories in a career (which Tiger would match in 2019) and was winning tournaments into his fifties. The event was held at Soboba Springs Country Club, a Southern California desert course, where the 70-year-old legend and the six-year-old prodigy would play a two-hole tournament on the 17th and 18th holes.

The 17th was a par-3 with water on the right side, and Woods' tee shot faded toward it and came to rest barely in the water. "Take it out and hit it again," Snead told the kid.

Tiger got other ideas, going down into the water to hit. He knocked it on the green and two-putted for a 4. Tiger ended up losing to Sam by a stroke, and afterward, the seven-time major winner offered his autograph; Tiger reciprocated by giving Snead his autograph.

Like Phil before him, Tiger accumulated golf trophies in such abundance that the Woodses ran out of room for them.

"It got to where it was way beyond what I initially thought," Duran said. "He was unbelievably good at golf at five years old. When I first met him he was four and a half and hit some balls on the driving range. I had never seen a kid hit a ball like that. You see parents with their kids, hitting balls, balls going everywhere. But Tiger carried this little canvas golf bag. He had a 2½-wood, a 7-iron, and a putter that he carried with him.

"Oh my gosh, he hit these teed-up shots perfectly. They weren't more than 50 yards. But it was unbelievable. At the chipping green, he was hitting pitch shots high and low with that 7-iron. Back then, he had a slight stutter and he would just say, 'I'm going to hit it high.' As time went on, we played quite a bit of golf. He was able to manage his game, and he was clearly better than I was. He just didn't hit it very far.

"How low can you shoot when you only hit the ball 60 yards? But when he got around the green, pitching, bunker shots, putting . . . it was unbelievable how good he was at those things."

And he would get better. Much better. Duran kept working with Tiger for six years, and by then he was enough of a presence around the Navy course that some of the longtime patrons got annoyed with this 10-year-old kid—who was so good—having his run of the place.

All the while, Duran stuck with a game plan that Earl put forth, and he encouraged Tiger to play within his age group. Although Woods was clearly good enough to step up and compete with older kids, the well-grounded idea was it served him better to play with those his age and continue to beat them.

Winning begets winning. Winning when you are supposed to win provides its own kind of pressure. Such a mandate proved beneficial years later when Woods dominated the pro game.

"That was definitely part of the motivation," Duran said. "I don't know if I influenced that at all, but I was never in favor of playing up. Kids play up and they learn to lose. They're put up into a position where they don't win.

"My philosophy was, and I believe Earl and Tida supported it, that winning tournaments meant you're learning to win. Lose every tournament and you're learning to lose.

"At some point, you do need a higher level of competition, and he eventually did. But he was a little kid. He just stayed in his age group, and dominated the age group."

When Tiger turned 10, Earl decided a coaching change was necessary. Not due to anything Duran did wrong, but Tiger was literally and figuratively outgrowing Duran. Earl wanted someone to help Tiger improve his swing as he got taller and stronger. And he became aware of a teacher named John Anselmo, the head pro at Meadowlark Golf Course in Huntington Beach, which was about 13 miles south of the Woodses' home in Cypress.

Anselmo, already in his sixties, had experience working with young up-and-coming players.

"Dad said he had never seen a kid that age with so much ability," said Dan Anselmo, also a teaching pro and the son of John—who passed away in 2017 at age 96.

"In my own teaching, I would give my students something to work on. And they would come back and wouldn't change. I wondered if I was doing something wrong. I'd ask my dad if he ever gave Tiger something to work on and he didn't accomplish that. And he said no. He said that was unusual. Change is very difficult.

"Tiger had this laser focus. When he would commit to doing something and make any kind of change or improvement, it didn't take him long to accomplish things. [My dad] shared a story about one time following a lesson, [Tiger] would work on a knockdown shot out of the trees. Hitting a fade. Hitting a draw. My dad would show him how to do it. And he'd get up and duplicate it. He had such an amazing ability to see something and then translate that into a feel immediately. It was an amazing thing for my dad to really watch and be a part of."

Perhaps that is why, later on, Woods was so comfortable with changing coaches and swings. During the height of his professional career, he did this to the chagrin of many observers.

Both Duran and Anselmo took joy in their sense of accomplishment with Tiger. They never asked to be paid nor were they offered. And neither man ever expressed any resentment about it. They knew what they had in Tiger was special, and the opportunity was gold in itself.

Throw in Earl, Tida, and sports psychologist/caddie Brunza, and Team Tiger did quite well.

If Tiger was thinking about Phil in those days, it wasn't apparent.

They might not have lived far away geographically, but they were many miles apart in the golf stratosphere. Mickelson was making a name for himself in his circles, Tiger in his.

"By the time Tiger was 14, his focus was on being the best golfer in the world," said Joe Grohman, an assistant pro at the Navy course during Tiger's teenage years. "His sights were way, way, way higher than beating somebody. He was really focused on that. His main goal at the time was beating Jack Nicklaus' records at the same age. Tiger was about 14 when he showed me the list. He had already surpassed Jack at the same age.

"It's his whole career, but we were on the first inch. I remember at [age] 24, I'm thinking 'a 13-year-old is more mature than I am.' It was pretty incredible."

Grohman said when he first arrived at the Navy course, he was unaware of Tiger and his growing legend. Introduced to him by Earl, Grohman figured Tiger was like a lot of good, young players—just not *that* good.

"He was 13 and he beat me; and he beat me soundly," Grohman recalled. "I was so mad I had to walk off 18 and compose myself before I shook everyone's hand. Earl was like, 'You've never heard of my son?' and I said, 'Earl, you have to get him into junior golf.' I hadn't heard of him and he said, 'I'll tell you all about him.'

"I was this hotshot junior golfer from upstate New York. I knew about all the junior golf events. And here Tiger had already won the Rolex, already had five Junior Worlds. These are all the events I only hoped and prayed I could qualify for, and this kid had won them. Phil, I think, had won two. But five? As soon as I heard, that, I thought, 'Oh my God, this is the Second Coming.' I tell you, I tried to take as good of care of that kid as I could. I thought he can't miss."

Grohman said he was a scratch golfer at the time and learned that Tiger played off a 2.3-handicap at the Navy men's league. During that round they played together, he could already sense the competitiveness.

"He was beating me and I was giving him crap," Grohman said. "He was all jovial and I tried to get into his head a bit. Instantly, the smile went off his face. He got really, really quiet. I asked Earl what I did, and Tiger just took it to the next level and killed me. He was talking smack, and I was really impressed that I was intimidated by a 13-year-old."

A story from Strege's book highlights perfectly just how good Tiger became—and how his game was drawing attention.

When Woods went to Western High School in Anaheim, he was immediately the best player on the team. Craig Black, a senior, worked throughout his time there to become the No. 1 player, only to become despondent when he watched Woods play.

"I'll never be No. 1, will I?" he said to Western's golf coach, Don Crosby.

"No, Craig, I don't think you will be," Crosby replied. "But don't worry about it. You'll be No. 1 ahead of everybody else. Nobody's going to be No. 1 here but Tiger for the next four years."

For example: in 36 nine-hole matches as a freshman, Tiger was an aggregate 1-under par.

By the time he was 15, Woods has established himself as the best junior player in the country. At the age of 14, he won the Optimist Junior World for the fifth time, won the Big I Junior Classic, reached the semifinals of the U.S. Junior Amateur, and was a first-team Rolex Junior All-American.

In 1991, Woods became the youngest at age 15 to win the Optimist Junior World 15–17 age division, won the California Interscholastic Federation Southern Section individual title, two events on the American Junior Golf Association tour, and a smattering of other junior titles.

His best achievement was winning the 1991 U.S. Junior Amateur title at Bay Hill Club in Orlando—where he would go on to win Arnold Palmer's PGA Tour event eight times—defeating Brad Zwetschke 1-up to become the youngest winner in the history of the event.

Grohman gushed some more.

"His mastery of his short game, his putting; it was magical," he said. "The shots he could hit . . . it was ridiculous. He had all the shots. One day I go to the range and he's working through his bag. He's on his 7-iron. I came back about four hours later and he's on his 5-iron. 'Something wrong?' 'Oh no, this is what I'm doing.' He's hitting low, middle, high, draw, straight, fade. All until his liking. And then goes through the whole process again. I was like, you've got to be kidding me. It was unbelievable."

Like Mickelson's, Woods' name is littered throughout the AJGA record. He won eight times—tied for second behind Phil's 12—and he twice won four times in a season. He also won the U.S. Junior Amateur three consecutive years.

That latter accomplishment probably separates his junior days from Phil's. Nobody won the U.S. Junior Amateur so young. Nobody won it three straight years. Both were remarkable, early, and often.

Pat Perez has some perspective on Phil's and Tiger's junior records. A veteran PGA Tour pro, Perez played college golf at Arizona State and is the same age as Woods. But he grew up in San Diego, so he was keenly aware of Mickelson. The name was too prominent in local golf circles, and Perez admired Phil's game and accomplishments, even if he was too young at that time to compete against him.

"You just know who is around you," Perez said. "I just played and my focus was on Tiger. He was so unbelievable. He won everything. You knew who he was. He was our guy. But everyone knew Phil, too. Because he was such a great player at that time. He was older than us, so we didn't worry about him.

"Each summer, there'd be 30 tournaments, and the same eight kids would fight for the win. And when you got to the bigger tournaments, you knew who you had to beat. I met Tiger when we were eight, and he was at Presidio Hills with his dad. He had this great little swing. You just knew he was the guy to beat. He was just different. And better than everyone else.

"And that is something that doesn't always come out about Phil. He's had an amazing career, and he was damn good back in those days, too."

THERE IS NO DENYING THAT BOTH TIGER AND PHIL WERE PHE-nomenal as junior players. Was one better than the other? You could probably make an argument on either side. Tiger won all those U.S. Ju-niors, but Phil was dominant in his own way, winning all over Southern California and attracting the same type of attention from college recruit-ers that Tiger would later garner.

Along with their success came a certain confidence. Cockiness? Per-haps. Brashness? Yep. But certainly they were both acquiring a love for the stage, the big moment. Tiger might not have been as outgoing, but he loved the spotlight in his own way.

Stephen Hamblin, the longtime executive director of the American Junior Golf Association, saw plenty of Tiger and Phil back in the day. Clearly he is well aware of the numerous trophies they both accumulated. But there were other examples of their greatness.

Playing for the first time in the 15–18 division, Mickelson was the youngest player in his group at a tournament in Lake Tahoe. Hamblin recalls a tough golf course with plenty of wind and Mickelson shooting 70 the first day to lead after winning the younger age group the year prior.

"A reporter was interviewing him at the end of the first round and asked him if he ever thought as a 15-year-old he'd be leading his age group," Hamblin said. "Phil's comment, and I'll never forget it: 'Sir, with all due respect, every time I tee it up I think I'm the one to beat.' I thought, 'How does a 15-year-old say that?' That's the confidence Phil had in himself. He was just being honest. Out of the mouth of babes. It told me everything about him. And he lived up to that."

Another time, Mickelson was practicing for a tournament in Columbus, Indiana. Hamblin recalled him working on difficult shots, such as hitting drivers out of divot or trying to hook a wedge. He was on the driving range with another player, the only two there, and the other boy looked at Phil trying to do all that strange stuff and asked if he'd like to play a three-hole loop before it got dark.

"Phil said he was just going to practice, but then the kid says, 'We could play for a little money,'" Hamblin said.

Phil's ears perked up. "How much?' They agreed to play for $5 a hole, and Mickelson birdied all three to earn $15.

"You're not the left-hander I was reading about in the paper, are you?" the kid asked as he handed over the cash.

"Yes, I am," Phil replied.

Tiger was just as brash. Hamblin recalled a time when he played with Woods in an event in which the reigning long-drive champion Art Sellinger was going to be hitting shots on a particular hole for the group, this one the 15th.

When he arrived at the Las Vegas course they were playing, Woods asked Hamblin, "What hole is Art on today?"

For most of the round, Hamblin said, Tiger was a bit unfocused. But as the 15th hole drew closer, he started to get dialed in. "You could see his antenna going up," he said.

When they got to the 15th, all the participants hit their drives before it was Woods' turn. Sellinger teased him. "Hey, Tiger, this is my show. Get your ass up there and hit your drive."

Woods hit a sweeping hook that "was mammoth," Hamblin said. "It hit in this hard pan and worked itself into the fairway. I saw Art and it looked like the blood had drained out of his face. He knows this is a big drive. So Art hits this shot, and it sounded like it was out of a cannon. It went up high and far and it was the most beautiful drive I'd ever seen in my life.

"Art comes up behind us in a cart, one drive is 400, the other is 405. This is with steel shafts and persimmon woods . . . and Art gets him by five yards. He walked back to the cart with me and put his arm around my shoulder and said, 'Don't say this to anybody, but that's the best drive I ever hit in my life.'"

Put Tiger's and Phil's junior records side by side, and there is a good argument to be made for each player as to whose was better. Does it matter? The bottom line is they were accomplished beyond their years at such an early time, a fact that guaranteed them nothing but nonetheless shone a big light on what lay ahead.

3

AMATEURS

When Tiger Woods was born on December 30, 1975, Phil Mickelson was already pretty fashionable with a golf club in his hands. Phil was born on June 16, 1970. His dad, Phil Sr., was an avid golfer, keen to carefully pass on his wisdom, and Phil got good at the game at a rate that would see him dominate kids and junior tournaments throughout San Diego.

It wasn't long before Tiger was chasing him. Perhaps not knowing exactly who Phil was, Tiger pursued the same kind of young-kid goals that seemed to consume both players in their youth.

At an early age, neither seemed content with being regular kids. Their parents gave each of them the golf opportunity, and they seized it. And the drive that saw them both become Hall of Famers with some of the best records in the history of the game was clearly sewn into the fabric of their being from a time they can hardly remember.

Although they were not from the same town, Tiger and Phil grew up close enough that at some point the exploits of each player registered on their respective radars.

When Woods started to horde trophies in his Cypress, California, home, Mickelson was already being wooed by college recruiters as he dominated the American Junior Golf Association ranks—as Tiger would soon do himself.

And even as Mickelson was winning three NCAA titles and a PGA Tour event while in college, it would have been hard for him to miss the exploits of another California kid, another prodigy, who began getting media attention almost out of the crib.

Given their age difference—a full five and a half years—and the tunnel vision often associated with youth, it makes sense, however, that neither guy thought too much about the other at this stage.

"I remember the Junior Worlds because it was right here," said Phil's mom, Mary Mickelson, of their big-time junior tournament played at Torrey Pines in San Diego. "And this little guy named Tiger used to come down. It was kids from all over the world, really, and they would play. And I remember Tiger. You knew his name and what he was doing. He won the 10-and-under, and I think when he was 11 or 12, he won also. Yes, his name was known to us at that time.

"But we didn't think much about it. The boy in Southern California we heard about a lot was Bobby May [another AJGA standout]. But we did hear about this young kid Tiger, although we didn't think much of it at the time.

"Philip [her son] and I have talked about that. He's always had a great admiration for Tiger, and he's told us that. Tiger pushed him. He was lucky to have Tiger come along at that time."

That is a subject that could be debated and dissected without ever coming to a proper conclusion. How might Mickelson's career have gone had there been no Woods? Would his victory total have risen into the sixties? Might he have achieved the No. 1 ranking in the world? How about more major championships? What about PGA Tour Player of the Year, an honor that, amazingly, Phil never claimed?

Then again, how much did Tiger drive Phil to become the player that he became? It makes for fascinating after-hours banter.

But back then, in their formative years, as teenagers? Not so much.

"Everyone knew who Tiger was at six or seven years old," said Kevin Riley. "The first time I saw him was at the Southern California Amateur. Everyone knew him. I saw him play, and he was beating men when he was 14 years old. And there's good amateur golf in California. Whenever he played, he won.

"I played him in the quarterfinals of the California State Amateur at Pebble [Beach], and I had him down two after six holes. I played well, and he beat me 3 and 2. He's amazing. Obviously, his record growing up was so good. I don't remember going to a tournament where he didn't win. It's crazy. Like the craziest thing ever. Phil is world-class and you compare him to anybody else, and it's no contest except for one guy."

Woods pursued Jack Nicklaus from an early age, wanting to accomplish goals at the same age or earlier than Jack. In 1986, *Golf Digest* published a list associated with the Golden Bear, and it's not the major championship record of 18 titles that is so often cited.

Tiger clipped the article from the magazine and kept it in view in his room.

Among the feats, Jack broke 50 for nine holes for the first time when he was nine. Tiger did so at age three.

Nicklaus first broke 80 at age 12; Woods was 8.

Nicklaus broke 70 at 13; Woods was 12.

Other achievements were also noted—a big, huge bull's-eye for Tiger—such as Nicklaus winning the Ohio state high school golf title at age 17, his first U.S. Amateur at 19, and his first major championship at 22.

Those were Tiger's very early aspirations, but it would have been difficult to miss what was going on with Phil. Already, Mickelson was showing a flair for showmanship, an ability to easily engage with teammates, media members, and those around the game.

And he did his own dominating. He was winning an NCAA title before Tiger was in high school. And while he may have been aware of Tiger—whose name was already gaining traction—he wasn't paying much mind to a kid racking up all those junior trophies.

"Yes, you knew about Tiger," said Harry Rudolph, a San Diego rival and friend of Mickelson's. "But Phil was beating everybody."

Rudolph was a junior golf, high school golf, amateur golf, and college golf rival of Mickelson's. They saw each other often in San Diego and all the way through college.

A highly sought-after recruit himself, Rudolph began his college career at powerhouse Oklahoma State before transferring to the University of Arizona, putting him in the same Pac-10 conference with Mickelson, who went to Arizona State.

Mickelson won NCAA individual titles in 1989, 1990, and 1992; the year he didn't win, Phil won the PGA Tour's Tucson tournament.

"Phil kicked all of our butts back then," Rudolph said.

When Mickelson won the NCAA title for the third time in matching a record held by Ben Crenshaw, Rudolph finished runner-up, although UA won the team title. Two years earlier, Mickelson led ASU to a team title while also capturing the individual crown.

"He had the greatest amateur record, junior record since Nicklaus," said Dean Reinmuth, Mickelson's first coach. "He was clearly that good. Nicklaus, Crenshaw, and Phil. He won three NCAAs. He won the U.S. Amateur. He won a tour event as an amateur. Qualified for the San Diego Open at 16. He played in the L.A. Open. There wasn't anyone close to him until Tiger came along."

Soon after that Arizona team championship, Rudolph got his first in-person glimpse of Woods at a sectional qualifier for the U.S. Open along with a couple of his teammates.

"We had just won the national championship, and we were among the best golfers," he said. "It was in San Francisco, and in the practice round, somehow Tiger wanted to play with us. It was the first time I ever played with him; he was maybe 15. It was noticeable to me at that point that he was something special.

"He was the only one who had a gallery in the tournament. We didn't have anyone watching us, but he had 100-plus following him.

"He had incredible speed at that age, and it was eye opening as far as what we were seeing. He was hitting stingers, just ripping them. And the sound of the ball, the flight of the ball . . . I was not surprised to see what he was accomplishing shortly thereafter. We were all kids. He was a skinny little kid but damn good."

But Phil was still Phil.

"It's possible that Tiger was more aware of Phil than Phil was aware of Tiger," Rudolph said. "What Phil was accomplishing as an amateur and college golfer . . . he was doing the things that Tiger wanted to do someday. And Tiger at 12 years old, I'm pretty certain, had a list of goals that were similar to what Mickelson was accomplishing: U.S. Amateur, NCAA, first-team All-American, Walker Cup team. At the time, Tiger had not won any of those things. Phil was doing it. Phil was beating up on those guys."

———

THE FIRST TIME WOODS AND MICKELSON PLAYED IN THE SAME tournament, it is quite likely they never laid eyes on each other. There was awareness, maybe even curiosity, but certainly not at the level of obsession.

The age difference was one thing; the stage was another: the 1991 U.S. Amateur.

The U.S. Amateur is the leading event for nonprofessionals in the United States. It dates to 1895 and is as old as the U.S. Open, both played in the same year and at the same place, Newport Country Club in Rhode Island.

A long list of the game's great players have won the Havemeyer Trophy (Theodore Havemeyer became the first president of the USGA in 1884), including Bobby Jones (who won five times), Jerome Travers (four times), Woods (three times), and Jack Nicklaus (twice). Woods is the only player to do it three consecutive years.

Arnold Palmer, Lanny Wadkins, Craig Stadler, Jerry Pate, John Cook, Mark O'Meara, Hal Sutton, Justin Leonard, Matt Kuchar, and Bryson DeChambeau are among the many U.S. Amateur winners who went on to have significant professional success.

Fred Ridley, the Masters Tournament and Augusta National chairman, who also is a former president of the USGA, won the title in 1975—and is the last player to win the tournament who never turned pro.

There is also a long list of winners who never did much as pros. Some of that is due to the vagaries of the pro game. Some can be traced to the randomness of match play. It is the great equalizer. All who play at a top level would agree that 72 holes of stroke play is a better gauge of a true champion. Match play allows for more flukes, more upsets. It evens the field. And you don't have to beat everyone.

In a head-to-head match, you could have a poor day, shoot over par, and still win your match and advance. But that over-par round in stroke play could be the difference. Meanwhile, a great under-par score could lose to an even better one in match play. It happens all the time.

Throw in the fact that some 312 competitors start off at the U.S.

Amateur and must endure 36 holes of stroke play, qualifying to reach the 64-man match play field, and winning the tournament becomes an impressive feat.

It is what makes Woods' three consecutive U.S. Amateur titles (not to mention three straight U.S. Junior Amateurs) so impressive. It also explains why Mickelson captured the tournament just once. There is no shame in having "only" one U.S. Amateur title.

So the 1991 tournament in Chattanooga, Tennessee, presented contrasting opportunities. With the main portion of the tournament played at the Honors Course, a difficult Pete Dye–designed layout, Mickelson was the defending champion, having defeated Manny Zerman in the U.S. Amateur final a year earlier at Cherry Hills in Denver.

At that point, Mickelson already captured a U.S. Amateur title and two NCAA titles, among numerous other college victories to his name. He was 20. He was the king of the amateur game and one of the great up-and-coming players.

Tiger? For all his fanfare, he came into the tournament looking at it as a nothing-to-lose proposition. He earned his place in the starting field by winning the 1991 U.S. Junior Amateur at the Bay Hill Club in Orlando, Florida, defeating Brad Zwetschke 1-up to become the youngest winner in the history of the event. He was just 15.

And he arrived in Tennessee only eight hours before his Tuesday tee time due to a 10-hour journey from Colorado, where he competed in a junior event called the Canon Cup. To save money, Earl Woods devised a curious airline route that took him on two stops before landing in Chattanooga.

When Woods teed off at 8:42 A.M. on just four hours' sleep, he was the only Black player in the field as well as the youngest competitor. And after two opening bogeys, it appeared this was all too much. Woods didn't want to skip the junior event, as he enjoyed the camaraderie of the team competition with players his own age. Earl believed that having that experience was important, more so than a tournament where his son would be at a distinct disadvantage. He also knew there'd be plenty of U.S. Amateurs.

But without much game or motivation, Woods still gathered himself enough to shoot 6-over-78. That might not sound great, but the first two days of the U.S. Amateur comprise 36 holes of qualifying for the match play portion of the tournament. The idea is to be somewhere among the top 64. And Woods still had a chance to attain that on the easier Cleveland Golf and Country Club course used as part of the qualifying.

Woods shot 74 the following day with his half brother Kevin caddying for him. He also had his first coach, Rudy Duran, along for the tournament as well as Earl. But that total of 152 was not good enough to advance to match play. Because they bought prepaid, nonrefundable airline tickets, the group stayed in the area while the rest of the tournament proceeded.

Mickelson did advance from the 36-hole stroke play qualifier but was defeated in the third round by unheralded Rick Southwick, blowing a 3-up lead through 10 holes.

This was not just an unlikely victory for Southwick; he was fortunate to even be in the tournament. He finished fifth in a four-spot qualifier just to make the field. When one of the players who beat him withdrew, Southwick got in, making the most of it by not only advancing to match play but also getting to the match with Mickelson and advancing to the quarterfinals.

"I never thought this could possibly happen," Southwick said afterward. "My dream was to come here and play Phil Mickelson. But it's amazing that I'm even here."

As disappointing as it may have been for Mickelson—he skipped an opportunity to play in the PGA Tour's World Series of Golf to defend his title—he had plenty to be pleased about heading into his senior season.

Although he didn't win the NCAA individual title—he tied for fourth—he possessed that victory back in January at the PGA Tour's Northern Telecom Open.

A YEAR EARLIER, MICKELSON TIED FOR 19TH AT WHAT WAS ALSO known as the Tucson Open. The event was played over two courses: three rounds at TPC Star Pass and one at Tucson National. (In 1990, it was TPC at Star Pass and Randolph Park Municipal Golf Club.) In 1991, Mickelson opened the tournament with scores of 65–71–65 to take a two-shot lead into the final round.

This in itself was a huge achievement. No amateur had won on the PGA Tour since Scott Verplank in 1985. Prior to that? Nearly 30 years (since Doug Sanders won the 1956 Canadian Open). Amateurs, namely college kids, didn't win at this level. Even experienced players like Phil and Tiger were woefully unprepared for the rigors of professional golf at that age. Or so it seemed.

And here was Phil out in front. The third round was notable for a shot that personifies Lefty. He hit an approach that barely trickled into the front portion of a bunker, leaving a very difficult chance to get the ball close to the hole and save par. The safe play was to hit the shot out to the side; getting behind the ball and hitting it toward the pin was nearly impossible.

Instead, Mickelson decided to play a shot that he'd practiced numerous times but was audacious under the circumstances. He aimed away from the hole, back down on the fairway. And with the ball on a slight upslope, he hit a shot that went over his head, backward, and toward the hole. It stopped close enough for a tap-in par.

"I just want his parents to make sure he stays in school two more years," Tom Purtzer, who tied for second, marveled afterward.

Victory did not come easy. Mickelson went from leading to trailing by two shots after making a triple-bogey 8 on the par-5 14th hole. He twice hit shots into unplayable lies. Only four holes remained.

But he parred the next hole, birdied the 16th, then parred the 17th, and found himself tied with Purtzer and Bob Tway. Both players made mistakes of their own that let Phil back into the tournament.

Knocking his approach to eight feet, Mickelson made the birdie putt to win, joining Verplank (1985 Western Open), Doug Sanders (1956 Canadian Open), Gene Littler (1954 San Diego Open), Frank Stranahan (1948 Miami Open, 1945 Durham War Bond Tournament), Cary Middlecoff (1945 North & South Open), and Fred Haas (1945 Memphis Invitational) as one of the only amateurs to win on the PGA Tour.

Purtzer and Tway shared first- and second-place money because Mickelson could not take the $180,000 prize as an amateur. (They each received $144,000.)

"He's just on a different level," said Tway, who won the PGA Championship five years earlier.

"Guys like Phil and [Jack] Nicklaus and [Tom] Watson don't come down the pike very often," Purtzer said.

"He didn't give up; he didn't change anything," said Mickelson's father. "Somebody came back a little bit, and all of a sudden, he was tied for the lead and birdied the final hole to win. After almost giving it away on the par-5, and then to come back, I thought that was so meaningful of an event that he could carry that with him for a long, long time. If you have a bad hole, it doesn't mean you are out of it."

Funny how that proved prescient, as Mickelson's scrapes with disaster throughout his career are legendary. And yet, so often he flicked away the distress and went on attacking, looking at the unbelievable as shots to be pulled off, not put off.

The victory served another purpose. It took away the sting when he failed to win a third consecutive NCAA individual title that spring and when he was bounced from the U.S. Amateur.

Those were disappointments, to be sure. But Mickelson was undeniably set up for an incredible future in the game.

While he could not take the prize money, his victory assured him a two-year exemption on the PGA Tour beyond the 1991 season. That meant he could return to school for his senior year, turn pro in the summer of 1992, and be a fully exempt player with no pressure to qualify.

Mickelson briefly entertained the idea of turning pro sooner but ultimately determined it would be better to return to school and pursue a few more amateur goals. And he quickly realized that he was not necessarily mentally prepared for the grind of pro golf.

"It was unbelievable to me how, as soon as the tournament was over, everybody was hurrying to catch a flight for Hawaii" and the next tournament, Mickelson said in a *New York Times* interview a day after his win. "I was so drained and tired. There was no way I would have been able to play this week. That's why right now I don't feel that I'm ready to turn pro and play every day, week after week."

In other interviews, Mickelson deftly handled the question of turning down the first-prize money (he couldn't take it anyway at that point) and the potential windfall he might have reaped if he turned pro then.

"People say I am losing money by staying amateur," he said. "But I feel the money will be there later, and it's not my motivation for playing in tournaments. Winning is."

He also grasped the idea that his game might still need some work and that playing against his amateur rivals might better suit him for the long haul.

"Granted, I won, but that's a little bit irrelevant," he said. "I did gain a little respect from the players, but real respect on the tour is based on consistency and being in contention and more than just winning one tournament. Right now, I'm honing my game here at ASU, and I'm also using the opportunity to get an education. So it is working hand in hand."

While Mickelson was heading for his senior year in college, already a U.S. Amateur champion and a PGA Tour winner, Woods was still in high school. For all their later greatness in the pro game, they were incomparable at that point in time. Both enjoyed amazing junior careers. But Tiger had yet to do anything on the amateur level other than win the U.S. Junior—an enormous feat as the youngest player to do so, but still miles away from what Phil was achieving.

"It would have been great to see the two of them at the same age," said Brett Avery, who covered Woods and Mickelson through their amateur and college careers for *Golf World*. "At that point, those five years were like light-years. They weren't going to be in the same environment until they got out on tour."

The fact that Mickelson already won on tour was a remarkable feat in itself.

FOR MUCH OF THE GAME'S EARLY HISTORY, AND THROUGH THE first few decades of the 20th century, amateur golfers ruled, while professionals were dimly viewed, treated mostly as second-class citizens by the game's establishment.

At some places, professionals—despite their high level of skill—were not allowed in the clubhouse. That led Walter Hagen, who won 11 major championships mostly during the time when Bobby Jones dominated the amateur game, to champion the cause for his colleagues.

At the 1920 Open played at Royal Cinque Ports in Deal, England, Hagen—as was the custom—was denied access to the clubhouse and told he needed to change his shoes in the pro shop. Instead, Hagen would dress at his hotel and have a rented limo drive up to the club, park on the lawn by a flagpole in front of the clubhouse, and change his shoes there.

Hagen was a showman who reveled in putting on a glamorous, partying front—and then cleaning up against the more "proper" amateur players of the day.

Throughout the 1920s, Hagen—who won the PGA Championship five times when it was contested at match play—fought those kinds of battles. And with a game to match, he gradually helped change the feelings toward professionals to the point where after Jones retired in 1930, amateurs were rarely as successful in open events.

No amateur has ever won the Masters, which began in 1934, and John Goodman was the last amateur to win the U.S. Open, in 1933. Jones was the last amateur to win the Open, doing so in his grand slam season of 1930. The PGA Championship has always been a tournament for professionals.

Even the Western Open (now called the BMW Championship), which dates to 1899 and was on equal footing as the majors of the day prior to the Masters, had just one amateur winner prior to Verplank in 1985—Charles "Chick" Evans Jr., who won the title in 1910.

Woods never came close to winning a tour event as an amateur. But his amateur record overshadowed any disappointment there might have been in Tiger's relatively modest results in professional events during those years.

FOR TIGER, THERE WAS NOT MUCH DISAPPOINTMENT ABOUT FAILing to advance to match play of the U.S. Amateur, as 1991 was very good to him, with victories in multiple amateur events, including the U.S. Junior and four American Junior Golf Association titles.

He was also gaining a measure of celebrity. People all around the game knew his name. Woods was doing things that were impressive for his age. Big Canyon Country Club, an exclusive club in Newport Beach, California, that at the time sold memberships for north of $100,000, gave Woods an honorary membership—which drew the attention of the USGA.

The governing body determined that Woods could have access to the course as an honorary member, but none of the other perks of membership. So no bag storage or gym access? The arrangement also raised concerns with the NCAA, which eventually signed off on the relationship even though Woods was still some two years away from going to college.

By 1993, Woods was getting too good and too big for junior golf. The legendary Byron Nelson—who in 1945 won 11 consecutive tournaments and 18 overall—wrote Tiger a personal letter inviting him to play in the Byron Nelson Classic later that year.

Nelson, who left the game at the relatively young age of 33 in 1945, remained relevant as a sometimes competitor, confidant, TV analyst, and later tournament host. His tournament, which continues today, became the first to have a former tour player's name attached to the title in 1968.

Getting that letter from Nelson was like gold to Woods, who also accepted an exemption to play in the Los Angeles Open again after having missed the cut there in his first attempt a year earlier. The Honda Classic in Florida also invited him to its tournament.

Later that summer, Woods was attempting to win his third straight U.S. Junior Amateur, this time at Waverley Country Club in Portland, Oregon. His opponent was Ryan Armour, who'd lost to Woods in the tournament quarterfinals a year earlier. This time he had Woods down two holes with two to play. No matter.

Tiger birdied the 17th to extend the match to the 18th hole, a par-5 where Woods found a bunker in two, blasted his approach to eight feet to make birdie and win the hole, then winning on the first extra hole.

Years later, Armour was paired with Woods at the 2018 BMW Championship. It was the first time they played together as pros in a span of more than 20 years. Now a family man who was grinding on the tour for two decades, Armour was no longer in awe of the man who tilted golf off its axis.

But Armour appreciated the greatness.

"He's unbelievable, the greatest player of our generation," Armour said. "I remember getting done that day, and this was the year he came back [2018] and had done really well. I remember telling my wife, 'He'll win soon.' Sure enough, he won two weeks later [at the Tour Championship]. If he drives it in play, he can beat anyone. Sure enough."

Armour knew way back then, as did many, what lay ahead. But a lot still needed to happen. Woods had yet to win a U.S. Amateur or even play a college tournament. And when he bowed out of the second round of match play at the 1993 U.S. Amateur, it turned out to be a blessing.

Played at Champions Golf Club in Houston, the U.S. Amateur was near Lochinvar Country Club, where instructor Butch Harmon worked. Harmon was well known in the game. He had a brief fling as a tour player, winning the 1971 B.C. Open. But he would gain fame and acclaim for his teaching ability.

Butch's full name is Claude Harmon Jr., and he is the son of another prominent teacher, Claude Harmon, who won the 1948 Masters for his only professional tournament title. The older Harmon became known for his work at two of America's more prominent clubs, Winged Foot Golf Club in New York (home to six U.S. Opens) and Seminole Golf Club in Juno Beach, Florida (a favorite of Ben Hogan). It was no coincidence that Hogan and Harmon were good friends.

Claude's four sons—Butch, Craig, Bill, and Dick (who passed away in 2006)—all joined their dad in the golf business.

But it was Butch who eventually saw some of the game's biggest names come under his guidance. Greg Norman was working with Harmon when he won the 1993 Open at Royal St. George's and continued to do so for a long period as the No. 1 player in the game.

Earl Woods decided that for Tiger to ramp up his game, he needed a strong teacher, such as Harmon. Earl did his homework, and he was impressed with what Harmon had accomplished with Norman. Harmon agreed to become Woods' coach, and even though Tiger was just 17, it was one of the most impactful decisions of his career.

"You could see the natural ability, a beautiful swing," Harmon said. "He was real thin in those days. He wasn't real strong, had a flippy swing. He'd just bomb it out there, and wherever it was, he'd go get it and get it on the green and make a putt. He just had so much raw, natural talent that you could see, boy, if you could harness all this talent and polish it up, it could be something special."

And yet it didn't matter that Tiger was working with a high-profile coach or that he was the most decorated junior in history or a first-team Rolex Junior All-American for four straight years or *Golf Digest's* Junior

Player of the Year or that he won those three straight junior Amateur titles.

He still returned to Western High for what he hoped would be a normal senior year, one that saw college recruiters becoming a bigger part of his life. Woods decided to narrow his list of schools to three: Arizona State, where Mickelson already made his mark; the University of Nevada, Las Vegas; and Stanford, the school he would eventually choose.

Before getting to Palo Alto, California, for the start of his freshman year, Woods achieved his biggest victory to date in the late summer of 1994 when he captured the U.S. Amateur at TPC-Sawgrass in Ponte Vedra Beach, Florida, with the match play portion played on the Stadium Course made famous by the annual Players Championship. Woods had a memorable final match against Trip Kuehne.

There was more drama earlier in the week when he faced former U.S. Amateur champion Buddy Alexander, who was then the golf coach at the University of Florida.

Alexander tried his hand at the pro game before regaining his amateur status and won the 1986 U.S. Amateur—which meant a spot in the 1987 Masters and a tee time with the reigning green jacket winner, Jack Nicklaus.

When he faced Woods at Sawgrass, Alexander was 41 years old and had coached the Gators to a national championship a year earlier. Woods was 18 and had yet to play a college match.

By the time their match reached the 13th hole, Alexander held a 3-up lead and a short putt to extend the advantage to 4 with just five holes to play. But he lipped out a three-footer for par that would have won the hole, giving Tiger life. "If he had made that putt, it was basically over," Woods admitted.

And then Alexander fell apart. He bogeyed each of the next four holes, his three-hole advantage now a one-shot deficit with one hole to play. Both players made a double bogey at the 18th, meaning Woods won 1-up—and offered the perfect example of how, in match play, you can win even if you're not playing your best.

In the 36-hole final, Woods found himself way behind again, only to fight back against Kuehne. On the famous (some say infamous) island hole par-3 17th—it is technically not an island because there is a small pathway leading to the green from the back left—Woods took dead aim at a precarious back right pin position.

From 137 yards, Woods fired at the flag and saw the ball land to the right of the hole, take one hop, and stop in the back corner of the green only a few feet from the railroad ties that bordered the green.

Woods surveyed the putt, and standing nearly on the edge of the green, he rolled in the right-to-left, 14-foot putt that broke some 12 inches. Wearing shorts, a baggy shirt, and a straw-brimmed hat, Woods furiously pumped his fist in celebration, a precursor of many memorable celebrations.

That birdie gave Woods a 1-up lead after rallying from 6-down, and he won the 18th hole as well to finish off a 2-up victory and become the youngest winner of the U.S. Amateur.

By making it to the final, Woods secured a place in his first major championship—the 1995 Masters. And the victory also got him spots in the U.S. Open and the Open.

"This feels great," Woods said afterward. "I had to play some of the best golf of my career. Being the youngest champion hasn't set in yet. It's a weird feeling to win like this. The only time I felt I had won was when I hugged my father [on the 18th green]."

THAT FIRST U.S. AMATEUR VICTORY WAS TALKED ABOUT FOR years. The way Woods came from behind was one thing. But to continually battle when it looked like he was done was simply a testament to a trait that followed him into his pro career—very few times could it ever be said that Tiger didn't give his best effort, and his ability to make cuts and continue to contend so often as a pro was strong evidence. The victory at Sawgrass was only a hint.

Woods was just a few weeks away from enrolling at Stanford, and he did not disappoint when he began playing collegiate events. His first was the William H. Tucker Invitational at the University of New Mexico, and Woods shot a final-round 68 to win by three strokes. A few weeks later, he tied for fourth in his second event at the Ping/*Golfweek* Preview at Ohio State.

Those on the team at the time knew who was joining them. In fact, as far back as 1992, when Woods was still a junior in high school, Notah Begay and Casey Martin asked coach Wally Goodwin if they could redshirt. Both saw issues in their games they wanted to work on away from the glare of competition while getting ahead in the classroom, allowing more time to concentrate on golf as juniors and seniors.

"And," Martin noted, "we wanted to be ready for our fifth year, to stack the tables. We had heard Tiger looked good to come to Stanford."

In the spring of 1994, Stanford won the NCAA title without Woods, with Begay setting an NCAA record by shooting 62 in the second round in McKinney, Texas. When Woods came on board that fall, the anticipation was huge for a sleepy sport such as golf.

In October, the team went to Birmingham, Alabama, for the Jerry Pate Invitational at Shoal Creek, a place that earned its own bit of infamy around the time of the 1990 PGA Championship when the club's owner—and a member at Augusta National—Hall Thompson sparked a controversy concerning a racist comment about prohibiting African American members.

Thompson let it be known that admitting Blacks "just wasn't done" in Birmingham, creating an uproar that saw all of golf's governing bodies agree that it would not take any of its championships to clubs that discriminated based on race or gender.

By the following spring, Augusta National was introducing its first African American member. Cypress Point, long part of the rotation for the annual Pebble Beach Pro-Am, was no longer part of the tournament. The Western Open moved from its all-male home of Butler National. And so it went.

At the time, Woods was too young to understand, but he became fully aware of the club's background by the time he arrived for the college event.

"But from what's been said and written about it I understand much better now," he said. "I think it was a sad situation. It's not supposed to be like that in the '90s. Isn't this America? Aren't we supposed to be one big melting pot? Then again, it woke everybody up to the fact that this kind of stuff still happens."

Woods shot 67 in the final round to win by two shots, the last tournament he won during his freshman season.

Despite his fame, Woods did not escape the kind of freshman hazing you would come to expect. He was a star, but he was not above doing what was required by the upperclassmen. Begay particularly reveled in the high jinks, calling Woods "Urkel" whenever the freshman wore glasses, a nod to the character on the popular television show *Family Matters*. He also made it clear that freshmen were to carry the golf bags to the team van.

With considerable fanfare, Stanford advanced through its spring schedule and to the NCAA championship in Columbus, Ohio, where the No. 2 ranked Stanford Cardinal went shot for shot with No. 1 ranked Oklahoma State.

The Oklahoma State Cowboys produced eight team titles during the season while the Cardinal captured five as they flip-flopped atop the rankings all season. With Woods on board, Stanford was considered the favorite to defend its title.

But for Tiger, it was a long year. His U.S. Amateur victory the previous summer meant a spot in his first-ever major championship in April at the Masters, where Woods shot scores of 72–72–77–72 to win the sterling cup awarded to the tournament's low amateur. He tied for 41st with Mark Calcavecchia, Jeff Sluman, and Payne Stewart.

Finishing behind Tiger that year were major champions such as Seve Ballesteros, John Daly, Hal Sutton, Fuzzy Zoeller, and Ernie Els. It was a good showing, but Tiger's Stanford teammates were stunned.

"We were like, if that's how Tiger stacks up against Tour players, we're all in trouble," Steve Burdick, an All-American two years earlier, told ESPN.

"We'd been watching Tiger play since September, and he was even more impressive than what we'd heard," Martin said. "The contact he made was like nobody else I'd ever seen. It was a different sound, so crisp every time. His divots were tight and shallow. Never a clunker. And he was the best clutch putter I'd ever seen in my life. Big putt? Pick it up?"

At Ohio State's Scarlet Course, Woods shot an opening-round 73 and drew a rebuke for an outburst in which he smashed a club against his golf bag and broke it. Another warning would have meant a two-stroke penalty. Woods rebounded to shoot scores of 72–70–71 and ended up fifth in the individual competition.

And after both Begay and Martin missed short birdie putts that would have clinched the victory for Stanford, Woods came to the last with a chance to be the hero. He faced a 25-footer for birdie that seemed destined to go in and give the Cardinal a dramatic title.

But Woods' putt skimmed the edge of the hole, meaning a par, with the team headed to a playoff.

All five players on each side took part, with the low four counting. The Cardinal had four par-4s but the Cowboys had two birdies and two pars to win. That dream Stanford team came in second, one of the rare times in the early part of his career that Woods was not a victor.

THERE WASN'T MUCH TIME TO WALLOW IN DEFEAT. ANOTHER hectic summer lay ahead, which included the U.S. Amateur, where Woods would be defending his title. The tournament was to be played at Newport Country Club in Rhode Island, a place of historic significance in the U.S. game.

Founded in 1893 and overlooking the Atlantic Ocean, Newport was one of the first USGA clubs. And it hosted both the first U.S. Amateur and first U.S. Open in 1895. To commemorate the 100th anniversary of the Amateur, the tournament returned to Newport.

Joined by his coach, Harmon, and father, Earl, Woods hoped to join Bobby Jones and seven others as the only players to win the championship twice, and once again, Tiger made it to the 36-hole final and faced a tough foe who was not in awe of all the accolades bestowed upon his opponent.

George "Buddy" Marucci was an accomplished amateur player, 43 years old, and a Mercedes-Benz dealer from Pennsylvania. He didn't have a professional golf career ahead, obviously, or any other big golf goals. But winning the U.S. Amateur and beating Woods would be a huge accomplishment, and yet he was a heavy underdog and could play with some level of freedom.

Marucci took a 1-up lead through the first 18 holes, then extended it to two with a birdie on the first hole of the afternoon round. Tiger fought back and took a 1-up lead to the final hole, where Marucci found the green and needed a 20-footer for a birdie that would tie the match and send it to extra holes.

Woods had 140 yards left and chose an 8-iron for a knockdown shot he was working on with Harmon. The yardage called for something less, probably a 9-iron or even a pitching wedge, if Woods chose to hit it hard. But he decided to try a shot that was not yet perfected in competition—and he pulled it off perfectly, as it spun back to the hole and left him with two feet, clinching a second straight Amateur title.

In the celebratory aftermath, Earl Woods announced: "I am going to make a prediction. Before he's through, my son will win 14 major championships."

It was an odd number to choose, ridiculous if you think about it, but eerie in years well past Earl's death. Woods, at the time, was not being set up to chase Jack Nicklaus' record of 18 major titles. Perhaps in his own mind, sure. But he was still a year away from turning professional—and at the time, that was far from a given. The idea of winning multiple majors, let alone 14, seemed preposterous and was somewhat embarrassing to Tiger. He was not into that kind of hyperbole.

Years later, when Woods, indeed, got to 14 majors—at the 2008 U.S. Open—those words from Earl would seem prophetic as Woods went through a number of personal problems exacerbated by the public eye, and a litany of injury woes and went 11 years before his 2019 Masters victory.

Woods had yet to celebrate his 20th birthday. A big sophomore year awaited, one that would see him win the Pac-10 Championship with a record-breaking 61 in the first round, add another victory at the NCAA West Regional, and then fire a second-round 67 on his way to the NCAA individual title. He ended the college season with the lowest scoring average and was ranked No. 1 in the Rolex/Nicklaus Individual Rankings.

Sure, not everything went perfectly. Woods missed the cut at the Masters, shooting 75–75 just a few days after Jack Nicklaus declared that Tiger would dominate Augusta National for years to come.

"Both Arnold [Palmer] and I agree that you could take my Masters [six] and his Masters [four] and add them together and this kid should win more than that," Nicklaus said after a pre-tournament practice round in which Palmer and Woods took part.

"This kid is the most fundamentally sound golfer I've ever seen at any age. I don't know if he's ready to win yet or not, but he will be the favorite here for the next 20 years. If he isn't, there's something wrong."

Woods did not yet show much when competing against pros, however. He finished 82nd at the U.S. Open. He missed the cut at the Scottish Open. At the Open, played at England's Royal Lytham & St. Annes golf course, Woods shot an opening-round 75.

But he bounced back with a 66 in the second round to make the cut, then added scores of 70–70 on the weekend to finish as the low amateur, with his score of 281 matching the record set by Englishman Iain Pyman in 1993.

It was his best effort in 14 tries in pro events after having missed the cut in his first seven pro tournaments. He never contended, but the Open performance gave him a boost and ultimately played a clinching role in his decision to turn pro.

"That gave me so much confidence," Woods said years later. "I tied the amateur record at the time for 72 holes. At the time, it gave me confidence that I could do it at a high level. And the fact that I shot that low round—I made seven birdies in a 12-hole stretch—I thought for an amateur in a major championship, that was a big step."

He gained enough confidence to convince him to turn professional and not return for his junior year at Stanford. There is evidence to suggest that the decision was already made, that the performance in England was not really a factor, given all the planning that went into such a decision.

Still, playing well against the pros didn't hurt, and it certainly was one more piece of validation—if any were still needed.

But first, there was one more amateur event to play, and Tiger would be attempting to do what no one had ever done—win the U.S. Amateur for a third straight time.

4

TURNING PRO

Phil Mickelson slept poorly the night before the final round of the 1996 NEC Invitational. He knew what was at stake over those 18 holes at the venerable Firestone Country Club in Akron, Ohio. This was a major championship-type venue, and a victory—perhaps save for his first as amateur—would be the biggest of his young career.

Mickelson led by three and had a few rough patches of poor play, but he eventually prevailed by the same margin.

The win was huge for several reasons.

It was Mickelson's fourth of the year, a monumental achievement for any player, after he won early in the season at tour stops in Tucson and Phoenix and also at Byron Nelson's tournament near Dallas. It might even put him on track for PGA Tour Player of the Year, an honor bestowed by the players via a vote of the membership.

Mickelson also posted a runner-up finish at the Nissan Open played at Riviera Country Club. He was third at the Masters, where Greg Norman blew a six-shot, 54-hole lead to Nick Faldo, who won a third green jacket and sixth major championship—while Norman was left to wonder how he never prevailed at a venue so seemingly suited to him. Those same questions would dog Mickelson for a time as he struggled to win any major championship for the first decade of his career.

The Firestone victory held importance for other reasons. Mickelson was in contention through 36 holes of the PGA Championship at Valhalla a few weeks earlier, only to let it slip away over the weekend, tying for eighth. While that was unlikely to linger, a win at a prestigious tournament so soon afterward would be welcome.

And now, just a little more than four years into his professional career, he reached the top 10 in the world for the first time and won nine PGA Tour events at age 26, achieving that total faster than anyone since Jack Nicklaus more than 30 years prior. (Mickelson was ninth in the world, one spot behind Corey Pavin and one ahead of Mark O'Meara. Norman was No. 1, followed by Colin Montgomerie and Ernie Els, with Faldo fourth.)

At that point, Mickelson's résumé included significant victories. There was the win in Tucson (Northern Telecom Open in 1991) as an amateur. There was his first PGA Tour victory as a pro in 1993 at the Buick Invitational of California, played in his hometown of San Diego at Torrey Pines. He won the International later that year, a tournament that employed a unique modified Stableford scoring format that awarded points for eagles and birdies and subtracted for bogeys and worse.

In 1994, he won the season-opening Mercedes Championship, a tournament comprised of the previous year's winners. (Mickelson was later sidelined due to a broken leg suffered while skiing that spring.)

He added a second victory at Tucson in 1995, and then posted the big breakout season in 1996, winning four times. At the time of his NEC Invitational victory, Mickelson was the youngest player ranked among the top 10, with only Ernie Els being close to his age. He was a star in the making.

Although he had yet to win a major championship, Mickelson, then 26, seemed poised to do so. In 14 major starts as a pro, he posted six top 10 finishes, including three top 5s. Four of the top 10s came in the latest two years. Given his ranking among the top 10, his victory total, and his abundance of moxie and skill, winning a major was the next logical step.

"This one had a lot of meaning and a lot of things that went along with this," Mickelson said after his win at Firestone. "This is a major championship course and having the 10-year exemption and all the other things as the year comes to an end, so it was a very important victory for me and it was something that I kept thinking about and wanted so bad."

In hindsight, it is amusing to consider that Phil was concerned about the exemption that came with winning the tournament that would three years later become a World Golf Championship event. At the time, having that kind of job security was huge, even if it appeared that Mickelson would continue to win often enough and earn enough money every year for that never to be an issue.

And sure enough, it would be another 20-plus years before Mickelson would dip outside the top 20 in the Official World Golf Ranking. The idea of job security was never a concern for him the rest of his career.

All of this should have dominated golf headlines. A young, superstar golfer wins for the fourth time in a season. He has a good chance to be voted Player of the Year, perhaps lead the money list. He's now top 10 in the world and climbing. And he does it at a stout course against a loaded field of pros.

But on August 25, 1996, another story took considerable attention away from Phil's achievement. Three time zones away in Portland, Oregon, Tiger Woods won the U.S. Amateur for the third straight year, in dramatic fashion. And he was hours away from turning professional.

Mickelson's thunder may not have been stolen, but the intensity of its boom did not equal his accomplishment at such a big tournament on the PGA Tour's schedule. To suggest his party was rained on was certainly accurate. The bigger noise was coming from the West Coast, and it would rumble through the game for decades.

WOODS, 20 YEARS OLD, MOVED THE GOLF NEEDLE MORE THAN any nonprofessional since Bobby Jones—who never won three straight U.S. Amateurs. Jones, generally regarded as the best amateur in the game's history, captured seven professional majors while never accepting a dime for winning them. He also added five U.S. Amateurs and a British Amateur title, victories that were considered major titles in his 1920s era.

In 1930, Jones, at 28, won the Amateur Championship, the Open, the U.S. Open, and the U.S. Amateur, becoming the only player to win all four in the same year. It was called the "Grand Slam," and nobody has come close to duplicating that feat because few players of Jones' stature would remain amateurs long enough into their careers.

Had Jack Nicklaus—who considered remaining an amateur—or Woods done so, perhaps we'd be talking about a different kind of history.

But as the game evolved, and as the pro game prospered, the major championships took on a different look. The Masters, which Jones founded, wasn't even around when he played in his prime. And he never played in the PGA Championship, because it was open only to professionals.

Woods was well aware that he could become the only player to win the event three straight times, a history-making achievement. And he also knew he wouldn't be around long enough to match Jones' tally of five Amateur titles.

"The greatest players ever, Nicklaus and Jones, never did this," Woods said prior to the tournament. "I like to be unique, to accomplish things that have never been done."

Despite playing the Masters, the U.S. Open, and the Open—an amazing trio of major championship golf for any amateur player—Woods put his entire focus for the year on the U.S. Amateur at Pumpkin Ridge Golf Club in Oregon. And with 312 players in the field, nothing was guaranteed.

Although Woods expected to advance to the match play portion of the tournament, he still needed to shoot the scores over 36 holes of stroke play to make the cut to the final 64.

With business deals, a move across the country, and the decision to turn pro providing all manner of distractions, Woods was helped by the team that his father, Earl, assembled. Tiger's longtime friend Bryon Bell (who still works for him today as part of Woods' golf course design business) caddied for him during the match play rounds.

So much for any concern over Woods qualifying for match play. He shot scores of 69 and 67 over the two courses at Pumpkin Ridge, and not only did he easily make the top 64 but he was also the medalist. That mattered little to Tiger, who only cared about being one of the 64. Being the No. 1 seed was a bonus.

During the third round, Woods ran into Charles Howell III. Howell, who would later star at Oklahoma State and go on to a highly lucrative—if not measured by victories—pro career, was just 17, and it was the first time Woods faced someone younger than himself in the U.S. Amateur.

Howell's game impressed Woods, but he still managed a 3 and 1 victory.

"I didn't lose 10 and 8," said Howell, who hung in for 17 holes. "So I'm happy."

D. A. Points, another successful future tour pro, was the next opponent, and Woods took him out 3 and 2. Then came Stanford teammate Joel Kribel in the semifinals. Kribel posted an impressive summer himself, winning the Pacific Northwest Amateur and the Western Amateur—titles that Woods had won two years prior.

Unlike other opponents, Kribel was not in awe of Woods, simply because he witnessed him perform so many feats so often. They roomed together on the road and were friends, often practicing and playing together. But as was pretty obvious, it was all business now for Woods, who found himself 2-down through 10 holes.

Three back-nine bogeys for Kribel doomed his chances at an upset. The only hole he birdied, Woods eagled, turning a deficit into a 3 and 1 victory and a spot in the finals. Woods didn't make a bogey during the match.

"I know what Scottie Pippen feels like now," Kribel joked afterward, referencing Michael Jordan's longtime teammate with the Chicago Bulls, who often played in his shadow.

As Woods stood one match from history, Kribel could only marvel at what he saw and experienced.

"To win two in a row is just phenomenal," he said. "And to be playing in the finals for three, that's unbelievable, as far as I'm concerned. If you have just one bad match, that's all it takes. And if one person gets hot, that's all it takes. You can be beat at any time. To win 18 straight matches [if Tiger were to win the final] would just be unheard of."

IN THE 36-HOLE FINAL, WOODS PLAYED STEVE SCOTT, WHO WAS heading into his sophomore year at the University of Florida. His girlfriend (now wife), Kristi Hommel, worked as his caddie, and they became quite the story themselves. Their upbeat, enjoy-the-moment nature resonated with those following the tournament—which was a significant number, given the interest in Woods.

And it stood in contrast to the businesslike Woods, who wasn't much for small talk or any feel-good stories that might stand in his path.

A year prior, Scott reached the semifinals of the U.S. Amateur and nearly met Woods in the finals at Newport Country Club. In his match against Buddy Marucci, Scott built 1-up leads three times, only to lose in 19 holes. He also acquitted himself well at the NCAA Championship a few months earlier, finishing in the top 10. Now he was in the U.S. Amateur final, having defeated Robert Floyd, a University of Florida teammate and son of Hall of Fame golfer Raymond Floyd.

Woods won that individual NCAA title by four shots over Arizona's Rory Sabbatini despite shooting a final-round 80 at the Honors Course in Ooltewah, Tennessee. Scott, with a final-round 70, finished 10 shots back of Woods in a tie for eighth.

At the Amateur, Scott was undaunted by a huge crowd mostly there to see Woods. He rattled off six birdies in the morning round. When he made a four-footer for birdie on the 18th hole at Pumpkin Ridge Golf Club, he led by five holes. His thoughts?

"Just that it's not good enough," he said. "I wouldn't have been happy until I had him 10-up or something. You can't get that. He's that tough. Against Tiger Woods, no lead is secure at all."

Scott recalled just how big of a deal it was to be competing against Tiger in those days. The match began early in the morning, and yet more than 15,000 people were there, many lining both sides of the first fairway.

And Scott knew full well what he was up against, doing his best to calm his nerves while taking his mind off the person he was playing—a nearly impossible task. Hearing Woods strike the ball did not make it any easier.

"It was just as crisp a sound as you could ever hear," Scott said. "I didn't want to get caught up in what he was doing in his golf swing. So I just listened to him all day."

During the lunch break, Woods went to the driving range to work out issues in his game with his coach, Harmon, who noticed some posture problems. Scott went . . . to the merchandise tent. Kristi suggested they do so. They had not had a chance to do it all week. And they thought it would be a good way to take his mind off of things.

Harmon recalled years later that after helping Woods fix his posture problems, he felt he needed to tell Woods something, anything, to get him fired up.

"I know he's ticked off," Harmon recalled. "So I put my arm around him and said, 'Have you noticed that every time Steve Scott wins a hole, that cute little girlfriend of his is laughing at you?' Tiger turned to me and said, 'You noticed that, too?' I knew that was all I had to say. I remember after he made that [birdie] putt on the 35th hole, he sprinted past me going to the 18th tee. He slapped me on the butt and said, 'She ain't smiling now!' He never missed a step."

And Woods barely missed a shot in the afternoon. As expected, he rallied, winning three of the first five holes to cut the lead to 2-up. If you were adding up strokes, Woods shot 65 over the 18 holes.

"What I witnessed the day we played was his ability to flip a switch from average or below average in the morning 18 to just superhuman," Scott said more than two decades later. "For him to do what he did, he's usually been kind of a slow starter and works his way into the events. And he definitely did it that day. He started as slow as he could that day."

Woods made his customary comeback, but Scott managed to hold him off as they played the 16th hole, still clinging to a 2-up lead. Scott holed a lob wedge for a birdie to win the 10th, but Woods responded by crushing a drive 357 yards at the 11th, hitting a 5-iron to 45 feet—and then he rolled in the putt for eagle. A missed four-footer by Woods, however, meant Scott held a 2-up lead with three holes to play.

Tie Woods on two of the remaining three holes and he'd be the upset winner. Capture the 16th outright and he'd be the champion right there.

So, typically, Woods dialed in. He hit his approach to the hole just six feet from the cup, setting up a birdie opportunity that would bring him within one hole. Scott hit his approach in a bunker and blasted to 10 feet. He needed to make that par putt to force Woods to make his birdie, thus edging that much closer to a jarring takedown of Tiger.

And that's where things got interesting.

Woods' ball on the green was on the exact line of Scott's, a few feet closer to the hole. And so, as is custom, Woods used his putter to move the mark out of Scott's line, and then he replaced it to the original spot before trying his birdie putt. Standard stuff.

"The probabilities in that moment were pretty remarkable," Scott said. "If you think of the probability of somebody else's ball marker being exactly in your line . . . in a two-person match . . . it never happened the entire day. I don't think it happened the whole week for me, honestly. I have to hole my par putt to force him to hole his birdie putt. And then if I walk off the green in a different way and don't look, who knows what the result would have been?"

Scott did make his par putt, putting the pressure on Woods to convert the six-footer. And for some reason, Scott looked back to see Woods in his crouch behind the ball, lining up the putt—and he noticed that Tiger failed to return the marker to its original spot.

Had Woods putted the ball from the wrong place, he would have lost the hole; the Rules of Golf stipulate a loss of hole in match play for such a violation (Rule 14.7a). But Scott stopped him; he reminded Tiger to return his mark, and Woods holed the putt to pull within one hole. A lost hole there for Woods would have meant Scott would be the U.S. Amateur champion, and the underdog would have scored a 3 and 2 victory.

"It's kind of mind-blowing," Scott said. "Think of Tiger Woods losing the U.S. Amateur on a technicality, almost a knucklehead move."

Scott spared Woods a huge mental error. Woods birdied the 17th hole to tie the match—he made a 35-footer—for the first time since early that morning, then saw Scott convert a tough five-footer on the 18th to send it to extra holes, where Woods won with a par on the second extra hole.

"Given the circumstances, this has got to be my best round," Woods said.

For the third straight time, Woods was the U.S. Amateur champion. He won 18 consecutive matches and endured 36-hole qualifying over three years. Add the three straight U.S. Junior Amateurs before it, and you have a remarkable run in USGA competition.

"There's really no words for it," Scott said. "'Ridiculous' almost doesn't begin to talk about it. You think in one match something could go wrong. I remember my college coach, Buddy Alexander, had him on the ropes [during Woods' first U.S. Amateur triumph]. He had a putt on the back nine to go up 4 with 5 to play. And he missed it. And Tiger ended up coming back to win the match.

"You make your own luck. You have to hit unbelievable shots at the perfect time. It's almost like he got down in matches to show everybody how he could come back. It's not like he was leading all the time. One of the matches could have gone sideways. Even in the junior ranks. Think of all the ones he won. All it takes is one missed putt when you are supposed to make it."

Throughout his career, Woods always made the putts he was supposed to make. But that one at the 16th at Pumpkin Ridge? Scott finds a sense of satisfaction in how it played out.

And it didn't hurt that, years later, Woods acknowledged that gesture, giving credit to Scott for his sportsmanship while also acknowledging that he marks his ball differently whenever he moves it—so as to remember to move it back.

"We all play roles in life," said Scott, who later became a club pro. "Tiger Woods was meant to be what he has turned out to be. He was meant to go on to greatness. He was meant to change golf in so many ways. But that moment right there, if it turns the other way—who knows what happens? Would it have stopped him from going on to play great golf? Probably not. Would it have been a weird way for him to turn pro? Does he not go on and win two Tour events [that year]? It's almost like this perfect script that you couldn't imagine writing yourself."

For Tiger, there was nothing left to prove. The pro game—and all its riches—beckoned.

THROUGHOUT THE SUMMER OF 1996, WOODS' TEAM BEGAN THE task of putting a blockbuster plan together to turn pro. All of this was kept under wraps as Woods continued to compete, including during the U.S. Amateur triumph where it turned out all had been done but the signatures to make it official.

To that point, Woods had achieved middling success playing in pro events. Unlike Mickelson, who won the Northern Telecom Open as a junior in college, Woods never contended in a pro event as an amateur. The first time he made a cut was at the 1994 Johnnie Walker Classic, a European Tour event won by Greg Norman; Woods tied for 34th.

In all, he played 17 times in pro events as an amateur starting with the Los Angeles Open in 1992, missing cuts in nine events. His best finish was a tie for 22nd at the 1996 Open.

After opening the tournament with a 75, Tiger even got some

counseling from Jack Nicklaus, who at 56 ended up finishing a few shots behind Woods in the Open.

"I don't ever want to see you shoot 75 in the first round of a tournament," Jack said.

"He gave me a little lecture," Tiger said. "It was kind of neat, that he cares about me that much. I came to understand that to win a major, or any golf tournament, you can't win it on the first day, but you can lose it on the first day. And I lost it on the first day. When you're not playing well, you still need to get in the clubhouse around even par. I learned it the hard way."

Woods followed that opening 75 with a 66 and added a pair of 70s on the weekend to tie for 22nd with Steve Stricker, Jay Haas, and Mark James. He was 10 shots back of winner Tom Lehman but still was emboldened by being the low amateur and bouncing back from the poor start.

His 72-hole score of 281 matched the amateur record set by Englishman Iain Pyman in 1993, a mark that held until 2015 when Jordan Niebrugge posted 277 in finishing tied for sixth at St. Andrews.

"I've thought he should turn pro the last three, four, five months," said two-time U.S. Open champion Curtis Strange, an analyst for ABC at the time. "He's ready physically. He's mature enough. He has nothing else to prove whatsoever in amateur golf.

"The quicker he gets out here, the quicker he gets to be the best player in the world. You learn how to play golf out here; you don't do it in the amateur ranks. I personally think the day he gets his card he'll be a top 30 player, and he'll do nothing but improve, with the potential to be the best player in the world someday."

The performance at Royal Lytham and the victory a little over a month later at Pumpkin Ridge helped frame the decision to turn pro and, in retrospect, made it seem all but the easiest of moves.

But the truth is those results likely did not matter.

The evaluation that led to signing lucrative endorsement deals and turning pro almost immediately after the Amateur was in the works for months. Had Woods not won the U.S. Amateur, it seems highly unlikely he would have gone back to school. And it didn't take much of a sleuth to figure that out.

Woods long before accepted a sponsor exemption to play the Greater

Milwaukee Open and the Canadian Open. These would be events he could play as an amateur, but why? If he were going back to school, it would be time to get situated at Stanford.

Then there were the deals that were all but ready to go.

Five years and $40 million to sign with Nike to wear the company's logo on his cap and shirt. (Later, Woods would play with Nike clubs and balls, as the company started a golf equipment company on Tiger's back.)

Five years and $20 million to sign with Titleist to play with the company's golf balls and clubs.

That's $12 million a year before Tiger ever stuck a tee in the ground as a pro. And contractual obligations for that kind of money do not come together in the two days from the end of the U.S. Amateur to the news conferences in Milwaukee previewing an otherwise sleepy fall PGA Tour event.

At this point, Tiger and Earl (with the help of his team) already decided to establish a corporation and move to Orlando, Florida, which was presented as a great place to play golf year-round but was more likely attractive for the lack of state income tax. A Californian, Woods was more than willing to relocate, given the millions he would save by not having to pay income tax to the state of Florida.

"I had a pretty good suspicion going back to May of that year because he had gotten sponsor invites to Milwaukee and a couple of others," said John Strege, the *Orange County Register* reporter. "I thought he was going to turn pro, no question. The on-the-record quotes from Earl were about trying to get experience.

"But it was very awkward. We're in the reporting business, but Earl told us [a few reporters] four or five weeks ahead of time that he was turning pro after the U.S. Amateur. But he said we couldn't write it. He told us before saying anything that it was off the record. So we couldn't do anything with it.

"Whether that's right or wrong from a journalism standpoint, I'll leave others to decide. But knowing this and you can't write it? It was extremely awkward. You know other guys have it. It was not a great situation. But the indications were all there anyway. The performance at the Open, a top 25. Butch [Harmon] said his game was ready. There were plenty of indications. But the fact he had committed [to Milwaukee] back in May was the indication to me."

Strege's confidence level was high enough that he booked a plane ticket from Portland to Milwaukee, knowing Woods would be there.

Missing from Milwaukee: Mickelson.

He was coming off a busy stretch that saw him play four consecutive weeks, capping it with a victory. And he was looking forward to a week off before a trip to Japan for the Suntory Open, a tournament where he would finish third and collect a hefty appearance fee, likely in the low six figures.

There's no way he—or anyone, really—could know what was about to take place. "Tiger Mania" was about to unfold, with all its madness, changing the way golf was viewed, consumed, and played; the way players were compensated; and the way the average sports fan couldn't help but take notice whenever Woods played.

5

Hello, World

Nearing the end of his fourth season on the PGA Tour in his third separate foray onto the circuit, Jeff Hart epitomized the heart and soul of the game at the highest level. Not everyone can be a superstar, and for some, fame is extremely fleeting—if there is any at all.

For every Tiger Woods and Phil Mickelson, there are at least several dozen guys like Jeff Hart: excellent golfers fighting their way to play among the elite and fighting to stay there. No private jets, no swanky hotel rooms, no guarantees.

They were almost certainly local junior stars and played college golf—as Hart did at the University of Southern California—and could likely beat 999 out of 1,000 players they came across in the world.

All of which highlights the elite level at which Tiger and Phil played. If someone can beat nearly everyone else on the globe, but has little to no chance against Woods and Mickelson, what does that say about how far and beyond the Tour everyman the game's two iconic stars were?

Hart was 36 years old and toiled on the various developmental and mini-tour circuits, including the Nike Tour (now called the Korn Ferry Tour). And the 1996 golf season was not going particularly well. Hart was on his way to losing his PGA Tour card and would need to earn it back in order to play a full schedule in 1997.

By the time the Greater Milwaukee Open rolled around late in a long year, Hart was well out of the running to finish among the top 125 on the final money list, the cutoff point for establishing exempt status for the following season. A victory would take care of everything. A high finish, and the resulting payday, would go a long way toward giving him a chance.

And then, as fate would have it, he was eating lunch early during tournament week at Brown Deer Park Golf Course outside of Milwaukee in Glendale, Wisconsin, and decided to look at the pairing sheet for the first two rounds of the tournament.

"Back then they put them on a sheet of paper and then posted them in the locker room and in the dining area," Hart recalled. "One of the tournament officials came and put the pairings in the lunch room. I was having lunch with Carl Paulson. I went up with Carl and looked and he said, 'Guess who you're playing with?' I knew instantly it was Tiger. That's all they were talking about that week."

Only two days prior, Woods, 20, shook free of Bobby Jones, laying claim to one of the greatest amateur records that the game ever produced in winning the U.S. Amateur. But while Woods was chasing history, various aspects of his decision to turn pro swirled in the background. And it was a decision he hoped to keep secret until a Wednesday afternoon news conference in Milwaukee. But if anyone was listening, there was one clue. On the way to Portland for what would be his final amateur event, Tiger quipped to his father, Earl, "I'm never flying coach again."

It is almost laughable now, but Woods intended to play the Wednesday pro-am as an amateur, hoping to drop his decision at a news conference later that day. But that simply was not going to fly, as too many people knew that Tiger, if not officially declared, was already a pro. John Strege, the *Orange County Register* reporter, had been aware of the decision for weeks, as were other writers who had been tipped off by Earl.

Still, Woods played the pro-am—with another pro, Duffy Waldorf, and three amateurs, as if the original plan was still in place.

Woods released a statement later that day saying he was, indeed, now a professional. He was whisked to Milwaukee, after all, on a Nike private jet—and he would address questions at his scheduled Wednesday news conference.

The golf world buzzed with anticipation. But Mickelson took the week off after his Sunday victory at the NEC Invitational, one that gave him more wins than any other PGA Tour player that year. He was but another player in Tiger's world, and he could not have been farther from Tiger's mind.

EVEN WITH ENORMOUS ATTENTION FOCUSED ON WOODS, THERE were still plenty of reasons for Mickelson to feel good about himself. He was having the best year, arguably, of any player on the PGA Tour, with four wins. Although he did not win Player of the Year honors in 1996 (the award went to Tom Lehman, who won the Open that year at Royal Lytham), Mickelson compiled numerous other achievements, including finishing second on the money list. And winning four times is an achievement we came to take for granted in Woods' time, but one that is hardly diminished.

Those nine victories at age 26 were big. Throughout history, just a handful of players had won so many tournaments so quickly. He was the youngest player to reach that lofty total since Jack Nicklaus. The win at Firestone also came with a 10-year exemption, something he never needed to worry about again in his career.

By the time Woods turned pro, Mickelson was fully entrenched and headed toward the greatness he would attain, already a star in his own right.

And there was legitimate reason to believe he would have a better pro career than Tiger.

Looking back, in light of all of Woods' accomplishments, it seems a prophecy in utter lunacy.

But think about how each entered the pro game, both with incredible credentials but Mickelson already having loosened the shackles on exempt status. Even the best players struggle to get on the PGA Tour in the beginning, and Mickelson never faced that problem.

His win in Tucson as an amateur was a rare feat and portended success. It was no fluke. Woods, meanwhile, never contended in a pro event as an amateur, his best finish the tie for 22nd at the Open six weeks prior to turning pro. He missed more cuts than he made, and while his skills were lauded by the likes of Jack Nicklaus, Arnold Palmer, and Greg Norman, no crystal balls could have predicted such greatness.

"I would suggest that if you look hard at their games—and this is not to take anything away from Tiger's six USGA titles, because match play is incredibly difficult, but Tiger's M.O. was to play sloppy, give away a few early, dig himself a hole, and then suddenly something happened," said Brett Avery, who covered both Mickelson's and Woods' amateur careers extensively for *Golf World* magazine. "He would rush ahead, and it was almost like the end of a mile race or a horse race where he just got his nose in front at the wire. He pulled it off again and again and again. He won a remarkable number of matches 1-up or 2-up or 2 and 1. Phil won his U.S. Amateur final 7 and 6. If you look at Phil's match play record, he was putting people away.

"So I'd want Phil's formative years rather than Tiger's from the standpoint of so many strong performances throughout. Tiger never really got close in a Tour event. That is the big thing that shocked me when he started playing as a pro. I knew he was going to be good, but because of the way he had played in Tour events [as an amateur], I didn't expect him to do what he did as quickly as he did.

"Alternatively, I didn't expect Phil to go out in his first year as a pro and kind of slash it around. You would have thought it would have been the other way around."

Mickelson might be excused if his pro career got off to a slower start than Tiger's, simply because he packed in so much at the end of his amateur career. After winning the Tucson event, Mickelson made the cut at the Masters, U.S. Open, and the Open in 1991. He played a full college schedule through the spring of 1992, when he won his third NCAA title. Soon after, he was heading to 36-hole qualifying for the U.S. Open and making his pro debut at the U.S. Open.

"So many people talk about his short game and the touch he has," Avery said. "But especially from an early age, it was the imagination. With Tiger it was the ability. They both could see a shot. Tiger would see the correct shot, and he'd want to be two yards in another direction, because then he's got the precise angle and distance to the hole.

"Phil could envision a shot that nobody else could. Which do you go with? Do you go with the technical, the tactical? 'I can see checkmate seven moves away.' Or do you go with the guy who is like a jazz musician, hand him one of the instruments, and see what he does?"

Jim "Bones" Mackay certainly learned quickly what he was dealing with in Mickelson. From Phil's first moment as a pro in 1992 through midsummer of 2017, Mackay was Mickelson's caddie, the relationship coming together through Mickelson's college coach and future agent Steve Loy.

"The first time I ever caddied for him was at U.S. Open qualifying in Memphis and he was an amateur," Mackay said. "I didn't really know him at all. We had a couple of five-minute conversations over the phone. And we didn't play a practice round. He had just won the NCAAs. He flew in and said, 'I'll see you on the tee.' And off we went.

"There were something like 80 guys for 16 spots. He shot 69 in the first round and broke the course record the second round. It was an amazing day for me. It was incredible how talented he was. He shot 62 and then it was off to Pebble."

Mickelson missed the cut in his first pro tournament, but Mackay knew he was working for a potentially special player.

"It was such a fascinating job to have because he played so differently," Mackay said. "At that point, I had worked for Larry Mize and Scott Simpson and a little bit for Curtis Strange and a couple of other players.

"All of a sudden I'm working for this guy who hits the ball much farther than any of the other guys I had ever worked for. A guy who is, 'I can pull off this shot. I can do this.' It was incredible. He's hitting it over trees; I'm looking under, he's looking over. So for me, I had to really adjust. This is the way he plays. I enjoyed it."

FROM THE TIME WOODS TOOK OFF IN PORTLAND AND LANDED IN Milwaukee, he went from poor college kid to multimillionaire without seeing a penny hit his bank account. The various deals with Nike and Titleist made it clear that he would never be stressed for money again.

Except he was still "broke" for the time being. As Strege reported in *Tiger,* Woods paid for a Tuesday dinner with a gift certificate. On the way to the course on Wednesday, Butch Harmon asked Woods if he had his checkbook. Woods was flummoxed.

"You have to pay the entry fee," Harmon told him.

"Butch, I don't have $100," Tiger said.

So Harmon loaned him the money.

Upon arrival, Woods transferred his golf clubs from a Ping carry bag into a big, new Titleist tour staff bag with his name stitched on it. And he reveled in some of the new swag he got as part of the Nike team.

"The best thing about getting all this stuff is the bags," Woods said. "I swear. The Nike bags have so many pockets. They're awesome."

Nike shipped him numerous shirts and pants, and sent in Nike bags. Waiting in his locker were three-dozen Titleist Tour Balata golf balls and four new Titleist golf gloves. It wasn't Christmas, but for a kid who became accustomed to coveting all the various perks that came to him for playing the game, this was the closest thing.

Naturally, Woods was adorned in Nike apparel, head to toe. The Nike Swoosh was everywhere—including on clothing worn by Earl and Tida, his parents.

Meanwhile, the media contingent swelled far beyond what was ever seen at a sleepy fall event that arrived well after the last major championship and in the middle of America's passion: college and pro football. The tournament attracted just four of the top 30 money winners and was eventually won in a playoff by Loren Roberts over Wisconsin's Jerry Kelly. Another Wisconsin resident, Steve Stricker, finished a shot back.

But all the attention was focused on Woods.

"I find it unfortunate that it has to be that way," Greater Milwaukee Open executive director Tom Strong said of the way Woods was dominating the pre-tournament discussion. "There are a lot of good players who don't get the recognition they deserve. What we have to keep in mind is, he's one of 156 players here. We want to do what we can to be sure Tiger's stay in Milwaukee is successful, but we'd do that for anybody who is attracting this much attention."

It became the way the golf world operated. Strong and a multitude of other tournament directors learned that for a good part of Woods' career, there were "Tiger tournaments" and then the rest. Through no fault of their own, these events were often judged on whether or not Woods played.

And if he did, it required a special diligence and attention to detail to accommodate Woods. It became a real issue; he was not big on giving people much advance warning. When Woods played, more media showed up and attendance spiked, meaning more concession venues, restrooms, and parking were needed. Hard costs increased for the necessary extras, but the payoffs included more ticket sales and far bigger television ratings for the title sponsor. Tiger boosted the PGA Tour and its tournaments unlike anyone else, adding headaches and the need for plenty of planning.

Woods was a media magnet. Other players were bound to get jealous or annoyed or put off by all the Tiger talk. But as we've seen time and again throughout the years, it was justified beyond the anecdotal evidence.

Only days after pushing past Bobby Jones, Woods was being showered with millions of dollars without yet having his name announced on the first tee as a professional. And people were interested.

Ratings for the final round of the U.S. Amateur were astronomical for a golf event, let alone the Amateur. Although the viewing times didn't match up exactly, Tiger's final match drew a 5.3 overnight rating, which roughly translates to five million viewers—something surpassed only by major championships. And to think, on the same day, Mickelson was winning a tournament in which he was grouped with Greg Norman— the "Great White Shark" who was ranked No. 1 in the world.

Understandably, ESPN chose to televise the first two rounds of Woods' professional career and altered its viewing schedule to make sure he was in the TV window on both Thursday and Friday.

After being introduced at the news conference, Woods broke into a smile and delivered the words that remain famous today: "Well, I guess . . . hello, world."

That seemed a pithy way to greet the audience, but it turned out to be part of a marketing slogan that Nike would later unveil: "Hello World."

He went on to explain his decision to turn pro and how it was in consultation with his parents and other trusted confidants, how his play of late factored in, and how his game could suffer from stagnation if he remained an amateur. The time was right, he said.

All the while, Earl basked in the glory. Never one to shy away from a reporter with a notebook or an interviewer with a microphone, Woods' dad was understandably proud of how his son's career had evolved to this point. Earl talked big, and Tiger delivered.

Unlike Mickelson's father—who was never out front, never before the cameras, never part of the story—Earl relished the spotlight. He gave several interviews that day, including one in which he said that if Tiger hadn't gone into golf, "he would probably be a 400-meter runner, and he'd be kicking Michael Johnson's ass. If you think his swing is pretty, you ought to see him run.

"There is no comprehension by anyone on the impact this kid is going to have not only on the game of golf but on the world itself," Earl said. "He'll cut your heart out in a heartbeat and think nothing of it."

If that didn't cause some eye rolling among the rank and file on the PGA Tour, then the Nike campaign certainly got everyone's attention. In a Nike commercial, Tiger said, "There are still golf courses in the United States that I cannot play because of the color of my skin." It was an immediate jolt, and it sparked controversy. Two days following the announcement that he had turned pro, 30-second and 60-second spots, along with numerous print advertisements, were rolled out.

While assuredly true that discrimination was still prevalent in various golf precincts, including the denial of membership for Blacks and women, it was almost certainly untrue in Woods' case. He was too famous and too connected to ever be denied a spot at any course he wanted to play.

While Tiger approved the ad, the bluster seemed—and remained— out of character.

The ad campaign didn't last long, but the words and the resulting reaction were a quick realization of the new world Tiger had created.

THE NEXT MORNING, TIGER'S PRO CAREER BEGAN. WITH CADDIE Mike Cowan—on loan from veteran tour pro Peter Jacobsen—Woods was about to embark on his new journey. Grouped with Jeff Hart and another pro named John Elliott, Woods faced a 450-yard par-4 that was lined with all manner of human beings, a simple foreshadowing of what would become a constant in his career.

First tee shot: 336 yards down the right side of the fairway. "Pretty good, isn't he?" Elliott said to the gallery.

"I had just never seen that kind of talent before," Hart said. "What stood out to me was his first hole, the first shot he hit as a professional at Brown Deer. I'm a straight hitter, and I'm worried about hitting the fairways. My first shot as a professional was in a mini-tour event down in Florida, and I can remember how nervous I was. It was a lifelong dream of wanting to be a pro golfer.

"And Tiger got up there and just ripped it right down the middle like it was nothing. You could see the intent and the focus was there from the get-go. That impressed me as much as anything he did. Mine was in total obscurity and I remember being really nervous. He's got 8,000 or 10,000 people [watching]. Then there's ball striking and distance. I had not played with anybody who hit it that long. Nobody hit it more than 30 yards past me. Here's a guy hitting it 60 or 70 [yards past]. That's just a huge advantage—20, 30 yards is negotiable . . . 50, 60, 70 yards . . . it's hard to beat someone like that."

Woods made an eagle during his round and shot 4-under-par 67. Not bad for the first time out playing for pay. He added another under-par score in his second round and yet was eight shots back, a bit of a wake-up call to the world of professional golf. With a so-so field on a rather unremarkable golf course, Woods played very nicely and was in the middle of the pack. A 2-over-73 in the third round knocked him out of contention, and by then he seemingly hit a wall—understandable given all the golf he played, the fanfare, the new contracts, the travel.

Tour veteran Bruce Lietzke, who played with Woods that day, was more than impressed after the round, despite Tiger's inconsistencies.

"He handled himself wonderfully, even though he was struggling with his game," Lietzke said. "I think he's going to be a real good representative of our game. Lord knows, we need it at the top. If he does become the next ambassador of golf, I believe the game is in real good hands."

The following day, hopelessly out of the tournament, Woods still did not disappoint. At the 14th hole, a par-3 that measured 202 yards, Woods hit a 6-iron that he believed he mishit, given he was trying to keep it low under the wind.

But the ball still flew the intended distance, and sure enough, rolled into the cup for an ace. The crowd, naturally, erupted, and Woods could have floated to the green.

In his first tournament as a pro, he made his first hole in one, the ninth of his life. (Woods would also make aces on Tour in 1997 and 1998—and then never again.)

A final-round 68 meant a tie for 60th and a check for $2,544 capping an eventful week that left the golf world buzzing.

AFTER ALL THE EUPHORIA, EXHAUSTION WAS INEVITABLE. AND RE-
ality was about to set in. Woods had no intentions of having a leisurely,
low-key entrance to his pro career. There would be no feeling-out process, no tiptoeing along to get himself established among the pros, almost all of whom were older and had little in common with him.

Today, it seems comical that there was legitimate concern about how
Woods would fare in the seven tournaments in which he was given sponsor exemptions to try to earn his PGA Tour card for the 1997 season.

Remember, Woods had no PGA Tour status. Like everyone else, he
needed to earn his way among the elite-level Tour membership, and
there were a couple of ways to do that. The most common at the time was
through the annual PGA Tour Qualifying Tournament, better known as
Q-School.

Mickelson never faced this fate. By winning the 1991 Northern Telecom Open, Phil cleared his path to pro golf more than a year before
he began accepting pay for play. A win on the PGA Tour comes with
an exemption that extends two years beyond the current season. So
Phil's win meant he was fully exempt for the rest of 1991, plus 1992 and
1993—regardless of how much money he won. (And Mickelson's 1993
win at the Buick Invitational of California, his first as a pro, meant he'd
be exempt through at least 1995.)

The Q-School was a stomach-churning tournament that caused sleep-
less nights and cold sweats. Stories abound about the agony of the experience. Careers hung in the balance, and it was the ultimate meritocracy.
Those who shot the lowest scores made it; those who didn't faced another year of uncertainty. Many entered a slew of mini-tour events, where
the pay was low and a glorified gambling element existed. Purses mostly
came from entry fees and the payouts beyond first place were small.

The Q-School encompassed as many as three stages, depending on
various qualifying criteria. Making it to the final, held in early December, at least meant having some status on the PGA Tour's developmental circuit, then known as the Nike Tour, now the Korn Ferry Tour. But
that was never going to satisfy Woods. The idea of playing on a lesser
tour seemed preposterous. And while he undoubtedly still would have

received his allotment of sponsor exemptions without full status, the safest way to the big tour was to succeed on the little one.

To avoid the developmental tour, he faced the 108-hole gauntlet—six rounds—for 40 exempt spots on the PGA Tour. It was the crapshoot of all dice rolls of all lottery picks. The idea of him showing up at La Purisima Golf Course in Lompoc, California, left the ultimate golf geeks salivating. The sleepy event where nobody could breathe would turn into a circus. And the intensity was akin to a high-wire walk across the Grand Canyon. There was simply no guarantee he'd succeed, even for someone as heralded as Woods. One bad day, an injury, an illness . . . the scorecard only knows numbers, not fame.

But there was a way to skip all of that.

Make money.

Woods would never have to worry about cash for the rest of his life, but the numbers beyond the dollar sign as it related to his PGA Tour earnings meant everything at this point. Long before FedEx points became the standard, cold, hard cash and the amount earned was how you were judged.

If Woods could earn more than the 125th finisher on the season money list—the cutoff for full-exempt status—as a nonmember of the PGA Tour, he would gain his status for the following season.

That seemed daunting, even for Woods. As an amateur, he'd never even posted a finish among the top 20 players at any PGA Tour event. In his first foray into the pro ranks, amid all the fanfare in Milwaukee, he tied for 60th and made less than $3,000. The projected sum he needed was in the $165,000 to $170,000 range. And he needed to fare a lot better than he did in Milwaukee. Quickly. And often.

As a nonmember, Woods was allowed to take up to seven sponsor exemptions, places reserved in the field for players who otherwise were not eligible. They were given to the title sponsor of the event as a perk, a way to reward an up-and-coming player or one who was down on his luck. Typically, it was done to get publicity and sell tickets. That meant Woods would easily be able to secure these exemptions.

During the summer, when Woods was an amateur and the world wondered if he was turning pro or returning to Stanford, his father quietly lined up sponsor exemptions to five tournaments beyond the two he was scheduled to play following the U.S. Amateur: the Greater Milwaukee Open and the Canadian Open.

So, secretly seven were already secured, an exhausting schedule that saw him set to play the Quad City Classic, the B.C. Open, the Buick Challenge, the Las Vegas Invitational, and Texas Open.

But why think small? While the rest of the golf world wondered if Woods could earn his Tour card in such a small number of tournaments, Earl told author Tom Callahan, when presented with the challenge, "Seven tournaments ought to be enough to win one of them."

Following Milwaukee, with just six more opportunities, Woods headed to the Canadian Open, where the tournament was shortened to 54 holes due to weather. A final-round 68 meant an 11th-place finish and $37,500. Then came the Quad City Classic, now called the John Deere Classic, a small-town event in Coal Valley, Illinois, that always possessed a "we-can-overcome vibe."

The PGA Tour has seemingly never done it any favors, placing it in undesirable spots on the schedule. In 1996, Quad City was played the same week as the Presidents Cup. The relatively new tournament—the PGA Tour created it as a counter to the Ryder Cup—would pit a team of Americans against an international squad of players outside of Europe. That meant most of the game's best were at a venue outside of Washington, D.C. Mickelson was a player on the U.S. squad, along with reigning Open champion Tom Lehman and Fred Couples. The international side boasted Greg Norman, Ernie Els, and Nick Price.

If the golf world was to tune into a tournament that weekend, it would be the Presidents Cup.

Of course, nobody saw Woods coming to steal the spotlight from the Presidents Cup. He opened with scores of 69 and 64 to take a one-shot lead into the weekend at the tournament on the Illinois-Iowa border. A third-round 69 helped Woods maintain a one-shot advantage heading into the final round, and a slew of media bailed on the Presidents Cup and headed to one of the smallest outposts on the PGA Tour.

Was Tiger really going to win a PGA Tour event in just his third attempt as a pro?

As it turned out, no. For one of the rare times in his PGA Tour career, Woods failed to turn a 54-hole lead into a victory. (His record is an astounding 56–4 on the PGA Tour with at least a share of the 54-hole lead; the Quad City tournament was one of just two times out of 47 that he failed to win when holding the outright lead.)

A quadruple-bogey 8 on the fourth hole turned an early three-stroke lead into a one-shot deficit. Ed Fiori, a veteran player known as "The Grip" or "The Gripper" for the unorthodox way he put his hands on the club, was everything that Woods wasn't—short, stocky, 43, and trying to hang on—and he produced an unlikely victory.

"It was kind of like the rat snake getting the cobra," Fiori said.

Woods was understandably annoyed. He let an excellent chance get away. And while he expressed frustration, Woods also possessed enough perspective to realize that he improved in each tournament. His tie for fifth meant $42,150, and all of a sudden his earnings reached $82,194. He was about halfway to his goal in prize money and ranked 166th on the money list, needing to leapfrog some 41 players, with four more sponsor invites to go.

Now it was on to the B.C. Open in Endicott, New York, where scores of 68, 66, and 66 saw him tied for third, three shots out of the lead. For the second time in four tournaments, the event was shortened to 54 holes due to rain, and that meant Tiger could not improve or chase victory. But it meant two straight top 5s, and now his money total reached $140,194, putting him 128th on the money list and within striking distance of the top 125.

But before he could earn another penny, Tiger's first bout with serious controversy hit him squarely between the eyes—and altered the way he would approach entering tournaments for the rest of his career.

IT WAS AN AMAZING FIVE-WEEK RUN, STARTING WITH THE U.S. AMateur victory, followed by the big turning-pro week in Milwaukee, then solid performances at the Canadian Open, Quad City Classic, and B.C. Open that saw him finish in the top 11 three times.

Even for a 20-year-old kid, it was draining. The high-level golf. The travel. The scrutiny. And while he was playing terrifically, it was inevitable that Tiger was going to run hard into a brick wall and feel the pain. And that happened in Pine Mountain, Georgia, site of the Buick Challenge. He played a nine-hole practice round and was wiped out. He decided he needed a break, a reasonable assumption and one that players make all the time.

On any given week on the PGA Tour, a player who signed up for the event weeks in advance changes his mind and withdraws (a procedural element required players to be entered and able to play by the Friday before tournament week). Some do it before traveling to the site. Others get there and realize it's best to not play. At times, an injury forces them out. Every week, there are withdrawals that garner little if any attention.

A few weeks into his pro career, Woods learned the hard way that pulling out of a tournament, for whatever reason, would mean headlines. Woods had every reason to bail, and who could blame him? Well, those who were set to be at a Thursday night banquet, where Woods was to receive the Fred Haskins Award, given to the top collegiate player that year, could. By withdrawing from the tournament, Woods was also skipping the dinner, which was planned months in advance, and skipping that dinner turned out to be a bigger mistake than skipping the event itself.

To put it kindly, Tiger was roasted. Media, other players, all corners. Criticism came from journeymen to Hall of Famers, notably Arnold Palmer.

"Tiger should have played," Palmer said. "He should have gone to the dinner. The lesson is you don't make commitments you can't fulfill, unless you're on your deathbed. People will forget about it in a week, but once you do what he did the second time is probably a little easier. And you can't fall into that trap. The important thing is how he handles it from here."

Those words coming from Palmer hurt. While in college, Tiger shared a friendly lunch with Palmer at Stanford. (Even that caused a stir when it was learned Palmer picked up the check, a secondary violation of NCAA rules. Tiger was declared ineligible until repaying Palmer.) When one of the great icons of the game calls you out, and does so quite directly, it can't be dismissed. Missing the dinner was the big no-no. Woods could have skipped the golf, attended the dinner in his honor, and left. Several people traveled to Georgia for the festivities. Without Woods, the event was canceled.

Tiger was stung and apologized to all involved. He admitted he should have stuck around for the dinner, at the very least. And a valuable lesson was learned. Woods wrote a column in *Golf World* magazine explaining what happened and admitted, "I realize now that what I did was wrong."

Woods went to his adopted hometown of Orlando for a few days of rest but with a new resolve: to never be criticized for something like that again. From that moment, Woods made a habit of never committing to a tournament well in advance. Even if he knew for weeks or months where he would show up, he waited until the week prior, usually the day of the deadline, to announce his intentions. That could be hugely problematic for tournaments planning for his presence or anyone else who needed to be there because of him.

But to Woods, avoiding the troubles that the Buick Challenge caused was all that mattered. A late commitment meant he wouldn't be letting anybody down if he decided not to play—even though those commitments are nonbinding, they are a necessary step in order to compete. That way there could be no issues for signing up and pulling out.

PERHAPS SOMETHING GOOD CAME OUT OF WOODS' ILL-FATED trip to Georgia. The nine-hole practice round included Davis Love III, by then an established star who was 32 years old, had won 10 PGA Tour events, and was known for his long-hitting prowess.

Because of Love's own association with instructor Butch Harmon, he knew of Tiger before many knew of Tiger. He could see it coming—perhaps not the way the onslaught eventually hit the golf world, but Love certainly was not surprised when it arrived.

"One of my favorite stories that Butch would tell me back then was that if this kid ever figures out how to hit a wedge, you won't be able to beat him," Love recalled. "I was like, ' Are you kidding me?' 'He has no idea how far a wedge goes. When he figures it out, you won't be able to beat him.' I thought Butch was exaggerating. And it turns out he was right, wasn't he? For a long time, we couldn't beat him."

On that Tuesday at Callaway Gardens, site of the Buick Challenge, Love had a chance to talk with Woods and was surprised at what he heard.

"He told me, 'One of my goals is to beat you down the stretch,'" Love said. "I thought, 'Wow, this guy has a checklist.' He had us pegged and he didn't mind telling you, 'Hey, thanks for the practice round. And I'm coming for you.' And he did it."

Yes, he did—the very next week at the Las Vegas Invitational, then a five-round event that started on Wednesday and was played on three different courses. With low scores the norm, Woods' opening-round 70 put him well off the pace. But the extra day also allowed him time to catch up, and he did. The second round saw him shoot a 63 with twelve 3s on his scorecard. "He should have shot in the 50s," Harmon said.

Even with that low score, Woods gained just a shot on the lead, from eight back to seven. He got within six after a third-round 68. And a 67 in the fourth round left him four strokes back of Ronnie Black, with several big names, including Love and Fred Couples, ahead of him.

He was about to have that opportunity to take on Love "down the stretch."

Tied for the lead standing in the 18th fairway, Woods made par to finish with a 64 and then waited for Love, who was still on the course but unable to make a birdie on the final hole to win.

They went to a sudden-death playoff, where Love blinked first. He missed the green with a long shot into a bunker, and he was unable to get it up and down. Woods, who hit first from the fairway after hitting a 3-wood off the tee, knocked his approach safely on the green. He lagged his birdie putt close, and when Love missed a six-footer for par, Tiger was the winner for the first time as a pro—in just his fifth start.

"We've got to get used to it," Love said. "I think everybody had better watch out. He's going to be a force."

Woods earned $297,000 for the victory, but more important, that idea of going through Q-School was squashed. The money list didn't matter. He would be exempt for all of 1997 and 1998 and—with more victories to come, just like Mickelson—never needed to worry about his status again.

Mark Calcavecchia and Kelly Gibson missed the playoff by a stroke. Couples, Paul Azinger, and Paul Goydos tied for eighth, four strokes back . . . with Mickelson.

Phil never shot worse than 68 and was just two behind Woods entering the final round, where Mickelson carded a 66—and still finished four strokes back. It was the first time they played in the same event as pros.

It's unlikely Woods gave Mickelson much thought with so many players in contention during the final round, but Lefty was certainly on Tiger's mind later when he left on a late-night flight and fell asleep. At one point, Woods was jolted awake and blurted out "Fuck Phil!" with those around him likely just as startled.

"I was going to be caddying in a celebrity golf tournament the next day," said Mackay, Phil's caddie. "And we had dinner with the [band] R.E.M. guys that played in this Fairway to Heaven golf tournament the next day. Davis was friends with them, and so we all went out to dinner, and Davis was late because he was in that playoff with Tiger. Davis was like, 'I can't believe it,' like he was upset he didn't win. At the time, of course, nobody knew how great Tiger was going to turn out to be. And Davis was bummed that he lost."

Turns out there would be a long line of players with that feeling.

Woods went on to finish third at the Texas Open and then won the Walt Disney World Classic—a tournament he added to try to make it to the season-ending Tour Championship reserved for the top 30 money winners. Woods' initial goal was trying to make the top 125—he blew that goal away.

Playing the final round with Payne Stewart, then 39 and the winner of two majors, Woods held his own. Stewart shot 67, but Woods beat him by one. Although he later tied with Taylor Smith, it turned out that, inadvertently, Smith was playing with a putter that had an illegal grip. He was disqualified, and Woods won without needing a playoff.

Originally, the idea of trying to win enough money to earn his PGA Tour card seemed improbable. But in seven starts, he won twice, finished third twice, and posted a fifth-place finish. He earned $734,794 and qualified for the season-ending Tour Championship to be played at Southern Hills in Tulsa, Oklahoma.

In his first seven tournaments as a pro, Tiger registered five top 10s. For comparison, Jack Nicklaus had just one, a runner-up at the 1962 Phoenix Open, and no victories. Mickelson had just one, a runner-up finish at the New England Classic, but he also missed three cuts.

It was simply a remarkable start, among the best debuts to a professional career ever. He finished in the top five in five straight tournaments, a feat not accomplished since Curtis Strange did it in 1982.

After playing his last professional event as an amateur at the Open, Woods was ranked 431st in the world. He gradually climbed to 75th after winning in Las Vegas. He was 37th after winning at Disney, and even with a bit of a stumble at the Tour Championship—he was distracted after the first round by his dad's hospitalization due to chest pains—he tied for 21st and improved to 35th in the world. By the end of the year, Tiger was 33rd in the world.

Mickelson, in his only other appearance with Woods, finished 12th at the Tour Championship to cap a career year. He won four times and posted 10 top 10 finishes. He ended 1996 ranked seventh in the world and posted nine total victories.

Still, all the talk was about Tiger.

As the year came to a close, Woods was named *Sports Illustrated*'s Sportsman of the Year, a remarkable feat given his age and relatively short time as a pro.

In the accompanying story written by Gary Smith, Woods' father, Earl, said, "He will transcend this game and bring to this world a humanitarianism which it has never known before."

Among others who had been *SI* Sportsmen of the Year to that point: Muhammad Ali, Arnold Palmer, and Jack Nicklaus. Woods was about to turn 21.

The story did nothing to lower the expectations for Woods. Earl went on to call him "The Chosen One" and predicted he'd have "the power to impact nations. Not people. Nations."

This was a shock to all in golf, even to those who recognized Woods' amazing talents, because there were no guarantees. He'd notched two victories. He'd climbed well inside of the top 50 in the world. But he had yet to even compete in a major championship as a pro.

Mickelson, deferential during all this time, was not swayed. He was true to his convictions and focused on his own quest to win his first major championship. Coming off his best year as a pro, all the Tiger talk did nothing to dissuade him. He saw 1997 as a big year.

Little did anyone know.

6

THE MASTERS

Phil Mickelson had little reason to fear Tiger Woods—few confident players would ever allow for that kind of mindset anyway. At age 26, he was already a superstar. He took on the top guns of the day, players such as Greg Norman, Nick Faldo, and Nick Price, and staked his claim as one of the game's emerging stars, if not its brightest.

Already, he'd amassed nine PGA Tour victories as 1997 dawned. He was ranked among the top 10 in the world. He played on two U.S. Presidents Cup teams as well as a Ryder Cup team—and some believed he should have been a captain's pick as far back as 1993.

Truth is, while Woods was garnering all the headlines, Mickelson had every reason to believe the hype was surpassed only by the steep, rolling inclines of Augusta National. Sure, Tiger was good. Very good. But Phil knew how tough it is to win at this level and that you don't strut onto the PGA Tour, put your name on the golf bag, and start winning.

Mickelson himself went through some of those growing pains, needing seven months to win his first event as a pro, at his hometown tournament then called the Buick Invitational of California at Torrey Pines in 1993. And when he did, the burden was lifted. Although results were spotty after that—he missed eight cuts, including four in a row at one point—he tied for sixth at the PGA Championship and won the International.

Well on his way to greatness, Phil certainly might have been put off by the attention Tiger received after just a handful of events into his career.

He never suggested such, but one had to wonder. After all, Phil won numerous junior titles. He was a four-time All-American at Arizona State. He won three NCAA titles, for goodness' sake. And—unlike Tiger—he won a PGA Tour event as an amateur.

"Phil said to me very early on in his career, 'Listen, I'm going to win a lot.' That's an unusual thing to say," said Jim Mackay, Mickelson's caddie. "You might say that to your wife or your parents. But when you say it to your caddie, who's only been working for a few months—'Hey, man, I'm going to win a lot'—that's a guy with unbelievable confidence. Obviously he had incredible talent. But when he said that to me and started winning, you realize that this guy has a chance to be one of the greatest players who ever played the game."

And so Tiger's prowess, while impressive, meant little to those established at the highest level. Some might have felt envy, but others were waiting for him to get his comeuppance. Phil never expressed any angst or exasperation. He certainly never downplayed Woods' arrival or belittled all the fawning praise. Phil simply believed Tiger would need to back up all the talk.

Winning twice in his first seven starts, including Tiger's first win in Las Vegas where Phil finished eighth, certainly helped.

"Obviously he's played exceptional," Mickelson said at the 1996 Tour Championship. "He's earned the respect of all the players. And obviously he had great credentials coming out and so forth, but a lot of the players felt he hadn't proven himself at the PGA Tour level. And he has more than done that in a matter of seven weeks."

Throughout his career, Mickelson often heaped praise on Woods. For every poke or needle, there were 20 positive comments. Whether he believed them all is irrelevant. Mickelson figured out what was coming from Woods and saw the value in being reverential.

And yet, if he wanted to rationalize Woods' start, he could. Tiger won events during the sleepy fall period. Vegas and Disney were solid tournaments, but they were hardly considered among the upper echelon. Players who easily qualified for the Tour Championship mostly checked out. Let's see what happens. This is a marathon, not a sprint. Pick a cliché.

Of course, the hype train chugged into 1997, and Woods won the season-opening Mercedes Championship at La Costa, California, which was also known as the Tournament of Champions. It was a small-field tournament filled with winners from the previous year. A washout of the final round necessitated a sudden-death playoff on the only dry hole with the reigning Player of the Year, Tom Lehman. Woods quickly put the playoff to an end after knocking his approach to the par-3 green stiff, which added emphasis after Lehman missed the green. It was the third PGA Tour victory of Woods' young career.

But Woods did not win again prior to the Masters. He played in four more tournaments in which Mickelson was in the field, never going head-to-head, with Mickelson capturing Arnold Palmer's tournament the Bay Hill Invitational, where Woods finished ninth.

And that set the stage for the first major of the year.

Mickelson already played in the Masters four times, earning low amateur honors in 1991, then posting top 10 finishes in each of the two previous tournaments at Augusta National. The year prior, Mickelson narrowly missed playing in the final group with Greg Norman, and he eventually finished well back of the winner Nick Faldo, who overcame a six-shot final-round deficit to win his third green jacket.

The experience was simply another step in the process for Mickelson, who headed to Augusta National in 1997 having posted six top 10s in majors. The conventional thinking was it was simply a matter of time before Phil would rack up his first major title, and then add several more.

Woods, meanwhile, was playing his first major as a pro. His tie for 22nd the year prior at the Open was his best finish to that point in any PGA Tour event. Also in 1996, he missed the cut in his second Masters as an amateur. That meant he competed in just six rounds at Augusta National, and while Jack Nicklaus declared that Woods would "win as many Masters as Arnold [Palmer] and I combined," you needed to win the first one to get to 10.

And so it went. All the talk was about Woods. He was among the pre-tournament favorites, along with Norman, the No. 1 ranked player in the world.

To that point, Tiger had played in just 16 worldwide events as a pro.

And yet, the expectation was that he was going to win, although nobody could have predicted what was about to unfold.

We should have known. A few days prior to the start of Masters week,

Woods was playing at his home course, Isleworth, in Orlando. It is where he befriended veteran PGA Tour player Mark O'Meara, who was nearly 20 years Woods' senior.

The two became frequent practice round partners. O'Meara and his then-wife, Alicia, showed Woods the ropes around the neighborhood. They helped him get settled into his new home and recognized that he was still just a kid at heart, with no domestic skills, no decorating chops, no direction other than on the golf course. They looked after him.

And O'Meara was more than happy to play and practice with Woods. Not only did he enjoy the company but Tiger also inspired him to be better (O'Meara would, at age 42, win two major championships, including the Masters, in 1998). It helped him up his game as he already seemingly saw his best days on Tour.

But as if to forecast what was about to occur, on the Friday prior to heading to Augusta, Woods shot 59, an Isleworth course record. He shot 32–27 from the back tees, which then played to 7,179 yards and a USGA slope rating of 74.4. Basically, that means the course ranked among the toughest in Florida.

The next day, the duo decided to play again, and there was some money on the line: $10 automatic one-downs, meaning any time a player fell behind by a hole, a new $10 bet started from that point until the end of the nine holes.

Starting on the 10th hole, Woods birdied to immediately go 1-up, meaning a new $10 bet was triggered. At the 11th hole, a par-3, Woods had the honors and hit first.

"I haven't even gotten out of my cart, but he hits it and it's going right at [the flag]," O'Meara recalled. "It one-hops and goes into the hole for a hole in one."

Before even attempting his own tee shot, O'Meara quit.

"I put $100 on his cart and said, 'I'll see you on the range.'" O'Meara chuckled. "You're 16-under par for 20 holes. I quit. I'm outta here."

WE DID NOT QUITE KNOW IT AT THE TIME, BUT THURSDAY, APRIL 10, 1997, was the true beginning of what would become the legend known as Tiger Woods. Yes, he'd produced all those amateur exploits. He'd already won three times as a pro. He'd just turned 21 a few months prior. But the opening round of the Masters was also the start of something special.

Per tradition, the defending champion Faldo was paired with Woods, the reigning U.S. Amateur champion. The six-time major winner was coming off a victory (which would turn out to be his last PGA Tour win) at Riviera in Los Angeles. Despite having never played in a major championship as a pro, Woods was installed as an 8–1 cofavorite with Faldo and Greg Norman—the tough-luck loser to Faldo a year prior when he squandered a six-shot final-round lead.

It was not a smooth start, however, for Tiger. He appeared nervous on the first tee and hit an opening drive to prove it, launching it well wide of the fairway. He putted his ball off the green at the first hole and made bogey. He added three more on the front side, including the par-5 eighth and again at the ninth to take 40 strokes and stand at 4-over through nine holes.

But Woods gathered himself—he said he tried to return to the feelings of a week earlier when shooting 59 at his home course in Florida—and blistered the back with four birdies and an eagle. His 6-under-par 30 gave him a round of 70, just three strokes back of first-round leader John Huston (who holed a fairway shot for an eagle at the 18th, eliciting the *Augusta Chronicle* headline: "Huston, The Eagle Has Landed"). Faldo shot 75.

Woods got under par for the first time at the 15th hole, where he hit a pitching wedge to six feet on the par-5 and made the eagle putt to stand at 1-under.

"Going in it was, 'What do you think of Tiger?' Didn't ask you anything [about yourself]. It was so total Tiger," Faldo recalled. "It was unbelievable. It was so total Tiger it was annoying. He came in with such major attention. And he used it in his favor. No player before walked to the first tee with eight policemen around him. Suddenly Tiger decided he needed security. He had a whole different aura. An aura around him where everybody watched him and listened. And everybody wanted a piece of it. Yes, it was amazing.

"He went out in 40 and back in 30, and then we didn't see him for the next 14 years. He left us in the dust. It was a special day. It was the way he went out in 40 and then to win by 12. That's something pretty unique.

[It's like] you miss the first corner and then don't see him for dust. That's really what that week was."

Mickelson shot an opening-round 76 and was on his way to missing the 36-hole cut.

Woods was the center of attention. Instead of what appeared to be the calamitous beginning to his Masters, he turned it around stunningly and was in contention. He was in the second-to-last Friday pairing with Paul Azinger, who in 1993 won his lone major at the PGA Championship before a cancer diagnosis knocked him out for a year.

Azinger, 37 at the time, notched 11 PGA Tour titles but had not won since returning from non-Hodgkin's lymphoma in 1994. And he never fared well at Augusta National, his best finish coming in 1998 when he was fifth. Still, he was a veteran player who opened the tournament with a 69.

Woods was far more in control to begin this day, parring the first hole and then birdieing the second. His only bogey of the round came at the par-4 third, and from there he cruised to a 6-under-par 66 that included an eagle-birdie-birdie run at the 13th through 15th holes. He surged into the lead by three strokes over Colin Montgomerie at 136, 8-under par. Azinger shot 73 and dropped back into a tie for seventh, trailing by six.

When Woods made eagle at the 13th, hitting an 8-iron to 20 feet and rolling in the putt, he led the tournament for the first time.

"To me, I figured he'd be nervous playing with me," Azinger recalled. "Why should I be nervous playing with him? He was 21. I didn't even think about it. I doubled the first hole from the middle of the fairway, then played 1-under the rest of the day. I'm hitting 3-wood, 8-iron into No. 13. I'm hitting driver, 8-iron to 15. Those were big holes that changed the way it went. He hit 3-wood, pitching wedge to 13; I hit 3-wood, 8-iron. The first tee shot I'm thinking, 'Holy crap.' On No. 2, right down the middle, he's got 6-iron, 7-iron into the green. And he didn't miss a putt inside 10 feet. If you're going to drive it great and not miss a putt inside 10 feet, who is going to beat you?

"To succeed [on Tour], you have to drive the ball well. You have to make putts, and you have to be the best wedge player. That week, he was all three. If you're two out of the three, you can make cuts and make a living. If you have one of the three, you're going to starve. But he had all three. Even if he missed a fairway, he hit it a mile.

"He was unaffected by the magnitude of what he was trying to accomplish. That's what struck me. He wants to play well way more than he is afraid of failing. There were little things in my head that I envied in him because he wasn't afraid of screwing up. Not everybody thinks that way. That's an asset. You have to want it way more than you are afraid of failing. That was something that was very obvious to me. When people asked me about Tiger later in his career, I always said he wants it more than everybody else. That doesn't mean we don't want it. Best way to say it is the guy isn't afraid. He's less afraid of failure than anybody I've ever seen. As a result, he failed less often."

The azaleas and the dogwoods had no chance against the onslaught. Augusta National was on fire.

Not only was Tiger leading but Montgomerie also shot a second-round 67 to get into the last group on Saturday. He was three strokes back, but Monty was an accomplished veteran in the midst of winning the European Tour's Order of Merit (money title) seven straight years (through 1999). To that point, he posted five top 10s in majors, including playoff losses at the 1994 U.S. Open (to Ernie Els) and the 1995 PGA Championship (to Steve Elkington).

And he provided a bit of fuel for Tiger when he said following the second round, "There's more to it than hitting the ball a long way, and the pressure's mounting more and more. I've got more experience, a lot more experience, in major championships than he has. And hopefully I can prove that."

All Woods did was prove Montgomerie's experience didn't matter. He played a near-flawless third round with seven birdies and no bogeys for a 7-under-par 65 while Montgomerie made three front-nine bogeys on his way to a 74. He dropped 12 shots back into a tie for sixth while Woods led the tournament by nine.

It was a remarkable display from Woods, especially for a 21-year-old playing in his first major championship as a pro. Woods missed a single fairway and just one green—at the par-4 third, where he saved par with a 10-footer.

"I'm probably the reason he did what he did," Montgomerie said years later. "I played with Tiger on that famous day on the Saturday. I witnessed something very special that day. I thought I would beat him. I was wrong. And everyone else was wrong as well. But I admitted it. I'd just witnessed something very special. I thought I shot a very solid 74 until I lost to him by nine shots. I witnessed something that nobody else had seen. I was asked, 'Will he win?' He'll win by more than nine. Of course he did. He won by 12.

"I'll never forget it. I outdrove him on the first. I hit the back of the bunker, and it shot forward and I got him by a yard. I could have walked in. I don't think I saw him again all day. I think he was 60, 70 yards ahead of me all day. It was phenomenal to watch him. He knew it was going in, and his caddie knew it was going in, and I knew it was going in, and everyone knew it was going in. The belief that he had that a ball was going to go in. Now Augusta is the most difficult to commit to and believe that the ball is going to go in the hole. Tiger had that belief at 21 years old. Incredible.

"I'll never forget what I saw close at hand. I was the closest to it all day. That was very special playing with someone we'd never seen at the level. He shot 65, and it was the easiest 65 I ever saw. Just something different about it. Never witnessed anything like that. I didn't really know what he was capable of. I felt I had experience over him. We could do something. I sorely misjudged him. And we all were. Nobody could have said what was going to happen, and that was the writing on the wall over the next 20 years. Very lucky to have lived in the era of Tiger Woods."

Montgomerie spoke beautifully and admiringly of Woods and what he meant to golf. But there were numerous occasions during his playing career that he could be less than accommodating. His moods shifted with his scores, and among those who often covered his European Tour career, there was always a level of skepticism that his charm could be maintained. Monty waxed poetic on the Wednesday before a tournament; not so much when he missed a cut on Friday.

And so it was that the Scotsman surprised the assembled masses in Augusta National's media center early Saturday evening by showing up to talk. Nobody requested him; nobody in their right minds ever thought he would want to talk after the beatdown that just occurred.

But not only did Monty take a seat in front of the scribblers, he also wowed them with his praise of Woods.

If there was any doubt about the outcome heading into the final round of the Masters with Woods leading Costantino Rocca by nine strokes, Montgomerie did his best to dispel it the night prior. "We're all human beings here," he said. "But there is no chance humanly possible that Tiger Woods is going to lose this tournament."

Reminded that Norman let slip a six-shot advantage a year earlier, Montgomerie said, "This is different; this is very different. Faldo's not lying second, for starts. And Greg Norman's not Tiger Woods."

Rocca, from Italy, famously lost the 1995 Open to John Daly at St. Andrews after miraculously holing a long birdie putt from off the green and through the Old Course's "Valley of Sin" on the 18th hole to force a playoff. Although Rocca, then 40, was a veteran of European Tour golf, he'd competed in just nine majors and this was just his third Masters.

Woods put to rest any doubts about squandering the lead by the turn after he made two birdies and two bogeys over the front nine. Rocca never got closer than eight strokes. At that point, all that was left was the 72-hole scoring record, which Woods set by shooting 3-under on the back—and converting a tricky par putt at the 18th—to finish 12 strokes ahead of Tom Kite.

IT WAS A DAYLONG CORONATION, A STROLL AMID THE TOWERING pines toward history. Woods, a man of color, took his place among the game's greats at an event that did not invite its first Black player until the year he was born.

That man, Lee Elder, was in attendance at Augusta National when Woods made the world pay attention to golf. In fact, Elder wouldn't miss it. He flew to Atlanta from his Florida home that morning and was driving—too fast—to Augusta when he saw the red flashing lights in his rearview mirror.

As the officer, who Elder noted was also Black, began writing out a ticket, Elder made his case to the Georgia patrolman.

"I gave him the whole story," Elder said. "I was telling him, 'There's history about to be made in your state. Tiger Woods is about to win the

Masters. I'm just trying to get there before he tees off." He just kept writing and writing. When he got through, he gave me the ticket and said I either had to sign it or follow him to the precinct."

And then there was the final kicker.

"He told me, 'I don't know who Tiger Woods is, and I don't like golf,'" Elder said.

Few would not know the name Tiger Woods again after this day. Black workers at the club snuck a peek at him on the first tee and stood on the balcony of the old manor clubhouse, cheering him as he putted out on the 18th while his record-setting performance was witnessed, in part, by some 40.1 million television viewers during the final round.

Those who played with him could only wonder. At the time, they weren't contemplating the social ramifications of his play; they were simply marveling at what was on display before them.

Woods set the tournament scoring mark of 270, 18-under par, and became the youngest player to win the title. His 12-shot victory was the largest in any major championship going back to the 1862 Open at Prestwick. There Tom Morris Sr. won by 13 shots—in a field that saw just eight players and on a 12-hole layout that was played three times—at a time when Abraham Lincoln was the U.S. president and golf had yet to be established in the United States. Woods later set the standard when he won the 2000 U.S. Open at Pebble Beach by 15 strokes.

"It's always a pleasure to speak about him," Rocca said from his home in Italy years later. "He has done so much for golf. It wasn't surprising. I had played with him when he was an amateur at the U.S. Open [the year prior at Oakland Hills]. I saw the potential he had."

In the immediate aftermath of his victory, Earl and Tida greeted Woods behind the 18th green.

The hug with his dad aired a million or more times over the years and played repeatedly for comparison when Woods won the Masters for the fifth time in 2019 and hugged his son, Charlie, behind the same 18th green. It was but one part of the dream realized for Earl, who boldly predicted such days would be common.

And yet it was difficult for anyone to envision such dominance. A victory in any major is a life-altering occurrence, but to do so by 12 shots?

At Augusta National, where for so long Black players were denied their opportunity to play?

Before he could even get comfortable in the green jacket, Woods took a call from President Bill Clinton, and later described it as if it were a chat with one of his buddies.

"He just said he was proud of the way I played," Woods said. "He also said, what meant a lot, the best shot he saw all week was the shot of me hugging my dad."

Mickelson was long gone. He missed the cut. Phil didn't miss another Masters cut until 2014—the same year Woods missed his first Masters due to his first back procedure, one that was announced only a week prior to the tournament.

But certainly by that weekend in 1997, Phil knew what he was up against. As great as he was, Tiger was proving to be every bit the star and more.

"I sat at home and watched it on the weekend after Phil missed the cut," Mackay said. "I'm sitting there watching it, and I couldn't believe a kid his age could consistently back off shots because of wind changes and be as composed. His golf I.Q. was incredible. I remember thinking, look at this guy; he's backing off shots; he's waiting on his wind, which is the key to playing well at Augusta, in my opinion. We all knew about the swing and the putting stroke. But at that point, I'm realizing how smart he is on the course and how composed. That kind of blew me away."

All in the game felt the same way. Even though the final round was a foregone conclusion well before Woods even got to the course, it was riveting. Nobody could take their eyes off the proceedings. And it sparked even more interest in Woods and what he would do next.

Nobody knew what was coming, but they certainly would be glued to their televisions, as golf ratings soared whenever Woods played. A commitment to a tournament meant an almost-automatic run on tickets, with tournament organizers scrambling to add concession facilities, parking places, grandstands, hospitality options, and security. It was wild. And it virtually never subsided, no matter when and where Woods played.

7

PINEHURST

The beeper.

It was huge at the 1999 U.S. Open. That bygone product of communication was nearly as big a story as the championship itself.

Phil Mickelson could have turned it into a great endorsement opportunity if he so desired, but there were bigger things on his mind.

One: his wife, Amy, was due to have the couple's first child, although it was apparent that the baby was going to arrive earlier than the projected due date of June 30. She was on bed rest after five months and began to go into preterm labor.

And two: well, the U.S. Open is a pretty big deal, and Phil was a threat to win any major, including the one being played at Pinehurst No. 2 in North Carolina, especially after having tied for the first-round lead. In fact, you might say the pressure was on him to rack up a victory in one of the game's four biggest tournaments, giving his immense abilities and the number of times he'd already swung and missed.

Celebrating his 29th birthday that week, Mickelson was already playing in the championship for the ninth time, with two previous top 10 finishes including a fourth in 1995 at Shinnecock Hills where he was in contention until the final holes at the tournament won by Corey Pavin.

But for a time leading into the 1999 U.S. Open, Mickelson considered withdrawing without ever leaving home.

"I have a once-in-a-lifetime opportunity to be there [for the birth], whereas the U.S. Open takes place every year," Mickelson said. "That's the way I've tended to look at it. I didn't know if I'd feel that way or not."

Mickelson shot 3-under-par 67 in the opening round to share the first-round lead with David Duval, Billy Mayfair, and Paul Goydos. And the result was somewhat surprising given his lack of preparation. Mickelson only arrived in North Carolina on Tuesday night from his then home in Scottsdale, Arizona, due to a Tuesday morning doctor's appointment.

Only after that meeting with Amy and the doctor did Mickelson feel secure in heading to the U.S. Open. He expressed reservations about going because Amy had endured some complications during her pregnancy. But the doctor assured the couple that the baby was unlikely to arrive early.

"I walked the course on Monday, and at that point, I didn't think he was coming," said Jim Mackay. "He told me he may come; he may not come. In a practice round, I had gone with Fred [Couples] and Davis [Love III]. There had been no moisture there in a long time. And these guys had trouble making pars in a practice round. It was that hard in practice. And then it all changed because the weather changed. He was very curious about what lay ahead and then he finally told me he was coming.

"He gives me the beeper when he gets out of the car, and he very matter-of-factly told me, 'I don't care when this thing goes off—you tell me—18th tee on Sunday, first tee on Thursday.'

"He was flat-out going to go home, 100 percent."

Mackay said he'd never used a beeper before or since. He kept it in his pocket, and he would be alerted if a message came from Amy. That was the deal that Phil and Amy made before he left home. Mickelson also kept a cell phone in his golf bag so he could communicate further if necessary. And a plane was standing by at the Southern Pines, North Carolina, airport.

"I figure it'll be about five hours and 15 minutes from the time I get the beep to the time I arrive at the hospital," said Mickelson, a licensed pilot who joked about flying the plane home himself.

With 13 PGA Tour titles to his name, a major championship was clearly a priority. Just not the main one at this time.

"I care now more for my wife and my daughter than I ever would about the game of golf," Mickelson said. "When I was 19 or 20 years old, I would have had a hard time envisioning that. But in the cycle of life, things change."

MICKELSON WON TWICE IN EACH OF TIGER WOODS' FIRST TWO full years as a pro in 1997 and 1998 and kept hovering in or around the top 10 in the world. His record in major championships up until the U.S. Open in 1999 was good if not great, with no victories but eight top 10 finishes, including a tie for sixth at the Masters won by José María Olazábal two months earlier.

Woods, meanwhile, was slowly putting together what would be an epic season, with most of the wins occurring later in the year. After his breakthrough win at the Masters in 1997, Woods found the going not as smooth in subsequent major championships. Some murmured that the major haul of titles predicted for him might not be on target.

Other than the 1998 Open at Royal Birkdale—won by Mark O'Meara, in a playoff over Brian Watts—Woods was not a serious contender in the eight majors played following his first win at Augusta National.

Woods followed a third-round 77 at Royal Birkdale with a 66 to miss a playoff by one stroke but posted just two worldwide victories that year and only one on the PGA Tour as he worked through the first of many swing changes that caused a lot of head scratching at the time. But he won three times before the 1999 U.S. Open, including a win on the European Tour in May and the first of five subsequent victories at Jack Nicklaus' Memorial Tournament, just two weeks prior to Pinehurst.

Following that blowout Masters victory, Woods told his coach, Butch Harmon, that he wanted to tighten up his swing and become more consistent. Harmon, while on board, told Woods the changes might take some time. "He wanted to do it right away," Harmon recalled. "I told him he needed to be prepared for things to take longer." Harmon said they worked on keeping the clubhead square to the target line for as long as possible, requiring a more vertical swing plane. The technical aspects of that took some getting used to.

Maybe that's why Woods' success leveled off in 1998 and why he was still relatively quiet early in 1999.

At the Byron Nelson that spring, Woods called Harmon from the driving range and said: "I got it." The changes they were working on, in Woods' mind, finally jelled. His swing felt more natural, his confidence naturally evolved, and he saw success on the scorecard. Woods arrived at Pinehurst coming off victories in his previous two starts.

"I kept telling everybody that I'm making some changes in my game," Woods said at Pinehurst. "And it's going to take some time. And I didn't like the way I played in '97, even though I won some tournaments. I didn't really like it because of the fact that it wasn't consistent. Anybody can win when they're hot; that's not that hard. But it's hard to win when you're off.

"And you saw that at the Memorial on Sunday. I wasn't playing that well, but I managed my game well, I used my short game to my advantage, and I went ahead and beat Vijay [Singh]. These are changes that I've made over time. And it was a matter of time before it started clicking. It wasn't going to happen overnight. I knew that. They're not as severe as you might think. . . .

"But I did make some changes to my swing plane, my grip, the way I released the club, and a lot of it had to do with I wasn't happy with the way I was playing. I wasn't as consistent as I wanted to be. A player may not win every week, but they want to have a chance to win Sunday on the back nine every single time they tee it up. You know you can win your share, but it's a matter of getting there. And getting there means you have to be more consistent."

When a guy wins the Masters by 12 shots and wins three other times and goes to No. 1 in the world at age 21 . . . well, for many, it seemed foolish to mess with his swing. But Harmon, Woods' instructor, understood full well what Tiger wanted to achieve.

As great as he was in his first year as a pro, Woods simply had little control with his irons: he didn't know how far they were going, and this was certainly true when he was using his short irons. And that negated his biggest strength: his ability to drive the ball farther than just about everyone in the game. Given that advantage, Woods and Harmon knew some changes were necessary to develop that consistency.

The results were predictable. To move forward, he first needed to take a few steps back. And in 1998, it wasn't like Woods was awful. He began the year by tying for second at the Mercedes Championship. He then won a co-sanctioned European Tour and Australasian Tour event in Thailand. He added four more top 10 finishes including an eighth at the Masters won by O'Meara before winning the BellSouth Classic for his seventh PGA Tour title.

But while he posted nine more top 10s the rest of the year, victories eluded him.

He finally won the following year at the Buick Invitational, played at Torrey Pines, starting an immense run of success at the venue he seemed to love more than any other. He tied for second at the Nissan Open and later won a European Tour event in Germany before his victory at the Memorial.

The changes were starting to pay off, and Woods opened the U.S. Open with a 68, just one shot back of the leaders.

One of them was Duval, who emerged as every bit the threat to Tiger as Phil. When Duval won the Players Championship in the spring, he replaced Woods as the No. 1 player in the world.

Duval caught fire late in 1997, with his first three career wins on the PGA Tour coming in consecutive starts. He added four more titles in 1998 while Woods won just once.

Duval then won four times prior to the Masters in 1999, including the Bob Hope Chrysler Classic, where he shot a final-round 59. When he won the BellSouth the week prior to the Masters, Duval was among the clear favorites heading to Augusta National. But a second-round 74 was too much to overcome as he finished tied for sixth, five strokes back of winner José María Olazábal.

He had his own issues heading to Pinehurst, however. In a freak accident with a coffee maker, Duval suffered second-degree burns on his right index finger and thumb and had to tape up the injuries. That limited his practice going in, but he still managed the opening-round 67 to share the lead.

"Seems like nice timing," Duval quipped about his injury that day. "I was obviously worried and concerned. Luckily, right now, it seems to be okay."

For Woods, all the attention on Duval seemed to be a good thing. While it might have motivated him in some ways, it also relieved some of the unrelenting spotlight that engulfed him since his Masters victory.

The term "Tiger Mania" was used often at the time, and Woods felt the full brunt of it. There was little room for him to breathe during tournament weeks, and his recent nice run only served to accentuate that again.

"I have become more comfortable with it over the past year and a half. I've become more adjusted to it," he said. "I understand a little bit more about it. Plus, with David Duval playing as well as he has, he's taken a lot of that spotlight away from me, and trust me, I'm not mad at that. Heck, keep it. But now that I've won a couple tournaments in a row, the fans are a little more eager than they were last year, and Tiger Mania is not as high as it was after the Masters, but definitely not as high as the Byron Nelson in '97 [which Woods won in his first start after the Masters]. I think that's when it reached its crescendo. I don't think it will ever be as high as that."

PINEHURST NO. 2 WAS AS MUCH A PART OF THE U.S. OPEN STORY as Phil Mickelson, Tiger Woods, David Duval, or eventual winner Payne Stewart. The home of legendary architect Donald Ross, the No. 2 course became his virtual playground, and he nurtured and shaped the course over decades of his life.

Ross emigrated from Scotland where he famously worked with Tom Morris Sr. (known as Old Tom Morris) at St. Andrews. He was the "Keeper of the Green," who not only won four Opens but also worked as a greenskeeper, clubmaker, ball maker, golf instructor, and designer. Morris still holds the record for being the oldest Open champion at age 46 (in 1867). But his influences on the game were significant, including on Ross.

Morris' innovations included ways to grow turf and maintain bunkers and all manner of aspects we take for granted today. Ross learned his lessons and eventually moved to America, where he settled in North Carolina in the early 1900s and designed the first four courses at the resort.

No. 2 became the signature venue, one that would host numerous championships over the years, including the 1936 PGA Championship, the 1951 Ryder Cup, and the 1962 U.S. Amateur, along with scores of other professional and amateur events.

But it never staged a U.S. Open. This was not due to any fault of the course, which checked nearly all the boxes of a major venue. But the idea of playing championship golf in the heat of a North Carolina summer and the stress it would have on the greens made it an unappealing venue. Few U.S. Opens were contested in the South for those reasons.

And yet, the pedigree of Pinehurst and advancements in agronomy and technology were factors that the USGA could not resist. It awarded the U.S. Open to Pinehurst No. 2 for 1999, making it the first "new" venue to host the championship since Atlanta Athletic Club in 1976.

The U.S. Open proved so successful that it returned again in 2005 (won by Michael Campbell) and in 2014 (won by Martin Kaymer). It is scheduled again for 2024, 2029, 2035, 2041, and 2047, with the USGA making it part of its top venue rotation.

"This is a golf course you have to think and think about where you want the shot to finish, think about where you don't want to be, and if it gets hard and firm and fast, wow," Stewart said on the eve of the tournament. "It will be a lot of fun. You're going to see all sorts of different shots played from around the greens. You'll see lob wedges; you'll see putters. You'll see all sorts of different clubs being played. And I think that's going to be what's going to make this week so special."

FOR MICKELSON, THAT BECAME APPARENT AS HE CONTINUED TO play well. And the story about the beeper got bigger as his wife's pregnancy and his plight to win his first major championship collided in the North Carolina Sandhills.

If the beeper blared, Mickelson was resolute. "I don't care if it interrupts a swing," he said. "I'm getting a car as soon as I can and getting to the airport."

Even if he were leading on Sunday?

"Yes," Mickelson said.

And what if you were on the 18th green with a putt to win?

"Five minutes, okay?" he said, acknowledging that he'd allow himself those few moments to try to finish the tournament. "But I want to be there for the full process."

This led to plenty of conjecture and a sprinkling of good-natured fodder as well. Given his inability to win a major championship to that point, some theorized that with a Sunday lead, Phil might be more likely to go into labor than his wife.

At that stage, only three players—Jack Nicklaus, Gene Sarazen, and Horton Smith—won 13 tournaments at a younger age than Phil's. But the "major" thing—well, it was an albatross. A big one. Phil was seven full years into his professional career and had not won a major. Perhaps the impending birth of his daughter, Amanda, alleviated some pressure.

"Now I have something to take my mind off a major championship," he said.

He even came up with a secondary plan for the beeper. "We've got a little code in case somebody gets a wrong number and beeps us accidently. So, if she punches in the code, I'm getting out," he said.

Nobody could blame Mickelson for thinking this way. Perhaps in bygone eras, the idea of missing a child's birth was more acceptable. Nicklaus, whose son Steve was born just a few days after his 1963 Masters victory, famously fainted at the birth of all five of his children. When his only daughter, Nan, was born, his wife, Barbara, quipped, "He was in the recovery room longer than I was."

If Mickelson didn't hit the floor over the prospect of finally winning a major, he wasn't going to do so at the birth of a child for which he desperately wanted to be present.

Mackay said he never considered the possibility of not telling his boss that the beeper sounded. What other choice did he have? There was some speculation that Amy might not say anything, and sure enough, she was watching the final round of the tournament and was again having contractions.

But Mickelson was adamant that she would not hold back.

"I made it clear, and she understands, that I want to be there off the bat and that I don't want to miss it," Mickelson said. "This is the most important thing as far as our family is concerned. I would be very disappointed if she were to go into labor and not call me."

So the pressure was on. For Amy. And for Phil.

FOR ALL THE TALK ABOUT TIGER AND PHIL, THEIR POTENTIAL AND their established greatness, there were plenty of questions going into Pinehurst about both players. Yes, Tiger won his last two starts, but the relatively quiet 1998 still lingered. There were whispers that the 1997 Masters and the subsequent success was just a long hot streak that cooled.

For Phil, it was more about finally cashing in and winning a major. Did he have what it took? Sure, he had those 13 PGA Tour victories, but in just over two years, Tiger racked up nine despite a year of change in 1998. Mickelson was beginning to feel the glare of unrealized potential.

But Mickelson was in a good place mentally. He left on that Tuesday after the doctor visit and told Amy that he was going to win: "I'm going to come home, we're going to have the baby, and it's going to be the best week of our lives."

Little did he know that on Wednesday, when he was getting in his only practice round at Pinehurst, Amy visited the doctor again, and the situation became more serious. If it were that way a day earlier, the doctor said, he would have not advised Phil to go. "My heart sank," she said.

In the second round, Mickelson and Duval each shot even-par 70, while Stewart's 69 put him in a three-way tie for the lead. Woods shot 71 and was tied for fourth, two strokes back.

Woods said, "To be able to go around this golf course, and even though not swinging as well as I'd like, I was able to still keep it in play, make pars, make birdies, and just hang in there. There's no way I could have done that last year."

Mickelson, of course, got more baby questions than golf questions. He told the media afterward that Amy visited the doctor again that day, that it appeared the baby was doing her part by not showing up for at least another week. "I'm really not overly concerned," he said.

Mickelson didn't know that Amy dealt with initial contractions that day. She didn't tell him, not wanting to distract him any more.

The Saturday pairings put Woods and Mickelson in the second-to-last group ahead of Stewart and Duval. In 1997, Tiger and Phil played during the final round of the PGA Championship, but both players were well out of contention. You have to do some digging to find that pairing, one that was more curiosity than substance. (For the record, both shot scores of 75 at Winged Foot and tied for 29th, 17 strokes behind winner Davis Love III.)

This was far different. The vibe was intense, electric. There was the veteran Stewart, 42 years old, a two-time major champion, competing with the next generation and loving the challenge. Although his win earlier that year at Pebble Beach was his first in four years, Stewart worshiped the U.S. Open and the style of play it required.

A year earlier, he played poorly in the final round of the U.S. Open at the Olympic Club in San Francisco, blowing a four-shot lead as Lee Janzen surged past him to his second U.S. Open title. Stewart left yearning for his second, a grand opportunity squandered. Now he was going up against the game's top players, all a decade-plus younger, and he was right there with another chance.

After some early-week rain, Pinehurst No. 2 saw a piercing sun bake the course, turning it into the fiery test for which it was famous. "I've been asked many times what's the hardest golf course I've ever played," Janzen said afterward. "Now I have the answer."

How tough?

Duval made three bogeys and a double bogey in the first eight holes. Woods started double bogey, bogey. Stewart bogeyed the eighth, ninth, and tenth holes. And Mickelson led by three shots.

All the while, that beeper lingered in the back of Bones' mind.

"The thing that was interesting to me, at this point Tiger has been around now for the better part of two years," Mackay said. "And he's looking like he's going to win a lot of tournaments, a lot of majors. And this is a great chance for Phil. It's a chance to get the major monkey off our back. And I was thinking, 'What if he has an unbelievable chance to win his first major and has to leave?' Tiger hadn't won a major for two years, but it [the 1997 Masters] was a pretty big one in terms of what he won and how he won it. The first one is the hardest to win and we've got a good shot."

Phil couldn't dodge third-round troubles. He bogeyed the 11th, 15th,

16th, and 17th holes, while Stewart settled down to make seven straight pars through the 17th. Mickelson stood one shot back in the 18th fairway.

And that's when his confidence shined.

For much of that week, Mickelson found it difficult to hit a cut shot—one that flies right to left for a left-handed golfer. His go-to shot was a draw, or one that curved to the right.

But as he mulled that second shot on 18, the pin was to the far left. It called for a cut—the shot Mickelson couldn't execute. Best play? Hit it in the middle of the green, take the two putts, and par—and get ready for Sunday.

Not Phil.

"I want to birdie this hole and get in the last group, so I'm going to have to try and cut an 8-iron," he said to Mackay.

Mickelson did cut the 8-iron, and it stopped five feet from the hole for a birdie, placing him into the last group with Stewart, who, watching from the fairway, hit his own excellent approach to 12 feet and made the birdie to regain a one-stroke lead. Although he struggled for a good part of the round, Stewart's 72 gave him a three-day total of 209, 1-under par. He was the only player in the field in red numbers.

With a 73, Mickelson stood alone in second. He was one worse than Woods, who shot 72 and was tied with Tim Herron, two shots back of Stewart. Duval's 75 knocked him three strokes off the lead, and in a tie for fifth with Vijay Singh and Steve Stricker.

"I felt very pleased with my golf swing," Woods said. "I shallowed out nicely. I bowed the hand down when I needed to. My trajectory was good."

He was also the closest to the lead through 54 holes of a major championship since he led by nine strokes at the 1997 Masters on his way to a 12-stroke victory.

And it set up what was the first time Tiger and Phil were both in contention at the same major championship.

Unbeknownst to Phil, Amy was much closer to giving birth to their daughter. With the onset of contractions, she went to the hospital. Phil called her, but Amy said nothing. She wasn't really keeping up her end of the bargain, but she also didn't have the heart to interrupt what could be a career-altering moment for Phil. This wasn't just missing a day at the office. This was the U.S. Open, and for all Phil wanted to be at home, Amy couldn't bear telling him. Like her husband, she was determined to take her chances.

While in the hospital, Amy was monitored and put on a drug called terbutaline to slow her contractions. After a few hours, she was able to go home.

MICKELSON AND MACKAY SHARED A HOUSE WITH FRED COUPLES and his caddie, Joe LaCava, that week. They spent their free time watching the NHL and NBA playoffs.

"We hired a cook, and all we did was watch hockey and basketball," Mackay said.

On Sunday morning, Father's Day, a late tee time beckoned, giving them a chance to watch some of the European Tour event that was on the Golf Channel. Miguel Ángel Martin prevailed at the Moroccan Open, which was a long way from what was at stake at Pinehurst in a few hours.

Throughout the week, Mackay heard comments from fans in the gallery, some begging him to take the batteries out of the beeper and feign ignorance. But the beeper was there for Mackay to hear, and he, like Phil, hoped that Amy could hold off for another day while the biggest Sunday of his career was about to unfold.

Mickelson was paired with Stewart in the final group, with Woods and Herron playing one ahead. A cool, damp day dawned, and Stewart wore a navy rain jacket but used scissors to cut off the sleeves, creating his own type of wardrobe.

Woods birdied the first hole, and so did Stewart, setting the stage for a day of drama that would go down to the final green and the final putt. Tiger was ultimately undone by some uncharacteristically poor putting.

After hitting an excellent approach shot to 12 feet on the 11th hole, he pushed the birdie putt, then blew the two-footer for par to fall three strokes back.

"I just basically yanked it," he said.

Mickelson's only birdie of the day came at the seventh hole, and it brought him to within one shot of Stewart. (Duval dropped out of contention with two bogeys and a double on the front side.) And when Stewart bogeyed the par-5 10th, they were tied.

A bogey at the 12th for Stewart dropped him a shot behind Mickelson. Woods' 30-footer for birdie at the 14th sent the gallery into hysterics, and the fight was on. On the 13th, Stewart bounced back with a birdie to again get a share of the lead.

The 16th at 489 yards was the longest par-4 ever in a U.S. Open at that time. Singh bogeyed to end his chances. Woods hit a 4-iron into the wind from 210 yards that he drilled to 12 feet, then made the putt to pull within one stroke.

A hole behind, Stewart's bogey dropped him into a tie with Woods, a shot behind Phil. And the tension continued to build.

Mickelson needed three pars to win his first major championship.

Woods missed the par-3 17th green, drawing a 7-iron on the 196-yard hole into a greenside bunker. He blasted to five feet—then missed the crucial par putt he needed.

"That's the last important putt Tiger missed for a decade," Paul Azinger told *Sports Illustrated*.

Back at the 16th, Stewart knocked his pitch 30 feet past the hole, but miraculously made the putt for par, one that Mickelson later said might have trundled out to 15 or 20 feet past the hole and possibly off the green. Mickelson, who also missed the green, rued the chip shot he hit, one he called "easy."

"Biggest putt of his life," said NBC's Johnny Miller on the broadcast.

That week, Mickelson came armed with a Calamity Jane putter, a replica of the one Bobby Jones used to capture the Grand Slam in 1930. It didn't have a wooden shaft, and of course it was for a left-hander, and it had what looked like a butter knife at the end of the shaft. And Mickelson putted well throughout the tournament.

But Phil and Calamity Jane missed the eight-footer, pulling it to the right, Mickelson making his first bogey of the round.

"After Payne made that putt, bells started ringing," said Rick Smith, Mickelson's coach at the time. "There was a church across the street. You could hear it on the course. It was almost a sign."

What looked like it would easily be a two-shot lead for Mickelson with two holes to play was a tie instead.

Both hit excellent approach shots to the 17th: Stewart to four feet and Mickelson to six feet. Not quite sure of the read, Mickelson asked Mackay for help, and ultimately pulled his putt a tad to the right and missed. Two big misses in two holes. Stewart made his to take a one-shot lead to the 18th.

For years, Mackay beat himself up over that read. "It was probably left edge," he said, having told Mickelson that he thought it was basically straight. "That is the biggest moment of my career I'd love to have back."

Mickelson never put it on Mackay, saying he pulled the putt. And so much goes into making one putt, including pace, that it would be difficult to blame the caddie in such a case. Phil didn't, but it stung none-theless.

"It was that shot where he knocked it close where the realization that he could beat me entered my mind, because until then, I felt like I was in control, making pars, and that I was playing well," Mickelson said. "And as soon as he knocked that four feet, I realized that par might not be good enough. So I ended up hitting a very good shot in there but just didn't capitalize on the putt."

Now trailing by a stroke with one hole to play, Mickelson watched as Stewart hit his tee shot that kicked into the rough by only a foot. From there, the lie was prohibitive, meaning he would not be able to go for the green. Phil pounded his drive into the fairway; for a guy who constantly mocked his own wildness, Mickelson was remarkably accurate, missing just two fairways in the final round.

But he was unable to get his 7-iron approach from 178 yards close, settling for a 30-footer up hill. Stewart, who needed to chip out, left him-self just under 80 yards. With a lob wedge, Stewart knocked his third shot on the green and had 18 feet left for par—and the idea of an 18-hole Monday playoff loomed, with Amy trying to hold off childbirth in Ari-zona.

When Mickelson curled his putt up close and tapped in for par, it came down to Stewart's putt. Make it and he wins the U.S. Open. Miss it and it's 18 more holes on Monday.

Stewart drained the putt, letting out a scream and two hardy fist-pumps to the cheers of thousands. Mickelson started walking toward Stewart as the putt was on its way, and it was Stewart who cupped his hands on Mickelson's face, and in the midst of his greatest victory, said, "Good luck with the baby. There's nothing like being a father!"

Mickelson left as soon as possible afterward. He arrived home at midnight, and the following day—about the time an 18-hole playoff would have commenced—Amy went into labor, with Amanda born several hours later.

FOUR MONTHS LATER, AND JUST A MONTH AFTER BECOMING THE spiritual leader of the U.S. Ryder Cup team that rallied for a victory, Stewart died in a plane crash. The Learjet he was traveling on from Orlando to Houston for the Tour Championship lost cabin pressure and incapacitated the pilots. It flew for hours, uncontrolled, before running out of fuel and crashing in a South Dakota field, killing all six aboard.

Stewart's death assured the tournament, already considered a classic, would endure as one of the most memorable of all U.S. Opens, given the drama that unfolded that day and the tragic way the champion's life ended just a short time later.

In the big picture, Mickelson accepted his second-place finish as the right outcome, as if that is what was meant to occur. He'd made it home for the birth of his first child without having to make the difficult choice to walk away from the tournament, and Stewart's maturity as a player and the sportsmanship he showed in victory also made an impact on him.

For Phil, it was also the first of six agonizing runner-up finishes at the U.S. Open, the only major he failed to claim. There would be others that hurt more, for sure. But three holes from the finish, he led and could not close it out.

For the entirety of 1999, Mickelson did not win a tournament. He missed the cut at the Open played at Carnoustie. He tied for second at the WGC-NEC Invitational, where Woods shot a third-round 62 and then saw Phil make a run at him with a final-round 65, coming up one shot short. Phil would not contend in a tournament for the rest of the year.

Woods, meanwhile, was on one of the game's greatest runs. After finishing third at the U.S. Open, he won six of his last nine worldwide starts, with just one finish worse than seventh.

Among the victories was his second major championship, a one-shot win at Medinah Country Club, where he held off a charging Sergio García down the stretch to capture the PGA Championship. Steve Williams, new on the bag earlier that spring, helped Tiger with a crucial read on the 71st hole that helped seal the victory. Added to the six individual wins was a World Cup victory where he teamed with Mark O'Meara.

The win was one of more relief than joy. The 10 major championships played since his Masters victory seemed like they'd taken an eternity, and as outlandish as it seems all these years later, there were murmurs about Woods' inability to get another major, or the difficulty he would face in chasing the number so many thought inevitable.

Such analysis proved to be well out of bounds because Woods was about to go on a run of epic proportions. While nobody could see the tsunami that was about to engulf the sport, Mickelson felt on the verge of his first major title, too. He had been trending toward that breakthrough, and Tiger was not swaying him.

And yet, Mickelson's frustration would continue for several years, while Woods racked up hardware left and right, dominating like nobody before him. A decade of incredible golf was about to unfold, with both players having memorable moments of triumph and disappointment.

8

TIGER SLAM

It was an unlikely place to be in an ornery mood, unless you were down to your last golf ball. The views from the 18th tee at Pebble Beach are among the best in golf. A morning round, with the waves from Stillwater Cove crashing beneath, can be good for the soul.

But Tiger Woods had no interest in the alluring vista. It was early on a Saturday, and he was completing the delayed second round of the 2000 U.S. Open, and he had just hooked his tee shot into the ocean. Woods held his hand out, somewhat annoyed that Steve Williams didn't give him a ball. The caddie knew what the golfer didn't, and he first wanted Woods to hit another club. Woods was having none of it, steam coming off the water and out of Woods' ears.

"I don't want to sound negative, but he had just hooked a ball into the ocean and now we're down to our last ball," Williams said during an interview years later. "He was adamant he was hitting a driver for the second shot. 'Take your fucking hand off that' [the driver head cover]. We had a bit of an argument. I know it's our last ball. There's OB [out of bounds] right, water left. I can honestly say it's the only time I was actually shaking.

"He hit a great drive in the middle of the fairway. But his ball is directly in line with that tree. He wants to hit a big cut out over the ocean, and I can't tell him. I thought the nervousness was over after the tee shot, but it continued. I couldn't say anything."

As the completion of the second round began early that morning,

Williams did not realize that Woods took several balls out of his golf bag the night prior to practice putting in his hotel room. Woods never put them back, and Williams didn't notice—until Woods tossed one to a fan coming off a green. Now there were just two left. "I wanted to go to that kid and ask him for the ball back," Williams said. "But I couldn't do it."

"I hit one halfway to Hawaii," Woods said of his tee shot at the 18th—with just one ball now remaining. "All of a sudden Stevie suggests I hit iron off the tee, and I did not say nice words to him at that time. So, I went ahead and hit iron. And I had a simple 4-iron to the green, and Stevie wanted me to hit it up the right side of the hole, and I said, ' Why do I want to go up the right side?' So I started it out to the left over the ocean to cut it back, and it just went long over the back, and I got up and down for a bogey. I knew something was up, but I didn't say a word."

Woods finished the second round with a 69 and a six-shot lead over Thomas Bjørn and Miguel Ángel Jiménez.

And Williams' exhale could probably be felt on the other side of the Pacific.

Woods went on to win that U.S. Open by 15 shots, one of the top feats in the long history of the game. The Saturday morning exploits among the crashing waves remain but a footnote. But it did produce an interesting what-if.

If Woods ran out of golf balls, he faced the prospect of a two-shot penalty—for violating the one-ball rule if he used a fellow competitor's ball or for "undue delay" if Williams or someone in Woods' group needed time to find him one. That six-shot lead goes to four, and all of a sudden the romp to victory is perhaps not so imminent. Not to mention the embarrassment and anger associated with such a gaffe.

Woods was never aware of that potential problem until well after the tournament.

It turned out to be the only drama for him and Williams during the course of a record-setting event that would end with Woods' 3rd major title and 20th PGA Tour victory.

WILLIAMS WAS JUST 34 YEARS OLD IN 1999 WHEN WOODS AND HIS team came looking for a new caddie. But Williams was hardly new himself. He'd been caddying for years, having started at age six in his native New Zealand. As a teenager, he worked for five-time Open champion Peter Thomson of Australia, and later, Greg Norman, Ian Baker-Finch, Raymond Floyd, and others.

And his reputation was impeccable. Williams came to be known as one of the best caddies in the professional business, a no-nonsense guy who was anything but a yes man.

In 1999, Floyd was well into his fifties and playing on what is now called the PGA Tour Champions. They won numerous times together on the regular and senior tours, and Williams was not looking to move on.

But a call from Woods when Floyd was playing the Doral event in Miami more than piqued his interest. Tiger Woods? Who in their right mind would not at least listen? Given what was known about Woods and his unbelievable potential, Williams knew he needed to investigate. And so as soon as the Doral event was over, Williams drove to Woods' Orlando home for a meeting.

Woods became disillusioned with Mike "Fluff" Cowan, who was originally on loan from Tour veteran Peter Jacobson but ended up sticking with Woods for nearly three years, through his first victories on the PGA Tour, the Masters, and into early 1999. Cowan was a bit of a celebrity in his own right, more Grateful Dead than Hollywood, but apparently crossed the line when he disclosed his pay arrangement with Woods in a *Golf Digest* interview, among other transgressions that may or may not have been that big of a deal.

So Woods was in search of somebody else, and it didn't take long to settle on Williams, who spoke his mind as it pertained to golf—a complete opposite character from Cowan. Williams was a strong presence for Woods, not intimidated by the best golfer in the world. And Woods liked that. He was good with someone so confident in his abilities to push back. He didn't want someone confirming a yardage or a club selection just to take the easy way out. And he welcomed a presence like Williams, who would suffer no fools outside the ropes as well.

Hired almost immediately, Williams began working for Woods that spring, and it wasn't long before they won their first tournament together at the Deutsche Bank TPC in Germany, a European Tour event. Then came a win at the Memorial, a third-place finish at the U.S. Open, and another win at the Western Open followed by a seventh-place finish at the Open.

But when the PGA Championship at Medinah Country Club outside of Chicago rolled round, Woods was again getting questions about his inability to add a major title since his 1997 Masters win. He'd produced just one close call since, at the 1998 Open, where he missed a playoff by a shot.

It came down to a duel with Sergio García, who was just 19 years old at the time, and a crucial moment on the 17th hole, a par-3 over water where Woods missed the green to the left. He needed to execute a delicate chip shot, and then still needed an eight-footer left for par to preserve a one-shot advantage over García.

Throughout his career, Tiger has mostly read his own putts on greens, only occasionally bringing in Cowan, Williams, or later, Joe LaCava to do so. Woods has been a terrific green reader—an underrated aspect of his success. But sometimes an extra set of eyes is necessary, and this was one of those rare times. Woods felt the putt broke ever so slightly to the right, and so he needed to play the ball just left. Williams, from the practice rounds, saw it differently.

"The line is just inside the hole," he told Woods with confidence.

Williams portrayed no fear, but he was dying inside. "Shit, what if I'm wrong here?" he wondered.

Woods drilled the putt into the hole, looked at Williams, and winked. Later, Woods said, "Stevie said, 'Inside left,' and I said, 'Perfect,' trusted the read, and made a good stroke."

A par on the 18th hole and Woods captured his second major championship. And it's always fair to wonder what might have happened if the Spaniard prevailed. He'd have one major, the same number as Tiger. Instead, Sergio would take another 18 years before he'd win a major championship at the 2017 Masters.

There was a photo of Woods holding the Wanamaker Trophy that he later gave to Williams and on which he wrote, "Great read on 17, Stevie. Thanks for your help, Tiger." It was affirmation for Williams, and it was for Woods, too. A trust was born, and their partnership would last some 13 years.

The victory was huge in that it was a burden lifted. Finally, Woods secured that second major title. "That putt was a turning point for us," Williams said. "And it cemented our relationship."

The result was a fifth worldwide win in 1999. A few weeks later, Woods won the WGC-NEC Invitational, the first of four in a row that included the National Car Rental Classic at Disney World, the Tour Championship, and the WGC-American Express Championship.

Woods finished 1999 with nine victories for the year, eight of them on the PGA Tour.

Without much fanfare, Tiger passed Phil in PGA Tour victories. Mickelson went all of 1999 without a win, and Tiger's eight PGA Tour titles pushed him past Phil. He tied him at 13 with the Disney win, surpassed him with the Tour Championship victory, and went two ahead with the victory at the WGC event played in Spain.

Phil did beat Tiger the following February at Torrey Pines, stopping Woods' winning streak at six tournaments. But Tiger won twice earlier that year, including coming from seven strokes back over the back nine to win at Pebble Beach. Phil would trail Tiger in PGA Tour victories for the rest of his career.

REGARDLESS OF MICKELSON'S VICTORY AT TORREY PINES TO STOP the streak, Woods played at an unbelievable level, his exploits in the majors only adding to his achievements.

"No offense to Jack Nicklaus or anyone else, but I don't think anybody has played as well as Tiger played in that particular time," said Butch Harmon, Woods' coach through 2002. "Look at 2000, for example, when his scoring average was 67 and change. He won nine times, three majors. He was the second longest hitter in the game, and he was hitting 72 percent of his fairways.

"He was doing things no one has ever done. He was winning tournaments by ridiculous amounts. He won the U.S. Open by 15, the British Open by 8. The scores he was showing were unbelievable, every week. The thing that separates Tiger from everyone else is his thirst to never be satisfied. If he's leading by three, he wants to lead by five; leading by five, he wanted to lead by 10. He was never satisfied with his game. He always worked to improve.

"He didn't have any weaknesses. And I don't think we can say that about anyone else who has ever played the game. Tiger was the best at every part of the game. He was the best driver, he was the best at controlling his trajectory, he was the best at controlling distance. His short game was the best; he putted under pressure better than anyone. He was the best iron player. In my 77 years on this planet [in 2021], and being around golf nearly my entire life, I've never seen anything like it."

Woods failed to win the Masters, a big blow considering his form and all the hype surrounding him. He opened with a 75 that included a double bogey at the 10th and a triple bogey at the 12th. He was nine shots back after a second-round 72 with a third-round 68 giving him a chance.

Vijay Singh, the Fijian-born golfer who, along with Mickelson and Ernie Els, would challenge Woods at a higher level than anyone else, prevailed to win his second major championship. Woods was within three strokes with 11 holes to play but never got much going. It was David Duval and Els who applied most of the pressure.

Els got within two strokes with a birdie at the 15th but never closer. Singh went on to win by three shots, with Tiger finishing a solo fifth.

"For some reason, the golfing gods weren't looking down on me this week," he said.

ANY PROBLEMS HE ENCOUNTERED AT AUGUSTA NATIONAL WERE missing at Pebble Beach. The 100th U.S. Open was Woods' 100th PGA Tour start at a place where he won the AT&T Pebble Beach National Pro-Am a few months earlier by storming back from seven strokes down with seven holes to play.

Woods won 12 of his previous 23 tournaments. In 11 tournaments that year, Woods won four times and finished outside of the top 5 just once. And at age 24, he was the No.1 ranked player in the world.

If there was any doubt that Woods was going to win, Paul Goydos made his mind up before the first tee shots were in the air. He played a practice round with Woods, along with Mark O'Meara and John Cook, on Wednesday. He predicted afterward to a couple of reporters that Woods would win by 10.

"They scoffed at me," Goydos recalled. "I remember walking away knowing there was nothing I could do to what he was doing."

Goydos offered up an example for the 12th hole, a par-3.

"The green is rock-hard, and the green is not very big," he said. "I can't hit a shot that carries the bunker and stays on the green. It's 200 yards downhill. I hit a 4-iron, and I flew the bunker, and it one-bounced and went into the rough over the green. So Tiger gets up there and hits a shot straight up into the air. And it flies over the bunker and stops four feet from the flag. I looked at him thinking he hit a hard 7-iron, and I asked him what he hit, and he goes, '4-iron.' 'What?' The ball had reentry burns on the way down. He had such control of the ball. He took 20 yards off it, threw it straight in the air, and hit it exactly as far as he wanted."

"Okay, then we get to 18. It's reachable [in two shots] in the summer. I had 230 to the front and hit 3-wood into that green. And Tiger was on the right side of the fairway, about 230 from the green, and he has an iron in his hand, and he hits this rocket to the green. It lands on the green near my ball. So we're walking up, and I ask him what he hit. 'Four-iron.' 'What?' He hits his 4-iron as far as I hit my 4-iron, and he hits his 4-iron as far as I hit my 3-wood. That's not even fair. He hit a 4-iron 195 on 12 and a 4-iron 230 into 18 and landed both exactly where he wanted to. I remember thinking, 'What are we doing here?' That's crazy golf."

Woods opened the tournament with a 65 and never looked back. He made six birdies and no bogeys over the par-71 course and made it look easy. The second round was marred by that bogey on the 18th hole, but he still shot 69 to finish 36 holes at 134, 8-under par. He led by six shots.

"I always enjoyed playing with Tiger," said Jesper Parnevik, who along with Jim Furyk played with Woods during the first two rounds at Pebble Beach. "I always played well for some reason. He was special to play with. During those years when he was so good, I would say what was most impressive was his focus. He has all the amazing shots that a lot of people don't have. But his focus was the most impressive. I said he could will the ball in the hole by just looking at it. That's what it seemed like.

"At Pebble, those greens were not perfect by any means. They were very bumpy. Poa. [*Poa annua* is the type of grass on the greens.] A lot of traffic. They were actually quite firm. I think me and Lance [Ten Broeck, his caddie] were going through his rounds; we couldn't figure out if he didn't miss a putt under 20 feet the first two days. Which is amazing around there. It was things like he did back then. Of course, he played well, and his short game was incredible, and he putted like a god. Just very hard to beat."

One of the highlights of the tournament was the 7-iron shot Woods hit during the second round from the rough on the par-5 sixth hole. From four-inch rough, over a tree (that no longer exists), past a second fairway, and onto the green from 205 yards.

The shot was so incredibly ridiculous that NBC-TV's Roger Maltbie explained, "It's just not a fair fight."

"Tiger's approach shot out of the thick rough over the tree on the right-hand side of the sixth hole was a very gutsy shot," Williams said. "One part of Tiger's game when he was in his prime that didn't get mentioned very often was his ability to not only advance the ball seemingly impossible distances from thick rough but also his ability to control the distance from what would appear to be an absolute rip of a swing.

"I remember that shot well and know for sure no other player would attempt that shot going for the green. Tiger has a great ability to see the shot and then execute it. His brute strength allows him to hold the club face square and somehow control the distance. Tiger would not think about the potential dangers if a shot like the sixth hole didn't come off. Instead he focused completely on the shot that's required, and his mental will would seem to enable [him] to hit some incredible shots from heavy rough."

Because of a weather delay, Woods' second round did not begin until late in the afternoon, and the group was not going to finish. A horn blew signaling a suspension of play when Woods was on the 12th green. He was allowed to finish the hole—and rolled in a 30-footer for birdie, with his trademark uppercut celebrating the situation and ESPN's Mike Tirico signing off the broadcast "Good night!"

Even after the golf ball issue on the 18th hole and subsequent bogey, Woods secured the biggest lead through 36 holes of any U.S. Open, one of nine tournament records he matched or set. He played the first 22 holes without a bogey as well as the final 26.

But there was an unusual hiccup during the third round. On the third hole, Woods' approach came up short of the green, but not in a bunker.

He then needed two swipes to get the ball out of some serious rough. He still needed three more strokes to get down for a triple-bogey 7.

Few players can win a tournament making a triple bogey, even fewer a major championship. But Woods still led by six, and when he made a birdie at the seventh hole, he was back to even par for the round. He ended up shooting even-par 71, still the second-best score of the day. Ernie Els was the only player to shoot under par.

"I played with him in the third round, and after two holes I just sort of knew it wasn't going to turn out well for me," said Thomas Bjørn, who shot 82. "And you end up sort of watching. Apart from the third hole on Saturday where he made triple, he was absolutely faultless. It was just a question of how many was he going to win by. There was almost a feeling he was saying, 'I'm this good and the rest of you are this poor.' That was almost the feeling I got. It was a case of him being so much better than everybody else at that moment in time."

Woods' biggest memory from that day? Making up for that triple bogey.

"I just wanted to get back to even par," Woods said. "Somehow, some way, if it was going to take me all day to get there, I'd figure out a way to get back to even par for the round. That's what I was thinking. And I was able to do that. And it was a huge task, and it was the second lowest round of the day. That's how tough it was out there. That was a mini-goal. And I told myself that just because I got off to a slow start doesn't mean I couldn't have a good finish."

THE THIRD-ROUND 71 HELPED INCREASE WOODS' LEAD TO 10 strokes. Bjørn, who was six strokes back after the second round, tumbled down the leaderboard. Only Els managed to make up any ground, leaping into a tie for second but a whopping 10 strokes behind Woods. It was the largest ever lead through 54 holes of a U.S. Open.

"The enormity of it doesn't really hit you at the time because you are playing a tournament," said Els, who shot 72 that day and finished in a tie for second with Jimenez. "But afterward, reflecting back, it was very special.

"I felt he was really at his best. He was different, especially playing with all the confidence he had in 2000. He just hit it unbelievable. The ball flight he had in those days was the best I've ever seen. The ball flight and the velocity of the ball coming off the club. I've never seen anything like that."

With that big lead starting the day, Woods gave himself a goal of not making a bogey, one that he figured would erase any chance of being caught.

"When I got to 16 and had that 15-footer [for par], that was all I was thinking about. Bury it. Don't make a bogey. Do what you set out to do. And I buried it. And I did the fist pump, because to me, that putt, that par, meant so much. That putt meant more to me than people might think.

"Playing 18, I could have easily hit driver down there, but I knew it was a three-shot hole, so I hit a 4-iron down there, a 7-iron layup, and then a wedge to the green and made a two-putt par.

"What not many people know is, if you watch the video of the last hole, I hit the first putt past the hole, and when I go to mark it, you can see me almost fake slam the ball into the ground because I was pissed that I had run it by the hole so far. It was four feet by. And now I'm thinking I could three-putt and make a bogey after I fought so hard all day not to make a bogey, and I'd end my U.S. Open on a bogey, and it would ruin the day, so I was steaming. Granted, I was going to win the U.S. Open, but I cleared my mind, made the putt, and it was the perfect cap to the week."

Els, a winner of four major championships and a member of the World Golf Hall of Fame, dealt with his own hurdles as they related to Woods. In 2000, he was runner-up in the first three majors, twice to Woods. And he was second to Woods five times, more than any other player.

"Growing up a winner and then running into a guy like Tiger, there was some frustration under the surface," said Els, who also won two of his major championships with Woods as part of the story—the 2002 Open and the 2012 Open. "But it was a good time. I won a lot of tournaments around the world at that time myself. I wasn't quite winning the tournaments he was playing. I guess that was the frustrating thing."

Woods' 272 total matched the lowest score in U.S. Open history.

Nobody else was under par, and his 15-shot margin of victory remains a major championship record; Tom Morris Sr. held the previous record of 13 shots, set during the American Civil War at a 12-hole Prestwick layout that was played three times, winning by 13 shots in 1862 over a field of just seven other players.

The comparison was absurd, as Els humorously pointed out.

"If you put Old Tom Morris with Tiger Woods, he'd probably beat him [Morris] by 80 shots right now," Els said. "Hey, the guy is unbelievable, man."

His scores were 65–69–71–67, and for the week, he made 21 birdies, 44 pars, 6 bogeys, 1 triple—and no three-putts.

"I putted so well that week. And the funny thing is, earlier in the week I wasn't putting well," Woods recalled. "I was a little off. I was having a little trouble consistently hitting my line. I was making putts in the practice rounds, but I just didn't feel right. It was weird. I was hitting too many pulls. So, I went to the putting green Wednesday and just putted and putted for more than two hours and found it. My hands were just a hair too low, so I raised them, and that allowed me to release the blade down the line. Everything clicked from that point on.

"I hit it great. And on *Poa annua* greens, I never missed a putt inside 10 feet for the week. Not missing a putt inside 10 feet on Poa is a pretty good stat. But it starts with the ball striking. I was hitting it so well that I was leaving myself, even on those greens, how small they are, with a lot of uphill putts. Having those uphill putts, especially on Poa because it gets a little bumpy, makes all the difference in the world."

Mickelson finished tied for 16th and years later said, "What [Woods] did at Pebble Beach is still the greatest performance in golf of all time."

AFTER WINNING THE U.S. OPEN, WOODS WOULD GO ON TO WIN 10 of his next 22 starts, including three more majors to complete in what has become known as the "Tiger Slam." Starting with the 1999 PGA Championship, he won 21 of 50 worldwide tournaments through 2001.

It didn't end there as Woods collected the 2002 Masters and U.S. Open to make it seven wins in 11 major championships. As for the 2000

U.S. Open, and a performance that might never be matched, Woods acknowledged just how good it was, but added, "I actually played better at the [British] Open that year."

Of course, he won by just eight at St. Andrews a month later, setting another tournament scoring record in the process. And then he was part of the duel of all duels with Bob May at the PGA Championship, needing to hole a tricky eight-footer on the final green to force a three-hole aggregate playoff.

May, a Southern California phenom who was a contemporary of Mickelson's, never won on the PGA Tour and was plagued by back issues throughout his career. But he gave Woods fits at Valhalla Golf Club in Louisville, Kentucky, never backing down and forcing Tiger to fight until the end.

Woods finally prevailed in the playoff, but not before hitting a wild tee shot on the final hole that conspiracy theorists today believe was thrown into play by a spectator. The ball bounced off a cart path and for a moment was unseen to television viewers . . . only to come bounding out into play, a fortunate break. He endured the last hole to win his third straight major championship, a feat accomplished in the modern era only by Ben Hogan, who won the Masters, U.S. Open, and the Open in 1953 (and couldn't play the PGA Championship because it overlapped with the Open).

That victory set up a long wait until a highly anticipated 2001 Masters, where Woods would attempt to win a fourth straight major, something not done since Bobby Jones' historic Open and Amateur run in 1930 that saw him win the game's majors of the day: the British Amateur and Open as well as the U.S. Amateur and Open.

There was some quibbling about the accomplishment as it was not attained in the same year, but the feat of holding all four trophies at once could not be diminished. Those who sought to lessen it by suggesting it wasn't as impressive as winning them all in the same year no doubt failed to take into account the long wait between the 2000 PGA and the 2001 Masters—a period of eight months. Woods won a whopping 10 times around the world in 2000, although Mickelson clipped him at Torrey Pines and again at the Tour Championship. As good as Tiger was, Phil still produced his moments.

And, as it turned out, it was Mickelson who was presented the chance to knock the Tiger Slam sideways.

KEEPING ONE'S FORM OVER A PERIOD OF WEEKS IS DIFFICULT. Golf comes and goes. The best of the best often follow poor weeks with victories and vice versa. To think that someone would play at the level Woods did in 2000 for another extended period of time is the stuff of fantasy.

So when 2001 dawned—with the prospect of the Masters looming in a few months—every move was scrutinized. And when Woods didn't win every tournament, the questions started to mount. Was he in a slump?

Woods went six tournaments without winning, but his results were the kind that would have sent Tour pros on a spending spree. His two worst finishes? A tie for 13th. He posted three top 5s, including a tie for second in Dubai. Slump? If that was a slump, most players would be signing on for exactly that kind of downturn.

Heading to Arnold Palmer's Bay Hill tournament, Woods was clearly frustrated with the narrative.

"Well, it's annoying because of the fact that if you think that way, then you really don't understand the game of golf," he said.

Woods was the defending champion of the event and duly inspired. It didn't hurt that Mickelson was in the mix. After rounds of 71–67–66, Woods still found himself tied with Mickelson—who finished with a blistering 66—while standing on the 18th tee in the final round. Woods just slumped to his knees on the 17th green in disbelief when his long-range birdie putt nestled near the edge of the hole.

A wild drive well to the left of the fairway on 18 appeared headed for trouble. But it hit a spectator and was briefly picked up by another before being replaced where it came to rest near a cart path. Woods was given free relief for his stance, then hit his approach to 25 feet and drained the birdie putt to crush Mickelson, who stood by watching it unfold. Mickelson was holding his daughter, Amanda, in his arms.

"I played like I felt like I did what I needed to do to ultimately win, and Tiger did the same," Mickelson said. "He just did what he needed to do. And I know that he didn't hit it the way he had wanted to. I know that he hit a couple of tee shots that he would have liked to have had back. He birdied 16 and 18 to win by one, and I thought that was pretty impressive."

"Phil played an incredible last round, started several groups in front of Tiger," said Jim Mackay, Mickelson's caddie. "He shot 66 in the wind, and we're standing there thinking, 'Okay, we're going to win this tournament and beat this guy in the end.' Tiger rope-hooked it off 18, and it hit somebody, and he got a great lie in the rough and hit a 5-iron to 25 feet and beat us by one. And that hurt. That really hurt. Standing on the 18th green, watching it [which is what we did], that hurt."

A victory at the Bay Hill Invitational, just a month prior to the Masters, helped quiet the critics. So did a win at the Players Championship, the PGA Tour's flagship tournament and one often referred to as golf's "fifth major." Throughout Woods' career, he struggled at TPC-Sawgrass, home of the PGA Tour and the unique Stadium course. Woods won the 1994 U.S. Amateur at the venue, but showed little success there as a pro.

A year prior in 2000, he finished second to Hal Sutton, then won on his way to the Tiger Slam in 2001. To think that he added the game's most prestigious tournament outside of the majors, too, was simply stunning.

And when it was over, NBC's Jimmy Roberts unwittingly walked into the buzz saw. Earlier, Roberts joked about Woods' "slump," likening it to when the Beatles of a bygone era failed to have the No. 1 record in any given week. In other words, Roberts was pointing that out to say the idea that Tiger was slumping was ridiculous.

No matter.

"Nice slump, huh, Jimmy?" Woods said when Roberts attempted to interview him on live television after the Players victory. Woods simply walked away.

The Masters loomed in just two weeks.

"He was being asked about the Masters every week he was out there, but it never really bothered him," Harmon said. "Mentally, he and Jack Nicklaus and Ben Hogan were the strongest players. Sure, he didn't like all the questions because, really, what could he say? But it fueled the fire even more."

To those around him, Woods rarely spoke about completing the Slam. But deep down he knew this opportunity might never arise again. Think about it: Nicklaus never won three straight majors, let alone four. Nor did Arnold Palmer. Nor Gary Player. Nor Sam Snead. Nor Tom Watson. Nobody but Hogan, at a much different time, had accomplished that feat.

And he was going for four?

"Every year, he set up his schedule, and it was all based on preparing himself for those four championships," said Williams. "Every year, including 2001, he constantly worked on being able to hit the ball with a draw. The 9th hole [at Augusta National], the 10th hole, 13th hole. You had to hit a draw. And he'd practice that. He had to hit that draw on call, particularly with his 3-wood.

"When you think that the PGA Championship finished in August and Augusta doesn't start until April . . . the whole time there was constant conversation in the media. 'Can Tiger complete the Grand Slam at Augusta?' While it wasn't any different as far as preparation or anything, we never talked about it. The ultimate goal was Jack's record [of 18 majors]. But there was no more emphasis put on that tournament. He gave them all 100 percent attention. Prepared the best way he could and went about it the same way. But he was fanatical about having to hit a draw."

And for good reason. Hitting shots with a ball flight from right to left was not natural for Woods. And at times in his career when things were going poorly, that draw would turn into a vicious hook. It took work and trust to make sure he felt comfortable with the shot, and as Williams noted, it was needed on so many key holes at Augusta National. (Conversely, for a left-handed golfer such as Mickelson, the fade from right to left was far more comfortable for him.)

Woods opened the tournament with a 70, then added a 66 in the second round and was tied with Mickelson, two shots behind Chris DiMarco. Tiger shot a third-round 68 to take the 54-hole lead, with Phil shooting 69 to finish one stroke back.

That meant a final-round pairing. Tiger and Phil. Tiger going for history; Phil trying to win his first major—and deny Tiger the Tiger Slam.

"People forget about that," said Jim Nantz, the longtime lead announcer on CBS-TV's golf broadcasts. "It would have been an amazing thing had Phil been the guy who prevented the Tiger Slam."

After Woods bogeyed the first hole, he and Mickelson were tied until Phil made a bogey at the par-3 fourth. But Mickelson was playing well and bounced back with a birdie on 5, only to drop back with a bogey on 6. Not rattled, Mickelson birdied the seventh and eighth, a feat matched by Woods.

"I can honestly say that Phil's front nine was the best nine holes of golf I've ever seen from anyone," Williams said. "Exact precision. Place it in the exact spot it needed to be. He made the putts he could make. It was incredible for me to see Tiger hang with him. He was just grinding, grinding, grinding. Phil didn't maintain it on the back nine, which was probably impossible to do. And then Tiger flipped the switch on the back nine."

David Duval, like Mickelson trying for his first major title, was in the group ahead and birdied seven of his first 10 holes. He started the day three strokes behind and shared the lead three different times on the back nine until a crushing bogey at the 16th hole. He ended up finishing two shots back, alone in second.

"You just can't give a guy like Tiger Woods a chance to bury you," Duval said. "Whenever he had the chance, he buried you."

Mickelson ended up three back, his chances dashed when he made a bogey at the 16th hole when trailing by just a stroke.

"The 16th was the killer for me," Mickelson recalled. "I had pulled within one shot, had the honors, and pulled the 7-iron [shot]. I didn't give myself a chance to put more pressure on him.

"It was really frickin' hard to play Tiger back then. I've said the greatest golf in the history of the game that has ever been played was the 2000 U.S. Open. Back then, he hit it so far and so straight and he was such a clutch putter, you felt like you had to play perfect golf to beat him. And perfect golf was not my forte. My forte was to try and make a bunch of birdies and be aggressive.

"I don't remember the specifics of the round but I do remember coming to the last hole and I was two back and I knew he could fly the tree [on the right] and he'd have 60 yards or something to the hole and it was like, 'How is the guy going to bogey with a sand wedge going in?'

"I remember feeling distraught on the 18th tee. That round, as long as he hit it and as straight as he hit it, you just couldn't see him making any mistakes to open the door, and that's tough to deal with."

Leading Duval by one and Mickelson by two, Woods did exactly as

Mickelson expected—he hit a huge drive at the 18th, followed by a sand wedge to the green, which he converted for a birdie and exclamation point on a fourth straight major title and sixth overall.

Woods buried his head in his cap and cried.

"I finally had no other shots to play. That it was it," Woods said. "It was done. It was such a weird feeling. Then I started thinking, I had just won the Masters. Then I started losing it a little bit."

"It was a remarkable day, obviously, capped off by a historic achievement," Williams said. "It was about as much fun as you could have on a golf course. Certain players love certain tournaments more than others. But they absolutely love Augusta National and what it means. That day, Phil had as much chance to win. And you know in the back of his mind, he wanted to prevent another achievement, where Tiger was going to join a very select few. In that sense of the occasion, it was two players playing and how they played. If you combined Phil's front and Tiger's back nine, it was unreal golf to watch.

"I think the Tiger Slam is the single greatest achievement in golf. No player has ever been under greater scrutiny as Tiger was during the 2001 Masters. And to pull it off was simply incredible."

SOME OF THE NUMBERS ASSOCIATED WITH THE TIGER SLAM ARE absolutely remarkable.

For example, he played those four major championships in a combined 65-under par—or 45 strokes better than any other player across that time. The next best were Mickelson and Els, who both shot 20-under.

He was also consistently good, not just putting up a couple of good scores here and there. Woods produced 13 straight sub-par major championship rounds from the final day of Pebble Beach in 2000 through the final round of Augusta National the following spring. That is the best such run in major championship history, although Mickelson and Rory McIlroy both had 12 consecutive under-par runs from 2014 to 2015.

Not only was Tiger long off the tee but he also hit a lot of greens. Incredibly, in each of those four major championships Woods won, he led or co-led every round in driving distance and greens in regulation percentage. He also made 91 birdies across those four majors; the next best was Mickelson, with 60 birdies and 5 eagles to gain 70 shots to par.

Of course, if you are going to win at that rate, not only are you going to need to make a lot of birdies but you also need to avoid mistakes. In the 16 rounds that made up the four major victories, Woods dropped just 26 shots via 21 bogeys, one double bogey, and one triple bogey. The next best among players who made the cut in all four events was by Justin Leonard and Ernie Els, who dropped 46 shots. Leonard via 36 bogeys and five doubles; Els through 42 bogeys and two doubles. Mickelson dropped 50 shots with 36 bogeys and seven doubles. In other words, in mistakes alone, players were spotting Woods more than a shot per round. If that's not enough, Woods went the entire week on Pebble Beach's notoriously bumpy *Poa annua* greens without a single three-putt. And he played the Old Course at St. Andrews without hitting a single shot into any of the 112 bunkers.

It makes sense that if Woods was playing that well in the majors, he was simply playing well, period.

Across the 10-month span of the Slam, Tiger played in 20 tournaments, winning nine of them, including the four major championships and, sometimes forgotten, the Players Championship just two weeks before he completed the accomplishment at the Masters. His worst finish during that time was a tie for 23rd at the Western Open, his only start between victories at Pebble Beach and St. Andrews.

"To win four consecutive majors, if you look at my career, I don't think I have ever accomplished anything this great," Woods said. "It's hard to believe, really, because there's so many things that go into winning a major championship. You've got to have some luck. You have to get some breaks. You have to have everything go right. To have it go right four straight times, some of the golf gods are looking on me the right way.

"I have a better appreciation for winning a major championship. To win four of them in succession, it's hard to believe."

It was . . . and it wasn't. As remarkable as the accomplishment was for Woods, it almost seemed inevitable. The fact that his early-season "slump" was deemed to be some sort of indictment on Woods' game simply showed the level of ridiculous expectations he faced.

A common wager offered at the time was to take Woods against the field. The notion is preposterous on its face: who would pick one player over a field of 150-some others, given the nuances of the game? And yet, Woods was so dominating, so impressive, it seemed like he might never lose.

Mickelson, meanwhile, was losing ground and it was frustrating. He registered 21 victories by the end of 2002, nearly a Hall of Fame career to that point. And hardly anyone noticed. Woods already had 39 worldwide victories and six majors.

Not that Phil showed any outward animosity. He tried his best to remain complimentary of Woods and took his opportunities to be self-deprecating. One such instance occurred at the 2002 Tour Championship in Atlanta, where the two were grouped together.

On the first tee, the announcer introduced Woods by noting his numerous accomplishments that year: "winner of 34 PGA tour events, including the 2002 Masters Tournament, the U.S. Open, the Bay Hill Invitational, the Buick Open, the American Ex—"

And then Mickelson interjected: "Yeah, yeah, yeah, we know . . ." to considerable laughter around the tee, including a big smile from Woods as he was about to put his tee in the ground. It was well timed. And funny. And perfect.

And yet, friction between the two was inevitable.

9

TENSION

Despite their attempts to downplay any issues, to try and make nice, to even force smiles in each other's company over the years, there remains plenty of evidence to suggest that Tiger Woods and Phil Mickelson, at the very least, were simply not ones to get along.

They lived in different parts of the country, they came from different backgrounds, and they played the game in different ways. One was more introverted, the other more extroverted. Tiger built up a wall; Phil did his best to remove any barriers, especially to an adoring public that he seemed to embrace, at least on the outside.

Some suggest that their differences went beyond the simple personality traits. Of course there was race. Tiger's mixed heritage and skin color were underlying issues that never played out in any huge public way, but they bubbled beneath the surface. While Woods might not have faced racism the way his minority pioneers in golf did, he certainly was aware of its undercurrent and heard occasional derogatory comments from those in the gallery, not to mention letter writers and social media posters.

Phil had none of those concerns. Much like Arnold Palmer, he was viewed as a man of the people, the guy who would make eye contact and slap a high five. Tiger was more like Jack Nicklaus, who in his early years was stone-cold and focused—the opposite of Arnie.

As for the Woods-Mickelson interactions, they seemed to really go one way. While Phil was almost always deferential to Tiger, Woods paid him little mind and often tweaked him—usually behind the scenes—when possible.

Nobody will say that Tiger hated Phil, but there was a strong dislike. That is without question. What it stemmed from is mostly a matter of conjecture. Did Tiger see Phil as a threat? Was he annoyed that Phil got a lot of love from fans, while he didn't? Did he think that Phil was under-rated or underachieving?

All are possible. And while those feelings waned over the years, they were real for at least the first decade-plus of Tiger's pro career.

Phil? He almost always said the right thing. And if there was animosity, he never let on. Not publicly. And, really, not privately.

"I can confirm that off camera, he says the exact same thing," said longtime CBS-TV broadcaster Jim Nantz. "I've talked to him countless times. He has high regard for Tiger. Totally feels like [Woods] helped make him a fortune. He was the first guy who really said that. He said it first and he said it loudest. [Tiger] changed the dynamics out here. He changed the game for the betterment of everyone. That is truly how Phil feels. He does not have any hidden dislike, jealousy, envy of Tiger at all. It does not exist. I've never seen a hint of it. Nothing but respect."

Nantz has called all eight Masters victories between the two play-ers as well as their combined six PGA Championships, not to mention countless other victories. He's been the lead CBS golf commentator since 1989. And while he was more at arm's length with Woods, he certainly has a solid relationship with Mickelson.

But a decade or so into his pro career, Mickelson faced bigger issues than whether or not he needed to make nice with Tiger. He needed to win a major championship.

And as big of a deal as Woods became—the rock star of all superstars—and though that stardom came together for him so quickly, one fact re-mained for Phil: Tiger is hard to beat. Among Mickelson's team, such a hard-cold reality is what ultimately mattered.

At the 10-year anniversary mark of Mickelson's pro career, which came at the U.S. Open played at Bethpage Black in 2002, the major count was stunning: Tiger 8, Phil 0. That year, Mickelson finished third at the Masters and second at the U.S. Open. Woods won them both, becoming the first player since Jack Nicklaus in 1972 to win the Masters and U.S. Open.

It's a nice play on words, but it is also true that Mickelson had a "major" problem.

He was too good, too talented, too popular to be without one of golf's biggest prizes. Through 2002, Mickelson piled on victories, but none of the hardware that distinguishes the best of the best.

There were close calls, for sure. The U.S. Open at Pinehurst in 1999. The PGA Championship at Atlanta Athletic Club in 2001. In both instances, Mickelson was beaten by a player who missed the fairway at the 18th hole—Payne Stewart at Pinehurst, David Toms at Atlanta Athletic Club—and then took his medicine by getting the ball back in the fairway before wedging onto the green and making a par putt. Both times, Mickelson lost by one when a playoff seemed imminent.

Being in the mix at the 2002 Masters and U.S. Open while Tiger made more history could not have helped.

At the US. Open, Mickelson was tied for third through three rounds, five shots back. But Woods bogeyed the first two holes in the final round, while Mickelson birdied the first, opening the door ever so slightly. With that early momentum, Mickelson squandered it with bogeys at the fifth and sixth holes, and never got any closer than two shots.

Despite his inability to rein in Woods, Mickelson endeared himself to the Long Island galleries, who were in full throat for a majority of the tournament and cheering a guy who was 0-for-40 in the majors as much or more than the guy who kept winning them.

"I have never seen a crowd behind a player the way they were behind Phil today," said Jeff Maggert, who played with Mickelson.

It was a tough day at a brutal course that also included a 49-minute rain delay. While Mickelson went home disappointed, Woods looked forward to a trip to Scotland with the Grand Slam in mind.

WOODS FIRST HEADED TO IRELAND WITH HIS FRIEND MARK O'Meara to get a little R and R but to also prepare for the Open at Muirfield by playing several links courses. Once again, all the attention was on Woods as he arrived in Scotland with more history at stake. (Mickelson would become an afterthought, as he was for much of his Open career until he broke through more than a decade later; he tied for 66th.)

A little more than a year earlier, Woods completed the Tiger Slam when he won the 2001 Masters to win a fourth straight major. As unprecedented as that was, now Woods was attempting something just as remarkable—to complete a calendar-year Slam.

Nobody had even faced the opportunity since Nicklaus in 1972. He, too, would attempt the feat at Muirfield, the East Lothian course where the Golden Bear won his first Open in 1966—and later named his own course in Ohio, Muirfield Village, after the Scottish venue. Nicklaus was unable to prevail in 1972 despite a final-round 66 that was the best round of the day, finishing one shot back of Lee Trevino.

The first two days of the 2002 championship were relatively mild by Scottish summer standards. While not overly warm, the temperatures were comfortable. Woods, then 26, was grouped for the first two rounds with England's Justin Rose and Japan's Shigeki Maruyama.

Although Woods felt he left numerous shots on the course in an opening-round 1-under-par 70, his second-round 68 put him squarely in contention (although he took 63 putts over the first 36 holes). He trailed leader Ernie Els by two shots, was grouped with his buddy O'Meara during the third round, and seemed poised to put himself right there with a run at a third straight major.

His Saturday tee time was 2:30 P.M.

Meanwhile, 83 players made the 36-hole cut at 2-over par, meaning the entire field was within eight strokes of the lead. Among those to make it on the number was Australian Steve Elkington, the 1995 PGA Championship winner.

Elkington shot 71 and 73 during the first two rounds, meaning an early tee time on Saturday. He returned to the Auld Hoose, a pub just around the corner from where he was renting a place in the nearby town of North Berwick, Scotland.

"It sits just above the port there, and the harbor is so old that they have stone gates to let boats in and out," Elkington recalled. "After the Friday round, I go into the Auld Hoose and there's an old guy who has a silver jug that they just leave for him. They call him 'the harbormaster,' and he has this big, long beard.

"So I'm in there on the Friday night, and he pulls me off to the side.

'Listen to me. The weather is going to be shit at about 3 P.M. tomorrow.' He could tell from the current. 'I'm telling you, it is going to be shit.'"

Elkington got out early and shot 3-under-par 68, one of just four players to score in the 60s all day. Just nine of the 83 players shot under par.

"I come back to the Auld Hoose, and I went in the back to have a sleep in one of the rooms," Elkington said. "When I came back out, two hours later, I looked out the front door and there was a guy crawling along hands and knees trying to get in the pub, the weather was so bad. Now I'm watching the scoreboard, and I'm going from 40th to 30th and then into the top 10. It was a great break."

The weather was simply causing havoc. The old man was a bit off in his prediction, but not by much. The storm hit just after two o'clock, and after a few squalls, rain and howling wind arrived at 2:30—just as Woods and O'Meara were teeing off. The temperature became so cold that the wind-chill factor hovered below 40 degrees.

"It hit when we were on the putting green getting ready to go," Woods said. "By the time we got on the first hole . . . the temperature dropped, rain was coming sideways, blowing. And gusts were over 40 [miles per hour]. The fourth hole, a par-3, normally we were hitting 7 irons. I hit a 2-iron, and it probably should have been a 3-wood. O'Meara hit a 3-wood. And then the next hole was a 2-iron, 2-iron par-5, and I hit driver, 2-iron, 2-iron. And it was so cold."

Woods and O'Meara were in the seventh group from the end, and nobody among those final 14 players shot better than 72. Colin Montgomerie, who shot a course-record 64 the previous day, matched Lee Janzen with the high round of 84. Monty went 74–64–84.

Pàdraig Harrington, who was among a five-way tie for the lead through 36 holes, could do no better than 76. He ended up missing a playoff the following day by a stroke.

"It was the worst weather I've ever played golf in," the Irishman said. "I have played in conditions that were unplayable that weren't as bad as that day . . . and it wasn't unplayable [at Muirfield]. . . . The balls weren't rolling off the greens. What was happening is there were very strong winds. There was rain that wasn't flooding the greens. And there was seriously cold temperature.

"Now the seriously cold temperature meant the wind was accentuating the effect of what it was doing to the golf ball, and the wet meant the ball wasn't rolling off the green. So you had two factors that were making the wind seem extreme—cold and wet—yet the wet was stopping the ball from rolling off. It was the cold temperature, the fact we weren't prepared and wet thrown in on top of us. It was horrendous."

For one of the rare times in his career, Woods was dealt an exceedingly bad break. His first tee shot landed in the rough, and the worst day of his pro career to that point commenced with a bogey. He made another bogey at the fourth when he couldn't reach the par-3 green. He made double bogey on the par-5 fifth when his second shot went into the rough and his fourth flew over the green. He needed 42 strokes for the outward nine.

There was a poor chip at the 12th, he left a ball in a bunker at the 13th, he then bogeyed the 14th before playing the final four holes in 1-under par. The damage was already done. The two doubles, seven bogeys, and a birdie added up to 81, or 10-over par—the first time he failed to break 80 as a pro and the last for another 13 years.

Els, who suffered his share of torment at Woods' expense, bogeyed four of his first six holes but managed to hang on. He teed off an hour after Woods, and that difference meant some reasonably calmer conditions over the closing holes. Els called the day "the most amazing I've seen in an Open Championship. You can't believe how bad the conditions were."

He managed a remarkable 1-over-par 72, making pars on holes 7 through 10 and then four birdies coming in to take a two-stroke lead over Denmark's Søren Hansen. The average score of the final 14 players was 76.7, while of the nine players who broke par, none teed off later than 10:20 A.M.

Woods was 11 strokes back, in a tie for 67th—his Grand Slam dream derailed. The following day, Woods matched the tournament's best final round, a 6-under-par 65 that moved him into a tie for 28th. He ended up missing the playoff won by Els by six strokes, meaning if he been able to eke out a 75 a day earlier, the Sunday score would have been good enough for a playoff.

A month later, Woods finished second by a shot to Rich Beem at the PGA Championship, giving him two victories and a runner-up finish in the 2002 majors. After the PGA, he would part ways with instructor

Butch Harmon and not win another major until the 2005 Masters, the first of six through the 2008 U.S. Open.

As 2002 closed, Mickelson still saw a big goose egg next to his major tally.

TIGER WON SIX TIMES IN 2002; PHIL WON TWICE. HOWEVER, 2003 was defined more by off-the-course issues than anything the two players did on it. For one of the rare times, the duo did little winning. Mickelson didn't win at all; Woods won five times but was barely a factor in the majors.

But a story blew up nonetheless.

Whether Mickelson was complimenting Woods or ribbing him remains the stuff of hearty debate. Either way, it caught the attention of the golf world, as did anything involving those two that suggested any hint of negativity.

In an interview with *Golf* magazine, Mickelson declared that Woods was playing with inferior equipment. "He hates that I can fly it past him now," Phil said. "He has a faster swing speed than I do, but he has inferior equipment. Tiger is the only player who is good enough to overcome the equipment he's stuck with."

Ouch.

This, of course, did not go over well with Nike. The company, which Woods almost single-handedly put on the golf map when he signed with it at the start of his pro career, was paying him millions per year. In addition to the apparel he wore and started with in 1996, the company progressed into making golf balls and clubs.

After a careful vetting process, Woods eventually switched over to the Nike ball (in 2000) and the irons (2002), and then its driver and fairway woods. Mickelson's comments were a matter of perspective. To some, he was simply just dissing Nike, though his criticisms were ultimately true: the equipment Woods used was not up to standard. To others, he was poking Nike *and* complimenting Woods for his ability to play so well.

Mickelson was under contract with Titleist and Yonex and eventually switched to Callaway in 2004, so his comments could have been taken in many ways. Was it a compliment to Woods? Was he tweaking his rival? Was he knocking Nike to enhance his own endorsers?

Both players came out with statements trying to downplay the incident. "We talked and cleared the air," Woods said. "Everything is fine. No worries. As we all know, Phil can try to be a smart aleck at times. I think that was one of those instances where it just backfired on him."

Said Mickelson: "I did not mean anything malicious by it, or I wasn't trying to make a derogatory statement toward anybody. I still should not have gone in that area."

And yet, the story lingered. For one, Nike officials were furious. They poured millions of dollars into research and development, paid Woods handsomely, and had several other players on the payroll. Having such a high-profile and successful player as Mickelson say what he did— whether he was kidding or not—certainly caused some consternation.

"I challenged him about it one time," said John Cook, a veteran player, who like O'Meara was friends with Woods and had an endorsement deal with the company. "I was a Nike guy at the time as well. Phil said something about winning with inferior equipment. I think he had forgotten that David Duval had won with it and Justin Leonard. I played well with it. A lot of things Phil said, well, it was Phil. This one hit home. I was a Nike brand guy. I challenged it. We had a little chitchat on the putting green at Augusta. I challenged him. You can skew the numbers any way you want, but this is about results. We went back and forth and nothing really came of it. A couple of months later, Phil was with Callaway."

The truth is, Woods *was* using inferior equipment. But not necessarily because of the company whose name was stamped on the clubs. At that time, Woods was playing with a 43½-inch driver and a steel shaft. Many players by then moved to a longer shaft and sometimes played various forms of titanium or graphite.

Woods was not taking advantage of the technology available to him, but why would he? He was the No. 1-ranked player in the world by miles. He'd won eight major championships and 34 PGA Tour events at that point. And he was going to go to a longer shaft?

Cook felt the need to stand up not only for Nike but also for his friend.

"I had been friendly with Tiger through Mark," Cook said. "We played a lot of practice rounds from 1997 through those years. I was playing well at that time, and we just got to hanging out, got more and more comfortable. He asked a lot of questions about the wedge game, short iron play, controlling trajectory. That's kind of what I was known for in my day. In 1999, I was 42, and I think he helped me as much as I helped him. He injected the youth factor back into me. He got me working.

"We just developed a nice trustful relationship. We talked about short game theory, the wedge game, 150 [yards] and in stuff. It's not rocket science. But hearing from someone who was living it, you want to listen. I just think he developed a trust, and we had a confidence in each other."

Interestingly, Woods' caddie, Steve Williams—who never saw eye to eye with Mickelson and later got into an infamous spat with the golfer— understood what Phil was trying to say. Or, at least given the benefit of time, he came to make sense of it.

"Phil didn't mean it in the way that it came across," Williams said. "Tiger had this very tight relationship with Nike. And this was a chink in their armor. They were new to the market, and a top player making a comment like that . . . and Phil has a lot of pull and power. So that was a real dent. I actually believe, in an underhanded way, he was saying this guy is an unbelievable player and he's not even playing with the best equipment.

"I'm being 100 percent honest, there is some merit to that. It's hard to say Tiger would have won more tournaments. And he was never going to play any equipment he thought wasn't the best. But over a period of time, a lot of players who were contracted with Nike never stayed with Nike for an extended period of time. That tells you they would find equipment that was better. If you look across all the players who played with Nike, very few stayed with them. Phil's comment was more of a compliment; it just didn't come across that way."

And Hank Haney, who within two years officially became Woods' full-time coach, offered another take on the incident.

"Tiger knew what he meant," Haney said in an interview. "Because of the way the media made a big deal out of it, Tiger saw a way to gain an advantage. He knew Phil didn't mean anything, and he knew Phil was right in what he said. And he knew it was an opportunity to get a little edge. 'I can make him feel a little uncomfortable about this.' And how is that not a big thing? It was just a way for him to gain an edge. He never thought about that for half a second, that Phil meant anything by it. You know what? Everybody is a competitor. Why wouldn't he? Why let him off the hook?

"It's different now. Maybe today he would let him off the hook. But back then he wouldn't let him off the hook. Everything is to gain the edge."

"Tiger looked at Phil as a way to further motivate himself to be better—basically a source of fuel," Haney wrote in his book *The Big Miss*. "In 2003, when Phil made the comment that Tiger was playing with 'inferior' equipment, I didn't think it was a calculated slam by Phil . . . on Tiger as a Nike endorser. Rather, I think Phil enjoyed noting—correctly—how slow Tiger had been to switch to new technology, like the largest-headed drivers, and how in Phil's view as an early adopter, Tiger was slightly handicapping himself.

"I'm sure Phil knew the quote was going to get some play, but I think it was him being mischievous more than anything else. But Tiger took that comment as negatively as possible to give himself a competitive jolt. I always thought Tiger was going overboard when he'd privately call Phil lazy or make fun of his body, but it was mostly the spillage from revving himself up. It was interesting that after Michael Jordan was criticized for bringing up petty grudges in his [2009] Hall of Fame induction speech, Tiger was asked about it. 'I get it,' he said. 'That's what it takes to be as good as MJ. You are always finding ways to get yourself going.'"

IT WASN'T UNUSUAL FOR MICKELSON TO TWEAK OTHER PLAYERS, but those instances simply did not generate the publicity that came with doing so at Woods' expense.

That same year, Mickelson was playing in the Open at Royal St. George's in Sandwich, England, where Woods contended before coming up two shots short of eventual winner Ben Curtis.

At one point, Mickelson faced a 40-yard pitch shot to the 10th hole, and it appeared he would have difficulty getting the ball close. One of the game's great short-game players, Mickelson made it look easy: he pitched the ball onto the green past the pin and saw it suck back with an amazing amount of spin to within easy distance of the hole.

Mickelson thought nothing of it. He routinely practiced spinning the ball and often mesmerized onlookers in practice sessions with his ability to do so.

But a fellow Tour player watching on TV did wonder if something was amiss. Michael Clark II, who was PGA Tour rookie of the year in 2000, thought it was too good to be true and wondered if Mickelson's wedges conformed to the rules regarding square grooves in clubs. Such grooves—now outlawed—were especially useful in putting spin on the ball.

When Mickelson played next at the Greater Hartford Open, a PGA Tour official approached him to say that his clubs needed to be tested. Mickelson, of course, was annoyed. And he found out it was Clark who turned him in. The clubs turned out to be legal, but that wasn't enough for Phil.

He knew that Clark was struggling that year (he made just nine cuts in 25 starts), and in danger of losing his exempt status, which would have meant a return to the PGA Tour's Qualifying Tournament, better known as Q-School.

So he penned a note to Clark and left it in his locker.

Dear Michael—I appreciate your concern. Good luck at Q-School this year. Phil Mickelson

The season was far from complete, but Clark finished 176th on the PGA Tour money list. Not only did he fall outside of the top 125 for exempt players but he also outside of the top 150, which meant he would have to attend the second stage of the Qualifying Tournament just to be eligible for the final stage. And he failed to advance.

Ouch.

MICKELSON POSSESSED A QUICK WIT AND A SHARP NEEDLE. HE used it on fellow players, caddies, broadcasters, media. Most of it was in fun. His poke at Tiger's equipment was meant to be just that, even if it elicited a far different reaction.

Tiger and Phil endured a few other uncomfortable moments over the years.

Dave Pelz, a short-game coach who works with Mickelson, caused a bit of a stir during the 2006 PGA Championship at Medinah, saying, "When Phil's at his best, I'm thinking nobody can beat him." Including

Tiger? "You bet," Pelz said. "If Phil's long swing is good, his short game, I believe, is the best in the world."

Pretty innocuous stuff, really. But anything that came across as a slight was magnified—to the point that both players weighed in.

"I think I'm pretty tough to beat when I'm playing well, too," said Woods—who had just won the Open at Royal Liverpool.

Mickelson simply made light of the situation: "My man [Pelz], he's enthusiastic. I have tried not to give you [media] too much to run with, so I'm paying other people now to do it."

After that brief "controversy," Woods said, "Phil and I are competitors. We've gotten to know each other over the years and we're fine."

That same week, Mickelson said that he had a "very unique relationship" with Woods. "I've enjoyed the opportunity to compete against him, and I've enjoyed the opportunity to play with him as a partner, the latter one probably being the better one."

Things escalated a bit more a few years later when during an event in his native New Zealand, Woods' caddie, Williams, drew the ire of Mickelson when he said, "I wouldn't call Mickelson a great player, 'cause I hate the prick."

In another interview a day later with a New Zealand newspaper, Williams piled on: "I don't particularly like the guy. He pays me no respect at all, and hence I don't pay him any respect. It's no secret we don't get along either."

Williams also told a funny story about a spectator shouting "nice tits" at Mickelson during the U.S. Open earlier that year—only the caddie got the tournament and the player wrong.

Nonetheless, the damage was done, and Tiger's sometimes offhanded comments about Phil were coming through via Williams.

Williams later said he was speaking at a local function, telling some stories, not thinking that any of his comments would leave the room. But the quotes were leaked to a local newspaper, which also ran them in an internet story, and it didn't take long before Williams calling Mickelson a "prick" made its way around the world.

"After seeing Steve Williams' comments, all I could think of was how lucky I am to have a class act like Bones [Jim Mackay] on my bag and representing me," Mickelson said.

Williams later apologized in an interview with the Associated Press, saying, "I don't deny that him and I don't get along. I shouldn't have said it, but no harm was meant. I was just having some fun."

Woods didn't think it was funny.

"I was disappointed to read the comments attributed to Steve Williams about Phil Mickelson, a player that I respect," he said. "It was inappropriate. The matter has been discussed and dealt with."

And so it went.

Butch Harmon, at this time Phil's coach and previously Tiger's, called Williams' comments "deplorable" and said that Mickelson was "one of the most popular players in the world, every bit as popular as Tiger Woods. He's a nice guy, all the guys like Phil, so I don't know where Steve was coming from with that comment. Personally, I would assume he would wish he'd never made it. I would have loved to have heard a recording of the conversation between [Williams] and Tiger. I worked with Tiger for 10 years and I can tell you he wouldn't have been very happy with that. Golf is a game of honor and integrity, and that was a very uncalled-for remark. I don't think it's any reflection of what Tiger thinks of Phil Mickelson."

Given his long tenure with Woods and how Tiger felt back in those days, Harmon was undoubtedly glossing over the truth. But he knew Tiger wouldn't challenge him on it. Whatever Tiger felt about Phil at the time, he'd never want it aired publicly. And he wanted to avoid controversy, period.

But it wasn't over. Not even close.

The following February, Woods was making his triumphant return from being away for nine months due to his ACL replacement surgery that occurred after his 2008 U.S. Open victory at Torrey Pines, where he was grouped with Mickelson for the first two rounds. The USGA, for the first time, saw fit to make several groupings by world ranking: No. 1 Tiger, No. 2 Phil, and No. 3 Adam Scott. It was the first time Tiger and Phil ever played in the same group at a major in which they were purposely paired together.

Tiger went on to win an epic U.S. Open in a playoff over Rocco Mediate while Mickelson watched it play out in his hometown.

The next time Woods teed it up in a tournament was at the WGC-Accenture Match Play Championship in Arizona. The return was much anticipated after a long wait following the U.S. Open and knee surgery, and the media turnout was immense, as every step Tiger took was analyzed.

So when Woods arrived early for a practice round—his customary procedure—he saw, much to his surprise, Mickelson in the parking lot as well. At first it was believed that Mickelson intended some sort of peace offering, a clearing of the air for the public to see. Instead, Mickelson was confrontational with Williams—who had called him previously to apologize—and awkwardness ensued.

Soon, both players were warming up on the driving range in the early-morning desert cool, steaming.

Mickelson's caddie, Bones, was loyal to a fault. He protected Phil at all costs, whether from fans, media, or other players. Like any good caddie, his job was to limit distractions and keep his player focused on the task at hand. Competitive just like Williams, Bones also wanted to win and loved the adrenaline associated with the pursuit.

But for him, there were never any dustups with Tiger. He might have wanted to beat him just as much as his boss did, but Bones never uttered a negative word about the game's best player. It was the ultimate in respect, and Tiger appreciated it. In fact, Woods' attitude toward Mickelson softened as Phil piled up more trophies, and he came to appreciate Bones even more for his role in that success.

Williams, meanwhile, never really knocked down that wall, although years later and upon reflection, he gave a more measured take.

"I wouldn't say it was bad feelings," he said during a 2021 interview. "You just get some people that rub you up the wrong way. As a player, I absolutely respect Phil. Some of the things he did absolutely rubbed me the wrong way. But as a player, I totally respect his game. It's not that I didn't dislike the bloke; his character wasn't in line with my character, if you like.

"Also, when you're working for somebody like Tiger, every time Tiger played with Phil, he had to shoot a better score. Most of the time when that happened they were in contention. There was a rivalry there and you couldn't help feel that rivalry. And sometimes my rivalry was a little bit different than Tiger's."

A random example occurred at the 2002 PGA Championship, where Rich Beem prevailed by one stroke over Woods for the last of his three

PGA Tour titles. Woods was coming off a victory the week prior at the Buick Open and looking for a third major of the year, having won the Masters and U.S. Open earlier. Only Ben Hogan (1953) and Woods (2000) accomplished that triple. It would have been another monumental achievement.

But Beem proved to be a pesky interloper. He was playing some of the best golf of his life, having won two weeks prior at the International. And he built a six-shot lead through 13 holes of the final round, then nervously played the last five as Woods—a group in front of him—birdied four straight holes. Beem played beautifully, but said later he faced all he could handle to finish the round, let alone worry about Tiger.

Beem hit 13 of 14 fairways that day, and after a bogey at the 14th hole, he made a birdie at the 16th to give himself a three-shot lead heading to the 18th tee. With Woods birdieing the hole ahead of him, a final-hole bogey gave Beem a one-shot victory. He later quipped that "I'm an excellent 19th-hole kind of guy," when asked about the prospects of a playoff with Woods.

Tiger was understandably disappointed but not to the level you would expect. Upon signing his scorecard, he watched the 18th play out on a television monitor, and while Beem was doing a celebratory jig on the green, Woods let out a scream in the scoring area. "Yes!" he bellowed to no one in particular.

Fred Funk, who played the final round with Woods, was stunned. What? He was in the scoring area, too, and wondered why Tiger was reacting in such a strange manner. Didn't he want a shot at Beem in a playoff?

"That's Rich Beem one, Phil Mickelson zero!" Tiger barked, relishing that Mickelson was still without a major title.

It was an unusual response, to say the least.

"It just shows you that back then there wasn't a whole lot they liked about each other," Beem said. "It's kind of funny."

Never mind that Mickelson was nowhere in that picture that day, having tied for 34th. Or that Woods was unable to capture his ninth major championship.

Woods' consolation was that it wasn't Mickelson celebrating his first major win. And that was satisfaction enough. The longer Phil didn't win a major, the more the pressure built. Tiger knew and relished it.

10

Finally

A golf ball is expensive for everyday golfers, especially knowing they go for upward of $55 per dozen for the high-end stuff. However, tour professionals have no worries when it comes to golf balls. They are given an endless supply.

But that's not to say it isn't costly to lose one, especially in the heat of competition.

When Tiger Woods' tee shot at the opening hole of the 2003 Open sailed wide right of the fairway at Royal St. George's in Sandwich, England, he had no clue just how much that missing ball would cost him.

Such a scenario playing out seemed preposterous. All manner of spectators lined the fairway ropes, even more than usual because Tiger was playing. Marshals, media, television spotters, you name it. All there saw where the ball flew and thought surely it could be found in the time allotted him, even if it buried into the thick seaside rough for which Open venues are known.

A year earlier, when the Open's final moments were playing out at Muirfield, English pro Gary Evans was furious when nobody could find his ball on the 71st hole. He ended up finishing one stroke out of a play-off won by Ernie Els.

"They would've found it if it were Tiger Woods' ball," Evans bemoaned afterward.

Not everything is as it seems. When Woods' tee shot missed the mark on the 442-yard opening hole at the southernmost venue used in the Open rotation, nobody could locate the Nike ball that had "Tiger" stamped on the side.

Playing partners Luke Donald and Sergio García trudged along, too, in the rough, seeing if they could find the ball. A marshal did locate a golf ball, but it said "Titleist 4," not "Nike 1." And the search continued but to no avail.

"The spotters didn't know where it landed," Woods said. "The gallery was telling us where they saw the ball go in and heard it go in, but we just couldn't find it."

García's assessment was blunt: "It was a bad spot to hit it. It was a jungle in there."

After the five-minute time limit (it has since been shortened to three minutes) to find a ball expired, Woods had no choice but to solemnly head back to the tee and reload. The stroke and distance penalty were especially harsh. The excitement of starting a major championship soon turned to dread. And when Woods missed the fairway again, he chopped it into the left rough where he hit a spectator in the knee. He then wedged on and two-putted for a triple-bogey 7 to begin the tournament. The results were devastating.

Woods played the remaining holes in 1-under par, a victory in his mind as he ended up shooting 2-over-par 73, just five shots back of the leader. After the round, Woods said he could not recall ever losing a ball in competition as a pro.

That is part of the charm of an Open; the quirky links courses in Great Britain and Northern Ireland can bemuse and befuddle.

But when it was over, Woods was not laughing. He ended up missing a playoff with unheralded Ben Curtis by two strokes—those two strokes given up to a lost ball and an opening-hole triple bogey. He ended up tied for fourth.

His finish was the closest Woods would come to winning a major championship in 2003. After capturing seven of 11 from the 1999 PGA Championship through the 2002 U.S. Open, Woods played six majors without a victory. He wasn't a factor at the Masters, U.S. Open, or PGA Championship, where he tied for 39th. In 28 major championships as a pro to that point, the PGA finish was his worst. He averaged an 11.6 finishing position in those 28 major starts.

But Woods did win five times on the PGA Tour that year, including two World Golf Championship events. He was a solid No. 1 in the world throughout. He compiled 39 PGA Tour wins, which equaled the total of the legendary Tom Watson.

Mickelson? No victories. Just a single top 3 finish, a third at the Masters. And only seven top 10s in 25 worldwide starts.

BY THIS POINT, MICKELSON WAS ROUTINELY BEING QUESTIONED about the way he approached major championship golf. The gusto he embraced did not lead to glory. Phil coveted the thrill of the journey rather than arriving safely at his destination. Aim for the pin or bust.

And Mickelson seemed to suggest he'd be just fine if that meant not winning a major championship.

Nonsense, to be sure. Mickelson wanted a major as much as he needed air itself, but he seemed to be cushioning the blow of not winning one more than 10 years into his career.

During the 2002 Players Championship at PGA Tour headquarters in Ponte Vedra Beach, Florida, Mickelson got defensive while explaining his offensive style. He contended, correctly, that he was one of the few players to stand up to Woods—although that didn't look like such a great boast when Woods led him in majors 6–0.

"I have won more tournaments than anybody playing the game right now other than Tiger," Mickelson said. "And I haven't seen anybody step up to the plate and challenge Tiger the way I have, winning the '98 Mercedes, winning the 2000 Tour Championship, winning the 2000 San Diego tournament head-to-head with him.

"He's the best player in the game, and I am not going to back down from him. And I see these other guys wilt, and it's unbelievable to me that they haven't been able to play their best golf when he's in contention."

Els might have wanted a word, and Vijay Singh (who won nine times, including the PGA Championship, in 2004) certainly enjoyed his moments against Woods.

But Phil's combative words were both welcome and yet somewhat puzzling. Sure, there were highlights. Tiger did not always prevail, and as Mickelson noted, there were some head-to-head encounters where he came out in front.

The scoreboard tells all, however. At the time of Mickelson's rant, Woods claimed 30 PGA Tour titles and six majors. Phil had 20 and zero.

Mickelson wasn't even leading that Players Championship, having shot a second-round 75 after an opening 64. He made a point to say that he simply played to his personality.

His comments came just a few days after he possibly let a tournament title get away from him at the Bay Hill Invitational. Mickelson led by one stroke with six holes to play but finished tied for third, five shots behind Woods. He was second-guessed for trying to hit a shot through trees and over water to the 16th green when a pitch out might have been the better play. Mickelson chose the bold play and found the water.

"That's just Phil," said PGA Tour player Chris DiMarco. "Doesn't matter who is in the lead. He plays that shot. He's just thinking he can do everything. He never not believes in himself. Sometimes he gets in trouble, and sometimes he hits the miraculous shot that gets on the green. If he feels like he can do it, he does it."

And appropriately, in the aftermath of that tournament at Bay Hill, tournament host Arnold Palmer wrote Mickelson a note.

"You never would have won as many tournaments as you have by playing a more conservative game," Palmer said. "Keep playing to win. Keep charging. Your majors will come."

Palmer loved Phil's style because it was *his* style. The winner of seven major championships himself, Palmer nonetheless rued some of the ones that got away.

And typically, Mickelson would rationalize any misfires as poor execution rather than planning.

"I won't ever change my style of play," he said. "I get criticized for it, but the fact is I play my best when I play aggressive, when I attack, when I create shots. That's what I enjoy about the game—that challenge. And if I were to change my style of play, I won't perform at the same level, nor would I enjoy the game as much."

Mickelson, then 31, admitted he had expected to win multiple major championships by that point in his career. He had 14 top 10s and no victories; the best chances were his 1999 U.S. Open close call with Payne Stewart and the 2001 PGA Championship where David Toms prevailed.

"I have had a number of chances to win majors, and I wouldn't have had those chances had I played any other way," he said. "Now I may never win a major playing that way. I don't know. I believe that if I'm patient, I will. But the fact is, if I change the way I play golf, I won't enjoy the game as much and I won't play to the level I have been playing. So I won't ever change. Not tomorrow, Sunday, or at Augusta or the U.S. Open or any tournament."

Mickelson reasoned that playing more conservatively actually hurt him. He cited the 1997 U.S. Open at Congressional as an example. He tied for 43rd.

"When things didn't go well, it upset me so much that I wasn't able to perform my best," he said. "Now if I hit a shot in the water on a par-5, I can live with that. If I make a bogey laying up, I have a tough time living with that. And I just feel like for me to play my best, I need to attack. That's the bottom line.

"I've taken it on the chin pretty good the last few years, but that's fine. It's just part of the deal for being on Tour. But I'd rather be criticized for not winning than be criticized like a bunch of players for not putting themselves in a position to win."

MICKELSON DID NOT WIN A TOURNAMENT IN 2003—A FIRST SINCE 1999. In 23 PGA Tour starts, his best was third at the Masters. From there, he didn't finish among the top 30 on the money list. And he went 0–5 for the U.S. team against the International team at the Presidents Cup in South Africa in a contest that ended in a tie.

It was not a good year off the course, either.

In addition to making a "dumb, offhand comment about Tiger Woods having inferior equipment" and that "I felt bad that I might have said something that came across as disrespectful," Mickelson also endured a personal crisis.

On March 23, Phil and Amy's third child, Evan, was born. But the pregnancy was not easy. In fact, the baby was two weeks late and labor was induced. According to Mickelson, after Evan was born, nearly seven minutes elapsed before the baby took his first breath.

Amy was in distress as well. She lost a lot of blood and was in "hemorrhaging shock," as Mickelson described it in his 2005 book, *One Magical Sunday.* The golfer said he overheard nurses in the hospital waiting room say, "It's just so sad, isn't it, that those three little children are going to grow up without their mother."

"The next hour was the longest, most agonizing hour of my life," Mickelson said.

"I was with Amy's mother," Phil's mom, Mary Mickelson, told *USA Today.* "And they were racing Evan out of the room. We heard Philip shout, 'Amy, Amy.' He said, 'Mom, you go with Evan. I'm going with Amy.' Philip had this terrified look on his face, a look I'd never seen him have. It was almost like he was in shock. Doctors and nurses were racing in and out, saying get this, get that, get doctor so and so. Soon Evan's coloring started to get better, but Amy was almost in a semi-coma. I remember hearing a nurse say, 'What a shame. She has two other little ones at home.' The nurse didn't think Amy was going to make it."

Mickelson considered skipping the Masters until Amy encouraged him to play. "Philip was very close to leaving golf," Mary Mickelson said. "Amy just kept saying, 'This will pass. It will get better. This is what you've worked for. This is what you've wanted.'"

The harrowing situation made Mickelson take stock of his life and his family, and once the golf season was complete, he didn't touch a club from mid-November until the beginning of 2004.

He used the break to work with his trainer, Sean Cochran. He focused on losing weight and eating better. And when he started practicing again, he spent considerable time with his coach Rick Smith, trying to put in play a controlled fade, a shot he knew would serve him well.

"I was determined to put everything to good use," he said.

And as 2004 began, Mickelson was determined to look ahead and not dwell on the past. That's why he has barely mentioned the situation involving his wife and son in any media interviews.

His first tournament of the year was the Bob Hope Chrysler Classic near Palm Springs, California, and Mickelson won it to break a 19-month winless stretch. He shot a final-round 68 and was 30-under par in the five-day event but tied with Skip Kendall, who shot a 65 the last day.

But Kendall couldn't match Mickelson's birdie on the first extra hole, giving Phil a much-needed win and a bright outlook for the new season.

"He almost lost his child and his wife," Smith said. "We got to the Masters [in 2003] and he hadn't even hit balls. He hadn't practiced, he hadn't played. He was devastated. And it took a while. But he was driven by adversity. I was excited for him to get going in '04. And after he won the Hope, he knew he was so dialed in, and it just got better from there."

When asked about the previous year, Mickelson focused on the deficiencies in his golf and not the family issues that might have led to them.

"Last year my confidence just slowly, slowly dwindled, and so that's why I really don't even want to think about last year," he said. "I started the year with a ton of confidence, with a ton of—I don't even want to say momentum but just the feeling that I could play well. And I just couldn't wait. I was so excited for the year to start. I can't wait to get back to Phoenix next week . . . and all the people we get out there. I can't wait to play again. This is the most fun I've had in a long time playing golf."

Mickelson followed the victory with a tie for seventh in Phoenix. He was third at Pebble Beach and tied for fourth at the Buick Invitational. He then tied for fifth at the WGC Match Play. The first time he was out of the top 10 was a tie for 24th at the Ford Championship at Doral, but he tied for third at the Players Championship in his next start and was 10th at the BellSouth Classic the week prior to the Masters.

Aside from more victories, it's hard to envision a better run-up to play at Augusta National.

"I think that being positive and working on having a direction, knowing what I want to do with mechanics, with short game, with putting, as opposed to searching last year, trying to fix things, and working out of the negative . . . I think that's the biggest area mentally is that I'm working from a more positive frame of mind," he said.

AS THE 2004 MASTERS APPROACHED, MICKELSON WAS IN A FAR better state of mind than he was a year prior.

"It's fabulous," he said. "Things couldn't be better with my family doing well and me playing well. It's been a lot of fun. It makes practicing easier, and it makes playing much more enjoyable. It's a lot easier to keep my mind on the game and on the golf course, the shot at hand, than it has been in the past.

"I have clicked onto something that has helped me out dramatically in my ball striking, and my ability to hit fairways feels night and day different."

The drop in form in 2003 cannot be overstated. After three straight runner-up finishes to Woods on the PGA Tour money list, Mickelson fell to 38th. Ranked second in the world in 2002, he fell to 15th at year-end and dropped another spot in early January. Turning the calendar meant everything, as did a fresh outlook on the majors.

He headed to Augusta leading the PGA Tour on the money list with more than $2.3 million. He ranked first in scoring average at 69.11. He was hitting 70.3 percent of his greens in regulation, ranked first in strokes gain metrics for his overall tee to green game and his approach game.

"Phil Mickelson has done something," Davis Love III said going into the tournament. "I don't know what he's working on, but he's doing something. He's hitting nice, controlled shots into the fairway. He's playing real smooth and graceful. He doesn't look out of control. I expect that he's pretty confident with his game and that he's ready for a big year. His game is very under control."

Woods was in an oddly unfamiliar place. More than a year earlier, he parted ways with his longtime coach Butch Harmon and never announced a replacement. Harmon was never officially told. It just sort of happened after the 2002 PGA Championship that they were no longer working together.

Thus, Harmon was never given a reason, although he believes it had to do with the way his own fame was growing at the same rate as Tiger's—and perhaps the idea that Harmon was getting too much credit. While all conjecture—and Woods and Harmon never said an ill word about each other over the ensuing years—it nonetheless left Woods trying to figure things out on his own.

There were murmurings that he might work with Hank Haney, longtime instructor to his friend Mark O'Meara. Haney employed a different approach to the golf swing from Harmon's, and some of what O'Meara suggested started to become noticeable in Woods' game. When they played practice rounds together, Haney was there with O'Meara, and the sense was he was also helping Woods.

Much of the questioning centered on how far removed Woods' swing was from his epic 2000 season and why he would change what he was trying to accomplish. Woods was often coy, but throughout the rest of his career, there would be questions about his decisions to change coaches and philosophies as he did.

"How's my swing different from now and then? It's pretty close to where it was then," he said. "The takeaway isn't as solid as it has been. That's one of the things I've had to work on to get back to that so the rest of the positioning takes care of itself. If you don't set yourself up on the way back initially, then you have to make a lot of compensations throughout the golf swing. I basically went back to basics on that."

That was code for Woods not being comfortable yet. He won the WGC-Accenture Match Play Championship in February, but it turned out to be his only victory in 2004 on the PGA Tour. He added the Dunlop Phoenix Tournament later in the year in Japan, giving him just two worldwide victories. But heading into the Masters, his results were ordinary. He tied for 46th at the Bay Hill Invitational and he tied for 16th at the Players Championship.

Then he shot 75 in the first round at Augusta and was never really a factor. He tied for 22nd. It was his worst showing in eight Masters as a pro.

ARNOLD PALMER WAS PLAYING HIS 50TH AND FINAL MASTERS IN 2004. He thought he'd said his goodbyes at Augusta National two years earlier, when then-club chairman William "Hootie" Johnson let past champions know in a letter that he preferred the aging ones step aside for the good of the tournament.

Palmer was 72 in 2002 and hadn't made a Masters cut in nearly 20 years. Nobody cared. Everybody loved Arnie, an Augusta National member no less. Decades earlier, he helped put the tournament on the map with his dashing style that played beautifully on the medium that was taking to golf, television.

His run of green jackets ended after his fourth in 1964, but not even prostate cancer kept Arnie from playing in the Masters. And the way it was coming to an end was harsh. Johnson overplayed his hand, and several past champions let him know it. He eventually rescinded what he laid out in the letter, although those who were struggling to break 90 on an increasingly longer Augusta National got the hint.

That meant Palmer would stretch his streak to 50 straight Masters, a remarkable achievement in its own right. Mickelson always seemed to be tied to Palmer the way Woods was to Jack Nicklaus.

In each case, one was far more gregarious and outgoing, prone to painful defeats. The other enjoyed the far better record, but sometimes waned in popularity compared to his rival due to never-ending focus and strong will.

Mickelson often cited Palmer's final U.S. Open in 1994 at Oakmont Country Club outside of Pittsburgh. That was Arnie country. He grew up in nearby Latrobe, and Oakmont remains among the jewels in American golf. That's where Nicklaus won his first Tour event and major championship at the expense of Arnie. At times, the crowd became unruly enough during that 1962 U.S. Open that it took to calling him "Fat Jack," something that irritated Palmer, who believed in sportsmanship.

The two were tied after 72 holes and played off on Sunday (then the tournament played a 36-hole final on Saturday) with Nicklaus prevailing. It was a huge win for Jack, but a bitter defeat for Arnold, who would lose three U.S. Opens in playoffs.

Now back at Oakmont for a final time in competition, Palmer, 64, received a special exemption from the USGA. It was the fifth time he received a pass into the tournament, a perk with which nobody could have a problem. When he missed the cut in sweltering heat, there was not a dry eye at Oakmont, including in the media center, where a typically cynical bunch of reporters gave Arnie a standing ovation as he fought back tears.

After the first round, Mickelson witnessed Palmer go into the volunteer tent and sign autographs, thousands. He signed for everyone who was there, everyone who wanted one. Until he was done.

That stuck with Phil, who became known for doing many of the same things, at times drawing the wrath of his peers, many of who believed he was insincere. In media circles, it was often wondered whether or not Phil was a fraud. That was basically a matter of conjecture, opinion. And the bottom line is this: whether he liked doing so or not, Mickelson made himself available to fans at a significant rate for someone of his stature. And did the smiling kid who got the autograph, a memory for life, really care if Phil didn't want to be there?

A few years prior to Palmer's U.S. Open departure, Mickelson asked him if they could play a practice round together at Augusta National. Palmer put together a group that included Nicklaus and Hale Irwin, with Arnie and Phil being partners.

What always stood out to Phil? Palmer birdied the seventh, eighth, and ninth holes during their match.

That was the kind of karma that Phil could really use now.

JUST PRIOR TO CHRISTMAS, PHIL'S GRANDFATHER, AL SANTOS, passed away at the age of 97. A former caddie at Pebble Beach, Santos took a great interest in his grandson's golf career. Mary Mickelson's father, Al appreciated that Phil gave him a flag from each of the tournaments he won, and they hung about Al's kitchen, one for each of Phil's 21 PGA Tour victories.

But not long before he passed, Santos told Phil that he believed 2004 was the year that a major championship would finally come. No more flags from regular events, he said. Only the majors.

So Phil went to Augusta National that spring with some emotional baggage. His grandfather's death. And the relief that his wife and son survived a harrowing childbirth that led to his worst year on Tour.

After 17 top 10s in majors, including three straight third-place finishes at the Masters, the time to win one of the big ones was upon him.

And as Palmer was playing his final hole in his 50th Masters to the roars and ovations of thousands, Mickelson was on the 17th, pouring in a 30-footer for a birdie that helped him shoot a second-round 69 and get within three shots of leader Justin Rose, in a tie for fourth.

The off-season renewal was also beneficial for Phil's game. He realized he needed to make changes if he was to compete at the same level as Tiger. Not only did Mickelson work to get in shape but he also spent considerable time with Smith, honing his swing.

"The best I've ever seen him swing it in my life was '04, '05, '06," Smith recalled. "He was ripping long cuts. Just a beautiful swing. It was a matter of him gearing himself to realize that Tiger was the guy. I think during that time was some of the most exciting made-for-TV stuff you've ever seen.

"The major strategy was more control. Learning how to cut the ball properly. And once he won one, I knew the floodgates would open for him and the confidence would soar."

But to that point, Phil was 0-for-46 in majors.

Things were different now, however. The week prior to the Masters, Mickelson walked the entire course with Smith and his short-game guru, Dave Pelz. He studied every blade of grass, plotted his strategy, and put in place a plan that would serve him well for many majors down the road.

And what transpired through the course of four days at Augusta National was a more cautious, a more measured Phil. Instead of firing at flags with abandon, he thought through the ramifications first. If he could take it on, fine. If not, play safe and live to play another hole.

Through three rounds, Mickelson led the field in greens in regulation at 75.93 percent. He hit more than 70 percent of his fairways. He played his last 32 holes without a bogey. These stats were unheard of for Phil-the-Thrill. But it was working. For the first time in his career, Mickelson was the 54-hole leader at a major championship. As for his nemesis, Tiger was in 20th place.

"Well, it doesn't suck," Mickelson joked in his news conference afterward when asked about Woods being so far back.

Now came the hard part. Closing the deal. And that was never going to be easy, especially with Ernie Els in the picture. A future Hall of Famer himself, Els was a Mickelson contemporary who went back as far as their junior days, when the South African traveled to Phil's hometown for the World Junior Amateur at Torrey Pines.

The "Big Easy," as he was nicknamed, already possessed three major championships—the 1994 and 1997 U.S. Opens as well as the 2002 Open at Muirfield. He was dealt his own frustrations with Augusta National but now surged out in front during the final round with some stunning golf of his own.

Mickelson, meanwhile, showed some weaknesses. He missed a short putt on the third for a bogey. He left a ball in a bunker on the fifth for another bogey. And by the time he got to the famed par-3 12th in the middle of Amen Corner, he trailed Els by a shot but could see the South African on the par-5 13th in two strokes.

So it was time to return to firing Phil. Conservative golf was not going to work now. Thus, he took on the flag at the daunting 12th, the one that always lurks on the far right side of the green on Masters Sunday, Rae's Creek beckoning below for any poorly hit shot.

Mickelson always believed that he had an advantage on that hole as a lefty. Hooked shots tend to go longer. As a left-hander, he could aim at the flag and feel secure that a misplayed hook would go long and not land short on the bank and roll back into the water. A righty, he reasoned, might fade a shot into that pin and see it come up short. The hole has proven the undoing of many challengers over the years.

Phil aggressively hit his tee shot to 12 feet, a feat even more incredible than it sounds given the way an unmistakable roar went up just as he began his swing. Els eagled the 13th and was suddenly three in front of Mickelson.

Under the spotlight and knowing he needed to make a move, Mickelson refused to yield. He made the birdie putt to begin his comeback. At the par-5 13th, he faded a driver around the corner, hit a 7-iron to 20 feet, and two-putted for birdie. He was within one stroke, but Els made a birdie ahead of him at the 15th, the lead again two. Ernie played beautifully, having gone 6-under par for nine holes.

Jim "Bones" Mackay played a key role on the 14th, talking Phil into hitting a pitching wedge rather than the 9-iron he preferred, believing a hard, aggressive swing with less club would produce the spin needed to get the ball close. Bingo. Phil knocked it to within inches.

Trailing by a stroke at the par-3 16th—the same hole that doomed his chances three years prior when he was trying to interrupt the Tiger Slam—Mickelson faded a 7-iron from right to left that stopped 15 feet away for another birdie. Mickelson and Els were tied.

———

THERE ARE ANECDOTES ABOUT THE WAY TO WIN A MAJOR CHAM-
pionship. A ruling a day earlier might have ultimately stymied his
chances at victory, and Mickelson certainly didn't need any more psychological hurdles in his path at this point.

Playing in the group behind Els, Mickelson saw the entire scenario
unfold. Els hooked his drive into the trees left of the 11th fairway. The
ball came to rest in an area of stacked limbs that workers compiled
during a storm. The debris was well out of play, but nonetheless, Els' ball
found its way into the mess. Els believed he was entitled to relief under
the ground-under-repair rule. Without such a ruling, he'd be required to
declare the ball unplayable and then would need to take a penalty drop.

The first official on the scene, Jon Brendle, a respected PGA Tour
rules official, did not grant Els' request. He believed that Els needed to
either play the ball or take a drop. Another rules official concurred.

Els disagreed. "I just felt they could have moved the stuff offsite, off
the golf course," Els said. "In South Africa, we call that 'greenskeepers'
rubble.' I felt pretty strongly about that."

So Els sought a third opinion, and Augusta National's Will Nicholson
was summoned. A longtime Augusta member who served as the Masters
director of rules and competitions, he was essentially the chief referee. A
former USGA president, Nicholson ruled in Els' favor.

This was not unusual. Augusta National has a history of siding with
players in such instances. Palmer got a famous favorable ruling on his way
to his 1958 Masters victory when he argued his embedded ball on the 12th
hole should have led to a drop. Another example? Woods' infamous drop
on the 15th hole in 2013 in which he could have been disqualified for signing an incorrect scorecard. The Masters cited a rarely used rule to assess
the two-shot penalty and keep Woods in the tournament.

Adding to the drama was the fact that, before Nicholson arrived, Els
attempted to remove some of the debris. In doing so, the ball appeared
to move, which would have been a penalty. It was determined that the
ball only oscillated. Then, given a drop, Els was able to pitch out to the
fairway, limiting the damage to a bogey.

While an important break for Els, for Mickelson it was another bad one on the way to trying to win his first major.

Months later, while playing a practice round for the PGA Championship at Whistling Straits, Nicholson—75 at the time and working the event as a rules official for the PGA of America—came upon Phil in a golf cart. Mickelson, never one to miss an opportunity to brandish his needle, dismissively said, "Hey, Will, if you're looking for Ernie, he's a couple of holes behind us."

"Phil, go fuck yourself," Nicholson said, then drove off.

Nicholson later came back and apologized.

YOU COULD NOT ASK FOR MORE FINAL-HOLE TENSION. ELS SHOT a remarkable 67 that included two eagles and was in the clubhouse, awaiting his fate. He later headed to the putting green, which is within 50 yards of the 18th green, to begin practicing for a potential sudden-death playoff. He could not see, only hear, what was going on just a short distance away.

"You're in another guy's hands," Els said. "There's nothing you can do."

It turned out to be a particularly frustrating year for Els in the majors—all of which he could have won. He was in the final pairing at the U.S. Open with eventual champion Retief Goosen and tied for ninth, he lost in a four-hole aggregate playoff to unheralded Todd Hamilton in the Open at Royal Troon, and he missed a playoff by a stroke at the PGA Championship, tying for fourth.

At Augusta, standing on the putting green, chewing on an apple, he was helpless.

Mickelson's approach came to rest 18 feet above the hole, and destiny was in his hands. He could put an end to all the talk about being "the best player without a major," all the negativity that dogged his pursuit of big titles.

Behind the green was Amy, her parents, Phil's parents, and the kids, including Evan—whose birth was so traumatic and who'd just celebrated his first birthday.

As he studied the right-to-left putt, Mickelson got a break: Chris DiMarco's approach from off the green came to rest just beyond Phil's ball. He was in nearly the same spot, meaning Phil could get a good look at the line DiMarco's ball took. When he missed, Mickelson saw a picture in his mind of what he needed his ball to do.

"Chris' ball was hanging on that left lip, and when it got to the hole, it just fell off," Mickelson said. "And my putt was almost on the identical line. Instead of falling off, it caught that lip and circled around and went in."

That's where Phil felt there might have been some divine intervention.

"I can't help but think my grandfather pushed it in," he said.

Mickelson birdied five of the last seven holes. His celebratory leap after the winning putt drop is so iconic that it resulted in his own personal logo—despite all the quips about the lack of light between the ground and his feet.

He shot 31-over the closing nine for a 69, beat a three-time major winner in Els, and at 33, finally won his first major championship.

"He knew it was time," Smith said. "The focus was very deep. The course management. His swing. His short game. It was getting dialed in, and he knew once he had the recipe it would be hard not to succeed. All things fell into place.

"He had to feel less reckless, but on that back nine, he was very aggressive, extremely aggressive, and he knew he had to be. When you go back and watch that back nine, you could just see everything coming out 100 percent. He went for every flag and it was amazing. Phil was always expected to do it, and deep down inside, I think it certainly created more pressure.

"And once he did it, everybody felt it: how many more can he win?"

"I really don't know what to say, to tell you how awesome it feels," Mickelson said. "It just feels so good. I don't think any Masters will ever compare to the 1986 Masters [won by Nicklaus at age 46], but for me, this one does."

The major tally: Tiger 8, Phil 1.

That didn't matter to Woods, however. He was not content with any previous success or a wide gap in major victories. As annoying as it was to see Mickelson wearing a green jacket, it was more of a bother that Woods was nowhere in the picture to prevent it from happening.

Mickelson contended at the U.S. Open, the Open, and the PGA Championship, finishing ahead of Woods in all of the majors in 2004. Both felt frustration: Mickelson for not winning another major, despite the opportunities; Woods for not even being a factor.

Neither player would win again that year on the PGA Tour, although Woods won in Japan in the fall. His game finally seemed to be coming together. Mickelson's was there. Another drama-filled year awaited.

11

Doral

At various times throughout Phil Mickelson's career, especially when he was in contention and had a late weekend tee time, he would conduct a double practice session. He would arrive midmorning, go through a full-range session with his coach, hit all the shots through the bag, work on the short game, putting—all aspects.

Then he'd take a break. Maybe eat lunch. Converse with his coach or his agent. Perhaps get some time with his trainer, stretch, before heading back to the range prior to the start of the round for a more casual warm-up session.

That was the plan prior to the final round of the 2005 Ford Championship at Doral.

The longtime PGA Tour event played annually since 1962 at the Doral Resort outside of Miami hit the lottery and jackpot and was gifted some lucky charms, too. Not only did it attract Ford endorser Mickelson but it also attracted Tiger Woods, who decided to play the tournament for the first time since 2002 and just the third time overall.

And then the dream scenario unfolded: not only were both players shooting good scores each day and in contention but they also managed to get into the final pairing on Sunday, a rare, colossal encounter that years later cannot be overstated.

Going into Sunday, Mickelson held a two-shot lead. He won twice earlier in the season and was coming off a year in which he was a contender in all four major championships, winning his first at the 2004 Masters.

Woods won earlier that year at the Buick Invitational, but was coming off a bleak 2004 season that saw just a single PGA Tour victory. And he had not won a major championship since 2002. Still, he was ranked second in the world, and he was stoked for the challenge, shooting a third-round 63 to get into the final group with Mickelson.

As Sunday dawned, the anticipation built, and fans streamed into the resort, Mickelson was following his plan when his coach, Rick Smith, came up with another idea after the lengthy morning session.

"Why don't we do something different," he recalled. "Everybody goes out to the practice tee. Everybody is there. Tiger is there. NBC is there. Why don't we pull a little Walter Hagen? Let's just go have lunch. Don't hit balls. Don't warm up. Just stretch and do a warm-up indoors. He's hitting it great, what's the point? We were sitting in the members' grill and having lunch. Let them wonder where you are. So finally it's about six minutes until his tee time, it was time to go, and he just walked right out to the first tee.

"That was kind of cool. Where is he? Is he sick? Did he pull a muscle? It was something different. We already had our morning practice. He had gotten a great session in, he was really hitting it good. What are we going to do, hit balls again and look for something wrong? I'll never forget him walking straight out to the tee, nobody has any idea what was going on."

EDDIE CARBONE WAS IN A BIT OF A DAZE, TOO, FLOATING ON THE proverbial Doral clouds. In his first year as the Ford Championship tournament director, Carbone arrived in Miami with the idea of giving the event a boost with more marketing ideas and incentives to get a South Florida audience with plenty of springtime options and diversions to attend a golf tournament.

Like every tournament director, Carbone had Woods on his mind. He started his new job the previous summer and spent time recruiting players, including Tiger, never knowing for sure if those efforts would pay off. As was his custom, Woods never committed until almost the last moment. And while Carbone had a good feeling that Woods would be involved, he didn't know for sure. Until he did.

"It was my first year, so it was all incredible and amazing," Carbone recalled. "The crowds were so thick and deep. There were a lot of tickets in the marketplace, so the crowds were off the charts. On the weekend, we had to shut the gates around 3 P.M. We weren't sure what was going on. It was pretty epic.

"We had this thing then where we had high school kids selling tickets for $5. I didn't even know about it; someone put that in place before I got there, and it was never a big thing. I was like, 'Where the hell are all these people coming from?' I'm on StubHub and all these tickets are on there for $10 that have a face value of $5. It was mayhem. And because it was Miami, where they expect top names, because Tiger wasn't there every year, it was this added excitement. It was crazy."

The scene on the first tee was no less chaotic. Mickelson arrived there having played coy, and thousands lined the tee box and the fairway on both sides of the par-5 hole.

"I was on the practice putting green, right there by the first tee, before they teed off and talking with Rick Smith about how amazing it was," Carbone said. "It was like a boxing match. And our theme for the [pro-am] draw party was boxing. And so it was sort of like walking into a boxing ring on the first tee. I remember, 'Oh my God,' it was totally packed with people. The energy was off the charts. It was a total slugfest."

Mickelson relished this opportunity. And he loved that Woods was in the hunt. He wanted Tiger there in the final group with him. The festivities had the atmosphere of a boxing match, even though Vijay Singh and Zach Johnson also began the day with a chance to win.

And so it was that at 1:45 P.M. they teed off, with a mesmerizing four-plus hours ahead, Woods wearing his trademark red shirt, Mickelson in olive, both wearing black pants.

Much like six months earlier, when they were U.S. Ryder Cup team-mates and were supposed to be on the same side, they could not have looked more apart. There was not going to be much banter. Tiger talked to his caddie, Steve Williams. Phil chatted with caddie Jim "Bones" Mackay as well as NBC's Roger Maltbie. Nobody expected they'd be chatty with each other.

Woods cut the lead to one stroke with a birdie at the fifth hole and then tied him with another birdie at the par-5 10th. The 12th was a stout par-5, measuring 600-some yards, and Woods was the only player to make eagle there during Saturday's third round. He did it again on Sunday, blasting a 3-wood from 300 yards to 25 feet, and then draining the putt to take a two-shot advantage.

Most figured it was game over at this point. Even with six holes to play, it's demoralizing to go from two shots ahead to two behind in the span of 12 holes. And nobody was better at closing out tournaments than Woods, something Mickelson knew plenty about.

Phil was not swayed. "When he made eagle on 12, I loved it," he said. "I want a chance to compete against him at his best. I didn't want him to be giving it to me. I wanted to go after it."

That was the first time Woods led all week. And then he got Phil's best. Mickelson drilled a 3-iron close at the par-3 13th for a birdie, then stuffed his 7-iron approach to five feet at the 14th for another birdie; Woods' congratulatory shout-out for the shot was inaudible amid all the thunderous cheering. With four holes to play, they were tied.

"It was huge for him to suck it up like that," Woods said. "He comes back with back-to-back birdies. That shows what kind of competitor Phil is, what kind of player he is. Don't forget what he did on the back nine. That was impressive to watch."

Mickelson gave himself a good chance at the 15th but failed to convert and later lamented, "That's where I had a chance to take control."

Woods struggled on the 16th on his way to his first bogey in 40 holes, and Mickelson could not take advantage. He never discussed it, but it's possible he was distracted by a photographer whose camera accidentally went off while Phil was attempting a chip shot. Mickelson missed the green but was faced with a chip he thought he could make. Somehow, he knocked it six feet past the hole, then missed the par putt, and they remained tied with two holes to go.

And that's where Woods broke free. He drained a 28-footer for birdie at the 17th, a feat that Mickelson could not match. It was Tiger's 27th birdie of the week. But there was still some drama to play out.

Mickelson missed the green to the left of Doral's closing hole, and faced a 30-foot chip shot to tie that he stalked like a putt. It was tracking toward the hole before catching the edge and staying out. "I thought it was in," he said. Tiger still needed a testy five-footer to preserve the victory, which he holed for a very satisfying win.

"It was tense," Woods said. "We were both excited. I can't speak for Phil, but I was certainly nervous out there. If you're not nervous on a day like this, you're not alive."

Make no mistake, Mickelson took little consolation in defeat. He relished the opportunity and openly said so. He wanted a crack at Tiger, and he figured he was playing well enough to accomplish the goal. The way he bounced back after relinquishing the lead spoke to his resolve.

With so much success for Mickelson to that point, it was difficult to conceive anything going wrong. He shot 60 during the FBR Open in Scottsdale, Arizona, to win and shot 62 on his way to victory at Pebble Beach. For 10 consecutive stroke-play rounds on the PGA Tour, he led or was tied for the lead.

The Sunday showdown with Woods presented a rare opportunity: it was just the third time that the two were paired together in the final group on the final day.

"It's pretty deflating," Mickelson said. "I really thought I was going to do it. I enjoyed going head-to-head with Tiger. I'm really in disbelief I fell short. I thought it was going to be my day."

"It was a hell of a day," said Mackay. "It was very cool. But it stung to lose."

And it was a big boost for Woods. If there was any doubt at this point that Hank Haney was his coach, it was all but erased at Doral. The partnership that quietly began sometime in 2003 and grew in 2004 was no longer a secret.

Woods produced his second win of the year and was pointing toward winning his first major championship in three years. Beating Mickelson didn't hurt.

"That was a big deal," Haney said. "He set Phil back a little bit. That was a stomp on the throat deal. That's just the way it was. If you would list the tournaments, majors are number one. And then I'm not sure if the Players Championship is number two. And then you'd be thinking the WGCs and the FedEx events.

"To me, it's the majors and stomping on a rival. Those are the two.

That's how it gets ranked. It was going against a rival head-to-head. It was a chance to make a statement. And in Tiger's mind this could be an edge he could use in the future."

To add a bit more insult, the winner received a $140,000 Ford GT in addition to the prize money. Mickelson was a Ford endorser and could have probably gotten the car anyway. He certainly could afford to buy it. Woods, who represented Buick at the time, would not be caught dead in a Ford, so he gave the keys to Williams, who rubbed it in by telling Phil that he was too big to look good in such a car.

Years later, Williams toned down the story.

"I just had a bit of a joke with Phil," Williams said. "Tiger chucked me the keys to the Ford, and he knew I was a fanatical Ford person. And of course Phil was with Ford. I said something like the car probably wasn't made for you. I'm better suited for it than you. Even though he rubbed me the wrong way, he had a great sense of humor. And he laughed at that."

The golf world came away smiling. The duel at Doral was great for the game, a needed boost. A rare Tiger-Phil pairing with them giving it their best was all the rage, and the major championships were not set to commence for another month.

"Ten years after that, even today, people talk about it," Carbone said. "The whole thing just played out beautifully. The back nine was a slug-fest and all kinds of stuff happed. We ended up doing a video about it in 2006, reflected back on the pro-ams and the players. That was played in the rooms [at Doral], and Phil said that video tormented him."

WOODS' DORAL VICTORY SET IN MOTION A GLORIOUS TIME IN THE Tiger-Phil dynamic. They would trade green jackets at the Masters over the next two years. They would combine to win six of the eight major championships played in 2005–06. And for the three-year period from 2005 to 2007, they combined for 33 worldwide wins, with seven major championships and a Players Championship between them.

Mickelson's play during this period is underrated, mostly because nothing is going to stand up to Woods, who won 23 times over those three years. When he missed the cut at the Byron Nelson tournament in

Long before most had heard of Tiger Woods, Phil Mickelson was making a name for himself as a junior player, winning 12 American Junior Golf Association titles, a record, from 1985 to 1988. *Courtesy of the American Junior Golf Association*

Playing in an AJGA event in 1987, Mickelson pitches to a green. He was the only three-time Rolex Junior Player of the Year in the organization's history, winning it each year from 1986 to 1988. *Courtesy of the American Junior Golf Association*

Even as a junior player competing in American Junior Golf Association events, Woods attracted a gallery full of spectators. *Courtesy of the American Junior Golf Association*

A four-time first team Rolex Junior All-American from 1990 to 1993, Woods won eight AJGA titles, tied for second behind Mickelson in the organization's history. *Courtesy of the American Junior Golf Association*

Jim "Bones" Mackay was by Mickelson's side as a caddie for 25 years, from his first event as a pro at the 1992 U.S. Open through the summer of 2017. "Bones" was on Phil's bag for 41 of his 45 PGA Tour victories and five of his six major championships. *Al Messerschmidt*

Butch Harmon started working with Woods when the golfer was just 16 years old, and oversaw him as he won eight major titles. Harmon, whose father, Claude Harmon, won the 1948 Masters, later went on to work with Mickelson from 2007 through 2015.
Al Messerschmidt

Veteran caddie Steve Williams started with Woods in the spring of 1999 and worked with him until a contentious breakup in 2011. Their 12-year-plus run saw Tiger win some of his biggest tournaments, including 13 of his 15 major championships. *Al Messerschmidt*

Earl Woods, working with Tiger at a golf clinic, had a big influence on his son's career and started him by hitting balls in the family garage. He passed away in 2006 just a few weeks after Woods finished three strokes back of Mickelson at the Masters. *Al Messerschmidt*

Ernie Els, with Woods, won four major championships and more than 70 professional tournaments worldwide, several at the expense of Woods and Mickelson. He also had his share of heartache, finishing second in three majors in 2000—including two to Tiger—and finishing a shot behind Phil at the 2004 Masters. *Al Messerschmidt*

It seemed like forever between major victories when Woods hoisted the Wanamaker Trophy at the 1999 PGA Championship. He held off Sergio García by a shot at Medinah (Ill.) Country Club. It had been 10 majors since Tiger won his first at the 1997 Masters. *Al Messerschmidt*

Throughout his career, going back to the days prior to turning pro, Woods was a huge draw wherever he went and in high demand for autographs.
Al Messerschmidt

Woods celebrates a birdie putt on the 18th hole at Augusta National that put the finishing touches on his 2001 Masters victory while Mickelson looks on. The win was Tiger's fourth in a row in major championships and was dubbed the "Tiger Slam." Phil had a chance to be the spoiler but finished third.
Phil Sheldon/Popperfoto courtesy of Getty Images

When Mickelson finally won his first major title, he jumped off the ground in celebration, having holed a birdie putt on the 18th hole at Augusta National to win the 2004 Masters. Woods was well out of contention. *Augusta National courtesy of Getty Images*

The body language at Oakland Hills in 2004 said it all. Woods and Mickelson were not particularly chummy at the time, and their Ryder Cup pairing on the first day turned out to be a disaster as they lost both matches they played together. It was the only time in the eight Ryder Cups in which they both played for the United States that Tiger and Phil were paired as partners. *Al Messerschmidt courtesy of Getty Images*

Hank Haney began coyly working with Woods in 2004 and became his official coach in 2005, leading to a strong run of successes that saw Tiger win six major championships and 31 PGA Tour events through 2009. The two parted in 2010. *Scott Halleran courtesy of Getty Images*

Woods and Mickelson had their most epic duel at the 2005 Ford Championship at Doral near Miami, where they played the final round together in the last group. Mickelson led by two going into the day, saw Woods pass him on the 12th hole, then tied him only to see Tiger prevail by one stroke. *Matthew Stockman courtesy of Getty Images*

A year after Mickelson put the green jacket on Woods, it was Tiger who returned the favor for Phil in 2006, site of Mickelson's second Masters victory. It was the culmination of a three-year stretch in which Mickelson and Woods traded the coat given to the winner at Augusta National. Tiger finished three strokes back of Phil that year. *David Cannon courtesy of Getty Images*

After a wayward tee shot on the 18th at Winged Foot, Mickelson made a series of mistakes on his way to a double-bogey 6 that cost him the U.S. Open, the only major championship he did not win. Woods missed the cut in a major championship for the first time as a pro. *Ezra Shaw courtesy of Getty Images*

Woods could barely walk during the 2008 U.S. Open at Torrey Pines, where unbeknownst to all but his inner circle, he was playing with two broken bones in his left leg. He also was just a short time away from full ACL replacement surgery on his left knee, which would keep him from playing for the rest of the year. *Scott Clarke courtesy of ESPN Images*

Woods celebrates on the 18th green at Torrey Pines in San Diego after making a 12-foot birdie putt on the final hole of the 2008 U.S. Open to force a playoff with Rocco Mediate. Woods won the 18-hole playoff the following day for his 14th major title. *Scott Clarke courtesy of ESPN Images*

Woods and Steve Williams during the 2010 U.S. Open at Pebble Beach, one of Tiger's rare high finishes that season. With a chance on the final day to win his first major title in two years, he shot 75 and tied for fourth with Mickelson. *Allen Kee courtesy of ESPN Images*

Eighteen years after he began his pro career at the U.S. Open, Mickelson was back at Pebble Beach for another U.S. Open along with his caddie, Jim "Bones" Mackay. Phil was in contention for his first U.S. Open title but a final-round 73 left him in a tie for fourth with Tiger, three shots back of winner Graeme McDowell. *Allen Kee courtesy of ESPN Images*

Mickelson poses with the Claret Jug after winning The Open at Muirfield, Scotland, in 2013. A final-round 66 led to a three-shot win and a fifth major title. Woods began the round just two shots out of the lead but finished sixth. *David Cannon/R&A courtesy of Getty Images*

Woods rejoices after tapping in a bogey putt on the 18th hole at Augusta National, where he won the 2019 Masters for his 15th major title. The victory came nearly two years to the day after undergoing serious spinal fusion surgery that put his career on hold. He defeated Brooks Koepka, Dustin Johnson, and Xander Schauffele by a stroke for his fifth Masters victory. *Kevin C. Cox courtesy of Getty Images*

With spectators reveling in the final-hole drama, Mickelson hits his approach to the 18th green during the final round of the 2021 PGA Championship. His shot set up a two-putt par and two-shot victory over Brooks Koepka and Louis Oosthuizen. *Scott Clarke courtesy of ESPN Images*

Mickelson raises his arms in triumph after finishing his round out on the 18th green at Kiawah Island's Ocean Course, where he won the PGA Championship in 2021. *Scott Clarke courtesy of ESPN Images*

Mickelson holds the Wanamaker Trophy after winning the 2021 PGA Championship, where he became the oldest major champion in history at age 50. It was his second PGA, his sixth major title, and his 45th PGA Tour victory.

Scott Clarke courtesy of ESPN Images

2005, it ended a run of a staggering 142 in a row that dated to 1998. He won two majors in 2005, two in 2006, and one in 2007.

Phil produced a four-victory season in 2005, just the third of his career. He won a major at the PGA Championship at Baltusrol, his second, holding off Tiger in the process and then winning a second straight at the 2006 Masters. After hiring Butch Harmon as his coach, he immediately won the Players Championship in 2007.

When Woods arrived at Augusta National just a month after his victory over Mickelson at Doral, the attention was as intense as ever. He went 10 major championships without a victory, leading to all kinds of conjecture about dropping Harmon and bringing on Haney as his coach.

Once again, Chris DiMarco was in the mix, as he had been the year prior. A former college standout at the University of Florida, DiMarco played on a Gator team that lost to Mickelson's Arizona State team in 1990, when Phil won the second of his three NCAA individual titles.

DiMarco won just three PGA Tour titles in his career, but he had a stretch where he was very strong in the major championships, posting six top 10s. Two of them were playoff defeats. Another was a runner-up finish to Woods at the Open.

One of those playoff losses came at the 2005 Masters, where he appeared buried after Woods made one of the most remarkable chip shots in golf annals. Leading by a shot on the final day, Woods hit his tee shot at the par-3 16th in a place that was so unusual that Williams said he was embarrassed not to know anything about that part of the course.

"No player I had ever seen had hit it that far long and left of 16, and I'd not bothered to scout that corner," he said. "You simply didn't expect any player to be over there."

Williams was so unsure that he feared the ball might be in the water. It was safe, but DiMarco was on the green with a makeable 15-foot uphill birdie putt, and Woods was in trouble, looking at an impossible shot, "one of the toughest pitches on the entire [course]," said CBS broadcaster Lanny Wadkins. A bogey seemed certain, and if DiMarco converted, Woods would suddenly be trailing by a shot with two holes to play.

What followed was perhaps the most viewed shot Tiger ever hit: a pitch shot into a slope away from the hole with the idea that the ball would land, then turn back toward the cup ever-so-slowly. Williams said years later that Woods was aiming for a pitch mark on the green that was the size of a dime. The hope was that Woods would give himself some sort of chance at making a par putt. The fear was that if he didn't hit the shot with the proper speed, it would come back and roll into the bunker.

From 45 feet, Woods dug down on the ball, landing it on the mark he pointed out to Williams. The ball made a hard right and started trickling back down the hole. As it inched closer, those sitting in chairs around the green rose were holding their breath. The murmuring increased to cheering.

"Oh. My. Goodness," said CBS broadcaster Verne Lundquist from the 16th tower. The ball came to a momentary stop on the lip, the Nike Swoosh visible for millions around the world to see. Woods, who raised his left arm and club in salute as the ball was still a few feet out, fell to his knees; Williams couldn't believe it.

Then . . . "Somehow an earthquake happened," Woods said.

And the ball dropped in for an unlikely birdie. Woods sprung up from his crouch with a roar as loud as the spectators, producing a much-loved double fist pump before an aggressive high five with Williams. After retrieving the ball from the hole, Woods added more triumphant bellows.

"Oh, wow!" Lundquist exclaimed. "In your life, have you seen anything like that?!"

Lundquist's call—much like his 1986 "Yes, sir!" call when Jack Nicklaus holed a birdie putt on the 17th green to take the lead for the first time—is as iconic as Woods' shot itself.

And yet it almost didn't matter. After DiMarco missed his 15-footer for birdie, Woods held a two-shot lead with two holes to play—and bogeyed them both. In fact, at the 18th, where Woods was on his way to a bogey, DiMarco nearly holed a pitch from in front of the green, which would have won the tournament.

Woods later described it as "throwing up on myself."

And they went to a sudden-death playoff at the 18th hole that nobody saw coming.

Woods hit his 8-iron approach shot to 15 feet after a perfect drive; DiMarco missed the same green with a 5-iron. "For some reason, I hit two of the best golf shots I hit all week," Woods said. He drained the putt for his fourth Masters and ninth major title—but first in nearly three years.

Mickelson finished 10th in his title defense, then waited for the traditional green jacket ceremony that first occurred in Butler Cabin and again on Augusta National's putting green.

Tiger's mom, Tida, and then-wife, Elin, were there to greet him after the draining victory, but missing was his father, Earl, who was too ill to make it to the course.

"It's been a difficult year; he's not doing very well," Woods told the onlookers. "He made the trek to Augusta, but he was unable to come out and enjoy this." Fighting tears, Woods said, "This is for Dad. I can't wait to get back to the house and give him a big bear hug."

WOODS' VICTORY AND HIS WIN LATER THAT SUMMER AT ST. ANDREWS for his second Open title were vindication, not only for him but also for his new coach, Haney.

The swing changes he made since his last major title were the subject of immense debate and conjecture. And Haney was well aware of it. Back then, Haney did not refer to himself as Tiger's coach, although he had been working with Woods officially going back to the spring of 2004. For a time, they kept the relationship secret, although many made the leap because of Woods' friendship with Mark O'Meara; Haney worked with the golfer for more than 20 years.

As Woods won just once on the PGA Tour in 2004, the focus was clearly on Haney. Singh passed by Tiger for No. 1 in the world. He produced his worst year in the major championships as a pro, his best finish a tie for ninth at the Open. He was hitting a dismal number of fairways, ranking 182nd on Tour with just 56 percent. And he ended the year at the Tour Championship failing to convert a 54-hole lead for the first time in his past 12 attempts. He and Jay Haas led the field by four with a round to go, but Retief Goosen's 64 left Woods as runner-up by four shots. Unheard of.

The second-guessing was intense. Why would Woods ever leave Harmon and attempt to alter a swing that won so many tournaments?

"I think it's subtle," Haney said of Woods' swing changes then. "But it's kind of like what people say when they are having minor surgery. The only minor surgery is surgery that is not on you. With Tiger, there is not a big, huge change that you can see without a trained eye. But when you change anything, it's not easy. There's no way to predict how much time it's going to take before you feel comfortable with it."

A former golfer at the University of Tulsa, Haney gravitated toward teaching and by age 24 was the director of instruction at Pinehurst, where he met O'Meara in the early 1980s. He eventually settled at Stonebridge Ranch in McKinney, Texas, and in addition to his duties there, he coached the Southern Methodist golf team.

That is where he met Woods, who was playing for Stanford at the time. The relationship grew through O'Meara and eventually became formal.

"Hank and I have put some serious hours into this," Woods said. "I read some of the articles over the past year of him getting ripped. I'm getting ripped for all the changes I'm making. To play as beautifully as I did is pretty cool."

It was tough to argue. Woods won seven times worldwide in 2005, including two major championships. And Mickelson put together one of his best seasons.

Mickelson was finally denting the Woods armor. He would never fully penetrate, but there were plenty of nicks and dings that caused Tiger to stagger. While Woods won two majors over the preceding two years, so did Mickelson, who gave Tiger all he could handle at Doral and proved himself to be a worthy challenger.

It didn't hurt that he won the last major championship of 2005. It would be a long wait until the 2006 Masters, and Mickelson snagged the last one and its off-season bragging rights. He began 2006 ranked third in the world, with Tiger a solid No. 1, a spot he would not relinquish for nearly five years.

But Phil was about to make it interesting.

12

WINGED FOOT

He buried his head in his hands, elbows resting on knees, squatting on the 18th green at Winged Foot Golf Club, the Odyssey putter that would strike one too many shots leaning on his leg. Phil Mickelson looked as if he had just been run over by a golf cart. His face was a reflection of the moment, and the moment was a reflection of Mickelson at his best and worst.

Mickelson had just lost the 2006 U.S. Open. Not just lost it, but blown it. Not just blown it, but committed golf suicide on the world stage, with adoring New York galleries crammed 20 deep, all there to witness Mickelson's triumphant walk down Winged Foot's final fairway, to watch him tip his hat to the masses, to give that trademark grin, a combination of feigned humility and practiced confidence.

Oh, he knew he was good. He was better than good. He was Phil-f-ing-Mickelson. But what those fawning fans saw on that warm June day on the 72nd hole of the game's most difficult major championship was Mickelson reduced to despair. He listened to an inner voice, and that voice betrayed him in the most hellish of endings. It was brutal.

And a huge opportunity was lost. Not just the opportunity to win a tournament. Or a major championship. Or the U.S. Open, the lone major he failed to win in his Hall of Fame career.

No, this was beyond all that. It was a chance, for once, to surpass Tiger Woods. Not in the world rankings. Not in career victories. Not in majors.

It was a chance to be the top dog, with the Big Cat, for once, chasing.

A victory at Winged Foot would have meant three straight major championships for Mickelson, a feat accomplished just twice in the modern era, once by Woods six years earlier. It would have flipped the script, changed the narrative. Instead of Tiger chasing history, it would have been Phil.

And what a gloriously entertaining notion: the idea of Phil soaring over Tiger, even if for just a short time.

When Woods was going for four majors in a row in 2001, the notion was unimaginable. And now Mickelson would have his crack at it? Not only would he have joined Woods (2002), Jack Nicklaus (1972), Arnold Palmer (1960), Ben Hogan (1951 and 1953), and Craig Wood (1941) as the only players to win the Masters and U.S. Open in the same year, Phil would also have joined Woods and Hogan as the only players in the modern era to win three majors in a row. And now at Royal Liverpool he'd have a chance at four straight?

There was the Tiger Slam, but a Mickel-Slam conjured a different kind of ring to it, but Phil didn't care how it sounded. There were all kinds of possibilities attached to whatever anyone wanted to call it.

Perhaps more subtly, a certain sense of satisfaction would have been in order. For a good part of their careers, Woods viewed Mickelson as an annoying gnat on his Nike shirt to be flicked away with little regard. For a long time, Tiger saw Mickelson as an underachiever, a player not getting the most out of his immense talent, one unworthy of his respect. He dismissed Phil as effortlessly as knocking the dirt out of his spikes.

Now Phil was standing up to the task long expected. He won the Masters, dealing Tiger a bitter defeat. And he was on the verge of capturing the most difficult of the majors, the one where Phil's biggest flaw—missing fairways—could be exposed. And yet he excelled anyway, with Tiger helpless to do anything about it.

Woods was not even there as all this drama unfolded. He was mourning the death of his father, Earl, who passed away on May 3, 2006. Tiger had not played since the Masters, where he failed to win the last major championship his father would witness—the one where he put the green jacket on Mickelson—and arrived at Winged Foot unprepared, missing the cut for the first time in a major championship as a pro. His thoughts were a long way from the suburban New York course, and frankly, for one of the rare times in Woods' historic career, the eyes of the golf world were not focused on him.

Phil had the stage to himself and stumbled into the orchestra pit. He crouched on the 18th green, a crumpled bundle of yellow short-sleeved shirt, black hat, gray slacks. He was embarrassed, in pain—and it was all self-inflicted. Know-it-all Phil handed the U.S. Open to a thoughtful, pleasant Australian pro named Geoff Ogilvy, who never won a major before and would never win a major again. In fact, he would never finish in the top 5 of a U.S. Open for the rest of his career. (Imagine the irony when, just a short time later, Ogilvy moved into the same Scottsdale, Arizona, neighborhood as Jim Mackay, Phil's caddie.)

And when Ogilvy was making a six-footer on the final green for a par that would give him a score of 2-over 72—he parred the last four holes and chipped in at the 17th—he could have no inkling that an hour later he'd be holding the U.S. Open trophy, with Mickelson at the ceremony, still down for the count.

"I'll tell you what," NBC analyst Johnny Miller said as he watched the carnage unfold, "Ben Hogan has officially rolled over in his grave."

And at that exact moment, Mickelson probably wished he were six feet under as well.

JOHNNY MILLER WAS NEVER ONE TO HOLD BACK. A BOLD PLAYER known for shooting low numbers, he evolved into one of the game's most outspoken golf analysts by 2006. Now 16 years into the gig and possessing the gravitas of someone who had won the U.S. Open, Miller found no problem with brutal honesty and wasn't worried about upsetting anyone. It sometimes made for uncomfortable moments, especially when he invoked the word "choke." But Miller—a Hall of Fame player who captured 25 PGA Tour titles, including two major championships—was true to his audience, not the Tour players he was critiquing.

So calling out Phil in the heat of battle at Winged Foot—or Tiger, when warranted—was Miller being true to his broadcasting ethos. It was also him being true to his U.S. Open roots, which suggested a player needed to hit fairways and greens to win. Mickelson was doing very little of the former.

Miller unwittingly played a role in what transpired at Winged Foot in terms of the course's perceived difficulty. At least that was the notion going back to the time Miller shot a 63 in the final round of the U.S. Open at Oakmont, the suburban Pittsburgh course that to this day is considered one of the toughest championship venues in the world.

Miller's 63 in 1973 was the lowest-ever score in a major championship and has since been matched just five times in the U.S. Open. It took until 2017 for anyone to go lower than 63 in a major when South Africa's Branden Grace shot 62 in the third round of the Open at Royal Birkdale. Just two 63s have ever been shot at the Masters.

Over the years, Miller has never been shy about talking about that round, and he referenced it on more than few occasions on the air. Then again, if ever there was a round to boast about and recount, the first 63 ever shot in a major championship would seem to qualify. Still, Tiger and Phil might be justified in rolling their eyes at such history.

Both players shot a score of 63 in majors. And both narrowly missed a putt on the 18th hole to shoot what would have then been a record-setting low round in a major championship.

Woods shot 63 in the second round of the 2007 PGA Championship at Southern Hills Country Club in Tulsa, Oklahoma. In sweltering, 100-degree temperatures, Woods lipped out a birdie putt on the 18th for a 62. He later described his round as "a 62½." Woods went on to win his 13th major championship that week.

Mickelson's 63 came at the 2016 Open at Royal Troon in the opening round, and he also believed he made a putt to shoot 62. "I want to shed a tear right now," he said. "That putt on 18 was a chance to do something historical." Mickelson played one of the best tournaments of his career, but finished second to Henrik Stenson—and was 11 shots clear of third place.

In 2000, *Golf* magazine ranked Miller's 63 the best round in golf history, and while there are undoubtedly other contenders, there is no denying its place in the annals of the game, especially as it came in the final round and helped him win.

"That's why it was voted the greatest round," Miller said during a 2016 interview. "There have been 59s shot; I shot several 61s in my career. But to shoot 63 at Oakmont on the last day to win by one is what makes the round what it is.

"If it had been on Thursday or Friday, it would have just been a terrific round. To go past all those guys who were in front of me and the fact I birdied the first four holes. Then I choked the next four holes thinking I had a chance to win. I had to go through that gauntlet of thinking. Then putting the hammer down and finish well, hitting every green in regulation.

"It's nice to have that one round that people will remember. Until someone does something like that or better, it'll always be thought about."

And it led to plenty of speculation when conditions were brutal at Winged Foot a year later. Did Miller's historic score unwittingly—or intentionally—turn the USGA devious as it sought to set up the next venue?

The scoring average on the par-70 Winged Foot course in 1974 was 76.99. During the first round, no player broke par. And some of golf's greatest players struggled. Nicklaus putted a ball off the first green, bogeyed his first four holes, and shot 75. Palmer shot 73. Miller shot 76. The 36-hole cut came at 13-over par. Hale Irwin's winning score was 287, 7-over par.

Although nobody at the USGA—which runs the U.S. Open—ever admitted so, many believe the organization reacted strongly to Miller's closing 63 a year prior. The general thinking was "We're not going to let that happen again."

"Well, that could have been part of the setup, yes," Irwin said. "I don't think the USGA looked kindly upon one of their setups being done in with a 63."

Winged Foot was another historic venue in the organization's long list of storied courses. Located in New York's Westchester County, it is where Bobby Jones won the third of his four U.S. Opens (1929), where Billy Casper one-putted nine greens in a row to win the first of two (1959), and where Greg Norman suffered the first of many agonizing defeats in majors, losing an 18-hole playoff to Fuzzy Zoeller (1984).

It is also where Tiger and Phil were paired together for the first time in the final round of a major championship: during the 1997 PGA, when both were well out of contention.

None of those previous majors were dubbed the "Massacre at Winged Foot."

"I think Winged Foot was a watershed Open," said the late USGA president Sandy Tatum, who was in charge of setting up the course that year. "It did set the premise for Open course setups, and I think that has carried on today."

A Tatum quote from that U.S. Open has lived on. Asked if the USGA was trying to embarrass the best players in the world, he said, "We're trying to identify them."

Woods and Mickelson saw their share of difficult major championship venues, led by the 1999 Open at Carnoustie, where the bizarre setup led to all sorts of anomalies, such as first-round leader Rod Pampling nose-diving on the second day and missing the cut and Sergio García, then an amateur, leaving the course in tears after missing the cut. Paul Lawrie won in a playoff after shooting 290, 6-over par.

The winning score at the 2005 U.S. Open at Pinehurst No. 2 was 280, even par.

The 2006 U.S. Open was the first at Winged Foot since Zoeller's victory in 1984. It is also where Davis Love III won the PGA Championship in 1997, although the layout was far more benign.

Designed by famed architect A. W. Tillinghast in 1923, Winged Foot was set up as the longest in U.S. Open history at the time, measuring 7,264 yards. But it wasn't the course's length that caused consternation. It was the narrow fairways and brutish rough, which, for the first time under USGA setup man Mike Davis, saw graduated rough that was more benign closer to the fairway but got worse the farther away the ball strayed.

It was the kind of U.S. Open course that Miller the analyst and Miller the U.S. Open competitor loved. It tested your ability to hit the ball in the fairway; it penalized you severely if you missed.

"I haven't seen rough that thick and dense I don't think ever," Mickelson said following a practice round at the course prior to tournament week.

In the 31 U.S. Opens following the "Massacre," the winning score was par or over just six times, including the year prior in Michael Campbell's win. Although the U.S. Open scoring record was achieved four times during that span, all were viewed as aberrations.

Winged Foot was setting up to be another week from hell, making Mickelson's exploits all the more remarkable given his propensity to miss fairways.

MICKELSON WAS PLAYING SOME OF THE BEST GOLF OF HIS CA- reer in 2006. After winning the 2005 PGA Championship at Baltusrol to cap a four-victory season, he was outside the top 14 just once in his first seven starts of 2006. Then he won in back-to-back weeks, claiming the BellSouth Classic in Atlanta as a warm-up to his second Masters victory a week later.

He arrived at Augusta National having shot 28-under par and winning by 13 strokes in Atlanta. Concerns about peaking too soon were quickly dismissed, and Phil being Phil, he employed a new strategy that saw him put two drivers in his bag. One would be used when he wanted to fade the ball; the other was designed for a draw that gave him extra roll.

The extra distance was especially useful in a year in which several changes had been made to the course, sometimes referred to as "Tiger- proofing" since they were made to combat the advantage that the now four-time Masters champion seemingly achieved in manhandling the layout in his nine attempts as a pro.

Six holes were lengthened by a total of 155 yards, and understand- ably Woods was still considered the favorite. He won twice earlier in the year.

Mickelson took a one-shot lead into the final round, and he was two ahead of Woods, who for the first time in his Masters career bogeyed three straight holes at Augusta National in the third round.

Phil parred the first six holes on Sunday, which saw a five-way tie for the lead before he birdied the seventh and eighth holes and held the lead for good. Tiger putted poorly, with three three-putt bogeys and two good opportunities for eagles missed at the 13th and 15th holes.

Failing to capture that Masters stung Woods about as much as any tournament he did not win. Knowing his dad was dying simply added to the pressure of trying to prevail.

Mickelson birdied the 13th and 15th and his bogey at the last was meaningless, meaning a two-shot victory over Tim Clark. Tiger, masking huge disappointment, slipped the green jacket onto Phil in the Butler Cabin ceremony and again during the formal prize-giving green jacket ceremony in front of all the dignitaries on Augusta National's putting green. They both smiled, but inside, Tiger was fuming.

"What I'm most proud of is that I didn't let other people back into it," Mickelson said.

Phil now had won consecutive major championships. After going more than 10 years and 46 majors without winning one of the four most coveted prizes, Lefty secured three in his last nine attempts. And he would put full effort into winning a third straight and four out of 10 when the U.S. Open at Winged Foot dawned.

As became his custom, Mickelson went on elaborate scouting missions at major championship venues. Swing coach Rick Smith and short-game guru Dave Pelz would also make the journey, and Phil would spend hours on the course, not playing a simple practice round but learning the various nuances of every angle of the course.

He took copious notes and along with his team did all he could to study every bit of real estate, to best position himself when the tournament rolled around. As fate would have it, on one of Mickelson's visits, dots on the greens that signal pin positions had been painted, ostensibly to give the grounds crew and USGA officials feedback. That was a clue to Phil, and he did his best to study them, hitting putts and chips to the various spots. And sure enough, during the first round, while playing off the 10th tee to start, Mickelson found the cup in a similar location to where he saw it in practice, holing a birdie putt from over a ridge to get the tournament started beautifully.

Mickelson intentionally played the final four holes in twilight during his pre-tournament trips to the course, hoping to simulate those major championship conditions that he would face as one of the leaders grinding down the stretch. He asked Callaway's club designer, Roger Cleveland, to make him a 64-degree wedge specifically made for Winged Foot, and that club was one of the reasons he remained in contention.

"It's like having [Arnold] Palmer the scrambler and [Jack] Nicklaus in the same body," Smith said at the time.

On the weekend before the tournament, Mickelson arrived at Winged Foot to get in more practice and play the course and happened upon Woods, who was also making an early visit to prepare for the U.S. Open.

Tiger had not played since the Masters due to Earl's death some six weeks earlier. That caused him to skip events he might have otherwise played that spring, including the Memorial Tournament in early June, an event he would eventually win five times and typically used as a tune-up for the U.S. Open.

And that meant Tiger was uncharacteristically unprepared, more so than he was for any tournament in his professional career. As we would learn, his heart was not in it. But the weekend prior still meant hope, and Woods was going to try and cobble something together as best he could.

He went to the driving range to warm up, as did Mickelson. They were located a few spots apart, hitting balls, going about their business, when a Winged Foot member who scheduled a round that day decided to drop his practice balls in one of the hitting areas between the two legends, who never seemed to notice. The man, clearly out of his element, flailed away amidst the two Hall of Famers—who would never say a word to each other.

KENNETH FERRIE WAS A U.S. OPEN ROOKIE, A 27-YEAR-OLD WHO played his way into the final pairing with Mickelson but lacked the experience necessary in such a pressure-cooker situation. The tall Englishman had recently lost more than 50 pounds, and he possessed the confidence to wear a Superman belt buckle. Ferrie played two years of junior college golf in Texas and won twice on the European Tour. All but unknown to Mickelson, Ferrie quite clearly knew plenty about Lefty.

"Phil faced a lot of polarizing opinions back then; people loved him and people hated him," Ferrie said. "But he was an absolute gentleman with me. He wouldn't hole out on the green. He would put a mark on his ball and wait to finish so the crowd wouldn't run away while I was putting.

"We had nothing really in common. We were just drawn together on this Sunday, and we each said, 'Good shot' when the other hit a good shot."

Ferrie shot himself out of the tournament on the front side, eventually shooting a 76 for the round. But he had the perspective to enjoy his view of history, and Ferrie stood in awe of what he kept witnessing from Mickelson.

"There's not another player in the world who could have managed his game that day like that," Ferrie said. "If I hit it in the places he did off the tee, I wouldn't have broken 80."

In truth, Phil's swing was seemingly patched together that day with masking tape and glue. He was hitting the ball all over the New York suburbs, and miraculously saving himself time and again, somehow still leading, on one of the most treacherous courses he played.

Case in point: Mickelson hit just two of Winged Foot's 14 fairways during the final round. It's impossible to contend, let alone win, doing that. And yet, there he stood with a chance to win the U.S. Open in plain view.

Despite all the mishaps, Mickelson led by two heading to the 16th tee, where a bogey saw him joined on top with perennial major championship loser Colin Montgomerie. Monty held the mantle of "best player without a major" from Mickelson after Phil won the 2004 Masters. But now, he buried a long-range birdie on the 17th to tee up his own chance at a fairy tale finish.

Two groups behind the Scot, Phil launched another wayward drive at the 17th, this one left of the fairway and, believe it or not, into a trash bin, allowing him a free drop. From there, he hit a bold, curving approach that set up a two-putt par.

As Mickelson stood on the 18th tee, it became clear he likely needed par to win; a bogey likely meant an 18-hole playoff the next day with Ogilvy. But perhaps Montgomerie's struggles ahead were a precursor of what was to come.

Monty ultimately tied for second with Mickelson after he double-bogeyed the final hole. It was a tortuous demise given how he'd hit a good drive but then missed the green with a 7-iron, chipped on, and then three-putted.

Afterward, in the heat of the hectic moment, Montgomerie

unwittingly pushed a police officer, causing USGA officials to scramble and intervene on his behalf, avoiding an embarrassing scene. It was a wild day.

Mickelson was aware of Montgomerie's undoing while waiting on the tee, thanks to a nearby scoreboard change and fan reaction. With just the unheralded Ogilvy a shot behind him now, the stage was set.

"It was like watching an absolute master," Ferrie said of Mickelson to that point. "Seve [Ballesteros] was a superstar magician, but I never saw Seve in his prime. Watching Phil was like watching someone who was superhuman. For him to be hitting it left and right on that course, and to be standing on the 18th at 2-over [for the day], it was one of the best rounds of golf I've ever seen."

It is a reminder of Phil's genius, and defined his career. There wasn't a snake pit from which he could not emerge, no shackles from which he couldn't become untethered. And there was simply no shot he wouldn't take on. Sometimes, he prevailed; other times he paid the price.

A day earlier, Mickelson played his best nine holes of the tournament, hitting his last five fairways to shoot 2-under 33. He knew a big day was ahead, and yet he sensed victory. There had been struggles, sure, but Winged Foot caused fits for everyone.

"Your mind races," Mickelson said. "It's that greatest feeling, that nervousness."

But those good vibes were gone when Mickelson hit the range on Sunday. He hit the ball poorly on Friday and was doing so again now. He needed a fix that wasn't coming. And the amount of time he spent on the range looking for a solution cost him time he dearly needed on the putting green.

And yet, there he was, one par from victory.

From the broadcast tower, Miller implored Mickelson to hit anything but a driver off the tee. But neither Mickelson nor Mackay thought that play was prudent. A 4-wood into the wind was no guarantee to reach the dogleg—and frankly, it was no guarantee to find the fairway, either.

So Phil pulled out the driver, teed up his ball on the far left side of the box, and planned to hit what he called his bread-and-butter shot, one he often employs on the par-5 dogleg left 13th at Augusta National—a baby, carved slice. But the moment the club struck the ball, Mickelson knew he came out of the shot too soon, the ball sailing way left toward the roof of the Champions Pavilion, a hospitality tent. "Oh, no," Mickelson said, grabbing his head as he watched the ball bound off the tent.

The shot eventually led to a double-bogey 6 that cost him the only major championship he has never won. His résumé, by his own doing, still has a giant bruise mark on it. It is the one bruise that time has never fully healed. And it left Mickelson trying to explain the unexplainable.

With the win, Mickelson would have joined Hogan (1953) and Woods (2000) as the only players in the modern era to win three consecutive major championships. Not even the great Nicklaus accomplished that feat. Nor Palmer. Nor Sam Snead or Byron Nelson. Nor Tom Watson or Lee Trevino or Gary Player.

And with such a victory, Mickelson would have headed to the Open at Royal Liverpool on the cusp of the unthinkable: matching Tiger's feat of holding all four major championships at the same time. But all that changed with a series of decisions that still boggle the mind, some far easier to question in hindsight.

Winged Foot's final hole—admittedly a muscular, 460-yard par-4 designed by Tillinghast to make a player's knees wobble and hands shake—was all that stood between Mickelson and such chatter. It was a coffee-is-for-closers type of situation: the kind of situation that Woods has historically excelled at: a lead . . . one hole to play . . . a major championship at stake.

Instead, Mickelson sprayed that tee shot so far left that it flew over the gallery and caromed off the top of that hospitality tent, which might as well have been a circus tent.

"He didn't have his best stuff that week," Mackay said. "It was somewhat of a miracle he was leading."

Davis, the USGA official who was officiating the Mickelson-Ferrie group, cleared spectators away from Mickelson's ball, then took a look at the slight downhill lie that saw the ball in a small clump of grass. To him, the lie was not as clean as TV made it look.

"I just remember before he played the shot thinking, 'This is why tournament pros are so much better than the rest of us,'" Davis said. And then he wondered, "How can you possibly get over or around this big maple tree?"

From there, slapstick comedy ensued as Lefty made a bad situation worse by trying to curve his 3-iron second shot from 210 yards around the big, gaping tree and onto the green, the hero shot for which he came to build his reputation. The ball had other ideas, flying flush into the tree, which spit it back out at him mockingly, just 30 yards closer to the hole.

Mickelson tried too hard to make a 4 when a 5 would have gotten him into a playoff. He actually got a great break that his drive came to rest where it did. He was in a cleared area. There was a shot to be played: curve it around the tree and onto the green, in a similar fashion to the way he pulled off his approach one hole earlier.

"I was there on the 18th hole when the ball went left over there, and when I got to where the ball was and saw where it ended up, I thought it was ideal," said Phil Mickelson Sr. "He had just played the exact same shot on the previous hole. Now he's got the same shot again. 'This is going to be easy.' I'll be darned if it just didn't go a foot and a half left of ideal and hit that darn tree.

"All he needs is par there. I thought he was in the catbird's seat. When the ball hit the tree, that changed the whole dynamic."

Mickelson's decision-making can easily be second-guessed. It was that day and will be forevermore. Sure, Phil possessed the ability and wherewithal to pull off the shot. It's what makes Mickelson, well, Mickelson. Hit the shot around the tree and onto the green, two-putt for par, win the U.S. Open.

But clearly it wasn't that simple, as the resulting struggles made clear. The argument: why not punch a shot down the fairway, leaving yourself a wedge shot to the green, setting up the possibility for a winning par putt but assuring a two-putt bogey and a playoff?

Similar scenarios played out to Mickelson's detriment in his career. Remember, Payne Stewart missed the fairway on the final hole in the 1999 U.S. Open and needed to play back into the fairway, leaving himself a wedge shot to the green. He holed the par putt to win in front of Phil, one of golf's most iconic scenes—a scene that would inspire a statue of Stewart's celebratory pose that now sits behind the green honoring the accomplishment.

Two years later, playing the final hole of the PGA Championship, Mickelson again was there with a chance to win, only to see David Toms do exactly as Stewart did, wedging onto the final green at Atlanta Athletic Club, then holing the par putt to deny Phil another major.

It seems Phil could have done the exact same thing at Winged Foot.

Ferrie expected Mickelson to give himself a 100-yard shot to the green after punching his second shot down the fairway. "I couldn't see him ending up more than six feet from the hole," he said.

But having gone for the green, he was now in real trouble, the par he needed to win all but a pipe dream. "It looks like he aged five years on that shot," Miller said. Mickelson was left with no choice but to try and take his third shot up over that tree, and in a bit of a daze, he was unable to get to the green. Not only did it find a greenside bunker but it also buried: the ultimate death sentence. The NBC cameras flashed periodically to Ogilvy and his wife in the scorer's room in the clubhouse, a look of disbelief on their faces. Ogilvy made a clutch par to post at 285, 5-over.

"This is a nightmare right here," Miller said. "Absolutely you couldn't have worse decisions than he's had on this hole. I don't care who you are—I know you all love Phil, but c'mon, you just have to make par on this hole.

"You don't have to run down the stretch on a white stallion. You can limp in there and say, 'Thanks for the trophy.'"

Mickelson's shot from the bunker for an unlikely par never had a chance. With the difficult lie, he could hit the ball with no spin, as it rolled off the far side of the green and into ankle-deep rough. His fifth shot, to force a Monday playoff, didn't come close. He made the putt for a double bogey, but it hardly mattered at that point. He shot a final-round 74. He finished 6-over par at another brutish Winged Foot test. Ogilvy was the one celebrating.

Nobody noticed that Ferrie did exactly what Phil needed to do: hit the fairway and green for a stress-free finish, a par that helped him tie for fifth and qualify for the 2007 Masters. "I was gutted for him," Ferrie said.

So was a good part of the golf world, it seemed.

"I still am in shock after I did that," Mickelson said later to a room full of reporters who were just as dazed. "I just can't believe that I did that. I am such an idiot. I can't believe I couldn't par the last hole. It really stings."

The "I am such an idiot" line brought to mind the famous quote of

Roberto de Vicenzo following the 1968 Masters. "What a stupid I am to be wrong here," the Argentine golfer said after it was learned he signed an incorrect scorecard and was required to take the score he signed for— one stroke higher—than the one he actually shot.

Instead of playing off against Bob Goalby for the green jacket—which is what the scoreboard reflected—he was runner-up by a stroke due to a clerical error and part of one of the most awkward award ceremonies that sport ever witnessed.

At least Mickelson's gaffe was with his clubs and not a pencil—not that it made things any easier. A month later, when Phil showed up early to practice at Royal Liverpool—site of de Vicenzo's Open victory the last time the event was played in the town of Hoylake in 1967—he wasn't trying to hide the pain.

"Well, I'm not going to ever forget that," he said. "I don't think many people who watched it will either, but for me, I won't ever forget that."

It would be impossible.

The end was swift and cruel. Mickelson stayed in the scoring room for a good while, consoled by his wife, Amy, still trying to make sense of it all. Amy would later say he was in a trance. Truth be told, Mickelson did not play all that well during the final round. He missed all those fairways and the fact that he held the lead was remarkable—although typical of the way Mickelson played the game. It is why his longtime caddie "Bones" still tells anyone who asks about the incident that while it was a crushing loss, it wasn't *the* most crushing loss in a Mickelson career filled with them.

"At least not to the level you might imagine, because you know what? It's a 72-hole tournament," Mackay said. "And it's a hard hole. It's pretty easy to say you make a 4 here and you win the U.S. Open. It's not that simple. You're playing a 460-yard par-4 and he was having trouble with his ball striking that day. There you go. You have to play them all."

Still, Mickelson led by two strokes after 15 holes. He held a one-shot advantage with one hole to play. At worst, he should have been in a play-off.

"To be honest, one of the worst collapses in the U.S. Open history by Phil Mickelson," said Miller, who simply articulated on the air what everyone else was thinking. Including Phil.

If not for Jean Van de Velde's cartoonish implosion on the 72nd hole of the 1999 Open at Carnoustie, Mickelson might be number one on the list of collapses. The French golfer needed only a double bogey to win but clanked an approach shot off a grandstand and considered playing a shot out of a knee-deep creek called the Barry Burn, which protected the green (he took off his shoes and socks and waded in before coming to his senses), before dumping another shot in a bunker.

Van de Velde can at least argue that the triple bogey he made on the last hole of regulation still ensured him a place in a three-man playoff—which, of course, he lost to Lawrie.

There were others lamenting on that Sunday. Montgomerie was clearly one. Another was Jim Furyk, who bogeyed two of the last four holes, including a short miss for par on 18. He joined the tie for second at 6-over. Pàdraig Harrington bogeyed the last three holes, a day after closing with a triple-bogey 7 on 18, to finish two shots back.

Woods said he watched both weekend days. "That was my punishment," he said for missing the cut. As the broadcast went to break before the presentation, a producer garnered a few chuckles by saying, "Somewhere in a boat off the Atlantic, someone is smiling." Woods spent the tournament week on his yacht on the nearby coastline. The suggestion was his "punishment" had turned less harsh by the end.

And Woods wasn't exactly exuding a sympathy vibe when asked about it a few weeks later. Privately, Woods texted an acquaintance to get a sense for what happened, and derisively asked what body part Mickelson tripped over. Publicly, it was more G-rated.

"With Phil on the tee, anything can still happen," Woods said. "He could still make bogey on that hole. I thought it was Monty's tournament, put the ball on the green and it's over. Obviously that didn't happen, and then Phil had his mistakes. It was a very interesting finish, one that none of us who are involved in the game of golf probably ever would have predicted we would have seen happening."

MICKELSON'S TIE FOR SECOND MARKED THE 21ST TIME TO THAT point that he finished seventh or better in a major. And his Masters victory two months earlier was not making him feel better. Not in any way.

While he broke through to win majors, Mickelson also kicked away a few chances as well. His total stood at three, which was historic in the overall scheme of the game but still left many wondering how many it could have been.

He was leading the 2004 U.S. Open at Shinnecock when he three-putted from five feet for a double bogey on the 71st hole to finish second to Retief Goosen. They were the only two players to finish under par. A month later at the Open, Mickelson held the lead at Royal Troon with seven holes to play, only to let it slip away, with Ernie Els losing in a play-off to Todd Hamilton. Stewart made that putt on him at the Pinehurst U.S. Open in 1999, and Toms did the same on the final hole of the 2001 PGA Championship.

But those defeats were nothing like Winged Foot.

"This one hurts more than any [other] tournament because I had it won," he said. "I had it in my grasp and just let it go."

Just more than two years prior, Mickelson captured that elusive first major, starting a green jacket–sharing run with Woods that seemingly followed in the tradition of the greatest players of their era.

While Woods was having one of his worst years as a pro to that point and going through swing changes, Mickelson emerged to challenge him. Then Tiger bounced back to win the Masters in 2005—his first major in three years—only to see Phil steal the year-end thunder by capturing the PGA. When Mickelson won the Masters the following year, it was Woods who put the green jacket on him.

And it mirrored some of the other great rivalries in the game. Starting in 1951, Hogan and Sam Snead alternated winning the Masters through 1954 and were among the first to take part in the green jacket ceremony, a tradition that began in 1949 when Snead won the Masters for the first time.

A generation later, it was Arnie and Jack—along with Gary Player. Palmer, who won the first of his four Masters in 1958, won it again in 1960, then in 1961 put the jacket on Player (after double-bogeying the last hole to lose by one), who helped Palmer back into it in 1962. Nicklaus won the first of his six Masters in 1963, but did the honors in 1964 for Arnie, who returned the favor when Nicklaus won in 1965. When the Golden Bear became the first player to defend his Masters title, the club chairman, Clifford Roberts, helped him with the ceremonial duties in 1966.

The Phil-Tiger-Phil exchange commenced in 2004, when Mickelson was finally able to shed the label of "best player without a major championship."

Woods piled up eight major championships by that point and—deep down—wondered how Mickelson could squander all that ability. Despite how Woods might have been dismissive at times of Mickelson, he also knew there was plenty of talent lurking. Woods was long an admirer of Mickelson's short game, and he was well aware of the junior, amateur, and college exploits. Woods privately surmised that Mickelson was either soft, or perhaps reckless, which helped form a less-than-flattering opinion of his older colleague.

But Mickelson finally winning a major helped change that. Grudgingly, not publicly, not all that fondly. But slowly, and over time, Woods' perception of Mickelson began to evolve. Certainly Phil winning at Augusta helped. So did their 2005 duel at Doral, where Mickelson gave Woods everything he could before coming up one shot short in what was perhaps the best head-to-head battle between them.

And even though Tiger would win two majors in 2005—his first since 2002—it was Phil who bagged the last one of the year at the PGA Championship. When he added the Masters in 2006—denying Woods a green jacket he dearly coveted—the two players combined to win four of the last nine major championships.

When Woods won the Masters in 2005, he paid tribute to his father. It was one of the rare times where Woods revealed his human side. Earl could not make it to the tournament due to illness.

"This one's for Dad," Woods said. "He's struggling. That's why it meant so much for me to be able to win this tournament, maybe give him a little hope, a little more fire to keep fighting."

Woods won the Open later that year at St. Andrews for his 10th major title followed by Mickelson's PGA title at Baltusrol. And when they arrived at Augusta the following spring, Woods' dad was again on his mind as Phil prevailed.

It was Phil's second straight major, and Woods could only grit his teeth, put the green jacket on Phil, and seethe.

"I've lost tournaments before, and I've been through some tough defeats over the years, but nothing like that because I knew my dad would never live to see another major championship," Woods said. "At the time, going into that final round on the back nine, I pressed and I tried to make putts that instead of just allowing it to happen, I tried to force it.

"I know he was at home watching, and I just really wanted to have him be part of one last major championship victory. And I didn't get it done."

That set the stage for Winged Foot, where Woods arrived rusty and distracted. "I'm here to compete and play and try to win this championship," he said. "I know that dad would still want me to grind it and give it my best, and that's what I always do. That's what I will certainly try to do this week."

Steve Williams, Woods' longtime caddie, knew better.

"I could have told you most likely before we teed off on Thursday that it was going to be tough," Williams said. "Making the cut was going to be tough. I would generally spend the weekend before with him, and his practice was certainly not great. His form was nowhere near where it needed to be to win a U.S. Open. Tiger was remarkable in that he won so many of his tournaments without his best form. But there you have to have your A-game. And a lot of times he won with less than that. But at a place that difficult, he just didn't have it."

As for his rivalry with Mickelson, Woods might have found new respect for Phil but was typically underwhelming in any praise. "You have had runs where Ernie [Els] was there for a little bit, then Vijay [Singh] and Goose [Retief Goosen]," he said. "And now Phil."

But Woods' game was clearly not up to the task. If ever he was vulnerable, this was the time. He was not the same Tiger, not by a mile. He bogeyed his first three holes, hit just three fairways for the round, and did well to shoot a 6-over-par 76. The drive, the ability to focus, to block out distractions were all woefully missing.

The following day, he double-bogeyed his fifth hole, and the typical fight was gone. He shot another 76 to miss the cut by three strokes, his first weekend off at a major since turning pro in 1996, a streak of 37 in a row. Tiger was hurting, understandably so. And Phil was in position to pounce, to sit atop the golf world with a third straight major.

But despite Woods being out of the picture, Mickelson was unable to deliver. At a time when Tiger would have stepped on necks to get the trophy, Phil could only sheepishly play that final hole with so much at stake, leading to that trancelike daze. It was his fourth runner-up finish at the U.S. Open (he would finish second on two more occasions), but more important, he blew a golden opportunity for that third straight major. It would take another four years before he'd win his fourth major.

Making matters worse?

Woods would go on to win the Open at Royal Liverpool, an emotional victory itself, as Tiger cried in the arms of Williams on the 18th green. And then he won again at the PGA Championship at Medinah. (In fact, after the U.S. Open, Woods tied for second at the Western Open, then won five consecutive tournaments.) Instead of Phil reigning with three straight majors, it was Tiger raining on Phil's stalled parade.

Mickelson's words—"I am such an idiot"—would linger for a lifetime.

13

TORREY PINES

If Tiger Woods knew anything about Andy Williams, it was because a golf tournament he cherished bore the singer and actor's name. Woods might have been hard-pressed to come up with the fun fact that Williams was nominated for six Grammy Awards. He cared more about Andy Bean, a golfer who he saw play in the entertainer's tournament.

Woods discovered the annual PGA Tour event at Torrey Pines Golf Course at a time when many events were named after celebrities. Williams' was attached to the San Diego tournament from 1968 to 1988. And it was late in that period when Woods first attended.

Riviera Country Club might have been closer to his Cypress, California, home, but Earl Woods took his son to the tournament that over time was called variations of the Andy Williams San Diego Open, later known as the Buick Invitational, and then the Farmers Insurance Open.

There Tiger learned about professional golf. He remembered seeing Bean hit a 1-iron. He homed in on California pros Mark O'Meara and John Cook, players with whom he would later forge important friendships. To Tiger, Torrey felt like home.

That's why, late in the 2002 season, news that might otherwise have been of little interest to him became of big importance.

It didn't matter that he won the Masters and U.S. Open earlier that year. Or that he won six times worldwide. Or that a U.S. loss at the Ryder Cup might have been eating at him.

"Torrey Pines Aces U.S. Open Bid," read a headline in the *San Diego Union-Tribune* on October 5, 2002.

It meant a lot to those who followed the game closely. The USGA announced that Torrey Pines, specifically the South Course, was being awarded the 2008 U.S. Open, making it just the second municipal facility to host the championship.

Earlier that year, Woods won the U.S. Open at Bethpage Black on Long Island, the first municipal course to hold the tournament. In part due to the success of that U.S. Open, Torrey Pines got its chance at a venue that staged an annual PGA Tour event, one Woods loved.

The news, of course, was big in San Diego, as that area would be getting golf's version of the Super Bowl. Southern California would stage a U.S. Open for the first time since Ben Hogan won at Riviera in 1948. And the golf world collectively nodded—then got on to more immediate concerns.

Not Woods. He already won two U.S. Opens, one by 15 shots. Five more U.S. Opens were scheduled before the tournament would venture to the scenic coastal bluffs that offered stunning views of the Pacific and ultimately presented one of the championship's most dramatic outcomes.

In the interim, Woods went on to hoist five more major championship trophies, but he always kept his eyes on Torrey Pines, to the point where he talked about that U.S. Open more than any other tournament he won or lost. He won the PGA Tour event at Torrey Pines six times prior to the U.S. Open, including five months earlier—by eight strokes.

"In all the time I caddied for Tiger, he had more of a fascination with that event than any other tournament," said Steve Williams, who caddied for Woods from 1999 to 2011. "When he had a chance to win the Masters [in 2001] and hold all four majors at the same time, the Tiger Slam, as it was called, there was a long time leading up to it. You would think there would be a lot of talk about it. He hardly mentioned it.

"But from the moment the USGA announced they were going to hold the tournament at Torrey Pines, he had a complete fascination for that event. And it was fascinating to me. I understand he grew up in that area, he won there, he loved the course. Whenever we played there, he was always like, 'I wonder if they are going to put the tee here, where are they going to put the pins?' He just had a complete fascination."

"The U.S. Open at Torrey Pines," Woods said, "was like going home. It meant more to me."

WOODS CELEBRATED HIS 32ND BIRTHDAY AT THE TURN OF THE calendar having just completed a remarkable 2007 season in which he won seven times, including the PGA Championship at Southern Hills, one of four victories in his last five starts. He was runner-up in the other.

The holidays didn't cause any rust. Woods began his year at Torrey Pines with the annual Tour stop then known as the Buick Invitational, cruised to his eight-shot victory, and set his sights a few months down the road on the same venue; capturing Torrey Pines became all but an obsession.

A week later, Woods traveled to the Middle East and won the Dubai Desert Classic by a stroke over Martin Kaymer. Three weeks later, it was a rout in the 36-hole final of the WGC-Accenture Match Play Championship, an 8 and 7 victory over Stewart Cink.

When he added the Arnold Palmer Invitational, it meant wins in six straight tournaments, including four for four in 2008 and eight of his last nine. "The whole thing is amazing," said Adam Scott, ranked third in the world in 2008, recalling those days. "When you think back to what it was then, how remarkable he was, how much better he was than anybody else."

The winning streak finally ended when Woods finished fifth at the WGC-CA Championship at Doral. And then at the Masters, Woods endured a somewhat frustrating week in cold temperatures that saw him six strokes back through 54 holes before finishing second by three strokes to Trevor Immelman.

Two days later, Woods announced that he underwent arthroscopic surgery on his left knee, which he portrayed as a simple procedure to repair cartilage damage. It was his third operation on the knee going back to 1994 and his second in five years. He was expected to miss a month while he recovered.

"I made the decision to deal with the pain and schedule the surgery for after the Masters," Woods said in a statement. "The upside is that I have been through this process before and know how to handle it. I look forward to working through the rehabilitation process and getting back to action as quickly as I can."

When Woods called Hank Haney to tell him about the surgery, it was the first time the coach, who now was in his fifth year working with him, was aware of it.

"The surgery was meant to clean things out, but it made it a lot worse," Haney said. "It set him back. Now he can't practice. How in a few weeks is he going to walk? He was going to try and play the Memorial [two weeks before the U.S. Open]. My initial thought when I first saw him was this isn't going to happen."

According to Haney, Woods hoped to alleviate increasing pain due to loose cartilage. But Dr. Thomas Rosenberg, an orthopedic surgeon based in Park City, Utah, discovered during the procedure that Woods' anterior cruciate ligament (ACL) was fully torn. Haney wondered if Woods was worse off for having done what was supposed to be a simple procedure.

The ACL is one of the two ligaments that cross in the middle of the knee—connecting the thighbone to the shinbone, helping to stabilize the knee joint.

"I needed it," Woods said during an interview reminiscing about the tournament 10 years later. "I had ruptured my ACL in July the previous year, in '07, and I played on it with no ACL and my meniscus was just, I was trashing it. My leg was sloppy. So I knew I had to go in there because I had fragments there. But my surgeons were saying that I also have to have the knee reconstructed. And I said, 'Well, we'll just do a cleanup job first.' Because I wanted to play the next three major championships.

"So we had the procedure done, cleaned out all the debris, and obviously there was no ACL in there. So I took time off after that surgery. When I came back, I was doing a photo shoot, and I was hitting a shot from a downhill lie, and that's when I cracked [the tibia].

"I was hurting and I didn't know what was going on, so I went to get an X-ray first and that's when it showed I had fractured it. From there, they were saying I was pretty much done for the year. I said, 'Ah, I don't know about that.' If I hadn't had the fracture, I might have been able to make it through the rest of the year. Maybe. Because I played basically from July of '07 through '08 with no ACL so I was kind of used to it.

"So I was hoping to get through the majors, have the reconstructive surgery after the PGA, and I'd have nine months to get ready for Augusta. But nothing worked out that way."

Not even close. Woods probably should have shut it down there. He could barely walk. Practice was a joke and Haney found it difficult to be positive.

"Tiger did that whole thing where they do the fake name and nobody knows he's the one getting an MRI," he said. "They get a doctor in Orlando to do it. Then Dr. Rosenberg flew in from Park City a few days later. He's explaining about the MRI, it's on his laptop, and he's showing there are two stress fractures [in the tibia of Woods' left leg] as well as the torn ACL. He's showing us everything, but Tiger is not really paying attention, not really listening.

"So I asked what was the normal procedure for a stress fracture like this, and he says stay off your leg for six weeks on crutches and then start rehabbing. I'm going through the schedule in my mind, and I'm thinking the season is over."

Woods won nine of 12 tournaments and had two seconds and a fifth during a time he did not have a fully functioning ACL. But playing the Memorial was soon scrapped and even the U.S. Open looked dubious.

"My thought was this is not going to happen," Haney said. "He's limping out of a golf cart to go hit 40 golf balls. How are we going to go play in a major championship in a few weeks? There was no chance."

Woods scoffed.

"Tiger looks up and says, 'I'm playing the U.S. Open and I'm going to win.' Just like that," Haney said. "Then he says, 'C'mon Hank, let's go practice.' The determination was absolutely incredible and clearly I'll never forget it."

ON THE MONDAY FOLLOWING THE MEMORIAL TOURNAMENT, 10 days prior to the first round of the U.S. Open, a series of sectional qualifiers for the U.S. Open occurred around the country. Typically less than half the field is exempt for the U.S. Open; the rest make their way into the tournament via sectional qualifying, now called Final Qualifying. They are 36-hole, one-day events.

Rocco Mediate, 45, was among 140 players at the qualifier in

Columbus, Ohio, conveniently set up to accommodate tour players competing at the nearby Memorial, making it one of the strongest fields but also one with the most qualifying spots. Mediate shot a final-round 69 at Muirfield Village Golf Club to tie for sixth at the Memorial, six strokes behind winner Kenny Perry. It was his 17th tournament of 2008 but his first top 10. He missed eight cuts and had withdrawn from another event.

In the sectional, Mediate shot scores of 72–67 to finish at 139, which was good enough to earn a spot in an 11-player playoff for the remaining seven spots. A total of 23 players earned their way to Torrey Pines from Columbus, including the likes of Davis Love III, Jesper Parnevik, Nick Watney, and a virtual unknown at the time, Dustin Johnson, who along with Mediate survived the playoff. Love qualified for his 18th consecutive U.S. Open. Pat Perez, a junior golf rival of Woods', who once beat him in the Junior World Amateur by eight strokes, and virtually grew up working at Torrey Pines, also made it.

It would be Mediate's 12th U.S. Open. He had two top 10s in 11 previous appearances, his best a fourth-place finish in 2001.

ONLY EIGHT DAYS BEFORE THE START OF THE U.S. OPEN, WOODS and Haney left Florida and flew to California, where the golfer played nine holes in a cart at Torrey Pines with no fanfare. He was wearing a knee brace that Rosenberg gave him with instructions to keep the number of balls he was hitting to a minimum.

The next few days were spent off property, and Woods never played more than nine holes at a time. Woods and Haney drove to Newport Beach to play at Big Canyon Country Club. A Saturday morning round did not go well.

"They gave him one of those big football lineman braces," Haney said. "He's wearing that thing and trying to practice and play, but he can't hit the ball. He played nine holes and lost like every ball. He had six or seven balls and lost them all, shot 47 or something. It was terrible. Didn't even finish the last hole. Some of that was the brace, and that was the last day of the brace. He basically said that whether or not he could make it was one thing, but he wasn't going to win using the brace. So he took off the brace, and he started hitting it a little bit better, but he hadn't walked."

Woods received an honorary membership to Big Canyon when he was in high school, an award that got scrutiny from the NCAA before the collegiate organization ruled he could accept certain perks at the club. He played there frequently at that time, knew the course well—but didn't know the kind of golf he was seeing.

"I was still trying to figure out how in the hell I was going to try and play with a knee brace," Woods said. "My knee was obviously moving all over the place and [the tibia] was broken, so I didn't know how I was going to play with a knee brace. So I played and shot 50-some-odd, and then on the way down there [to Torrey Pines] I threw it in the trash and was done with it. So I said, all right, I'm going to have to figure out how to play without a knee brace with this leg."

"One thing I could see," said Rob McNamara, Woods' longtime friend and vice president at Tiger Woods Ventures (TGR), "was he kept trying to find a swing that he could manage around. The thing that kept coming back to me was that his short game was still there. He could still putt. He'd hit a few, try to manufacture something, then he'd go to the putting green, chipping green. And that was still perfect. Then it was an awful lot of guts and willpower. That is what I think gave him the belief that he could manage his way around on a golf course he knew so well. That was the key."

Still, McNamara wondered if playing was wise, something he continued to ask Woods nearly every day.

"I was concerned for him," McNamara said. "Once he realized he couldn't hurt himself any more, that it was simply an issue of pain, and he decided he could manage the pain, it was just hard to watch. But he'd hit a shot, even at home in practice, hit one shot, do the sort of grimace and then go sit back down in a cart and then come back out and hit another shot. And that's what we did for a week."

Williams saw Woods for the first time since the Masters, and while he was aware there were some issues due to the surgery and missing the Memorial, he was in for quite a jolt upon meeting up with Woods for the first time at Torrey Pines on the Sunday prior to the U.S. Open.

"I had already had a heads-up from Hank Haney. 'Stevie, Tiger's got no right to be playing in this tournament.' I'll never forget those words," Williams said. "He went out there on the Sunday and I could absolutely see the discomfort he was in. The golf was not of the quality you would expect from Tiger Woods. No doubt, he was struggling."

FOR THE FIRST TIME, THE USGA DECIDED IT WOULD GROUP SEVeral of the top players based on their Official World Golf Ranking. Woods was No. 1 in the world, Phil Mickelson No. 2, and Adam Scott No. 3.

Mickelson rebounded from his devastating U.S. Open defeat two years prior to win four times in 2007, including the Players Championship. He also added two victories in 2008, at Riviera and Colonial. And playing in his hometown was an added boost.

But Mickelson never liked the Torrey course the same after Rees Jones, known as "The Open Doctor," renovated it in 2001—right after Phil won there for the third time. The design work was intended to make the course suitable for a U.S. Open, and it paid off as the USGA awarded the course the championship in 2008 and again in 2021.

It was a strange week for Mickelson, who was playing well enough to contend. But he made the curious decision to go without a driver—on what was then the longest course in U.S. Open history—for the first two rounds. And then in the third round, he three times failed to get a chip shot to stay on the 13th green, leading to a 9. He still managed to tie for 18th.

Because of the high-profile nature of such groupings, Mike Davis, then the USGA's director of rules and competitions (and later its chief executive), was alarmed when he received a phone call a few days prior to the U.S. Open from Woods' agent, Mark Steinberg.

"He called me and asked that I not tell anyone, not even others at the USGA. And I never did, but he said that Tiger essentially had a broken leg," Davis said. "I said, 'What?' I walked with his group as a rules official the last three days, and I remember thinking that this guy, from a mental standpoint, is unbelievable."

Woods shot 72 to open the tournament, and it was the first time he walked 18 holes since the final round of the Masters. But it was far more interesting than his 1-over-par effort suggested. He finished four strokes back of surprise first-round leaders Kevin Streelman and Justin Hicks, making a double bogey on the opening hole and another at the 14th hole. He managed three birdies over the first nine holes but none over the closing nine.

"If you take yourself back to that point in time, it was a very different set of circumstances surrounding all of us and especially in the middle of the most amazing run of golf for 10 years we'd seen," Scott said. "So it was obviously a heavily anticipated opening two rounds. With Phil the hometown boy and Tiger from up the road but also having won Torrey however many times he'd won there. And me going along for the ride."

Scott came into the tournament dealing with his own injury issues. He caught his hand in a car door a few weeks prior and suffered a broken finger but felt he was good enough to play, eventually tying for 26th.

"Going to the first tee Thursday was probably one of the unforgettable moments in my career," he said. "I don't think I've seen a scene quite like it. It was like 25 deep the entire hole. Looked up behind, not really a hill, but some elevated ground that was just packed. It was something else. It was more like the energy of a football game than teeing off at any golf tournament. There was real atmosphere there. Somehow I hit it in the fairway and Tiger made double at the first. That calmed me down nicely."

Mickelson recalled that Tiger struggled from the start: "I think he started the tournament with a double bogey. It was remarkable the way he fought and stayed in it. When you put yourself that far behind . . . it's just so hard to make birdies in a U.S. Open and he started with a double and he just played remarkable golf on a hard golf course."

"The shot that changed [Woods'] entire tournament around was at the fourth hole," said Mickelson's caddie, Jim Mackay, referring to a 488-yard par-4 that runs parallel to the Pacific. "It's probably the toughest hole on the course. He's in the right fairway bunker off the tee. The pin is front right. And he hits a 4-or 5-iron to about five feet and made a birdie. I remember thinking, 'Holy cow, that's some way to the right the ship on the hardest hole on the course,' to hit this long iron stiff. I remember being impressed with how composed he was. A nightmare start and then he hits that shot. Of the shots I remember other people hitting over the years, that probably has to be in the top 5 [of] all time."

And Woods' physical struggles continued.

"Watching Tiger on Thursday, I was first amazed that he finished the round," said Jim Vernon, the USGA president who served as a rules official. "Second, I was amazed he came back Friday to play. I couldn't believe how much pain he was in and how much he subjected his body to. That was special in itself. There was something remarkable about that. I was chatting with one of my friends afterward, saying that I wouldn't be surprised if he didn't make it out the next morning. Of course we were dealing with Tiger. But the pain was very apparent Thursday. It was awful. But again it's Tiger, and he has that extra something he can go to."

"I think I said to him on three separate occasions, asked him if it was the right thing to carry on," Williams said. "And I got the same reply each time: 'Fuck you, Stevie. I'm winning this tournament.' After three times, I wasn't going to say it to him again."

WOODS SHOT 68 IN THE SECOND ROUND, BUT IT STARTED POORLY. Along with Mickelson and Scott, he began on the 10th hole and bogeyed two of his first three. He got those two strokes back with an eagle at the 13th but made two more bogeys coming in. Then he got on a front-side roll, birdieing the first while playing his second shot from a cart path—at the hole where he would make double bogey three times—and went on to make four more birdies, trailing leader Stuart Appleby by a shot and in a tie for second with Mediate and Sweden's Robert Karlsson.

"We had been paired with Tiger before when he was hurting, but never like this," Mackay said. "I remember him driving it off the 18th tee, and he looked ill because he was in so much pain. It was hard to watch in a sense. And yet there he was near the top of the leaderboard. You had so much respect for what he was doing. He was just finding a way. He had a look like, 'They're going to have to carry me out of here.'"

"Tiger back then, because he beat us all the time . . . we didn't like him that much," Scott said. "The skeptic in me said he's a great showman. Even when he was playing great golf back in the day, he was milking everything to his advantage. Putts that were always a little bit low, he'd raise the putter and walk out and the crowd would be really into it. Just to have the crowd going. He used that to psyche out other players. The skeptic in me thought he was putting it on a bit. But I don't really know the extent that his leg was damaged. Obviously, like my hand was broken, his leg was, and he thought he was good enough to play and he won. He knew what he was doing. He got it around somehow."

A third-round 70 was surreal. Playing with Karlsson, a 38-year-old European Tour veteran, Woods again made a double-bogey 6 on the opening hole. He shot 2-over-par 37 for the first nine holes. When he bogeyed the 12th, he was 3-over for the round and three strokes back of Mediate.

Then he sent the large crowd into a frenzy.

It began with a stunning eagle at the 13th after Woods went flag hunting with a long iron from the right rough. His towering shot almost flew directly into the front-hole location before rolling all the way to the back fringe. From there, Woods sent his putt across the length of the large green, and when it curled hard right to left and disappeared, his double-thrusting fist pumps gave his leg some added shock.

A bogey at the 14th was a minor setback, when with an awkward lie beside a bunker at the par-4 17th, he chipped in for a birdie, sheepishly laughing as he pulled his hat over his face. Then to cap it off, Woods drained another huge eagle putt—a 60-footer at the 18th—and the place might as well have fallen off into the Pacific Ocean, the explosion of noise was so loud. For the round, Woods hit just 6 of 14 fairways.

"At the time [after the poor start], I was four back and I was honestly trying to not have that gap widen," Woods said. "If I could keep it the same, great. If I could narrow the gap, even better. And then I make the putt on 13, I bogey 14 with a tee shot way right, and then 15—that was the one when it really hurt. There were a couple of shots where I could feel the bone in my leg break. And the tee shot on 15 was one of them. I felt it crack.

"But I parred 15, parred 16, and then hit it way right on 17. I was just trying to get the ball into the left bunker and it ended up on the slope, which was even better because I could control the shot, and it came out really hot. If you read my lips, I say, 'Bite.' And it one-hopped in. And then 18, I just tried to hit a big slice, aimed as far left as I could. If I get it in play, I knew I could [reach the green in two] because they had the tee all the way up, and so I knew it would be a 3-wood or 5-wood into the green. And it hurt past impact again and I was pretty sore after 15 and I had to stop for a bit. But I hit the fairway, then hit the 5-wood on to the green, and lo and behold, I make the bomb."

"All Tiger had was a 40-yard cut, which he could hit," said Gareth Lord, Karlsson's caddie. "When he played that, he was fine. When he tried to hit normal shots, he was struggling. On the 18th tee, we heard it [his leg] go [snapping sound], no doubt. Then he blistered it down the fairway with a cut. Then a high 5-wood on the green for an eagle putt."

Said Karlsson, "It was just mayhem around us. It was just incredible to be part of."

"The putt on the [18th] green, I watched the whole thing, and halfway there I knew it was in," Lord said. "We came off the course, Robert and I looked at each other . . . and we went straight to the bar and had a large Johnnie Walker Blue each. That was it. It was about $90 a shot, I promise you."

WOODS WAS LEADING THE U.S. OPEN WITH ONE ROUND TO PLAY, despite his left leg getting worse. At the time, nobody outside of his inner circle knew that in addition to the ACL issue he was playing with two stress fractures in his tibia, the main source of his pain. Each night, Woods would get treatment from his trainer, Keith Kleven, trying to get ready to play the next day.

Woods, when asked if he ever thought he might not be able to continue, said: "Not 'I can't [go on],' but, 'Boy, this hurts.' I proved to myself in practice, even though I only hit four or five balls, I may have hit them pretty well, but I never hurt pre-impact. Whatever backswing I made, whatever downswing I made, the pain only got me just after impact. My whole focus for the week was to virtually try and hit perfect shots because nothing was going to stop me from making quality impact. Now post-impact I may not be able to walk for a little bit or it may throb but the impact part of it I could control. So all my focus was on making proper impact and if it hurt, it hurt."

"I'm not sure really sure how to explain it, but it was evident that because of the injury, it was almost like this is the ultimate challenge," Haney said. "'This is something that nobody could ever do, but if I could do it, that it would be the biggest mountain I've ever climbed.' That motivation was really strong for him.

"He seemed to only limp on the bad shots, so my thought process was

I just have to try to help him not hit so many bad shots. There's something he's doing in his swing that's hurting his knee, and there needs to be less times that he gets jolted. But I never felt like he wasn't going to make it. He's halfway up Mount Everest and he's going to turn back? No way. He's Tiger Woods."

The time away from the course wasn't much better for Woods. He found sleeping difficult due to the pain, and basically spent the nights trying to get himself ready to go through it again the next day.

His daughter, Sam, celebrated her first birthday that weekend and provided only a brief distraction.

"Sam had her little wooden club and she was hitting against the floor and it kept me from thinking about golf," he said. "But I could never get myself away from thinking about the pain. It was just constant. The treatment was constant throughout the night. I slept on the massage table. I had my knee drained, iced, elevated, worked on, just trying to get as much inflammation out as I could. Then somehow start activating it in the morning, and that was the hardest part because it was so wobbly.

"Once I finally got going it was okay. Keith was awesome. He did a hell of job in the morning getting me where I could go. Because at night, when I got back to the room, I was thinking there was no way I could play any more holes. I'm done. But can I somehow figure out a way to get it good enough to go tomorrow, and each day it progressively got worse. But Keith did such a great job."

FOR THE 14TH TIME IN HIS CAREER, WOODS HELD OR SHARED THE 54-hole lead at a major championship. On all 13 previous occasions, he went on to win. This time, he led by one over Lee Westwood, two over Mediate, and four over Geoff Ogilvy and D. J. Trahan. Woods played the final round with Westwood, an Englishman who climbed back from the depths of falling to 200th in the world. Mediate was in the group ahead with Ogilvy, the 2006 U.S. Open champion.

Once again, Woods doubled the first, then added a bogey at the second to drop three shots in two holes. Woods didn't claim a share of the lead again until the 11th hole, but he bogeyed the par-5 13th and the 15th to drop a shot back of Mediate.

"When the caddies sit around at the beginning of the week, we ask each other what we think will win," Mackay said. "Everybody to a man said this was a 9-, 10-, 11-under U.S. Open. The overwhelming memory I have of that U.S. Open is that Tiger carried so much weight in those days, guys would have trouble getting over the psychological hump of separating themselves on the leaderboard.

"I thought it was the ultimate week where Tiger's legend kept the scores low. The fact that 1-under ended up playing off was so shocking to a lot of us there. It spoke to his legend. The course was gettable. The fairways were not overwhelmingly narrow. The greens were not firm. But no one got away from Tiger. It's no disrespect to anyone there. You have it or you don't. No one could get away from him. Tiger was hanging around, chipping in and making eagles, and playing in a tremendous amount of pain."

Most of the rest of the world was unaware just how much distress Woods played under during that week.

"You could see Tiger was in a bit of agony," said Westwood's caddie, Alistair McLean. "He was struggling. He chopped it about a bit. It was around the seventh hole, he hit a tee shot and nearly collapsed. I remember saying, 'I don't think this guy can finish.' He struggled on and so much credit to him. He winced on every single shot and I can't remember any physios coming around. He soldiered on. He chipped and putted, got it around, and did what great players do."

SO IT CAME DOWN TO THE PAR-5 18TH, A 573-YARD HOLE THAT was guarded by a pond in front, leaving a small piece of fairway on the right side leading up to the green. Woods made the long putt on Saturday to eagle the hole, and if Mediate could birdie the hole ahead of him, Tiger would have needed another eagle to tie. But Mediate parred, meaning Woods needed a birdie to extend the tournament to an 18-hole playoff. Mediate set the clubhouse lead at 283, 1-under par. Both Woods and Westwood came to the last with a chance to tie or win.

"It wasn't a poor tee shot; it was just a little bit left of where you need to be [in a fairway bunker]," Williams said. "Immediately that takes 3 out of the equation. Then you need to hit a good layup you are comfortable with for that flag. But the layup was not very good and he hit it in right rough. Now you're not in the fairway, and that's always that much tougher to judge."

From the right rough, Woods had 95 yards to the front of the green, 101 to the hole, the pin cut toward the right side. He needed to decide between a 56-degree sand wedge and a 60-degree lob wedge.

That is where Williams' knowledge of Woods' game and the confidence he possessed in his own ability as a caddie became factors.

The yardage called for a 56-degree sand wedge, not the 60-degree lob wedge Woods ended up using. Williams was adamant that the club with more loft was the play. He correctly reasoned that adrenaline would cause Woods to hit it farther than normal and that such speed would cause the spin necessary to get it to stop as close to the hole as possible.

"My gut instinct told me that this ball was going to fly," Williams said. "It was not a [60-degree] wedge yardage. Tiger was hitting that club about 95 yards. [But] everything told me in my gut that in order to get that ball close, it was with a lob wedge.

"Tiger couldn't see the rationale. Usually in that situation when you're playing you want to be decisive. You don't want to be debating back and forth and create any doubt. But I was fully convinced. And I don't think we had ever discussed a shot for that length of time."

Ten years later, Woods disclosed that his ball was actually in a divot.

"It was a 56-degree number, but I needed the spin," Woods said. "Well, there were a couple of things that happened where I got lucky. One: that was still in the era of square grooves [which help get more spin on the ball but have since been outlawed]. And two: somebody had hit out of that same exact spot sometime that week, and I was actually in a divot. And so I could get clean contact so I could get my sand wedge on the back of the ball so I knew I could spin it. Stevie convinced me to hit 60, and I needed to hit it as hard as I could to get as much spin on the ball as I possibly could."

Before Woods played his third shot, Westwood was in the fairway contemplating his approach. He, too, found a bunker off the tee, then laid up into the fairway.

"Lee was left with an awkward number to approach the green," McLean said. "It was just too far for his sand wedge to hit it straight at the pin, and it was too close for a [pitching] wedge. And he hit a nice shot; it just released. He couldn't hit it hard enough to spin. You just can't take that chance from there. If you spin it back in the water, that's the daftest thing he could have done."

Now, after all the debate, it was Woods' turn.

"I remember when he laid it up," said Mackay, who was watching on TV. "The pin was front, and I thought he was in all kinds of trouble. You just wouldn't think he could generate enough spin to keep the ball around the hole. I remember reading that he had this conversation with Steve to hit the hard 60 and generate as much spin as possible. To me, the third shot was as crucial as the putt. You just don't realize unless you've been there to play that shot from that rough and to give yourself what he had and a shot to get in a playoff."

Mediate watched the whole scenario play out after signing his scorecard.

"He hits a horrible layup," Mediate said. "That's what was shocking. So, now I'm in the thing (scoring area) going, this thing might be over. It might just be mine. I thought he was going to pitch in, so I'm like all right, I'm still alive, as far as winning or playing tomorrow. Either one I'm good because I can't do anything else.

"And when he hit that pitch shot, something weird happened when it hit the ground. Because as you noticed, it stopped, it kind of trickled toward the hole. Well, come to find out, I think it was the following year, I asked him about it. One of the few things he told me, he goes, it was an old divot. I said, of course it was. Of course it was because you can't spin it out of that stuff. I don't care who you are. It's like a Brillo pad, but it's green. Are you kidding me? But my point is, you still got the shot. And then, he's still going to make the putt."

WOODS PURPOSELY AIMED A BIT TO THE RIGHT, IN CASE THE BALL came up short. But the ball landed just past pin high, stopped, came back, and rolled ever so slightly toward the hole. He left himself a 12-footer to tie. Westwood's approach came to rest 20 feet away but above and to the left of the hole if looking from the fairway. He had a downhill putt that he didn't hit hard enough, the ball trailing off before reaching the cup.

"It was sickening to not be in that playoff," Westwood said.

Now all eyes were on Woods. "We were just standing there," said Ogilvy, who played with Mediate. "Is he gonna; is he not. Is he gonna; is he not. Is he gonna; is he not."

"I always thought part of Tiger's genius was his ability to read greens," Mackay said. "And I think the ability to read greens is the most under-rated skill in golf. I was watching with my wife, and I remember telling her, he could push it, pull it, or miss, but he probably won't misread it. I just remember the camera being on Rocco—he was in the scoring area—and it's a little like standing in front of the firing squad. They're just not going to miss very much."

"It's funny: you're on the green there, and I'm just going through my mind thinking about tomorrow's round already," Williams said. "He had an uncanny knack or amazing ability to hole putts on the 18th green to tie or win. It was seldom that he missed one. I didn't have any doubt in my mind that he would make that putt. It wasn't a question."

Just 12 feet of tricky terrain remained before the ball began tumbling toward the hole, leaving the Nike Swoosh prominent with every revolution. But as Woods rose out of his stance and thousands around the green held their breath, those fleeting moments seemed as though they could be measured in days, weeks, months, and years.

To some, it was the greatest 72nd-hole putt ever in a major championship, a confluence of events that were surreal and yet standard for Woods. Still, the ball that bounced along the green, caught the edge, and dropped in for a birdie did not even win the tournament for Woods.

"I changed my stroke on that one a little bit because it was going to be so bouncy," Woods said. "I hit up on it a little bit to try and get the ball rolling earlier. Growing up on *Poa annua,* that's what I've always really done. I hit it more with my hands and I made sure I released it a lot. And I did, and I got the ball rolling, and it was bouncing all over the place. The stroke felt good. And then the ball took forever to break because it was bouncing most of the time."

Years later, Haney remained in awe.

"When the ball was like halfway or three quarters of the way to the hole," Haney said, "it hit a spike mark. That spike mark could knock it to the right, knock it to the left, or it could hit the spike mark and slow it down. That ball just barely lipped in on the high side. If it didn't slow it down it would have had too much speed to lip in. It slowed up just enough. That's luck. But there always has to be some luck in every putt. But when you're with Tiger, you always feel like he had this ability to will the ball in the hole. I know that's a little mythical, but I felt that was one of those cases. He just willed it in the hole. I don't know how he did those kind of things."

Woods, who after making the putt arched backward and shook his fists with putter in hand as he yelled, sheepishly mocked his own celebration.

"I remember screaming, and I remember realizing I was screaming at the sky," he said. "I was looking straight up. And then I put my head down quickly because I was wondering what I was doing."

FOR THE THIRD TIME IN WOODS' CAREER, HE WAS HEADED TO A playoff in a major championship. He won the 2000 PGA in a three-hole aggregate over Bob May, the 2005 Masters over Chris DiMarco. This would be over 18 holes.

For Woods, it was the opportunity to win a 14th major and fifth tournament in seven starts in 2008. For Mediate, he could become the oldest U.S. Open champion in its history.

At 9:00 A.M. Pacific time, the round began, with some 25,000 spectators on the grounds attempting to follow one group. Woods finally parred the first hole, and despite being one shot down through four holes, he built a three-shot lead through 10. But Woods made bogeys at the 11th and 12th, and Mediate birdied the 14th and 15th to take a one-shot lead. When Woods narrowly missed a long birdie try at the 16th and a midrange chance at the 17th, he was again faced with being one shot down playing the 18th.

Mediate again settled for a par on the home hole, unable to get a lengthy birdie putt to drop. Woods, who this time hit the green in two, knocked his eagle putt to within three feet, then made the birdie putt to force sudden-death after both players shot 71.

"They started the playoff at nine o'clock," said PGA Tour player Brandt Snedeker, who was in the San Diego airport that morning awaiting a flight home. "Nobody was at their gates; they were all at the sports bar that was there for five different flights. There were 150 people watching this playoff, hooting and hollering, going crazy. I haven't seen that for a Super Bowl or any event in an airport like that, not seen that many people around a television watching something. It was crazy."

"The cool story I remember from that week was the Travelers Championship had a [charter] plane for players to go from the U.S. Open to their tournament," said Streelman, who had a share of the first-round lead. "So Monday morning all of us jump on the plane to fly to Hartford, and we were taking off right when the playoff started. Every person on the plane—the players, their families—was watching the playoff on their TVs. Every single TV had the playoff on, about 60, 70 TVs. And we land in Hartford and Tiger and Rocco are going into the playoff hole. And no one got off the plane. Not one person got up to leave. It was an amazing sight. I looked out the window and saw the courtesy carts waiting for us, and no one got off the plane until the playoff was over. I'll never forget that."

The sudden-death playoff began at the par-4 seventh, a dogleg right par-4. If necessary, it would continue to the eighth hole and then the 18th. Woods hit a drive in the fairway and knocked his approach on the green to about 20 feet, but Mediate hit his drive into a fairway bunker, and then his approach went left and into the spectator grandstand, from which he would receive a free drop.

It almost became anticlimactic at this point, as Mediate pitched onto the green but was left with a long par putt that he missed. Woods lagged his birdie putt toward the hole and tapped in for the victory, accepting congratulations from Mediate and Williams on the green. A cart ride back to the clubhouse and the trophy presentation ceremony was like a coronation, as fans cheered him along the way. Not with him was Williams, who walked all the way back, carrying the bag.

"It's a sizable walk," he said. "I had to sort of collect myself. I just knew how much this guy wanted to win this tournament. I felt an inordinate amount of pressure all week long. He's a very good mate of mine; I don't like seeing him in pain. There seemed to be a lot of pressure and commotion. When he won the tournament and put his name beside Torrey Pines, he had obviously had success prior to that.

"But he wanted it so badly. I think I felt that pressure as well. It's great to thrive on that. When he won, it had been an unbelievable seven days here. Take it all in. It was unbelievably satisfying."

NONE OF WOODS' MAJOR CHAMPIONSHIP VICTORIES WERE LIKE this one. He won a Masters by 12, a U.S. Open by 15, and an Open by 8. For the most part, Woods dominated in his major victories or at least appeared to be in control, even if there were some notable slips along the way before righting himself.

Even in his two previous playoff victories at majors, Woods shot a final-round 67 at the 2000 PGA before defeating Bob May. At the 2005 Masters, he shot an opening-round 74, rallied with a 66 in the second round, and still trailed by six before a third-round 65 put him in front—only to bogey the last holes before prevailing over DiMarco with a birdie on the first playoff hole.

But the 2008 U.S. Open saw wincing, limping, and an inordinate number of poor shots. He made four double bogeys, including the first hole three times. He made two doubles in the opening round. Over 72 holes, Woods had 42 pars, 13 birdies, 3 eagles, 4 doubles, and 10 bogeys to get to 1. Both he and Mediate shot even-par 71 in the playoff, with Woods needing two birdies over his last six holes to force sudden death.

"The thing that stood out the most was that week showed you how tough Tiger was in those days," said Butch Harmon, Woods' former coach who worked for Sky Sports that week. "He was driving it terrible; he was hitting it all over the place. The putt he hit on the 72nd hole, if you see it from ground level, it's bouncing all over the place, and then it was like the hole just reached out and grabbed the ball.

"That was a typical moment for Tiger Woods, having the ability to will the ball in the hole. I've never seen anybody like him in my entire life. He just had that ability. When it came down to hitting a shot or hitting a putt or a pitch, he just knew that he could do it, and he pulled it off every time."

The euphoria was short-lived. As satisfying as the victory was for Woods, he knew more than anyone what lay ahead. Although he said nothing about impending surgery immediately following the victory, it was already scheduled.

Woods put everything he could muster into winning the U.S. Open and pulled off the remarkable, improbable win.

It was his last tournament of 2008. And nobody could have predicted what awaited. Woods eventually returned to great fanfare and plenty of success. But a series of personal and physical crises resulted in a decade of drama. And in the short term, he missed his first Ryder Cup.

14

THE RYDER CUP

Tiger Woods' U.S. Open victory over Rocco Mediate in a playoff at Torrey Pines was exhilarating. People around the world were riveted to the Monday playoff, which went to an extra hole as the two players were not only tied after 72 holes but also tied after another 18.

Finally, Woods prevailed with a par on the first extra hole, the par-4 seventh on Torrey Pines' South Course, winning for the fifth time in 2008 in just seven starts and posting his 14th major championship title.

At the time, ESPN's coverage of the playoff from noon to 2:00 P.M. was the highest-rated golf telecast in cable television history, with more than 4.7 million viewers. The final round on NBC topped out at 12 million viewers.

All along, the golf world knew he was playing the tournament in pain. But only those close to Woods knew just how bad it was and what lay ahead. Two days following the victory, Woods announced he would need surgery on his left knee and that his season was over—and that he suffered a double stress fracture in his left tibia that had been discovered just a few weeks before the U.S. Open.

On June 24, Woods underwent surgery to replace a torn ACL, a procedure that required a complete reconstruction of his knee. The surgery was performed by Dr. Thomas Rosenberg, who became quite familiar with the inner workings of the left knee that belonged to one of the most famous athletes in the world.

Rosenberg, along with Dr. Vern Cooley, performed the surgery in

Park City, Utah. Rosenberg proclaimed it a success, and said with "the proper rehabilitation and training, it is highly unlikely that Mr. Woods will have any long-term effects as it relates to his career."

That was the good news.

The bad news was that a remarkable run of golf came to an end. In his previous 12 worldwide starts, Woods produced nine wins, two seconds, and a fifth. And he accomplished the latest victory while more or less playing on one leg.

The surgery meant that for the first time as a professional, Woods would miss a major championship, having to skip both the Open at Royal Birkdale and the PGA Championship at Oakland Hills. Ireland's Pàdraig Harrington won both tournaments.

And for the first time since he turned pro, Woods would miss the Ryder Cup.

That seemed to be a big blow to the U.S. team that had been reeling in the competition. It lost the last three Ryder Cups, and both the 2004 and 2006 defeats were embarrassing blowouts. Now the No. 1 player in the world would not be part of a team that needed all the help it could get.

And yet the U.S. team captained by Paul Azinger won, giving the Americans their first victory in the competition since a remarkable comeback on the final day in 1999.

That win saw the Americans overcome a 10–6 final-day deficit for a dramatic 14½ to 13½ victory, with Woods and Phil Mickelson winning their singles matches, setting off a wild celebration that lasted well into the night.

It was the last time Tiger and Phil would celebrate a Ryder Cup victory together as playing teammates. In fact, it is the only time in eight Ryder Cup appearances that Woods was on a winning U.S. side.

For all his individual success, Woods' record in the Ryder Cup is poor. And Mickelson's is worse.

That the Americans were able to win a Ryder Cup without Woods led to the unfounded conjecture that the game's most famous player was actually a detriment in such a team setting. There was certainly a portion of the populace that believed Woods didn't care, that his individual record was all that mattered.

"No player who plays at that level and has the desire to win, whether it's a nine-hole practice match or the Ryder Cup . . . they don't want to lose," said Steve Williams, Woods' former caddie. "Guys who win and win often, they don't want to lose. There's no chance you could say he didn't care. He loves to win and hates to lose. Nobody hated to lose at match play more than this guy. I can't put a finger on why he didn't perform his best.

"When it came to putting your schedule together, the Ryder Cup wasn't a priority to him as far as being 100 percent ready to play in that tournament. He scheduled himself around the major championships. And then you have the Players Championship and the World Golf Championships and the Ryder Cup came after that. Would he give that the same amount of practice as the majors? Probably not. Every year he was trying to peak for one of those big events. And that probably played a part in it.

"But I can honestly say, in a lot of the four-ball and foursomes matches, a lot of Tiger's playing companions didn't play as well as they could play, either. That probably added to it. For a little while there, he was a little bit aloof, and a lot of guys were intimidated by Tiger, even his own countrymen and teammates. It wasn't until after he had competed in several that others players felt comfortable."

AT A TIME WHEN WOODS AND MICKELSON WERE BATTLING FOR the game's top prizes, their careers converging at unbelievable heights from the period of 2002 to 2007, they were on two American teams that suffered the most lopsided defeats in the event's storied history.

The two best American players of their generation disappointed in the biennial team competition that had grown into far more than a friendly exhibition. And their play has often been chided, dissected, and scrutinized, with no clear answers and numerous opinions.

"To be a successful player in professional golf, you've got to be a marathon runner, not a sprinter," said 2014 European Ryder Cup captain Paul McGinley—who in 2002 earned the winning point for Europe at The Belfry when he defeated Jim Furyk in Sunday singles. "You've got to train at marathon speed. You've got to be able to pace yourself over four days with all kinds of different things thrown at you. Weather conditions.

The draw. So many different dynamics go into being hugely successful like both of those players. And the skill set and mindset they had in four tournament rounds is a very different mindset that is required when you play in a Ryder Cup.

"You've got a partner. Both those guys are control freaks, and giving up control is not easy for either of them. And another dynamic is matches are based over 18 holes. They are 100-meter sprints, and they've excelled as marathon runners."

Something has to explain their records.

Woods is 13–21–3 in eight Ryder Cup appearances; the only time he played on a winning team was in 1999.

Mickelson is 18–22–7 in 12 Ryder Cup appearances; the only times he played on a winning team were in 1999, 2008, and 2016. Woods missed in 2008, 2014, and 2016 with injuries. Mickelson's 12 Ryder Cups and 47 matches are both U.S. records.

At the last Ryder Cup they played together at Le Golf National in France in 2018, neither player won a point, with Woods going 0–4 and Mickelson 0–2 as the United States was again defeated.

"I'm a little bit surprised how Tiger's record isn't better, because he was clearly the No. 1 player for so long," said Bernhard Langer, the two-time Masters winner from Germany who captained the 2004 European Team to victory and went 21–15–6 in 10 Ryder Cups as a player. "He clearly did not do as well as he would have done in majors or regular events. And I compare the Ryder Cup to a major, especially the way the crowds get behind it.

"Everything about the Ryder Cup is like a major. I would think that they were into it, that they were interested. They're representing their country and their team. I would have thought they'd take it seriously. None of us like to lose. Let's put it that way. You put any of us out there and we hate to lose. Especially Tiger and Phil. They are used to winning. And they know if they lose, they will get questioned. That's not fun to go through."

LANGER TOUCHED ON A THEORY THAT WAS OFTEN BROACHED over the years as U.S. Ryder Cup losses piled up and Woods and

Mickelson's individual records went from bad to worse: that they didn't care.

Given their competitiveness, their overall records, and their match play records as juniors and amateurs, it just didn't make sense.

And Mickelson proved as much at the 2014 Ryder Cup.

It was there that he put his reputation on the line and called out a legend in the game, Tom Watson.

The air was already chilly in Gleneagles, Scotland, after another U.S. defeat, this time a 16½ to 11½ whipping that left the Americans again searching for answers. It became downright freezing in the media center early that evening when Mickelson, just a few seats away from Watson, all but eviscerated the five-time Open champion for the way he handled his Ryder Cup captaincy.

"Unfortunately, we have strayed from a winning formula in 2008 for the last three Ryder Cups, and we need to consider maybe getting back to that formula that helped us play our best," Mickelson said during the news conference.

Watson, 65, was the last captain to win in Europe—in 1993. He was the surprise choice of PGA president Ted Bishop, who wanted to think outside the box and bring in a new voice and face, one who earned tremendous stature in the game. The problem was, Watson was also the oldest U.S. Ryder Cup captain in history, was no longer a regular player on the Tour, and hadn't attended a Ryder Cup since his captaincy.

Asked if Mickelson was being disloyal for expressing his views so strongly, Watson said, "Not at all. He has a difference of opinion. That's okay. My management philosophy is different than his."

As is Ryder Cup tradition, all 12 players and the captain are at a table for a news conference afterward. For the losing side, it's drudgery, the last place any of the players or captain or assistants wishes to be in such circumstances.

The 10th question went to Mickelson, and he was asked about what worked in 2008, a 16½ to 11½ victory for the U.S. under captain Paul Azinger and the only one since 1999.

Mickelson then went off.

"There were two things that allow us to play our best I think that Paul Azinger did, and one was he got everybody invested in the process," he said. "He got everybody invested in who they were going to play with, who the picks were going to be, who was going to be in their pod—when they would play, and they had a great leader for each pod.

"In my case, we had [assistant] Ray Floyd, and we hung out together and we were all invested in each other's play. We were invested in picking Hunter [Mahan] that week; Anthony Kim and myself and Justin [Leonard] were in a pod, and we were involved in having Hunter be our guy to fill our pod. So we were invested in the process.

"And the other thing that Paul did really well was he had a great game plan for us, how we were going to go about doing this. How we were going to go about playing together; golf ball, format, what we were going to do, if so-and-so is playing well, if so-and-so is not playing well, we had a real game plan."

Earlier that year, the subject of Watson's captaincy came up with Mickelson in a casual chat I had with him at the Scottish Open. Mickelson was the defending champion—he won the Scottish and the Open in consecutive weeks in 2013—and he was playing in the pro-am at Royal Aberdeen. Among those in his group were Alex Salmond, then the First Minister of Scotland, and Bishop, the PGA president.

It was casual, off-the-cuff stuff, but Mickelson's view of Watson as captain nearly three months prior to the Ryder Cup was hardly glowing. There was no sense that it would go as poorly as it did, but Mickelson questioned the appointment. No players were consulted and Watson didn't seem to have much contact with the current group of players. He was highly skeptical, but in no way was he trying to make a big deal about it either. Yet in retrospect, it's almost as if Phil knew something might go wrong.

Mickelson's main point at the news conference was the Americans were never put in a proper position to win. Now you can argue Ryder Cup strategy all the way back to the Cup's origins, when it was meant to be a friendly competition between the United States and Great Britain and Ireland. The competition was so lopsided in favor of the Americans that it was Jack Nicklaus, in the late 1970s, who suggested that continental Europe be included to make for a more robust team.

Be careful what you wish for, Jack. It took a few years, but by the time Nicklaus captained the U.S. team for the first time in 1983, the Europeans were suddenly competitive. Led by captain Tony Jacklin, the Europeans nearly pulled off an upset in Jack's Florida backyard. Two years later, at The Belfry in England, Jacklin captained the European side to its first win since 1957. And then, in 1987, he whipped Jack at his own club, Muirfield Village in Ohio, winning for the first time overseas.

Jacklin and Nicklaus provided the game with one of its great acts of sportsmanship when, in 1969 at Royal Birkdale, their match was not only tied on the 18th green but it was also tied for the rest of the competition. Jacklin left himself a putt just outside of two feet for par; Nicklaus holed his par putt from a longer distance, then picked up Jacklin's marker, conceding the putt.

The match ended in a tie, as did the Ryder Cup, 16–16. It was the first time since 1957 that the GB&I side did not lose. Nicklaus later said that he knew Jacklin would make the putt but feared the consequences for his friend in his homeland it he didn't. Thus, "The Concession" was born.

Jacklin concluded his four-time run as captain with the Ryder Cup's second tie in 1989, meaning he finished with a record for 2–1–1. And it was game on.

As the Europeans gained confidence and stature, there was a sense that camaraderie, bonding, and strong pairings led to success. And that the Americans were a bunch of individuals who found difficulty coming together.

Mickelson felt the players needed more of a say, needed to be more invested.

Asked if any of that happened during the week at Gleneagles, Mickelson said, "Uh, no. No, nobody here was in any decision."

Watson, when asked about Azinger's captaincy compared to his own, put the loss on the players.

"I had a different philosophy as far as being a captain of this team," he said. "It takes 12 players to win. It's not pods. It's 12 players. And I felt—yes, I did talk to the players, but my vice captains [Andy North, Steve Stricker, and Floyd] were very instrumental in making decisions as to whom to pair with. I had a different philosophy than Paul. I decided not to go that way."

It was a blunt, brutal assessment from Mickelson. And it didn't come without a ton of reaction and criticism. Many believed he could have delivered the message in a better way, at a better time.

"Should we go into this one hour after being defeated?" said Scotland's Colin Montgomerie, a victorious captain in 2010 and decorated Ryder Cup player. "You support your captain under all circumstances. In public, you respect and honor your captain. The PGA of America selected Tom Watson as the best choice to try to win the Ryder Cup back. Unfortunately, the team didn't perform for Tom."

Nick Faldo, who had his own issues as European captain in 2008, criticized Mickelson, as did Golf Channel analyst Brandel Chamblee, who took Lefty to task for "corrupting the experience of the Ryder Cup." "If you are looking for a reason why the United States continues to lose," Chamblee said, "you just saw it; you just saw it in one man."

Mickelson, undoubtedly, was speaking out of frustration. And the fact that he did so with such directness in such a setting should again put to rest any notion that the Americans don't care about winning the Ryder Cup.

But Phil knew what he was doing. He wasn't just venting. He had a purpose.

While saying what he said was a risk, Mickelson figured that saying those things behind closed doors would not have the proper impact. He feared that the powers that be would listen, then likely dismiss his concerns and go about business as usual. He was correct in viewing Watson's captaincy as a poor one. The eight-time major champion, who was beloved in Scotland and one of the all-time greats, didn't adapt to the modern Ryder Cup.

For one, Watson brought no entourage of assistant captains during his first captaincy. The Americans were also frequent winners back in his time. Now things were different, the U.S. was losing often, and for all his accolades, Watson had his struggles: he'd made a last-minute decision to pick Webb Simpson for the team over Bill Haas, then changed his mind about pairings.

Mickelson was willing to take the public relations hit, and it worked. Within weeks, the PGA of America, which runs the U.S. side of the Ryder Cup, put in place a Ryder Cup task force that brought together various entities, including Woods. The idea was to better prepare players and assistants to ascend to the captaincy, for both the Presidents Cup and Ryder Cup.

Tiger and Phil working together?

If there was any notion that Woods was disinterested, it changed when he got involved from afar in the 2015 Presidents Cup, constantly texting assistant captain Davis Love III and captain Jay Haas. By that point, Love had been named Ryder Cup captain for 2016, and Woods later became an assistant. He also assisted Steve Stricker at the 2017 Presidents Cup.

The world's most prominent golfer—in the midst of two years away from the game—was fully engaged.

"I am so happy to see how well thought through he has been," Mickelson said at Hazeltine, site of the 2016 Ryder Cup. "I can't believe our conversations, how detail-oriented he has been. The players, the pairings, the possibilities. Not just what match you will play, but where on the list. He has got us a good, solid game plan that is easy to buy into and get behind. I'm very impressed."

For once, the Tiger-Phil dynamic saw them on the same side, likely a far more difficult leap for Woods than it was Mickelson. He spent the better part of 20 years keeping Phil at a par-5 distance; now not only did they exchange phone numbers but they were also regularly texting each other to discuss strategy. Mickelson later apologized for his outburst toward Watson, but the bottom line is it helped usher in the changes he and many others sought.

MICKELSON SUFFERED SOME OF THE SAME BLOWBACK ABOUT not being invested that Woods did. But there are numerous examples that suggest otherwise, including the 2009 Presidents Cup—the Ryder Cup–like competition that sees a U.S. team play an International squad from everywhere but Europe in non–Ryder Cup years.

That year, U.S. player Sean O'Hair made it clear that he didn't want Mickelson as a partner during the competition at Harding Park in San Francisco. "He said their games didn't mesh," said Paul Tesori, O'Hair's caddie at the time. Phil was wild, O'Hair was a fairways and greens guy.

They played different golf balls, which could be a problem in the alternate shot format.

Mickelson, of course, found out. And Phil being Phil, he told captain Fred Couples he wanted to play with O'Hair.

"That Friday, we are playing terrible," Tesori recalled. "We're sure we are going to sit the entire Saturday [when there are two sessions]. But the pairings come out; we have Phil Mickelson. Phil says, 'Boys, this is what we're going to do. Sean, hate to bust you, but I heard you didn't want to be paired with me. We're going to play the TaylorMade. We'll hit your ball. I'm not going to play my best; you're going to play unbelievable.'"

The first competition that day was foursomes, or alternate shot. "I remember one hole," Tesori said. "Phil hit a terrible drive way left. We're trying to figure out a way to somehow wedge it onto the green. If we get lucky, we can maybe get it on the far back left half.

"Phil goes, 'Nope. I want you to hit 25 feet right of the green; I'll chip it up to 3 feet, you'll knock it in, and we'll win the hole.' And that's exactly what happened. Now Phil starts pumping Sean up. 'Man, the way you won Quail Hollow [earlier that year]. You hit it so good. You didn't make a putt outside 10 feet and yet you won. In fact, do you realize you're the only guy in the last 30 years on Tour who won without making a putt outside 10 feet?' Sean starts feeling confident and we win 5 and 3."

Mickelson and O'Hair were then paired again in the afternoon fourball (best ball) session.

"We played incredible," Tesori said. "On Sunday [in singles] we get Ernie Els, their best player, and Sean beats Ernie 6 and 4.

"Now why would you take the guy who's playing the worst on the team and said he didn't want to play with you and rise to that? Who does that? That's just so Phil."

Mickelson went 4-0-1 at that Presidents Cup. Woods won all his matches, going 5-0, as the United States defeated the International side. And for all their Ryder Cup woes, Phil and Tiger are at the top of the Presidents Cup when it comes to records.

Woods is 27-15-1, having gone 3-0 at Royal Melbourne in 2019, the first time Mickelson missed a U.S. team dating back to his first at the 1994 Presidents Cup. Mickelson is 26-16-13.

WITH NEW DIRECTION, WOODS' ROLE WAS FAR FROM CEREMO-
nial at the 2016 Ryder Cup. He didn't play all year due to the back problems that plagued him in 2015, but he was a big presence at Hazeltine
National in Minnesota. The U.S. team used a pod-like system employed
by Azinger in 2008. Under that formula, Azinger divided his team into
three groups of four players each. Those groups practiced together in the
days leading up to the Ryder Cup, and not deviating from that plan was
a clear sign that their partners in the foursomes and four-ball matches
would not come from anywhere outside that group.

Woods spearheaded a similar approach; behind the scenes, he was
crunching numbers and figuring out the best matchups among players. The other vice captains under Love were Tom Lehman, who captained the 2006 U.S. Ryder Cup team; Stricker, who was set to captain
the following year's Presidents Cup team; and Furyk, who would later be
named the U.S. Ryder Cup captain for 2018.

"He's taken Rickie [Fowler] and Justin Thomas under his wing," Love
said. "He's a different Tiger Woods. We know him now. We see him as a
friend and a teammate and also a really good golfer. Before it was, 'He's
Tiger Woods; we can't mess this up.'

"He started in '15 with the Presidents Cup. We were in Korea, and he
was at home, and he wouldn't stop texting us. My wife said, 'How cool is
it that Tiger is doing that, that he's so involved.' And it really is."

Among those in his pod was Patrick Reed, known as a bit of a loner
but one who loved wearing red on Sundays to emulate his hero. When
other players decided to call it quits after nine holes during practice,
Reed wanted to continue. Woods offered to go along with him.

"It was amazing," Reed said. "I learned so much just from that nine
holes walking around that I felt like that alone could save me so many
shots throughout my career—just by just thinking of the minor details.

"He'll answer any question, whether it's about golf, on the golf course,
off the golf course, anything."

With a raucous home crowd of upwards of 50,000 well-lubricated
spectators per day, the Americans thrived, winning the Ryder Cup 17½
to 10½. For once, the Americans were on the winning side of a lopsided

victory. Mickelson, who acknowledged feeling the pressure in the aftermath of being so outspoken, went 2–1–1, including a riveting singles tie (he made 10 birdies) against Sergio García.

THE U.S. PUT IN PLACE A NEW RYDER CUP FORMULA, BUT IT DIDN'T work for Woods or Mickelson in Paris at the 2018 Ryder Cup. They were both dreadful. Mickelson slumped late in the year and only played twice. Woods, coming off his 80th PGA Tour victory a week earlier in an emotional scene at the Tour Championship in Atlanta, was out of gas after the overnight trip to France and failed to win a match. The United States lost again and more questions arose.

One that remains difficult to answer is Woods' poor record and his inability to find successful partnerships.

To punctuate just how frustrating the process has been over the years, Woods has played with 14 different partners in 29 team matches—never winning more than two matches with any single partner.

The situation, this time, at least seemed different. The thought was that Woods was no longer the big target, nor expected to be dynamic. And finding a suitable partner seemed easier. Loads of guys wanted to play with Tiger, including the two who did in Paris—Reed and Bryson DeChambeau.

"Back then, he was trying to carry the whole team on his shoulders," said Love, a teammate of Woods' in four Ryder Cups. "He couldn't figure out his role. And then we kept asking him to play with different people. I remember not wanting to screw up a good thing.

"It requires a chance to prepare for a couple of weeks, and that's what Phil [Mickelson] has been talking about. I got thrown in on Friday night to play Saturday morning alternate shot with Tiger in an away game [2002], and that kept happening to guys. It was intimidating. When you feel pressure because it's your own teammate, that doesn't really help. Then he put pressure on himself to carry the team and his teammate. It just wasn't working."

It started out well enough. At Woods' first Ryder Cup, at Valderrama in Spain in 1997, he was paired with friend Mark O'Meara. It seemed the perfect team. Woods and O'Meara knew each other well. They defeated Montgomerie and Langer 3 and 2 in four-ball.

It was the last time Woods could claim a winning record at the Ryder Cup.

He didn't win another match in Spain and lost singles to Costantino Rocca—the Italian who played alongside him during his 12-shot rout earlier that year in the final round of the Masters—in a 14½ to 13½ U.S. defeat. It was the last time he lost at singles, going 4–0–2, until his defeat to Jon Rahm in 2018.

But the team aspect always remained a problem. Woods is 9–19–1 with partners. His best records are 2–1 with Love, 1–0 with Chris Riley (during a 2004 blowout loss), and 2–2 with Furyk. He seemed to find another good partner in Stricker, going 2–1 in Wales in 2010. But they were disastrous together at Medinah in 2012, going 0–3 when just a half point would have meant a huge difference in the outcome.

"Tiger is an intimidator even if he doesn't try to be one," said Azinger, who played one match with Woods at the 2002 Ryder Cup—and lost. "When I was his partner, I thought there was a standard he was expecting out of me and I had one I was expecting from him. And neither one of us reached that standard. He's intimidating to his partners."

When the subject of pairings is broached with Woods, he often goes inside baseball, viewing the situation from a technical standpoint rather than any kind of anxiety or personality issues.

Until the 2016 Ryder Cup, players were required to abide by a rule in place on all the pro tours that stipulated that a player must use the same brand and type of golf ball throughout a round.

This became a problem in the alternate-shot format because Woods' partner would then be required to play shots with an unfamiliar golf ball, one that was tailored to his skills.

"Tiger wasn't about to use his partner's ball," said Mark Calcavecchia, who played one match with Woods and lost at the 2002 Ryder Cup. "I actually didn't think it would be a problem. The Nike ball he was using back then was made by Bridgestone and I was fine with that.

"But I remember a couple of instances where I hit iron shots in alternate shot, and I flushed a shot and thought it was plenty of club and it would come up short. That ball he used all those years went nowhere! It spun a lot and went nowhere. It was hard for guys to get used to that in one match. I never understood why he didn't just use a Titleist, and it would be easier for his partner. Let's face it, Tiger could play anything. But sure, that had some influence on his partners."

Woods' lack of personal success in the Ryder Cup, combined with a couple of cryptic quotes about the competition in his earlier days, led many to believe that Woods was not fully committed.

Speaking once about his lackluster record, Woods asked the questioner if he knew Jack Nicklaus' Ryder Cup record. The point was that while most can rattle off Nicklaus' record of 18 major titles and that he won 73 PGA Tour events, his 17–8–3 Ryder Cup mark does not come readily to mind.

(Even Nicklaus at times struggled in the competition while never playing on a losing team: in 1975, he lost two singles matches in the same day to England's Brian Barnes when the format was different.)

Prior to the 2002 Ryder Cup at The Belfry in England, Woods played in the WGC-American Express Championship in Ireland. Asked if he'd rather win the tournament or the Ryder Cup the following week, Woods answered the former. "And I can think of a million reasons why," he said, a reference to the $1 million in prize money awarded the winner.

While comments such as those did not help his cause, they did not necessarily tell the whole story, either.

"He was tremendous on the team," said 2002 captain Curtis Strange. "He was the first in line to do anything. He was the first one to sign the memorabilia we had to sign, all the 200 things we had to sign. He was terrific. And he was a great teammate. And after [playing for] me, he became a little more of a spokesman. Back then he led more by example, and he was still young. But he has done it the last couple of times, and especially as an assistant captain. He was tremendous."

DESPITE THEIR POOR PLAYING RECORDS, BOTH WOODS AND MICKelson are a lock to be future U.S. Ryder Cup captains, if they so desire. (Mickelson's 2022 move to the controversial LIV Golf League, however, put that in question.) And why wouldn't they? Both have been shown to bring a passion to the event, especially in recent years. Both took part in reshaping the dynamic of U.S. fortunes at both the Presidents Cup and the Ryder Cup.

It came as a huge surprise when Woods decided to take on the role as U.S. captain at the 2019 Presidents Cup. The feeling is he did so because he might have believed his playing career was over in the aftermath of spinal fusion surgery in 2017. When PGA Tour commissioner Jay Monahan first approached him about taking on the role, Woods declined, believing it was too soon.

But his experience at the 2017 Presidents Cup seemingly swayed him. Woods was announced as the captain in March of 2018, when he was four events into his comeback. Little did Woods know that he'd play well enough the rest of that year and into 2019 to be a competitor, too. Nobody was surprised when he picked himself to be a member of the team that competed in Australia—where Woods went 3–0 as a player and led the Americans to victory.

"It's cool because I feel like it would be very easy for someone like him to say I'm just going to be a captain because it would be cool on my résumé and everybody wants me to be a captain and we'll just go over there and hopefully play better than them," said American Justin Thomas, who played both team matches with Woods in Australia.

"But, no, he has the full intention of getting the best team as possible sent out every day and for us to win every point that we play. So it's pretty cool to see how passionate he is about it."

Much the same could be said about Mickelson, who played on every U.S. Presidents Cup team from 1994 through 2017 and every U.S. Ryder Cup team from 1995 through 2018. His PGA Championship victory at age 50 in 2021 put him in the discussion for another Ryder Cup appearance in the pandemic-delayed competition in 2021. He ended up being an assistant on the team, his first foray into that role.

There's not enough time to change their records as Ryder Cup players. But both Tiger and Phil have an opportunity to write a different story as captains. Whether or not that serves to overshadow their lackluster playing records, it can't erase the fact that at the height of their careers, when they were vying for the ultimate prizes in the game, they were disappointments at the event that has come to be as popular as any in golf.

It is a unique aspect to their rivalry. They had little to do with each other in early Ryder Cups. They proved to be poor partners the only time they were put together in consecutive sessions on the same day. And where either could have given their résumés a boost, especially in relation to the other, it never happened.

And yet, as they got older, they worked together for the good of the U.S. team, an odd partnership that never would have seemed possible.

TROUBLE

The start to Tiger Woods' 2010 golf schedule was delayed considerably. For the second consecutive year, Woods was skipping the annual PGA Tour event at Torrey Pines, but this time injury was not a factor, unless you consider the self-inflicted variety of which the entire world was aware.

A Thanksgiving run-in with a fire hydrant outside of his Orlando, Florida, home led to a tabloid feeding frenzy and headlines far and wide. Woods was involved in an infidelity scandal that saw him in rehab and off the golf course. It was the first major negative in his career, and the impact was far-reaching.

Woods went into hiding, and his golf career was on hold. Events he was expected to play were skipped. Who knew when he would return?

In the absence of Woods, Phil Mickelson was left to fill the void.

And he didn't wait for any questions about Tiger when he made his season debut at Torrey Pines. He brought up the topic himself. In his first comments since Woods' highly publicized car accident on November 27, 2009, and subsequent leave from golf, Mickelson began a pre-tournament news conference by addressing the issue of Woods' absence.

"The game of golf needs him to come back," Mickelson said. "I mean, it's important for him to come back and be a part of the sport. But right now he's got a lot more important things going on in his life.

"Amy and I are good friends with both Tiger and [his then-wife] Elin, and we care deeply about how this turns out. But I'm going to choose not to talk about it publicly anymore, and I appreciate your understanding on that."

Mickelson added that he had "limited communication with the [Woods] family" and that "I don't want to talk about it publicly for the reason that we're friends and we have a personal relationship, and I just don't feel—I feel like it's a violation of our trust and our relationship."

Then 39, Mickelson won three times on the PGA Tour in 2009 despite his own personal issues. It was a trying year in which both his wife, Amy, and mother, Mary, were diagnosed with breast cancer.

He finished the season with a victory at the Tour Championship, then won the unofficial World Golf Championship event in China, the HSBC Champions. At both tournaments, he defeated Woods, the No. 1 ranked player in the world.

Mickelson was the best bet to step into the gaping hole created by Woods and give golf fans something else to talk about—if that was even possible.

Not that Lefty necessarily relished the role. But as the No. 2 player to Woods' No. 1, as a longtime rival to the game's best player, as one who had his own goals and aspirations coming off a personally trying and yet ultimately successful year, Mickelson found himself in exactly that position as his 2010 season started.

The game needed some sunshine after the storm clouds Woods produced over the previous two months. And Mickelson was undoubtedly the player with the most ability to deliver.

"I haven't thought about it like that," Mickelson. "I'm just excited to play golf. I'm excited to get back into competition and be a part of this. Again, I haven't really looked at it from that point of view, but nobody will be able to fill the shoes that are voided right now."

Mickelson expressed his hope that Woods would return from his "indefinite" leave from the game because "the game of golf needs him to come back."

In the meantime, however, the game needed Mickelson to get off to a hot start in 2010.

Throughout their battles over the years, Woods was the better player than Mickelson. But you would get a healthy argument about who is more popular. And with Woods gone, Mickelson was presented an excellent opportunity to aspire to a few goals that he, remarkably, never attained.

Despite 37 PGA Tour victories, including three major championships, Mickelson never won a PGA Tour money title, never was voted Player of the Year, never ascended to the No. 1 ranking.

"Well, my whole career I've been trying to get to No. 1, I just haven't had much success," Mickelson said. "But this year, whether or not Tiger is in the field, I still believe that this is an opportunity for me to compete in majors, to challenge him. I've had some great head-to-head success in the last year or two, and I expect this year, with or without him, to be one of the best years of my career."

Before Woods' troubles began, 2010 was shaping up to be an interesting year between the two players. Woods won seven times worldwide in 2009, but Mickelson produced one of his best seasons.

He won three times on the PGA Tour, including his first World Golf Championship event at Doral. He finished ahead of Woods at both the Masters and U.S. Open, then defeated him at the Tour Championship and the then-unofficial WGC-HSBC Champions in China.

The last seven times Mickelson and Woods were in the same group, Lefty shot the lower round five times and tied Woods once.

"I think he's going to be even better," said Mickelson's swing coach Butch Harmon, who had a big role in helping Mickelson overcome some of the mental hurdles he faced in playing against Woods. "Physically he got his body in shape. And with the work he's done swing wise . . . I was very happy with what I saw.

"He's extremely anxious to get going. This could be his best year ever, and he's looking forward to it. Sure, it puts pressure on him, but I haven't seen him this excited to start the year."

Mickelson's 40th birthday approached around the time of the U.S. Open, and yet he figured to be a force no matter what happened to Woods.

"The way Phil Mickelson played at the end of last year . . . the way he is hitting the ball," said Ernie Els. "Phil is hitting it as long or longer than anybody out there. He has really been working hard. Now his putting is coming around. I think Phil is probably the man to beat now.

"Even when Tiger stopped playing—even if you ask Tiger—I think Phil got right to his level. I think there is a new guy we've got to chase."

NO STORY LINES WERE MORE OUT FRONT THAN WOODS' WHEN the Masters rolled around in April. It didn't matter who was hot, whose games were trending, who seemed most likely to win the green jacket. It was all Tiger.

He was returning to competitive golf for the first time since the scandal broke. And he picked the most famous golf tournament and course in the world as his place to do it. In a way, it was brilliant. Woods would be protected from any unruly fan behavior. It simply wasn't tolerated at Augusta National. It was also a familiar place, one that brought back good memories, and where he also felt he could succeed again.

Woods was never going to avoid a media crush, but such a scenario was built in at Augusta National, which made the surprising decision to conduct Woods' interview on Monday of tournament week—away from all other player interviews. It was as if the tournament was saying, "Let's get this out of the way." Tiger was the only player who came to the media center that day.

He admitted that despite all his successes, golf was not fun because of the turmoil in his personal life.

"Look at what I was engaged in," Woods said. "When you're living a life that is a lie, life isn't fun . . . that's been stripped away. It feels fun again."

Woods' highly anticipated news conference before more than 200 reporters lasted 34 minutes and included all range of questions, such as why he chose to receive treatment from a Canadian doctor who had been accused of prescribing performance-enhancing drugs to other athletes.

For the first time, Woods disclosed that in addition to recovering from reconstructive knee surgery in late 2008, he also tore his Achilles tendon in his right foot late that year.

Woods admitted to having a procedure known as platelet-rich plasma (PRP) therapy, which helps speed the healing process. He said he chose

Dr. Anthony Galea because of his work with other athletes. The procedure is legal under the PGA Tour's drug-testing policy. "I've never taken any illegal drug in my life," Woods said.

His world—and that of golf—changed greatly since his SUV crash just outside of his Florida driveway.

That mysterious accident just yards from his home began a stream of negative publicity that continued with numerous reports of marital affairs, his leave from the game, a stint in undisclosed rehab, and a gradual return to the public glare.

Woods made his first public comments on February 19 at PGA Tour headquarters in Ponte Vedra Beach, Florida, apologizing to his family, friends, and business associates and promising to "make amends, and that starts by never repeating the mistakes I've made. It's up to me to start living a life of integrity."

Just less than a month later, on March 16, Woods announced that he would be returning to golf at the Masters. On March 21, he gave his first interviews, five minutes each to ESPN and Golf Channel. That Monday of Masters week was the first time he took questions in an extended format.

Typically, Woods would have fielded queries in a pre-tournament setting with topics such as why he had not won the Masters in five years or why he claimed just one green jacket in his past seven attempts.

But after a long break from golf, the answers to those questions were left for another day.

Woods said that his agent, Mark Steinberg, was contacted by federal investigators about Galea, who had been charged with dispensing illegal drugs in both Canada and the United States. Woods vowed his full cooperation.

Asked why he did not address the issue earlier—the *New York Times* first reported Galea's link to Woods in December of 2009—the golfer said it was because he did not have the forum to discuss it and wasn't asked about it in the two televised interviews.

And asked why he did not discuss any of his public relations mess sooner, Woods said he wasn't "in the right place" to do so in December and that he entered therapy—the type of which he would not disclose—in late December.

"A lot has happened in my life in the past five months," Woods said. "I'm here at the Masters to play and compete, and I'm really excited about doing that."

Earlier that day, Woods played a practice round with former Masters champion Fred Couples. They were joined by Jim Furyk on the 13th hole and played the rest of the way together. Although the crowd was cordial, it was not overly enthusiastic.

Woods made an attempt to interact with spectators—not typical for him—and even engaged in the tradition of trying to skip a shot over the pond at Augusta's par-3 16th. Nobody ever remembered Woods doing that.

"I was more nervous out there," Woods said. "I didn't know what to expect. To be out there in front of the people, where I've done some horrible things . . . for them to want to see me play golf again felt great . . . Today I took it in more."

GETTING THE MEDIA OUT OF THE WAY WAS ONE BIG STEP IN THE return process. Now Woods simply needed to get ready, and given all the time he'd missed, there was little to waste. Proper practice was essential, and Woods used the next two days to his advantage to cram all he could into his arsenal before his Thursday tee time.

But the day before the tournament, Woods was broadsided by something neither he—nor anyone—saw coming.

The annual Wednesday news conference is a tradition that dates to the early days of the tournament. The current chairman of the club and thus the Masters addresses the media, usually with updates on various club endeavors as well as course changes and anything else related to the tournament.

William Porter "Billy" Payne, presiding over his fourth Masters as chairman, was well known in the sports world. A former college football player at the University of Georgia, he took on a very public and encompassing role as president and CEO of the Atlanta Olympic Committee for the Olympic Games.

In essence, Payne, an attorney and Atlanta businessman, was the lead figure in bringing the 1996 Games to Atlanta and running the enterprise.

He later became a member of Augusta National, got involved in various committees, and on May 5, 2006, was appointed to the all-powerful role of Augusta National chairman, becoming just the sixth to hold the position in club history.

Payne is hailed for many positives that occurred during his tenure, including the admittance of Augusta National's first women members, embracing digital technology to help promote the tournament, and spearheading various grow-the-game initiatives, such as the Drive, Chip, and Putt Contest, as well as international amateur tournaments in Asia and South America that offered spots in the Masters field.

But nobody saw the remarks Payne blistered Woods with on April 7 coming.

"It is simply not the degree of his conduct that is so egregious here," Payne said of Woods. "It is the fact that he disappointed all of us, and more importantly, our kids and our grandkids. Our hero did not live up to the expectations of the role model we saw for our children."

Payne's comments were the most outspoken of anyone in an official capacity in golf. Woods was a four-time Masters champion, a revered figure in the game. And Augusta National accommodated his return news conference, at the club's insistence staging it on Monday to better cut down on distractions related to the tournament.

That takedown was particularly brutal.

Woods already played a nine-hole practice round with Mark O'Meara and left the course prior to Payne's news conference.

"Is there a way forward? I hope yes. I think yes," Payne said. "But certainly, his future will never again be measured only by his performance against par but measured by the sincerity of his efforts to change. I hope he now realizes that every kid he passes on the course wants his swing but would settle for his smile.

"We at Augusta hope and pray that our great champion will begin his new life here tomorrow in a positive, hopeful, and constructive manner, but this time, with a significant difference from the past. This year, it will not be just for him but for all of us who believe in second chances."

And with that Payne moved onto questions as those in the room were almost too stunned to ask what led to such a verbal beating.

As shocking as the revelations about Woods had been in the previous months, he did little but harm himself, his reputation, and his family. In no way did Woods impact the Masters—in fact, he was bringing even more attention to the year's first major with his presence—and Payne's reaction seemed heavy-handed coming from a place that was forced to deal with its own issues, ones that were all too apparent when Woods became the first Black man to win the tournament in 1997.

Woods wasn't about to get into any kind of a back-and-forth over Payne's comments. When asked about them following the first round, Woods said, "I was disappointed in myself, too."

But it clearly hit deep.

"That caught Tiger by surprise," said Steve Williams, his caddie. "That was a bolt of lightning out of nowhere."

ANTICIPATION WAS HIGH FOR THAT FIRST-ROUND TEE TIME, AND the Lords of Augusta made Woods wait. He did not begin play until 1:42 P.M., along with K. J. Choi and Matt Kuchar.

Hank Haney, Tiger's coach, noted later that Woods struggled in their practice sessions together. He cringed at the thought of how the first round might play out. And yet, Woods split the fairway on Augusta's first hole and went on to shoot 68—the first time in 16 Masters appearances that he broke 70 in the opening round.

So much for competitive rust.

Woods never shot better than 70 in his four victories, and he trailed 50-year-old Couples by two shots.

It was Woods' first round of tournament golf in 144 days, and the absence caused many to wonder just how well he could perform at one of the most exacting courses in the world.

But Woods shot his tournament lows for the first round on both the front nine, and overall, had two eagles in a round for the first time, and even pulled off a remarkable ninth-hole hook shot around trees to set up a birdie.

"Very pleased," Woods said of his first official round of golf since winning the Australian Masters on November 15. "For the most part, I think I hit the ball well all day. And I just didn't make a lot of putts. If I putted well today, it could have been a really special round."

Woods needed 31 putts and suffered several lip-outs, keeping his round from being even better. He hit 14 greens in regulation and missed just five fairways.

"To be surprised by a guy who won a U.S. Open on one leg . . . you kind of stop being a little bit surprised," said Kuchar, referencing the No. 1 player in the world's 2008 U.S. Open victory at Torrey Pines.

After admitting he was nervous about the reaction he would encounter from spectators when he played his first practice round on Monday, Woods received a warm, although not boisterous, ovation as he approached the first tee.

"The people were just incredible, incredible all day," he said.

Although there were no negative incidents on the course, there were two planes that flew overhead pulling banners that referenced Woods' off-the-course transgressions.

Woods said he did not notice them, and when pressed, said he was not surprised.

"It wouldn't be the first time," Woods said.

All in all, it was a good day: Woods was in a tie for seventh, trailing Couples by two and one behind Mickelson, Tom Watson, Lee Westwood, Y. E. Yang, and K. J. Choi. He was tied with Anthony Kim, Nick Watney, Ian Poulter, and Ricky Barnes.

Asked if he was surprised to see Woods' name on the leaderboard, Open champion Stewart Cink chuckled.

"Boy, have we gone a long way now," he said. "No, I'm not surprised."

MICKELSON MISSED A ONE-FOOTER ON THE FIFTH GREEN DURING the second round, shot 71, and was tied with Woods, who shot 70, two strokes back of leaders Westwood and Poulter.

Westwood surged ahead with a 68 on Saturday and was joined in the final-round group by Mickelson, who shot 67 to stand a stroke back with 18 holes to play. That included a run of eagle-eagle-birdie at the 13th, 14th, and 15th holes. Another 70 by Woods left him four strokes behind—and ruing his missed opportunities.

He three-putted three times during the round, among other things, but he did birdie the final hole to at least give himself a chance.

"I was fighting it all day," he said. "My warm-up wasn't very good. I was struggling there. I really struggled with the pace of the greens and fighting my swing. It was a tough day."

Woods was struggling. He was three days into his comeback, and just being there and competing wasn't enough. He was angry he didn't play better. He was angry Mickelson was leading. He was angry. Period.

And he clearly was not happy with his coach.

Haney came to Woods somewhat quietly in 2004, then oversaw the golfer as he won 31 PGA Tour events, including six major championships. While the number of majors under Haney wasn't as many as Woods achieved under Harmon (eight), his consistency was better.

Under Harmon, Woods won 38 times worldwide, with 13 seconds, 12 thirds, and 29 other top 10s for a total of 92 top 10s in 142 official starts. That means roughly 65 percent of his starts saw him finish in the top 10.

Under Haney, Woods won 35 times worldwide, with 15 seconds, 4 thirds, and 13 other top 10 finishes for a total of 67 top 10s in 88 starts. That means 76 percent of his starts saw him finish in the top 10.

The records under both coaches were phenomenal. But Woods, statistically, was better under Haney.

And yet Haney constantly felt he was under the glare, that the idea of Woods ever leaving Harmon was always a topic on people's minds. And, on occasion, he felt he didn't always have Woods' undivided faith in him.

That was apparent prior to the final round of the Masters, as Haney wrote in his book *The Big Miss*. Haney noticed a player who was shockingly not into it that day, almost in defiance. Woods did not embark on his usual structured practice session, and Haney was stunned that Tiger was not in a better frame of mind, given all he endured and how far he came to be in such a position.

Haney said that Woods' Sunday warm-ups were "traditionally works of art, especially when he's in contention" and that he could go through the entire bag "without missing a shot." But Tiger was taking too little time between swings, wasn't watching the flight of the ball, and was having a terrible warm-up session.

"He's acting as if I'm not there," Haney wrote. "I get nothing. Since emerging from his meal in the clubhouse, he's switched on that cold-blooded ability to leave a person—even someone close to him—hanging. Amazingly, right here, right now, Tiger is blowing me off."

Haney saw that as nearly the end of their relationship.

In an interview years later, Haney tried to explain that, for some reason, Mickelson leading the Masters, among other things, was part of what was bugging Woods.

"It had to have something to do with it," Haney said. "He was worried about Phil. If he's three shots down to Westwood, and he's four ahead of Phil, I don't think he has that attitude that day. Or if he was three shots down to Chris DiMarco, he doesn't have that attitude. But his attitude that day was it was over. He knows how good Phil is. He knows how good his short game is. And he knows how good Augusta is for Phil, too. So many factors.

"And he's never come from behind [to win a major]. The first time you're ever going to come from behind at a major is at the Masters when you've spotted Phil Mickelson three shots? Not likely. Augusta steepens the odds right there.

"Tiger was mad he didn't keep it closer the day before. He had three three-putt greens. And face it: the guy he was chasing was tough. It was the wrong guy to be chasing at the wrong course. And in his mind, he had kind of a limited arsenal [that week]. He probably felt like he had fired all of his bullets in his gun just to be where he was. And now I've fired all the bullets in my gun and I'm three strokes down to . . . pick any player who hasn't won [a major] before . . . but I'm down three shots to Phil Mickelson. It's a little different story, especially on that golf course. And it's not three shots down at the U.S. Open or the PGA where a wild one could get him."

Woods shot a final-round 69 and could never get close enough to the leaders. He struggled from the outset.

Mickelson had more than Tiger to worry about. Despite Westwood's lack of major hardware, he was still an accomplished European Tour player who contended in several big tournaments.

And Mickelson was not exactly on fire leading into the Masters. He posted just one top 10 in seven finishes.

As it played out, the man he still calls "Coach" was doing his best not to jump out of his chair and scream at the television. Steve Loy, Phil

Mickelson's longtime agent, tried to remain calm. After all, a bit of decorum is required inside the Augusta National clubhouse. But how do you hold it in?

The player he recruited as a teenager to play golf at Arizona State, then later went to work for, was involved in a riveting back nine Sunday, a major championship at stake.

And then, like the rest of the world, Loy could not believe his eyes. There was Mickelson in the pine straw on Augusta's par-5 13th hole, thinking about firing a shot through an opening in the trees.

As caddie Jim Mackay tried to talk Lefty out of it, Loy gulped. There was nothing left to do but watch and hope as Mickelson rifled his 6-iron and nearly caught one tree with his follow-through, the ball landing on the green and coming to rest three feet from the cup.

Fans who lined the hole went crazy, Mickelson pumped his fist and Loy could only sit back in his chair in disbelief.

"This hair used to be blond, not gray," Loy quipped as he held his hand over his heart, shaking his head.

It was the shot of the tournament, of the year, and maybe of Mickelson's career.

And it once again helped define Phil the Thrill.

He won his third Masters, this one by three strokes over Westwood, shooting a 5-under-par 67 with a series of great par saves and clutch shots.

But none was better than the 207-yard 6-iron that set up a birdie—which should have been an eagle—at the 13th.

Nobody would have blamed him if he laid up to a manageable yardage and tried to make a birdie with a phenomenal short game. There are all manner of instances in Mickelson's career where the heroic play didn't work out. But this time it did, and there were grins all around.

"You can't print it," laughed Harmon, Mickelson's coach, when asked what he was thinking as the decision unfolded. "I was praying he would lay up. I'm sure Bones was doing the same thing.

"But he made a great explanation. He had to go through the same gap to go for the green as he did to lay up. So why not go for the green? With all the birdies they were making in front of him, he figured he needed to make birdie. You know how confident he is on those kind of shots."

Had Mickelson converted the eagle putt, the shot to set it up would have gone down as one of the greatest of all time.

Somehow, Mickelson missed the hole with the three-footer, giving himself a longer birdie putt coming back. He made it, a crucial development as he kept a two-shot advantage over Westwood that he never relinquished.

"It's one of the few shots, really, that only Phil could pull off," said Westwood, who was also playing his second shot from the trees. "I think most people would have just chipped that one out. That's what great players do . . . pull off great shots at the right time."

Asked for a better shot he's seen, Westwood was stumped.

"Not around here," he said. "It was something special."

And it helped seal an emotional victory that saw tears flowing from the 18th green all the way down to Rae's Creek. Mackay, for one, basically lost it when he saw Mickelson's cancer-stricken wife, Amy, emerge just from behind the green, the first time she attended a tournament since the previous year's Players Championship just weeks before the Mickelsons announced her diagnosis.

Somewhere in the crowd were both Mickelson's and Amy's parents, their three children, and, of course, an adoring audience that cheered golf's feel-good story of the year.

"I was a bit of a mess there at the end," Mackay said. "It was an incredible week, obviously. I have to think down the road, at least for me, it will mean way more than any other victory he's had."

Mackay was there since the beginning, since before Mickelson turned pro in 1992. He was on the bag for all but one of Phil's 38 PGA Tour victories at the time and all four majors he won to that point. And he knows the reputation Mickelson has acquired, one of a player who gambled too much on the golf course for his own good.

"The biggest reason he won this golf tournament was because of how aggressive he played," Mackay said. "He played incredibly aggressive all week. You can make the argument that over the years a couple of things haven't worked out for him when he played aggressive, but he would not have won this tournament if he had not done some of the things he did."

The 2006 U.S. Open at Winged Foot is a good starting point for second-guessing his approach. Aside from the 2009 U.S. Open, where

Mickelson tied for second, he had not given himself many chances in majors since that debacle.

And if that shot catches the tree during the final round, who knows? But it worked beautifully, despite Bones' pleas for the safe play.

Mackay noted that Mickelson's aggressiveness actually helped him the day prior, when he fired a 7-iron onto the same green to set up an eagle.

"That turned his tournament around," he said. "That eagle on 13 gave him so much momentum. It's a pin you can't really get to. He makes eagle there, and then the ball goes in on 14 [for an eagle], and then in a sense you're feeling like, gosh, this could be our week."

Of course for the longest time, it wasn't looking that way at all. A stamen somehow fell from the sky and landed right in Mickelson's line as he putted for birdie on the second hole. Sure enough, the ball hit it and went off line.

He didn't make his first birdie until the eighth hole, then needed to get up and down for pars at the 9th, 10th, and 11th holes. It wasn't like Mickelson was knocking down flagsticks, which is why the play at No. 13 will long be remembered.

"The gap wasn't huge, but it was big enough, you know, for a ball to fit through," Mickelson said to laughter. "I just felt like at that time, I needed to trust my swing and hit a shot, and it came off perfect."

AS GREAT AS THAT WEEK WAS FOR MICKELSON, IT TURNED INTO dread for Woods—even though he should have been thrilled with his tie for fourth. Given all he battled, and how little he was able to prepare, breaking par in all four rounds was an impressive achievement, and even having a chance should have been viewed as a victory.

But Woods didn't see it that way; there were never any moral victories for him. Although he tied for fourth that summer at the U.S. Open played at Pebble Beach, that, too, was viewed as an opportunity squandered.

His Masters news conference with reporters afterward suggested anything but satisfaction.

"Yeah, I finished fourth. Not what I wanted," he said. "I wanted to win this tournament. As the week wore on I kept hitting the ball worse. I hit it better on Friday, but after that it was not very good."

And Woods wasn't giving himself a pass or lowering expectations.

"I entered this event, and I only enter events to win, and I didn't get it done," he said. "I didn't hit the ball good enough, and I made too many mistakes around the greens, but after that it was not very good."

Earlier in the week, Woods expressed a desire to enjoy golf more. To show a brighter, happier side. To interact with spectators. It was meant to try and soften his image and seen as a way forward after all the turmoil.

But by Sunday, that was gone. Perhaps it was too soon. Certainly it was too much to ask, especially in such circumstances. And to be clear, it was a rather ridiculous expectation. Woods spent his entire life playing and preparing one way. Now he was supposed to smile on the course to satisfy everyone else?

"I think people are making way too much of a big deal out of this thing," he said. "I was not feeling good. I hit a snipe [hook] off the first hole, and I don't know how people can think I should be happy about that. I hit a wedge from 45 yards and basically bladed it over the green. These are not things I normally do.

"So I'm not going to be smiling and not going to be happy. And I hit one of the worst, low, kind of low quick hooks on 5. So I hadn't hit a good shot yet. I'm not going to be walking around there with a pep in my step because I hadn't hit a good shot yet."

And so it went. Tiger wasn't happy. Phil was ecstatic.

Both had their issues, however, including not winning for the rest of the year.

It was an interesting time. For Tiger, getting back to his winning ways was seemingly the way to put his personal travails behind him and off the minds of those who followed him. But with every week that passed without a victory, it was easy to reference the scandal as some sort of demarcation point from which he needed to emerge. He came close at the Masters and the U.S. Open but largely struggled throughout the year.

And while Phil faced numerous chances to move past him in the World Rankings and finally get to No. 1, he could never cross that line.

16

The Coach
and the Caddie

For all of his Hall of Fame credentials, Phil Mickelson never got to No. 1 in the Official World Golf Ranking, a somewhat remarkable fact given all he accomplished.

Sure, he saw a big and imposing roadblock in Tiger Woods, who was atop the world rankings for a record 362 weeks. It's tough to get to No. 1 when someone else is so firmly entrenched in that spot, as Woods was for many years.

But even when Woods was in the prime of his career, he didn't always occupy the No. 1 position. And yet, Mickelson never replaced him, never even held the top spot when Woods was down.

It is a significant hole in Mickelson's résumé, almost fluky. How could he never get to the top with all those wins, all those majors? How much does it matter?

Perspective rules, and Mickelson undoubtedly cherishes his 2006 and 2010 Masters victories—both won when Tiger was No. 1. Same with the 2013 Open victory. That championship hardware means much more than being atop a list that is more about bragging rights than anything else.

Still, Woods' reign atop the rankings is impressive.

He first got there in 1997, less than a year after turning pro, having already won six times, including the Masters. But over the next year, the No. 1 spot would bounce between Woods, Ernie Els, and Greg Norman. Then, in the spring of 1999, David Duval moved into the picture. Woods regained the top spot after winning the PGA Championship that year and held it for more than five years.

That's where Vijay Singh stepped up. He put up an incredible 2004 season, winning nine times on the PGA Tour, including the PGA Championship. Woods won just twice worldwide that year and saw Singh grab the spot three different times.

When Woods finally wrestled No. 1 away from Singh in June of 2005, he held on for more than five years and a record 281 weeks.

That end coincided with his trying 2010 season, the one that saw him finish tied for fourth at both the Masters and U.S. Open but not able to do much else. He almost hit rock bottom at the WGC-Bridgestone Invitational at Firestone, a place where he won seven previous times, finishing 78th out of 79 players. By October, Woods relinquished the top spot to England's Lee Westwood.

Meanwhile, Mickelson had numerous chances to surpass him and was never able to do so, one of his best chances coming at the same Bridgestone Invitational where Woods faltered. Mickelson did, too.

It wasn't quite the same as failing to pounce on Woods when Mickelson didn't close out the 2006 U.S. Open at Winged Foot. But it was a lost opportunity in their battles, nonetheless.

LONG BEFORE HE LOST THE NO. 1 RANKING, WOODS LOST HIS coach. Hank Haney saw it coming when Woods was moody at the 2010 Masters, and things didn't change much after that. After such a good performance under trying circumstances, Woods was a mess in his next start, the Quail Hollow Championship, where he missed the cut.

And that is when the pressure on their relationship intensified. Haney did not accompany Woods to Charlotte for the Quail Hollow tournament, although he often did not attend regular Tour events. But when he skipped the Players Championship the following week, eyebrows lifted to the sky.

Golf is the ultimate individual game, the player who swings the clubs bearing the responsibility for where the ball flies and how many times it is struck. A golf coach doesn't call plays, doesn't make personnel moves.

He can't even give advice during a round, per the game's rules. So how was it that Haney was to blame for Woods' woes?

Going into the Players Championship, Woods played a grand total of six competitive rounds of golf, with an amazing performance at the Masters followed by one of his worst ever at Quail Hollow, where many observers believed for the rarest of times, he mailed in his performance. The incredible focus on his personal life undoubtedly took a toll. And hitting a little white ball was suddenly not something he could do without a million other thoughts possibly penetrating his head.

So the golf world was buzzing with speculation about Woods replacing Haney, who worked with the game's No. 1 player since 2004 and was in his employ while Woods won 31 PGA Tour titles and six major championships.

NBC analyst Johnny Miller bluntly called for a change on the eve of the tournament in a conference call with reporters to hype the Players Championship. Plenty of others speculated that Haney's days were numbered, too.

"He needs a new, fresh, either teacher or just go back to what is natural to his game," Miller said. "What he is working on now, I believe is . . . no disrespect for Hank Haney, but it is not working. And sometimes when it is not working, sometimes you have to get off the fork in the road and get back to what brung you there and what won all these championships for him. He needs to do that, and if he was here right now, I would tell it right to his face."

Haney said that he just received a quarterly payment from Woods' team and had not been told his services were no longer needed. And he said Woods was enduring a complicated time in his life that was bound to impact his golf.

But what Haney did not say was that Tiger could have probably done better by him in the public arena. Haney would not go there then, and it was understandable, but Woods did his coach no favors by not clearing up the matter.

"I'm still working with him, yeah," is all Woods said when asked about their relationship that week.

Then observers tried to put two and two together on the day prior to the tournament when Woods played a practice round at the TPC Saw-grass with Hunter Mahan and Sean O'Hair—both of whom worked with Orlando-based instructor Sean Foley, who worked a short distance from Woods' home.

Perhaps Woods was ready to ditch Haney for Foley?

It was fair to wonder if a swing coach was his biggest concern. Major championships at Pebble Beach and St. Andrews were in the immediate future, and those are places where Woods experienced great success. Just a year earlier, he won seven times worldwide. Swing changes?

The chatter was simply an example of the kind of scrutiny Woods faced. Mickelson never endured that kind of second-guessing, especially as it related to his coaches. Rick Smith worked with him for some 10 years, and the two were close—so close that Mickelson waited to dismiss him following his inability to win the 2006 U.S. Open. Smith was with him for three majors and what likely should have been a fourth.

It wasn't until the following spring that Mickelson made the move to Butch Harmon, who oversaw two major wins and a Players title. But the legendary coach could never cure Mickelson of his driving woes—certainly not consistently—a fact that never was cause for much criticism.

And when Mickelson parted ways with Harmon in 2016, it was done with nothing but praise.

Haney rarely got that kind of love from Woods. The greatest endorsement for the teacher was the fact that he helped Woods come back from major knee surgery to win six PGA Tour events in 2009. The achievement was somehow not given its due, perhaps because of Woods' shocking runner-up finish to Y. E. Yang at the PGA Championship, where for the first time in his career, Woods failed to convert a 54-hole lead in a major championship into a victory.

After missing his only cut that year at the Open, Woods went on an incredible run, finishing 1–1–2–T2–T11–1–2. He helped the U.S. Presidents Cup team to victory by going 5–0, tied for sixth at the WGC-HSBC Champions in China, then won the Australian Masters.

It also set up for a phenomenal 2010. Woods won seven of his 19 worldwide starts, the major venues were favorable, and nobody was over-analyzing Haney's work with Woods.

Then November 27 happened and the revelations of marital infidelity and an indefinite leave from the game amid the myriad distractions, tabloid reports, rumors, embarrassment, and all manner of gossip.

And three tournaments into the comeback it was Haney's fault?

Even Harmon, Woods' coach before Haney, suggested it was far more than swing mechanics.

"Tiger Woods is, to me, his game is in disarray," Harmon said in an interview. "There's no doubt about that. That's obvious. Anybody that plays golf can look out there and see that, that he's not Tiger Woods.

"But until he gets his head on straight, and he gets his things in his mind settled—with some professional help I would add—I think it's going to be a while before we see the old Tiger Woods. He will figure out the mechanical part of it, the physical part of it. It's the mental part of it, I think, that's hurting him right now."

Miller suggested that Woods view tape of his 15-shot victory at the 2000 U.S. Open and try to get back to the way he played when he won three straight majors and nine times on the PGA Tour. It was an incredible year, but it was also three knee surgeries prior for Woods.

There is no denying the excellent work that Harmon did with Woods from the time before he turned pro through the 2002 season. Some questioned why Woods would want to make a change, but he did, and by 2004 he was working with Haney, and part of the burden the instructor undertook was to alleviate the immense pressure on Woods' left knee.

Getting into swing theory is dangerous business. Who is to say what is correct? Such debates have raged for more than 100 years, and there is a reason why the likes of Haney and Harmon and others become famous. There is more than one successful way to do it, and not everything works for everyone.

Yet starting with the 2005 season, Woods won those 31 PGA Tour titles and six majors, had 57 top 10 finishes in 78 tournaments. In all that time, he finished worse than 30th just eight times, with five of them missed cuts. (For comparison, Mickelson had 15 wins and three majors, 42 top 10s, and 34 finishes outside of the top 30, including 10 missed cuts in 111 events dating to the start of 2005.)

Just two weeks prior, Woods reported on his own website that he made an albatross and shot 63 at Isleworth, then his home course and one of the toughest in the country. And then the week prior at Quail Hollow, Woods admitted he was finding difficulty taking his game from the range to the course.

"I've had moments where I didn't hit the ball very good coming in, and you've got to turn it around," Woods said. "That's the whole idea of practicing and really working on being focused on what I'm doing and being committed to what I'm doing.

"I know what the fix is, and I've proven it to myself, and it's just a matter of going out there and executing it consistently over 72 holes."

Haney skipping the Players added to the murmurings but should not have mattered; he went to just four tournaments in 2009—his first after Woods returned from knee surgery and the three U.S. majors, where the coach was only there for the practice rounds.

"His clubs are the same, his coach is the same, his caddie is the same, his putter is the same. What's changed?" Haney said. "I don't want to sound like I'm making excuses. I think it's obvious that he has a lot of things going on in his life. I'm sure that if people will give him a little bit of a chance that he'll be back to playing golf the way he knows he can."

But by Sunday of that week, things took a different turn. Woods' neck was bothering him and he ended up withdrawing just a few holes into the final round. He reported pain after hitting his tee shot at the seventh, then called over an official after hitting his second shot short of the green and told him he was withdrawing, leaving Jason Bohn to play the rest of the round alone.

Woods withdrew from just two tournaments as a pro to that point: the 1998 AT&T Pebble Beach National Pro-Am, which needed a weather-delayed finish, and the 2006 Northern Trust Open before the third round due to illness.

"Setting up over the ball is fine, but once I start making the motion, it's downhill from there," said Woods, who did not previously disclose any issues with his neck.

Just two days earlier, he was asked specifically about his left knee, for which he had the season-ending surgery in 2008, and his right Achilles, which he disclosed at the Masters.

Asked if there were any issues, Woods said, "No, zero. Absolutely 100 percent." Asked about the Achilles, he said, "No, I started back running again. Haven't had any swelling. I still feel that I'm explosive in all my exercises I'm able to do now, which I wasn't doing any of that last year. So it feels good."

Woods didn't volunteer anything about his neck, but Haney acknowledged that it was an issue going back before the Masters.

"Tiger doesn't make excuses, but I know it has been bothering him," Haney said. "I don't know how bad . . . Tiger is a tough guy. He played the U.S. Open on a broken leg. So when he says something is bothering him, it's probably not real good."

Woods didn't end up missing any time, but he did move forward without his coach. Haney contemplated quitting after the Masters, but was talked out of it by Woods' agent, Mark Steinberg. But there was just one following conversation between the two men—something Woods was not forthright about in his pre-tournament news conference at the Players.

On the morning of the final round, Haney said Woods called him again, complaining about his neck, and it was after that conversation that he made the decision he'd no longer be working with Woods.

Woods' lack of communication, Haney's own reticence about being a scapegoat, more than six years of scrutiny—it all added up.

A few days later, Haney released a statement in which he made it clear that it was his decision.

"I have informed Tiger Woods this evening that I will no longer be his coach," Haney said. "I would like to thank Tiger for the opportunity that I have had to work with him over the past [six-plus] years. Tiger Woods has done the work to achieve a level of greatness that I believe the game of golf has never seen before and I will always appreciate the opportunity that I have had to contribute to his successes."

Other than his tie for fourth at the U.S. Open a month later, Woods struggled the rest of the summer. In his return to St. Andrews after winning the Open at the Old Course in both 2000 and 2005, he was never in the tournament, finishing a distant tie for 23rd.

And when he finished 78th at the WGC-Bridgestone Invitational, Woods again slipped to a low point. His game was a mess, and his personal life was still unraveling with the news that he and his wife, Elin, were headed for divorce.

That was the same week that Mickelson, who was in contention through two rounds, had one of his best chances to surpass Woods in the Official World Golf Ranking and move to No. 1 in the world for this first time. Anything inside the top four would assure that ascension.

But Mickelson slumped on the weekend, shooting a Saturday 71 after opening 66–68. An 8 in the final round doomed him to a disappointing tie for 46th, and an excellent chance to get to No. 1 vanished.

Meanwhile, the following week at the PGA Championship at Whistling Straits, Woods was working with Foley. Their relationship would not become official for a few more weeks.

BY THE TIME THE BMW CHAMPIONSHIP ROLLED AROUND, WOODS was clearly working with Foley, whose teachings differed greatly from Haney's and Harmon's.

Nobody knew what it would mean.

Asked if Foley was his coach, Woods replied, smiling, "He's coaching me."

Semantics aside, Woods was spending time with Foley for more than a month. They worked together at the PGA Championship. They spent a few days together in Orlando—where Woods lived, where Foley was based—prior to the Barclays tournament.

And Woods saw steady progress, although a few weeks prior he hesitated to dive into a situation under Foley that was more about science and less about swing mechanics.

"That's one of the things I had to understand," he said. "I needed to understand the whole concept before I committed to what I was doing. It's nice when you get rewarded with results, and the shots that I'm hitting now, it's been a long time since I've been able to do that. That's always a good sign.

"I've committed to the concepts, and more than anything, I understand what he's trying to teach. So that's the biggest thing."

Unclear was if Woods was willing to regress or struggle with his game while he figured out the nuances of Foley's methods. It happened each of the previous times he overhauled his swing in search of long-term consistency.

After winning four times in 1997, including the Masters, Woods virtually started over with Harmon, won just once in 1998, and then went on a tear, winning 27 PGA Tour events, including seven majors, between 1999 and 2002.

In 2003, Woods won five times, but no majors, and split with Harmon the year prior. He started working covertly with Haney in 2004, a year in which he won just once and produced just one top 10 in majors. He then tore through the following years with Haney.

After Haney departed, Woods said he would push on alone. But after a few months, it was Foley's turn, and if the past was any indication of the future, Woods needed to invoke all of his powers of patience.

"That's where experience helps," he said. "I've been through it with Butch and I've been through it with Hank. I've been through it before, and it's taken some time, and I understand that. I have no problem with that, as long as I keep making progress along the way."

The problem for Woods was the immense amount of attention he received. He didn't win for a year on the PGA Tour. If Mickelson missed a cut, there was far less fanfare. Anyone else? It's part of the game.

Woods posted just two top 10s to that point in 2010. His 3-under par rounds to finish the Deutsche Bank Championship the week prior were the first time he strung together three in a row since the preceding year's Tour Championship. And every time he missed a fairway, the sirens started blaring.

A swing change is a complicated deal, even for Woods, which suggests he might not necessarily pile up the hardware with the amazing frequency of the past.

"When you're out there on the golf course playing, it's understanding how to fix it," Woods said. "That's the hardest part. You can do it on the range. You get into a rhythm or whatever it is and hit ball after ball after ball, but out here on the course, you hit a couple bad ones, how do you fix it?

"And knowing the answer and being confident in the answer, that took a lot of time with Butch and it took some time with Hank, and it's taken some time with Sean, but not quite as long."

Unlike his arrangement with Haney, Woods shared Foley with his peers. Foley, a Canadian instructor who relocated to Florida, taught the likes of Stephen Ames, Sean O'Hair, Hunter Mahan, Justin Rose, and Parker McLachlin. Foley said it would be no problem fitting Woods in.

"You don't need [exclusivity], it's not necessary, because you don't need that much time, especially when you live in the same area code," Foley said. "It's perfect."

Whether or not their work would turn into the kind of perfection Woods displayed previously was part of the intrigue.

DESPITE HIS TRAUMATIC SUMMER OF GOLF, WOODS SLOWLY BE-gan to show some signs of progress under Foley. Although he didn't contend in any of the remaining PGA Tour events—and missed qualifying for the Tour Championship for the first time in his career (non-injury division), Woods was one of captain Corey Pavin's picks for the U.S. Ryder Cup team.

There was actually some consternation over this, a feeling in some places that Woods didn't deserve the pick. His game was not great, and there was a suggestion he might be a distraction.

But once Woods professed his desire to be part of the U.S. team that took on Europe in Wales—and showed some semblance of form—it was a foregone conclusion that he would be picked.

And as it turned out, there was more quibbling about Pavin's fourth pick after Woods, Stewart Cink, and Zach Johnson: Rickie Fowler. The PGA Tour rookie hadn't won anything to that point. He became the first U.S. captain's pick who never won a tournament. He did not even finish among the top 30 in his previous four events and produced no top 10s since early June.

Pavin picked him anyway, which made the Woods choice seem tame.

As it turned out, both players were positives in another U.S. defeat.

Woods played three more tournaments the rest of the year and did quite well. He finished fourth in defense of his Australian Masters title and then lost in a playoff at the Chevron World Challenge to reigning U.S. Open champion Graeme McDowell at the tournament Woods hosted for his foundation.

All in all, it seemed as if Woods was putting his personal woes behind him, at least as far as his golf was concerned.

But the early part of 2011 saw no building on that success. In his first appearance at Torrey Pines since winning the U.S. Open in 2008, Woods tied for 44th. He went to Dubai and tied for 20th. He lost in the first round of the WGC-Accenture Match Play Championship. He tied for 10th at Doral but was a mediocre T24 at the Arnold Palmer Invitational.

All these places where he found success in the past and he was having none now.

It set up for an odd Masters for Woods, who was hardly a prohibitive favorite but clearly on everyone's mind again.

A second-round 66 seemingly put him right there; a third-round 74 seemingly knocked him out of contention. But the golf he played that Sunday was the kind many took for granted, the kind many came to expect.

Woods made an exhilarating charge, one that stalled on the back nine and was ultimately too little. Woods shot 5-under-par 67 and twice held a share of the final-round lead but ultimately could not keep it going, missing several key putts.

"Absolutely," Woods said when asked afterward if he left a few shots on the Augusta National course. "I should have easily shot 3- or 4-under on the back nine. I was right there in the thick of it."

Woods birdied the second and third holes but seemed to stall with a bogey at the fourth. At that time, he still was well behind third-round leader Rory McIlroy. But as the Northern Irishman began a gradual decline (McIlroy shot 80 that day), Woods kept moving up. He birdied the sixth and seventh holes, and when he knocked it on the green at the par-5 eighth and drained an eight-foot eagle putt, the tremors were felt throughout Georgia. Woods was right there.

He made an amazing par save at the ninth and was still at 10-under par when he hit his tee shot in the middle of the green at the par-3 12th. But from there, Woods three-putted—missing a three-footer for par. It was his sixth three-putt of the week.

And it would prove to be huge, especially when Woods could not make birdie at the par-5 13th, where he knocked his second shot over the green. At the 14th, he missed a 10-footer for birdie. Then, at the par-5 15th, Woods nailed a 6-iron approach from 207 yards, stopping it six feet from the hole. An eagle would have given him the outright lead, but he pushed the putt right and settled for birdie. It turned out to be his only birdie on the back nine.

"I hit it good all day," Woods said about just the second tournament this year in which he played his way into Sunday contention. "I hit it good all weekend. I got off to a nice start, turned in 31. The back nine I should have capitalized more."

South African Charl Schwartzel birdied the final four holes for the victory, winning by two over Australians Adam Scott and Jason Day. Woods tied for fourth, four back, and could look at that missed eagle putt on the back nine and the three-putt greens as his demise. He had now gone 17 months since his last victory at the 2009 Australian Masters.

Since returning after a self-imposed five-month break to deal with his personal issues in 2010, Woods' best finishes were a tie for fourth at the 2010 Masters and a tie for fourth at the 2010 U.S. Open.

The outcome at the 75th Masters was his best of 2011, just his second top 10 finish. Woods now saw 11 major championships without a victory pass, the longest major-less streak of his career.

But as it turned out, Woods faced bigger issues.

UNBEKNOWNST TO THE WORLD OUTSIDE OF WOODS' CIRCLE, HE suffered knee and Achilles injuries while hitting a shot from pine straw during the third round of the Masters. Woods made no issue of the problem either Saturday or Sunday, showed no obvious physical issues while shooting the final-round 67, and left everyone believing that his tie for fourth was a step toward returning to past glory.

Instead, two days after the Masters, Woods announced that he suffered those injuries and would be out of action. He ended up returning in May at the Players Championship, where he hit his first practice shots since the Masters on Monday of tournament week, and played just 18 holes of preparation.

Woods said that his injuries prevented him from hitting balls or playing until that week but that he was competing in the Players Championship because he needed the work to get ready for the following month's U.S. Open at Congressional Country Club outside of Washington, D.C.

"The whole idea is that I peak four times a year, and I'm trying to get ready for Congressional, and I need some playing time," Woods said, referring to the four major championships and the U.S. Open venue. "I missed playing last week [at the Wells Fargo Championship] at a golf course I truly love playing, but I really want to get out there and play and compete. This is a big event, and I want to be here and play."

He wasn't at the Tour's signature event long.

Those knee and Achilles issues were apparently still a problem. Woods shot an ugly 42 for the first nine holes at TPC Sawgrass, including a triple-bogey 7 on the fourth hole. He was clearly limping and withdrew from the tournament.

"I'm having a hard time walking," Woods said after his brief appearance that saw him hit just one green in regulation and make no birdies.

To that point, it was just the fourth time in Woods' pro career that he withdrew from a tournament after starting it. This time Woods was unable to make it to the 10th tee, and given his lack of practice and the way he looked, it was not surprising. He winced on several tee shots.

"The knee acted up and then the Achilles followed after that and then the calf started cramping up," Woods said. "Everything started getting tight, so it's just a whole chain reaction."

And it's around this time that Woods' injuries started to become a consistent problem. He missed two major championships in 2008 due to the ACL reconstruction. Now he faced more time away, possibly due to something that wasn't even apparent at the time.

Not only did Woods injure the same knee but he also injured his left Achilles—different from the one he injured in 2008–09.

"This morning, felt fine during warm-up, and then as I played, it progressively got worse. . . . The treatment's been good. It's been getting better. It just wasn't enough."

Woods said his doctors told him it was fine to play, that he wasn't risking further injury. "The more rest I get, the better it would be, obviously," he said. "Obviously it's a big event. I wanted to come back for it and play, and unfortunately I wasn't able to finish."

IT IS NOT A STRETCH TO SAY THAT THE INJURY INDIRECTLY LED TO the breakup of another longtime relationship, one Woods enjoyed with his caddie, Steve Williams. It's possible their partnership would not have lasted beyond the summer; player-caddie agreements come and go.

But this was such a unique and successful bond that it seemed it would never end. Woods' physical issues set in motion a chain of events that led to their split.

Woods and Williams were together for 12 years to that point, a rare occurrence in player-caddie relationships. Of course, Mickelson and his caddie Jim Mackay were in their 19th year working together, a tandem that would last a quarter century.

Although it could be argued that both players would have achieved the same level of success no matter who was on the bag, there is undoubtedly a benefit to such longevity, a comfort level that served both well.

And so the notion that Woods was having issues with his caddie became a big story.

As the U.S. Open approached in June, Williams thought that Woods was going to play. Not only did he make plans to travel from his home in New Zealand but his father-in-law, Ian Miller, had also made plans to be on the East Coast for the AT&T National—the tournament Woods then hosted on behalf of his foundation—two weeks later.

Williams understandably assumed that if Woods could play the U.S. Open, he'd be competing in his own tournament soon after.

But after Williams had already traveled to the United States, Woods announced he would be skipping the U.S. Open (Woods didn't return to action for nearly two months). Williams believed he could have been given more information, but he understood that if Tiger couldn't play . . . well, he couldn't play.

With that news, Adam Scott came up with an idea. If Williams was not working, could he work for Adam?

Scott ran it by Williams, who in turn reached out to Woods to ask for permission. Woods said yes, and Williams would attend the U.S. Open after all.

Then, according to Williams, Woods changed his mind. His agent, Mark Steinberg, called Williams to deliver the news. And Williams was disturbed.

Williams had given his word to Scott, and Williams had made plans to not only travel to the United States but also stay on to work at Congressional. He didn't like the idea of going back on his commitment.

"At that stage, I'd said yes to Adam on the basis that Tiger had given me his blessing and wasn't about to turn around and tell Adam that Tiger had reneged," Williams wrote in his book, *Out of the Rough*.

Williams said that Woods was ultimately fine with the decision, and perhaps that was the case. But he pushed it further when he asked to caddie for Scott at the AT&T National. With his father-in-law attending, Williams figured it would be nice to work again.

After first saying yes, according to Williams, Tiger changed his mind.

"I was furious," Williams said in his book. "I thought it was selfish of him to stop me doing this. My father-in-law had taken time off work to go on this trip; it was all planned. If he'd have been a real friend he would have understood. We were at a stalemate. I wasn't going to budge and he was digging in his heels."

Although there was some dispute about the actual wording and timeline, that decision effectively ended their time together. Williams said Woods told him they were done if he proceeded, and he went ahead and caddied for Scott at Aronimink Golf Club in suburban Philadelphia.

Woods attended the final day as host and met with Williams afterward, effectively firing him. Although those words were not used, Williams believed they were done before that meeting anyway. Regardless, one of the most successful partnerships in golf was stunningly finished.

Williams could understand it coming to an end, as many player-caddie tandems run their course. He couldn't understand it ending in this manner. He took issue with the way he was let go by Woods after 12 years of service—and 13 major championships in which they worked together—especially after he maintained that he stood by his employer in the aftermath of the extramarital affairs that put Woods' golf career on hold.

The split was not announced until after the Open, where Williams again caddied for Scott. Neither party wanted it to be a disruptive situation at Royal St. George's, where Woods missed his second straight major and fourth in four years.

It became a big deal just two weeks later, when Scott won the

WGC-Bridgestone Invitational at Firestone, a place where Woods and Williams registered so much success over the years.

After the tournament, Williams described it as "the best victory of my life," despite having been a caddie for more than 100 wins. In some circles, Williams comments got more play than Scott's victory.

And they carried over into the following week at the PGA Championship, where Woods was doing all he could to distance himself from the mess. Williams, too, backed off, saying he was emotional.

"When we were coming down the stretch, and all those people were calling out my name, I mean, I've never experienced anything like that," Williams said. "And when Adam won, all of a sudden that emotion poured out. But it's time to move on. The Tiger thing is over."

Woods was playing his first tournament since withdrawing at the Players Championship and his game was nowhere near up to standard. He tied for 37th, then missed the cut the following week at the PGA Championship, just the third time as a pro he missed the cut in a major.

A telling exchange occurred at Firestone following the second round where Woods shot 71 and was well back of the leaders. It was just his second full round of golf since the Masters, but his frustration was palpable.

At one point, I tried to ask Woods why his expectations were so high, given that he took a long time off and was coming back from an injury. Wouldn't it make sense to back off those expectations?

"No," he said.

Why not?

"Never have. Why show up at a tournament if you are not there to win? There's no reason to come."

Well, that's admirable, but unrealistic. Everyone, including Woods, needed repetitions in competition. Pro golfers have no minor-league rehab games to hone their skills. And nothing you can do equates to getting inside the ropes in the heat of competition.

Clearly it was a bad idea for me to continue down this road.

"I'm not other guys," he snapped.

Tiger's game remained as dark as his mood.

He failed to qualify for any of the FedEx Cup playoff events, and was done for the PGA Tour season, and yet was still picked to play for the U.S. Presidents Cup team by captain Fred Couples.

The rift with Williams more or less died down until later in the year when Williams took another shot at his former boss at a Friday night dinner in Shanghai as part of the WGC-HSBC Champions.

Williams was receiving a tongue-in-cheek award for "celebration of the year" in the aftermath of Scott's victory. The idea was to poke fun at Williams more than anything else.

And in accepting, he tried to have fun, too, but he went over the line.

"It was my aim to shove it up that Black arsehole," Williams said in "accepting" the award.

The Daily Mail quoted an unnamed caddie in attendance, who said, "Never have you been in a room and seen so many jaws drop at the same time. We knew he [Williams] was an idiot, but we didn't know he was a racist idiot. I was standing next to a European Tour official who said, 'Thank God he is not on our tour.'"

Several media outlets reported the comments, although no reporters were present at the private function, described as a lighthearted evening in which players and caddies alike take some good-natured ribbing.

Williams saw fit to post an apology on his website, admitting that his comments could have been "construed as racist. However, I assure you that was not my intent."

He was on the bag for more than 60 of Woods' worldwide titles, including 13 of his majors. There was the 15-shot victory at Pebble Beach in 2000, the tearful win at Royal Liverpool in 2006 when Woods won for the first time after his dad's death, the epic playoff win at the 2008 U.S. Open.

And yet, Williams described his win with Scott at the WGC-Bridgestone Invitational as "the best week of my life," an almost laughable assertion given the level of success he achieved with Woods—including having won the same tournament at Firestone seven times.

Williams was no stranger to controversy. He endured run-ins with fans and photographers, coming off as a bully. When he referred to Mickelson as a "prick" a few years earlier, that drew a rebuke from Woods and necessitated an apology.

The two met at the Australian Open—where Woods finished third the week prior to helping the U.S. team winning the Presidents Cup—to try and clear the air. But their relationship—Woods was Williams' best man at his New Zealand wedding—was never the same again.

By that point, Woods had already employed veteran caddie Joe La-Cava, the longtime looper for Fred Couples who was working for Dustin Johnson at the time.

Hiring LaCava was like a football owner deciding to go from a tough-guy coach to a player's coach. Their styles and personalities were completely different.

As it turned out, Woods would have a good bit of success with LaCava, too. And in a unique twist, Mackay and LaCava were good friends—something that was extremely unusual in the Tiger-Phil dynamic.

Tiger and Phil might have played the game in completely different ways: Tiger more calculating, Phil more gambling. But both players—despite immense talents and seemingly every reason to believe they could have just about anyone carry their golf bag—saw the value in having an experienced, loyal caddie.

Woods sought out the best in the game at three different times in Mike Cowan, Williams, and LaCava. Mickelson hired Mackay almost sight unseen but immediately took to him and trusted him for 25 years. When they decided to part in 2017, whom did Phil hire? His brother, Tim, a good player himself and a former golf coach at Arizona State.

It didn't hurt that Williams' own venom toward Mickelson was right there on the surface. He didn't hide it, and that friction only helped to heighten the interest in the two guys who hit the shots and made the putts.

17

Double or Nothing

Phil Mickelson owns a mischievous side that is every bit as sharp as his short game. The stories are endless, going back to his youth, such as the time he took a few bucks off an unsuspecting junior player who didn't realize until after their match that Lefty, already a name in the game, was the one who coyly set him up.

When Tiger Woods lost a practice round wager to Mickelson at the 1998 Nissan Open that made him reach for five $100 bills to pay off his debt, it was Phil who wasn't satisfied with the victory. He made copies of the precious green tender, wrote a note to Woods mocking him by saying the "Benjis" were very happy in their new home, put it in Tiger's locker, and reveled in his ingenuity.

Woods, perhaps not so amused, never played a practice round with Mickelson again for 20 years.

And he was never the practice round huckster like Lefty, who enjoyed such merriment.

This was in keeping with the miles-wide chasm between the two, and it wasn't likely they were going to start getting chummy during practice rounds.

Mickelson always loved the interaction with other players and was certainly keen for the heart-bumping action that such money games produced. Even into his fifties, Phil reveled in setting up such encounters, often taunting his prospective opponents on social media.

Tiger wouldn't want to give Phil the satisfaction. And for the majority of his career, he was a practice round loner, preferring to toil on his own with his caddie and coach, only later embracing more practice round partners.

But during the 2012 AT&T Pebble Beach National Pro-Am, Woods had no choice but to play with Mickelson. It wasn't a practice round, but the real thing. The last day, the final round of a PGA Tour event, with a tournament title at stake.

Mickelson was an annual commitment to the event, playing a venue he loved, a place where his grandfather, Al Santos, once caddied. Woods loved Pebble, too, and saw some spectacular success there. He won the AT&T in 2000, rallying to win from seven shots down on the back nine, and then won the U.S. Open there the same year, an epic victory that saw him prevail by a record 15 strokes, the only player to complete 72 holes under par.

After 2001, Woods vanished from the Northern California tournament until 2012. He didn't much care for the long rounds with amateurs in every group, the bumpy Pebble Beach greens, the often cool, sometimes rainy, temperatures. Despite growing up in California, Woods typically couldn't wait to get to Florida, where the greens were smooth and the temperatures warm.

Woods was at a different stage in his career in 2012. Aside from winning the Chevron World Challenge the previous December—the 18-player unofficial event that benefitted his foundation—Woods was going on 29 months without a victory on the PGA Tour.

To start that year, Woods ventured to the United Arab Emirates where he received a hefty seven-figure appearance fee in the $2 million range—the largest since emerging from his personal issues two years prior—to play in a European Tour event, the Abu Dhabi HSBC Championship.

When he signed up for the Australian Open a few months prior, Woods normally could have expected to receive the GDP of a small nation in order to get him there. It was prior to the Presidents Cup in Melbourne, and captain Fred Couples offered him an at-large pick with the not-too-subtle hint to play in Australia's national championship the week prior, with or without a big payday. Woods had little leverage at that point, anyway, and "settled" for a reported $1 million, a fee his agent, Mark Steinberg said would "never again" happen.

In other words, you're getting Tiger cheap. Enjoy. (After holding a share of the 36-hole lead, Woods settled for a third-place finish, two strokes behind Australian Greg Chalmers.)

At Abu Dhabi Golf Club two months later, Woods, of course, was the big attraction. This time, he shared the third-round lead but faltered in the final round and finished two shots behind an English journeyman named Robert Rock and another shot behind Rory McIlroy, in a tie for third. After a third-round 66, Woods could manage just an even-par 72 on the last day, his inability to close costing him a chance at that elusive victory.

Another chance awaited at Pebble Beach. Woods committed in part because he skipped Torrey Pines that year and wanted to get in a West Coast event. Also, Tony Romo—the Dallas Cowboys quarterback—put on a recruiting effort to get him to play as his partner in the pro-am format.

The event has a pro player with his amateur partner playing for three rounds over three courses—Spyglass Hill, Monterey Peninsula, and Pebble Beach. After 54 holes, there is a cut to the low 60 pros and the low 25 amateur teams. Woods and Romo qualified for the amateur portion as well, as did Mickelson and his partner, Skip McGee, a Barclays executive who found himself in the midst of golf royalty, an NFL star, and a national TV audience that had to wonder how *that* golf swing ever became part of this group.

The scenario of a final-day pairing came together on Saturday afternoon well after Woods and Mickelson finished. Movement on the leaderboard caused a shuffling in the order of play, the stars aligned, and Tiger and Phil ended up in the same final-day foursome. It was the 30th time in their careers that they were in the same group. Woods led in those head-to-head matchups 13–12–4.

More important to both was winning the tournament title, and they would be chasing Charlie Wi, who shot 69 at Spyglass Hill to take a three-shot lead over Ken Duke into the final round, to be played at Pebble Beach.

Those two players combined for exactly zero victories on the PGA Tour. The Woods-Mickelson tally to that point was 110.

Woods was four strokes back after a 67 in third place, with Mickelson two more strokes behind and tied for fourth with Kevin Na, Dustin Johnson, Brendon Todd, and Hunter Mahan. Woods' victory drought was a big topic, but Mickelson wasn't racking up victories either. He won the year prior in Houston but failed to overtake Woods for the No. 1 ranking and had just that lone victory in his last 37 starts. He was stuck on 39 PGA Tour wins.

"I know that I'm quite a few shots back," Mickelson said after his round. "But I also know that this golf course you can come out and get a quick start, make some birdies, and when that happens, it's tough to follow suit a few groups behind. So I'm in a nice situation where if I can get a hot hand early, I can make a run on the leaderboard."

At the time he said those words, Mickelson could have no idea he'd be firing at flags with Woods part of his audience.

FOLLOWING THE THIRD ROUND, CBS'S JIM NANTZ HOSTED A LAV-ish party at his home, which borders the Pebble Beach course—and even has a replica of the par-3 seventh hole. All manner of players and celebrities were in attendance. Among them that night prior to the final round were Mickelson and Romo—who would later retire from the NFL and become Nantz's broadcast partner on CBS's NFL games.

"Romo has been a friend for a long time, long before we started working together," Nantz recalled. "I've hosted that dinner for over a quarter century, sort of in the spirit of [Bing] Crosby. Bring a lot of people together from different realms. Have some fun, a lot of laughs. It's a good name-dropping event. Clint [Eastwood] comes every year. Through the years, I've had any number of people: Tom Brady, Peyton Manning. Ray Romano. Rush Limbaugh came one time. Aaron Rodgers, a lot of entertainers. And Mickelson comes every year."

In 2012, Nantz invited Romo and his wife, Candice. "And I sit Tony next to Phil," Nantz said, all but looking for trouble.

Romo already knew how this was going to look. He was sleeping with the enemy on the eve of their big showdown. And so Romo made it clear to Candice, "You cannot say anything to Tiger. Tiger cannot know. It would crush him."

The next morning was cool and cloudy. On the range, no words were spoken as pros with a smattering of amateurs warmed up. Mickelson was all business and acted as if he didn't know Romo.

"They get to the first tee, everybody strikes their shot, and Tony is walking down the pathway with Tiger," said Nantz, summarizing the banter. "And all of a sudden he hears Phil say, 'Hey, Tony. Hey, Tony. That was a great time last night. I really enjoyed dinner with you. It was fantastic.' And Tiger glared at him. Tony said, 'Uh, that was Jim Nantz's dinner. Jim hosts this dinner every year. I didn't know he was going to be there.'

"So Phil catches up to him and says, 'We had so many laughs. I loved that story about this and that. Like you said, we've got to get together.' Phil is smearing it in. And if you remember, Phil was lights out the first seven holes. He was 5-under through six. And as we were coming on the air, Tiger was 1-over through eight, and Phil was 5-under through eight."

Even if he didn't get under Tiger's skin, Phil still enjoyed trying to do so.

It was a fun day. Maybe not for Tiger. Well, absolutely not for Tiger, who couldn't get off the Monterey Peninsula fast enough and didn't return to Pebble Beach again until the 2019 U.S. Open.

But big picture, the Tiger-Phil dynamic was as good as any 17-Mile Drive vista. Mickelson more than lived up to his end during the final round; Woods did not. Just having them in the same group—even if the amateurs were unsightly nuisances during the final round—was welcome and not to be taken for granted.

For a generation plus, they were the face of golf, combining to win 112 PGA Tour events and 18 major championships to that point. And while it wasn't a duel like they produced at Doral back in 2005, it was compelling, nonetheless.

Few saw this kind of drubbing coming: Mickelson waxing Woods by 11 strokes, 64 to 75, and cruising to his 40th career PGA Tour title to move into ninth-place all time, ahead of Tom Watson and Cary Middlecoff. Mickelson came from six strokes back to win by two. He shot the lowest score of the day by three shots. He didn't make a bogey and twice made long putts to save par.

"Phil's a big-stage kind of guy," said Mickelson's caddie Jim Mackay. "I think it's fair to say that he enjoys what you saw out there today. He loves playing with Tiger. He loves having the chance to win tournaments. I think he gets fired up to have everybody watching.

"He has so much respect for Tiger, as obviously everybody out here does. He's close with Joe [LaCava, Woods' caddie], as I am. We know it's going to be fun. There's going to be a lot of people watching. It's a big stage. And that's what he likes. The one thing that has always impressed me about him is how comfortable he seems when there is a lot going on."

So imagine just how big that stage was for McGee. He was an executive with Barclays from Houston and thrust into the limelight, as nerve-racking a stage as any amateur golfer could imagine.

They made the cut to 25 teams, and there was McGee in the middle of the madness, actually playing his 15-handicap brand of golf alongside Mickelson, Woods, and Romo for the world to see with a real tournament title on the line.

"We'd be walking down the fairway talking about the economy, about work, about Barclays, about his golf course projects," McGee said of playing with Mickelson. "He's just a very engaging guy. I had to snap out of it at times to remember how big this was. It was such a privilege.

"It was very unique. I'll treasure this forever. It's something I'll tell my grandkids about."

No doubt. But it did provide an odd backdrop to the Tiger-Phil duel. While the tournament's tradition is based on the amateur format, it can get a little uncomfortable having guys chopping it around inside the ropes while the big boys are playing for the tournament title.

It certainly didn't bother Mickelson, and Woods has dealt with this kind of thing forever, though not as often during actual tournament rounds. But Romo is a scratch golfer who played quite well on the final day and was used to the commotion. And yet there was Woods, trying to win his first tournament in more than two years, his game seemingly trending toward that sort of breakthrough victory, and he was helping Romo read putts? Bizarre.

Woods never seemed into it. Early on, even when he was right in the tournament, he appeared lethargic, lacking energy. Woods seemingly found an opening when Wi four-putted the first green, but Tiger struggled with his own putting problems, hitting a ghastly birdie putt at the second from five feet that barely sniffed the hole. And he never got comfortable on the greens.

Asked afterward if he was ill, Woods said no, that he simply was walking slow, taking his time to deal with the inevitable pace-of-play issues that haunt the tournament because of its amateur format.

"There's no need to rush, no need to do anything quickly," he said. "So I just took my time, and unfortunately, I had to take my time on a lot more shots than Phil did."

That might have been the only time Woods laughed all day, and shooting the highest score of any player inside the top 49 certainly contributed to his mood. He missed five putts inside of five feet and took 31 for the day and dropped from third to a tie for 15th.

But even as late as the par-3 12th hole, there was a glimmer of hope, as Woods holed a bunker shot for a birdie while Mickelson found himself in trouble for the first time all day after a poor approach and an indifferent chip shot. Mickelson faced a 40-footer for par, and a bogey would mean Woods would be just three behind with six to play.

Of course, Phil drained it—just as he did a long par putt at the 15th while Woods couldn't make a four-footer.

It was that kind of day for Tiger, but it still didn't deter the fans, who seemed eager to see him back competing for such titles. They cheered him right up until the end, when he knocked it on the green in two at the par-5 18th. Woods, of course, three-putted for par, while Mickelson made his eighth birdie of the day to cap a memorable victory.

It improved Mickelson's overall record in head-to-head matchups against Woods to 13–13–4, including 8–3–1 since 2007. Phil used to suffer at Tiger's hands, but not so much anymore, something that was a source of great glee, even if he tempered his gloating in post-round comments.

"I feel like he brings out the best in me," Mickelson said. "But it's only been the past five years. Before, I got spanked pretty good. Let's not forget the big picture here: I've been beat up."

So had everyone. On that day, it was Tiger who took the beating, in shocking fashion.

_____

MICKELSON SIMPLY LOVED THAT KIND OF THEATER. HE LOVED THE game inside the game. He loved the action.

That's why a friendly Tuesday practice round among other Tour friends was more than just a game with buddies—especially if there were monetary stakes. Over the years, Mickelson often waged these battles as if they were the real deal on a Sunday. And his theory was that it toughened him. If you are playing for something early in the week, you're not going through the motions. You're preparing yourself for what lays ahead.

He also loved getting into the pockets of his peers; he was never one to let them out of a bet. Mickelson could dish the dirt with the best of them, but he also had the thick skin to endure the ribbing if he was on the short end.

And so there are dozens of stories of Phil putting together money matches, at regular Tour events, at majors, wherever. As his career progressed, he'd often recruit some of the younger players, seeing himself as a mentor who might help them learn to play under pressure while also having some fun at their expense.

One time, Mickelson engaged a couple of players in a match at the Open that was pure stroke play but the stakes were £1,000, and the players had to pay that sum to those who finished better than them. In essence, if you finished last among three players, you were paying £2,000. One of the players balked, wanting to make the wager more reasonable, like £100.

Mickelson wasn't having it. "If you can't play for a couple thousand dollars of your own money, how are you supposed to play for over $1 million when you're trying to win the tournament on Sunday?" Good point, Phil.

Among the highlights is a story from the 1999 Masters, where Mickelson teamed up with John Huston, a seven-time PGA Tour winner who earned his own reputation for early-week prowess.

Mickelson and Huston teamed up for some time in these sort of practice round matchups, becoming quite the bandits. Huston, known for his hot streaks (he once shot the tournament record at the Hawaiian Open and set a low-round scoring record at Muirfield Village, home of the Memorial), could make a bunch of birdies. On this day, they asked John Daly if he wanted to be part of it. The two-time major winner was more than keen on some action, too, and he was allowed to bring his own partner.

So on the Tuesday of Masters week, Daly showed up with Tour pro Tim Herron and said he'd cover his part of the bet, which was surely more than a few bucks. It was a simple best-ball game, meaning low score of each team counted. And when it got to the 18th hole, Mickelson and Huston had already closed out the match.

Daly asked if they could play the last hole for double or nothing.

Of course, Mickelson and Huston were more than happy to do so.

"Phil was just so into it," Huston recalled. "And losing didn't bother him. He enjoyed the winning so much that the losing was okay because he just enjoyed beating us way more. Still does."

Playing Augusta National's 18th hole that day, Daly hit his approach to the par-4 green, with the cup on the front right. He hit it past the pin and saw it spin back to within inches for a certain birdie and what appeared to be a winning hole for him and Herron. That would mean squaring the bet; at worst, the final-hole wager would be halved.

Huston had other ideas. He, too, knocked his approach close. Only it rolled into the cup for an eagle.

"It was that front right pin where it's kind of a funnel anyway," Huston said. "It's amazing people don't hole it more often when it's over there."

Maybe so, but under those circumstances, to make an eagle from the fairway on top of a certain birdie was remarkable. And it spoke to the competitive nature of those matches. Huston recalled the $3,000 that was earned at that point doubling to $6,000.

And it got better the next day.

"Daly came out with David Duval, who was No. 1 in the world at that time," Huston said. "It was pretty interesting."

Daly figured he'd found a ringer and was willing to double down on his efforts to recoup the prior day's losses. Mickelson and Huston were up to that challenge, too.

Huston, who loved the practice round action every bit as much as Mickelson did, was the star on this day. He birdied seven of the nine holes on Augusta's back nine. (How much would any of them pay for that during the actual tournament?) Mickelson eagled both par-5s. They produced a best-ball score of 25 for Augusta's 10th through 18th holes. And they cleaned up on a couple of guys who had to wonder what hit them.

Under the rules of their wager, the losers were required to pay up that day, in cash. And the sum was considerable, even for professional golfers. Huston recalled it coming to $14,000 each, "which back then was pretty big money."

Daly left Augusta National, presumably to get the money, and later came chugging down Magnolia Lane in a Cadillac courtesy car. He noticed Mickelson on the range that bordered the club's entrance at the time, stopped the vehicle, and got out and handed over the money—in a brown shopping bag. The Lords of Augusta National, if they witnessed this display, cringed.

Huston, who was playing in the Par-3 Contest, laughed at the memory of that scene.

But while he teamed up with Mickelson often, they were also adversaries at times, each getting the better of each other. In the 2000 Open at St. Andrews, Huston recalled making "a bunch of birdies in a practice round. Phil claimed I shot 62 or something. He didn't figure that I could play that way in the tournament, so he went to a betting shop [legal in the U.K.] and bet that I would miss the cut. Which I did. So he got all of his money back [that he lost in the original bet].

"That's cruel. And he loves that story. But I always felt playing money games was the best way to practice. And if I lose to Phil, it's a good learning experience. That's how I approached it."

MICKELSON WAS GOOD FOR A WAGER OFF THE COURSE, TOO. IN his early days, he made no secrets about gambling on the Super Bowl or his Fantasy Football team or other types of action.

He also enjoyed putting his prognostication skills to the test.

Mickelson became aware of Jon Rahm, the 2021 U.S. Open winner, before most. His brother, Tim, was the coach at Arizona State when Rahm played collegiate golf and was recruited from Spain, sight unseen. Such was Rahm's promise that Tim Mickelson left his coaching job to become Rahm's agent before leaving that job to caddie for Phil full time.

"This kid is going to be top 10 in the world within a year," Mickelson said just before Rahm turned pro in 2016.

Tour pro Colt Knost was intrigued. Really? Top 10? That's Tiger-type ridiculousness. He knew how difficult that climb to those heights would be. It's a long journey, and while he acknowledged Rahm's talents, Knost also knew there were no guarantees.

"I was like, 'How can you think he'll be top 10?'" Knost told the gambling website The Action Network. "He has no status on the PGA Tour. If he has to play the Korn Ferry Tour [the PGA Tour's developmental circuit], he has no chance."

Mickelson was nonetheless willing to take the risk. And he put the money up to prove it, proposing Knost give him 2–1 odds that Rahm would be a top 10 player in the world by that week in June the next year, 2017. And the sum was enough to make him think about it.

Knost figured it was easy money, and others agreed with him. Then one week later, Rahm finished as low amateur at the U.S. Open, tying for 23rd place at Oakmont.

The following week, Rahm turned pro and tied for third at the Quicken Loans National—which only put him in the top 300 in the world. A month later, after three more starts and a tie for second at the RBC Canadian Open, Rahm jumped to 142nd in the world, and also clinched special temporary membership on the PGA Tour. That meant no Korn Ferry Tour. And Rahm got to 137th by the end of the year.

When he won the Farmers Insurance Open the following January after holing a 60-foot eagle putt on the final green, Rahm was suddenly inside the top 50 just seven months after turning pro.

Now it seemed far more a given that Rahm would make it. By the Players Championship in May, Rahm was 12th in the world. And two weeks later, with Mickelson undoubtedly rubbing his palms in glee, Rahm cracked the top 10 with a second-place tie at the Dean & Deluca Invitational in Forth Worth, Texas.

"It once again shows how smart Phil Mickelson is," said Knost, who would not disclose the amount of the bet. "There was a comma involved," he said. "Let's just say it hurt me more than it helped Phil."

OF COURSE, WHEN YOU ARE TALKING ABOUT GAMBLING, NOT EV-ery story is a happy one. Certainly for all the success, there is bound to be failure. It's the nature of the element and why the bookies drive nice cars.

So surely Mickelson suffered some losses along the way. Nobody keeps records of that, nor is one apt to brag about it.

But when the government gets involved . . .

That's what happened in 2017 when Mickelson was implicated in a three-way insider-trading episode that ended with two people facing prison time and Mickelson getting a big break based on the timing of the case and never having to testify.

Mickelson long before became friendly with Billy Walters, whose complicated life involved an amazing level of gambling success. He was a "professional" gambler in every sense of the word and built a complex system that helped him make millions in Las Vegas.

He was also an avid golfer, and according to a *60 Minutes* episode from 2011, Walters said he won as much as $400,000 playing one hole. He also claimed he earned $1 million playing golf in a single round.

Mickelson and Walters were an interesting match. They are separated in age by approximately 30 years. But they shared a love for golf—and the action.

Lefty's gambling extended beyond golf. Mickelson liked to share stories about bets that went his way. Such as the time he and a group of partners allegedly put $20,000 on the winner of the 2001 Super Bowl and won $560,000. He also apparently won big on the Arizona Diamond-backs to beat the New York Yankees in the 2001 World Series.

Mickelson's gambling was serious enough that in the aftermath of his wife Amy's harrowing pregnancy that saw her and their newborn son nearly die in 2003, Phil pledged to put an end to that risky side of his lifestyle. He stopped gambling on sports and in casinos.

His mother, Mary Mickelson, said Phil wasn't losing huge sums. "But when it came out that he was seen in Las Vegas and supposedly gambling a lot, he said, 'If that's what people perceive, I'll stop.' And he did."

Perhaps the public gambling ceased. But Phil still loved the rush and preparation that playing money golf games gave him. And he still made sports bets, just more discreetly.

According to a 2017 *Golf Digest* story, Mickelson established a sports gambling account with Walters. And in a sworn statement by Mickelson's business manager, Steve Loy, on September 19, 2012, Mickelson paid Walters $1,950,000 to cover a debt "related to sports gambling."

There were other times that Mickelson owed similar amounts, according to Loy's statement, but Phil was also making huge amounts on and off the course. In 2012, for example, *Golf Digest* reported his income from prize money and endorsements to be $48 million. (Through the 2021 U.S. Open, Mickelson earned more than $94 million in official prize money in his career on the PGA Tour, second to the $120 million for Woods.)

Where Mickelson ran into trouble concerned Walters' dealing with a company called Dean Foods. Walters knew Tom Davis, a board member of Dean Foods, one of the largest dairy processors in the country. According to the Securities and Exchange Commission and federal prosecutors, Davis gave Walters inside information about issues impacting the stock price of Dean Foods. As a board member, Davis was committing a crime by divulging such information.

Mickelson got involved, according to the *Golf Digest* story, through Walters. It started in July of 2012, and Walters urged Mickelson to start trading the company's stock, using three brokerage accounts he controlled. When the stock price jumped approximately 40 percent about a week later, Mickelson sold his shares for more than $930,000 in profit. This then allowed Mickelson to repay a debt to Walters.

In 2015, Davis pleaded guilty to 12 counts, including insider trading and lying to the SEC and FBI. And he agreed to cooperate with the continuing investigation. By helping, he was greatly reducing his own sentence, which was a maximum of 190 years.

The situation was murky with Mickelson, who got this information from Walters. But did he receive it from Davis? And if not, was he guilty of committing insider trading?

A different inside-trading case had a significant impact on Mickelson. In 2014, the U.S. Court of Appeals for the Second Circuit, which includes

New York, threw out a conviction in which a person traded stock based on inside information that he received secondhand. It was basically the same position in which Mickelson found himself. According to the *Golf Digest* story, because there was no evidence of what Mickelson knew concerning Davis, he could not be charged under the precedent set by the other case.

So the U.S. Attorney in Manhattan charged only Walters with insider training, although Mickelson figured prominently in the trial as his name was used by the defense to suggest that Walters was too smart to involve a famous golfer in such a scheme.

Prosecutors, instead, built a case that Walters gave Mickelson inside information so the golfer could generate the funds necessary to repay Walters. According to records introduced at the trial, accounts controlled by Phil and Amy made 23 purchases of Dean Foods stock at a total cost of $2.46 million in a single month between July and August 2012. They sold for a profit of nearly $1 million.

Mickelson declined to testify, based on his Fifth Amendment right against self-incrimination. Walters was found guilty on all 10 counts against him.

The SEC named Mickelson as a "relief defendant," meaning that he was not accused of wrongdoing. Mickelson settled by agreeing to give back his trading profits of $931,738 plus interest of $105,291. He neither admitted nor denied the allegations put forth by the SEC.

Mickelson's representatives maintained that the golfer did not know Davis, thus he did not know the original source of the inside information. They point to the "relief defendant" status as indication and that if there was proof Mickelson violated the law, he would have been charged.

According to the *Golf Digest* explanation, a later case rejected the previous one that said that those who received inside information could be prosecuted even if they did not know the original source of the information. Mickelson had fallen inside of a window. He may have been prosecuted if his case came up prior to December 2014 or after December 2016.

In other words, Phil's timing was good as far as how this played out.

Even if he didn't know the source of the tip, Mickelson could have been prosecuted anyway.

Walters was later sentenced to five years in prison and fined $10 million for his involvement. Prosecutors argued that from 2008 to 2014, Walters made more than $43 million from trades of Dean Foods by both realizing profits and avoiding losses.

Twice during the investigation, Mickelson told FBI agents he had no knowledge of insider trading regarding Walters, who wondered why prosecutors never compelled the golfer to testify by offering him immunity.

"Here is a guy that all he had to do was come forward and tell the truth," Walters told ESPN in an interview just before going to prison in 2017. "That was all he had to do. The guy wouldn't do that because he was concerned about his image. He was concerned about his endorsements.

"My God, in the meantime, a man's life is on the line. He's going to go to prison. And you got prosecutors up there during the entire trial, the entire month—all they talked about over and over was me giving my friends insider information. That is all they talked about. And they knew those jurors were all up on the internet reading that stuff about Phil [profiting from the Dean Foods stock purchase]."

Mickelson never appeared in the courtroom, but he was still a big part of the trial. According to the ESPN report, he was mentioned by name at least 122 times during the three-week trial, the majority coming from prosecuting attorneys.

Walters received a commuted sentence from President Donald Trump on his final day in office in 2021. A White House release announced clemency for 143 people, including 70 who received commuted sentences.

As part of the White House release, Mickelson's name was erroneously reported as one of several people who wrote or spoke on behalf of Walters.

Mickelson said he did not write a letter or correspond in any way on behalf of Walters, and his attorney, Glenn Cohen, made a point to set the record straight.

"The reason we are upset is because it's untrue," Cohen said.

MICKELSON NEVER SPOKE IN ANY DEPTH PUBLICLY ABOUT THE
Walters mess. At the very least, he was fortunate to not have been in
bigger trouble. He moved on, and although there continued to be a limited amount of backlash, Mickelson's public image mostly survived what
could have been a major ordeal. Unlike Woods' own scandal nearly a
decade earlier, Mickelson managed to avoid the harsh and unrelenting
scrutiny that played out for months with Tiger.

Phil enjoyed, however, talking up a different, big Las Vegas adven-
ture: a winner-take-all match with Woods.

And it became clear that some of their practice round encounters—
the 2018 Masters, the 2018 Players Championship—were part of a plan
to partner in a business venture that would see them play a series of
matches against each other and with partners.

Their management companies—typically fierce competitors vying
for the same endorsement dollars—came together to put a high-stakes
match in place. It came to be known simply as The Match pitting Tiger
against Phil for $10 million in Las Vegas at the ultra-swanky Shadow
Creek—a golf resort known for catering to gamblers.

But first the PGA Tour needed to sign off. As part of membership,
players assign their media rights to the Tour. That means they can't simply go off on their own and play wherever they want, especially if television is involved. They essentially need permission, in the form of a
release.

And in the case of this event, played the day following Thanksgiving,
the PGA Tour took a role, got a licensing fee, and insisted that the purse
be reduced to $9 million. At the time, the PGA Tour's FedEx Cup cham-
pion received a $10 million bonus and the Tour didn't want any prize
that equaled that. So $9 million it was.

The match got plenty of hype. And 18 holes were not enough to decide the outcome. After one extra hole, they still remained tied, and so
they decided to settle it in true gambling fashion by making a makeshift
20th hole, played from the practice putting green behind the clubhouse
to a newly cut hole on the 18th green.

And they needed to play that three times before Mickelson finally prevailed, holing a four-footer to capture the winner-take-all match, 1-up.

"This has been very special," said Mickelson, who talked up the encounter for months and suggested it would help him get some small measure of satisfaction if he could win after a Hall of Fame career that was still in the shadow of Woods, who at the time had 14 majors and 80 PGA Tour titles.

"I know, big picture, your career is the greatest of all time," said Mickelson, who then had 43 career victories and five majors. "I've seen you do things that are just remarkable. But just know I will not ever let you live this one down. I will bring it up every time I see you. I will wear this belt buckle [another prize for the winner] every time I see you.

"It's not the Masters, it's not the U.S. Open, I know, but it's something. It's nice to have a little something on you."

Woods humbly sat by, taking the good-natured abuse he knew would be coming if he did not prevail.

"I had plenty of opportunities to make putts today, and I didn't make any putts to put a little bit of pressure on Phil," Woods said. "I had an opportunity on the last hole [the first playoff hole on the par-5 18th] to win the match, and I hit a bad putt, and then in extra holes—how do you not hit the green with a lob wedge? Twice?

"So that was an opportunity that went wasted, and Phil capitalized on it."

There were indications that Mickelson was more prepared, having spent several days in the previous weeks at Shadow Creek, including a good part of the holiday week.

Woods was only there for a practice round on Tuesday, then joined his family in Palm Springs, California, for Thanksgiving, and then returned on the morning of the match.

Both players shot 69 in the regulation holes, with Woods making six birdies and three bogeys. Mickelson made three birdies.

"The Match" had its moments, and it was well intentioned. The pay-per-view part of the deal suffered through some technical difficulties, allowing many to stream the event for free.

It is also difficult to believe that Woods wasn't compensated, despite the "winner-take-all" moniker attached to the day. With Woods' management company involved, it's unlikely he was doing something with so much attention and hype for free. Same for Phil.

An obscene amount of money, with a pay-per-view offering and a showdown between a couple of aging golf stars, helped draw plenty of interest. Excellent golf was required to carry the concept, an exciting back-and-forth of eagles and birdies with the longtime legendary rivals outdoing each other.

That did not happen to the degree that was hoped or needed.

At one point, former NBA star Charles Barkley, who was part of the broadcast team, bellowed, "You know, America, you're watching some really crappy golf."

Never mind that it was a worldwide broadcast, and that Barkley—who suggested he could hang with Woods and Mickelson on this day—is as awful at golf as he was great at basketball.

It was an outlandish overexaggeration, but the bottom line was that the golf wasn't compelling, especially considering that they played it on a beautiful course where earlier in the week Mickelson suggested the winner would need to shoot "63 or 64" in order to win the match.

Yes, there was some decent banter between Woods and Mickelson, but it was nowhere near the level of needling expected. As the match wore on, both players reverted to the grinding mode that served them well for the previous two-plus decades. "It's amazing how quiet it gets on the back nine," Mickelson said.

Even for guys who make $40 million-plus in off-course income per year, $9 million for one day gets your attention. And they are competitive, which is part of the reason they've been so successful.

The truth is, Woods appeared rusty and far less motivated to play at his best in a match that Mickelson made no secret about wanting to win.

"In the big picture, nothing is going to detract from the career and accomplishments he's had," Mickelson said of Woods. "For me to have a little something on him like this means a lot to me."

It was an odd end to what was an otherwise extraordinary year, especially for Woods.

Mickelson won the WGC-Mexico Championship, defeating Justin Thomas for his 43rd PGA Tour victory and first in nearly five years.

A week later, Woods contended at the Valspar Championship in just his fourth event following spinal fusion surgery and would go on to contend in two majors and win his 80th PGA Tour title at the Tour Championship.

Both golfers, of course, would go on to enjoy even greater triumphs, far bigger than a contrived made-for-TV gambling exhibition.

18

MUIRFIELD

For the length of Phil Mickelson's professional career to that point, Jim "Bones" Mackay traveled the world, lugging a golf bag and dispensing wisdom through a journey that saw his boss experience the ultimate lows, achieve the ultimate highs, and attain greatness.

But he never cried after a victory.

The tears flowed that Sunday evening in July 2013 in the Scottish mist, a most improbable win for Mickelson completed in stunning, awe-inspiring fashion at treacherous Muirfield in the tiny town of Gullane, where the wind whipping off the Firth of Forth was rivaled only by the way Phil blew past the field.

A final-round 66 closed out a decisive victory at the 142nd Open, with Mickelson coming from five strokes back to win his fifth major championship and capture the game's oldest trophy, the Claret Jug.

The win was beyond gratifying and could have very well capped Mickelson's career if he did nothing else beyond it. He was 43 years old. He'd won the oldest tournament title at a historic place, the course that serves as home to the Honourable Company of Edinburgh Golfers. And it didn't hurt that he overtook Tiger Woods in the process.

"You're with a guy for all that time, and it's pretty cool when you see him play the best round of his career in the last round of the British Open to win," Mackay said. "He played the best round of golf I've ever seen him play."

There have been a lot of great rounds for Mickelson in a Hall of Fame career, but the round played that day was extra special. He needed just 26 putts to match the best round of the tournament, but was the only player in the last 11 groups to break 70—and he did so by four strokes.

He birdied four of the last six holes and closed with a back-nine 32 to claim the third leg of the career Grand Slam. To that point, Mickelson had won the Masters three times, a PGA Championship, and an Open, meaning he needed a U.S. Open to have a victory in all four majors.

Mickelson's picture-perfect round looked even sweeter when compared to the struggles of those he chased for most of the day. Third-round leader Lee Westwood shot 75 to drop into a tie for third. Hunter Mahan, who played in the final group with Mickelson just a month earlier during Phil's heart-breaking sixth U.S. Open runner-up finish, was two strokes back of Westwood to begin the day, shot 75, and tied for ninth.

Adam Scott, who led into the back nine, made four straight bogeys to shoot 72 and tie for third along with Ian Poulter, who was one of the few to make a move, shooting a final-round 67.

Then there was Woods, who with Mahan was just two strokes back entering the final round and in prime position to end the major-less void that now reached five years. But he could manage no better than a 74—eight shots worse than Mickelson—tied for sixth, five shots back.

Not only did he see his winless streak in majors stretch to 17 but he also saw Mickelson celebrating the victory with Bones, Butch Harmon, and his family, including his wife, Amy.

It was the frustrating end to another major for Woods, who showed plenty of form over the previous two years in regaining the No. 1 spot in the world ranking and winning eight times worldwide.

But a 15th major remained elusive.

And it was worse because it was Mickelson who did what Woods could not on that final day. At one point, Woods offered little credit, saying the course was "gettable." He did acknowledge, however, that Phil going so low took some of the sting out as he was the only player in contention to do so.

And yet the closing charge he so desperately needed in the final rounds of a major over the past several seasons went missing again.

Woods was universally hailed for converting 14 of 15 third-round leads to win all 14 of his major championships. But it was mystifying that, when in position, he was never able to overtake a leader to get one.

"Well, I think if it does feel any better, it's that Phil got to 3-[under]," Woods said after finishing at 286, 2-over par. "If he would have posted 1-[under], it would be a different story. I think a lot of us would be a little more ticked than we are now. But he posted 3. That's a hell of a number."

As it turned out, Woods needed a 69 to tie Mickelson, a score not easily attained on this day. The fact that Mickelson bettered that number by three pointed to a remarkable performance on a world-class course under major championship pressure.

Woods produced a solid ball-striking tournament and put himself in the best position to win a major through 54 holes in four years. Still, he started shaky with bogeys on two of the first four holes, leaving himself long birdie putts that he could not lag well enough, leading to three-putt greens. From there it was a game of catch-up that he could never conquer.

"It was frustrating," Woods said. "I played well. I could just never get the speed [of the greens] right today. We started on the first day, and it progressively got slower. And that's usually the opposite at most tournaments. It usually gets faster as the week goes on, but this week was different. And today I had a couple of opportunities to make a couple of putts, and I left them short."

Asked about wanting this one a bit more than others: "I want every one, are you kidding me? I felt like I was really playing well today. Actually the whole week. I really hit so many good shots and really had control of my ball this week. As I said, it was just trying to get the speed, and I just didn't get it."

Woods made no excuses. There was neither a mention of the left elbow injury that affected him a month earlier at the U.S. Open nor a mention of his ensuing break to rest. And he noted that he was able to watch parts of the telecast on that Sunday morning and recognize that the greens were slower and not releasing as they did during the first few rounds.

He didn't make his first birdie until the par-5 ninth, which at the time got him within two strokes of the lead held then by Westwood. But

Woods could not sustain the momentum. He missed the fairway at the 10th and made a bogey, then made another one at the 11th. Birdies at 12 and 14 were too few.

After the Open, Woods had nine top 6 finishes in major championships in the 17 he played since the 2008 U.S. Open, the last of his 14 major titles. He was 25-over par in the third and fourth rounds of major championships in his last seven majors, compared with 8-under in the first two rounds. And his 74 tied his highest final-round score at the Open as a pro.

It led to more questions about the mental hurdles involved in getting to major No. 15, but Woods wasn't going there that day.

"Overall I've been very positive about how I played this week, and the frustrating part, as I said, is I didn't get the speed," he said. "As the greens got slower, I had a harder time adjusting and hitting the putts harder because that first day I think it got to a lot of us that played in the afternoon. They were really quick and they kept getting faster and faster. As the week went on, they got slower."

Mickelson ended up beating Sweden's Henrik Stenson, who shot 1-under-par 70, by three strokes. When he holed a 15-foot birdie putt on the 18th, it was all but over with nearly an hour of golf left to play.

"I didn't know that was out there," marveled Zach Johnson—who tied for sixth—to Mackay afterward, everyone in shock and awe at the score produced by Mickelson.

"I don't care how I got this trophy—I got it," Mickelson said. "And it just so happened to be with one of the best rounds of my career, which is really the way I've played my entire career. I've always tried to go out and get it. I don't want anybody to hand it to me. I want to go out and get it. And today, I did."

Mickelson continued the tradition of high-caliber champions at Muirfield. Going back to World War II, all of the winners at the East Lothian course were in the Hall of Fame, starting with Henry Cotton and followed by Gary Player, Jack Nicklaus, Lee Trevino, Tom Watson, Nick Faldo (twice), and Ernie Els. Mickelson was the first to win the championship while already in the Hall of Fame.

Mickelson may have been coming off a victory a week prior at the Scottish Open, but Castle Stuart is not a links in the same fashion as

Muirfield, which turned brutal despite sunny skies and moderate wind for most of the week.

Mickelson produced a disappointing career at the Open with just two top 10s in 19 previous appearances. He contended two years prior at Royal St. George's and in 2004 at Royal Troon, but generally was frustrated by this style of play.

But the Scottish Open victory gave him a boost and Mickelson sensed a good feeling about the final round, despite being five strokes back.

"He was just so calm and confident," said Amy Mickelson, who brought the couple's three children along to the Scottish Open the week prior before a detour to Barcelona and then to Gullane for the Open. "He's been relaxed all week."

And yet, Mickelson was five strokes back on a course that was not giving much up. Westwood, 40, appeared in good shape to get his first major title, holding steady at 3-under par through six holes. But he never made another birdie and bogeyed four of the last 12.

"I didn't really play well enough today," said Westwood, who has eight top 3 finishes in major championships, the most of anyone without a victory. "I didn't play badly, but I didn't play great. It's a tough course, and you have to have your A-game . . . I said in the press center last night, sometimes you play well and somebody plays a bit better, and sometimes you play poorly. I really didn't do either today, and Phil obviously played well."

When Westwood faltered with a bogey at the eighth, Scott and Stenson joined him in the lead before Scott took it outright with a birdie at the 11th to get to 2-under par. The Australian was bidding to become the first player since Woods in 2005 to win the Masters and Open in the same year.

But two holes later, Scott went on his own bogey binge, bogeying four in a row. A year prior at Royal Lytham & St. Annes, Scott bogeyed the last four to lose the title by one to Ernie Els.

"I let a great chance slip during the middle of the round, and that's disappointing," Scott said. "My game is in great shape, and that's the good thing to take from it, but I didn't get to the number that Phil finished on. Had I played a little more solid in the middle of that back nine, I could have had a chance coming in."

Mickelson barely got a mention on the BBC as he played the first nine, making a birdie at the par-5 fifth and then another at the par-5 ninth to get to even par for the tournament. He then bogeyed the par-4 10th, his momentum seemingly stalled, as he fell four strokes behind Westwood.

But his 5-iron to the par-3 13th changed everything. "It was a putt that was going to make the rest of the round go one way or another," Mickelson said. "Because I just thought if I made it, it would give me some momentum, get me to even par for the championship, a score I thought had a good chance of being enough.

"And that putt went in, and it just gave me a nice momentum boost, because it's very hard to make birdies out here. It was a critical putt."

Mickelson made another birdie at the 14th to get to 1-under and he was tied for the lead when Scott bogeyed the 13th. He made good pars at the 14th and 15th, then saw a big opportunity at the par-5 17th.

Getting to 2-under par would be crucial, as the other contenders were struggling to stay in the game. "That's the moment I kind of had to compose myself, because I hit two of the best 3-woods I ever hit," Mickelson said. "That is exactly why I don't have a driver in the bag. Those two 3-woods were the best shots of the week, and walking up on that green is when I realized that this championship is very much in my control. And I was getting a little emotional."

Mickelson two-putted for birdie to get to 2-under, then hit a 6-iron to the 18th, narrowly clearly a bunker but setting up a birdie putt that he knew clinched the tournament.

It was especially gratifying given his close call a month earlier at the U.S. Open, where he finished second for a record sixth time. "It was tough," said his coach, Harmon. "But you go back to work, and that's what he did. It paid off."

The victory was the 42nd of Mickelson's PGA Tour career and moved him back to No. 2 in the world for the first time since 2010. He still had yet to reach No. 1.

Afterward, Mickelson, as only Phil can do, was calmly talking to reporters beside the 18th green, raving about the 3-wood he loves so much, discussing how he was unsure if he ever had what it took to win this championship, when he suddenly realized he was in demand.

The trophy presentation was taking place on the green—where he was supposed to be—and as Mickelson chatted, his name was being announced as the Champion Golfer of the Year. He walked out, hoisted the Claret Jug, and gave a simple victory speech.

Off to the side, Bones sobbed some more, a man crying tears of joy.

Woods rebounded two weeks later to win the WGC-Bridgestone Invitational, his eighth victory at Firestone. He shot a second-round 61 and went on to win by seven shots, a rousing victory that saw him capture his fifth title of the year.

All was good—until it wasn't.

A week later, Woods played a lackluster PGA Championship, never sniffing contention. And while he didn't tell anyone, he suffered with some back stiffness.

And it was just the beginning of a journey filled with pain.

19

FIFTEEN

Joe LaCava started his 30th year as a caddie in an unusual position: with nothing to do. Like everyone else in the early part of 2016, LaCava was waiting and wondering when Tiger Woods, who'd recently turned 40, might be healthy enough to play competitive golf again.

LaCava, who spent some 20 years working for Fred Couples and various other employers, including Dustin Johnson, went to work for Woods in 2011 at a time when there were considerable questions about the golfer's game.

Asked why he made the move away from an up-and-coming player such as Johnson, LaCava said, "Because he's Tiger Woods."

It was a simple, understandable answer. But now LaCava was on the sideline and out of work. Woods endured not one but two back procedures in the time since he last played at Wyndham Championship in North Carolina nearly six months prior. (Caddies are typically paid a base salary plus commission, but only for the weeks they work.)

"I miss it, for sure," LaCava said a few months into 2016. "I never complain about being home, but I miss working in general. Then when you see a tournament like San Diego come along, a place he owns and you think, 'He's won at this place' . . . that stinks. I miss my buddies, some of the caddies, going out to dinner. But most of all I miss being in the hunt and winning. Definitely miss it, how could you not?"

LaCava, 52 at the time, enjoyed the perks of being at home in Connecticut. He got to see all of his son Joe's high school football games. He was able to drop his daughter, Lauren, off at college near Boston. A big sports fan, he attended numerous Giants, Rangers, and UConn games.

Then there's golf, and instead of caddying, he was playing. Often. LaCava, a 6-handicap, estimated he played as many as 50 rounds from September through November, some at New Jersey courses such as Ridgewood and Baltusrol, where the PGA Championship was scheduled for later in the year. "That's a ton for me," LaCava said. "Some days were 27 holes. And I had a blast doing it. And I'm surprised how many of many friends could take off, you know, guys with normal jobs. I never had trouble filling a foursome."

LaCava joked that he was home so much that his wife, Megan, wanted him out of the house. "Yeah, she's tired of me. That's automatic, isn't it?" he said. "I say that in a funny way. It's been nice to be home for many things."

It was a good bet that he would be home for a good bit longer. Woods' last public appearance was the week of the Hero World Challenge in early December, when his news conference took on a somber tone as he said any accomplishments from this point would "be gravy."

At the time, Woods had yet to begin rehabilitation from surgery, and there was little to indicate that much progress was made.

LaCava heard the negativity in Woods' comments but didn't get the same sense from the golfer when he saw him on two occasions later that month.

They attended a Giants-Dolphins Monday Night Football game together, and then LaCava returned to South Florida to celebrate Woods' 40th birthday on December 30, 2015.

"A week later [after the Hero], and certainly three weeks after, I didn't get that impression at all from him in the two times that I was down there," LaCava said. "When we went to the Giants game, it was guys having a good time. He knows how big a fan I am of the Giants, so he teases me, gives me a hard time. At that point, I know he's a ways from coming back, and I'm not going to press the issue. I want him to take this time. But this was a buddies trip, and in hanging out with buddies, I sense he's very positive about the future."

Still, all those months later, not working for all that time, not sure when you're going to work again . . .

"I understand what you are asking, and what I'll tell you is this: Tiger has been great to me since day one," LaCava said. "And he continues to be great and very generous with me."

LaCava understandably did not want to delve into those details, but as Woods suffered through injuries and layoffs, it was sometimes easy to forget that he'd won nine times with LaCava by his side—each with a first-place check of $1 million or more.

Since going to work for Woods starting at the Frys.com Open in 2011, LaCava caddied for Woods in 64 official worldwide events through 2015—and that doesn't count two Presidents Cups and a Ryder Cup or any corporate activities. During that time, Woods earned more than $16.4 million on the PGA Tour alone, with a pretty good commission going the caddie's way.

But Woods was not making any money on the golf course at that point, so it was fair to wonder if LaCava explored or was asked about any other opportunities.

"A couple of guys approached me—I don't want to name any names—but I said no; I hope it was politely said no," LaCava said. "My plan is to wait for Tiger to get back. I've told them I just want to work for Tiger and nobody else at this point. They were all nice about it; they didn't know what my situation was. I've elected to wait things out with Tiger, and that is my plan going forward."

LaCava enjoyed a long career inside the ropes. He began caddying for Ken Green in 1987. He then went to work for Couples in 1990, the start of a successful partnership that lasted more than 20 years in which La-Cava counted 12 victories, including the 1992 Masters and 1996 Players Championship.

Over the years, when Couples took breaks due to his own back issues that began in 1994, LaCava caddied for the likes of Mark Calcavecchia, Justin Leonard, Mike Hulbert, John Cook, Jay Haas, Bill Haas, and Camilo Villegas.

He stayed with Couples on to the PGA Tour Champions before the golfer encouraged him to go with a younger player who would be able to offer a steadier income. That's when he went to work for Dustin Johnson in early 2011; they contended at the Open that year and also won the Barclays.

But when Woods—who parted ways with Steve Williams earlier in 2011—inquired about his services, LaCava didn't waste much time fretting over the decision. "Because he's Tiger Woods," LaCava said. "It's a no-brainer. That's my thought: it's Tiger Woods, right?"

And that attitude persisted. Even though there were long bouts of inactivity in 2014 and 2015, and into 2016 and 2017 (and later in 2021 after Woods' car crash), LaCava said there were no regrets.

"None whatsoever," he said. "That's meant to be a positive toward Tiger and not a negative toward anyone. We all know what Dustin has done and what he is capable of. It's certainly not a knock on him. But I love working for Tiger. He's been fantastic to me. Generous from the get go. Is it frustrating at times? Of course it is. It is for him. But you can't do anything about those things."

LaCava was among many who were encouraged after Woods' performance at the Wyndham Championship. He tied for 10th after sharing the 36-hole lead, his best finish in 2015. He didn't qualify for the FedEx Cup playoffs. But after a break and more work with his then-instructor Chris Como, Woods was expected to play at least three fall tournaments with an eye toward being fully ready to go in 2016.

It didn't work out that way, as Woods needed a second microdiscectomy surgery September 16 on his lower back (the first was March 31, 2014). A third lower back procedure occurred on October 28 in the same area. Having to do it twice within six weeks seemed more than ominous.

"I was pretty optimistic the way he played, certainly," LaCava said. "I'm right next to him, so I knew he was in more pain than most people. I didn't know it would lead to what it would lead to. I don't know enough about it to talk intelligently; I just know it [back pain] comes and goes.

"But as far as the golf, I thought he played very well. It was looking like full steam ahead. Like I always say, more reps. I just liked the fact he was going to play more golf after the playoffs. I was looking forward to those. I was thinking at the time that he gets four or five weeks off to practice that stuff and start working on his swing and then looking forward to '16."

Now he was looking at a season of inactivity. Woods did not play a single PGA Tour event in 2016. He came back for the Hero World

Challenge in December, where he showed tremendous promise in the 18-player event in the Bahamas.

He then committed to playing the Farmers Insurance Open at Torrey Pines to open 2017, and then the Omega Dubai Desert Classic. Woods also marked down the Genesis Invitational at Riviera.

Those plans quickly went awry. Woods missed the cut at Torrey Pines and didn't look good doing so. Taking the 17-hour journey to the Middle East—even in Emirates Airlines Suite luxury—always seemed a questionable plan, a $2 million appearance fee be damned.

And Woods never looked right in Dubai. The first round saw him walk cautiously from the driving range to the first tee, swing tentatively for the first few holes, get off to a slow start, and never recover.

The result was his worst score in 29 rounds at Emirates Golf Club, a 5-over-par 77 that included no birdies, left him 12 strokes back of Sergio García, and almost assuredly would have him looking at plans to leave for home early.

Despite appearing to be uncomfortable, especially early on, Woods said there were no issues with his back. I asked him directly if he was in any kind of pain—the kind that appeared obvious.

"No, I wasn't in pain at all," he said. "I was just trying to hit shots and I wasn't doing a very good job. At the end, I finally hit some good ones but the damage had already been done. On top of that, I could have hung in there, could have shot something near even par if I would have made some putts, but I made nothing."

To all who watched, it was clear Woods was not being honest. Not in pain? The guy could barely move, and the way he swung the club suggested caution. He shuffled around the course like a 75-year-old man. He swung tentatively. Something was amiss. And sure enough, the next day he withdrew, citing a back spasm suffered the night prior at dinner.

His agent, Mark Steinberg, said the issue was not related to the back pain and nerve issues that plagued him for so long, but the long view makes that answer look preposterous. Still, then, it was viewed with relief. If it was something different from the usual back issues, maybe he'd be okay. There was even talk that Woods would be able to keep his commitment to the Genesis Invitational in a few weeks' time.

But that didn't happen. And neither did the Arnold Palmer Invitational or the Players Championship. Or the Masters. For the second consecutive year and third in four years, Woods missed the year's first major championship.

And as it turned out, that tournament week became a huge turning point that would make or break his career.

NOBODY EXCEPT PERHAPS HIS CLOSEST ADVISORS AND FAMILY—and some astute players who were there—knew just how bad it was for Woods when he arrived at Augusta National in April of 2017 to attend the Champions Dinner on Tuesday night of tournament week.

Woods needed help to be there and was in considerable pain. He told some of the past Masters champions that his career might be over. For three years now, he'd been dealing with nerve issues in his lower back. He had three procedures. He took nearly all of 2016 off, and here he was again, unable to play and unsure if he ever could again.

Something was bound to give, and Woods was finally convinced he needed to explore some other options. That is why he made plans to leave from Augusta that night and head to London for a consultation with a team of specialists who would give him some ideas on how to proceed.

Earlier that day, Woods met with CBS's Jim Nantz, who conducted an interview with the then-four-time Masters champion that was recorded and produced for Augusta National and never to be aired, meant for the club's archives.

Knowing what he knew based on that interview, Nantz could never envision what occurred two years later.

"I thought he was uncomfortable," Nantz said. "His every movement I thought brought pain. We sat down and I can't tell you how long it went. He just did a good job on that interview. He was so openhearted.

"There was a sense of resignation in his voice. He was talking in the past tense. He wasn't looking forward. He was reviewing his career at Augusta as if it had been completed. That's what struck me most of all. He wasn't talking like he was still in the game at Augusta. He was reviewing what he had done there without leaving any sliver of any indication of hope that he was going to be coming back there. He didn't say he was done. He talked like someone who was reviewing his playing days as if they were final.

"With all the highs and lows he had to live with and being very public in his life, I think the lowest of the lows for him was probably that very night: coming to the Champions Dinner and having to turn around and leave. From a golf perspective, it had to be the lowest of lows. He felt a sense of being done."

Woods attended that dinner needing a nerve blocker to deal with the pain, and the specialists in London suggested spinal fusion surgery, an operation that would remove the offending disk while "fusing" the spine at the location of the injury. The disc would be shaved down, and the fusion would provide more stability but far less flexibility. There were no guarantees.

Just 16 months later, after a rousing performance at the 2018 PGA Championship, where Woods finished second to Brooks Koepka in stifling St. Louis heat, the Tiger comeback was full on. He now contended in consecutive major championships and could easily have won both. A year earlier, he was barely hitting balls.

The resurgence captured golf fans and beyond. It was great theater, and the only disappointing aspect that the Masters was eight months away. Nick Faldo, the CBS-TV analyst and six-time major champion, went on the *Dan Patrick Show* a few days later and relayed a story not yet heard: Woods said at the previous year's Masters Champions Dinner that he felt his career was done.

It is possible Faldo heard the story himself or perhaps from one of the other gossipy past champions. Jack Nicklaus later joked that it was Gary Player who couldn't keep quiet. In any case, what of this story?

Woods' next tournament was the Northern Trust event in New Jersey, and when possible I would try to catch up with him for a few minutes during a practice round or pro-am round.

These were rare, special opportunities to get Woods away from the glare of TV lights and cameras. Our relationship was such that he knew he could speak freely, and often it was simply small talk, asking about families or travel or something otherwise mundane.

At times, I might ask Woods what he was working on, or engage with him and his caddie, LaCava, about trivial matters. If I was working on a story, I made it clear that I was hoping to ask him about something I wanted to use, and he almost without fault was accommodating.

But this Faldo story was different. Tiger hated to show any vulnerability. And he was loath to talk about any of the procedures he endured in great detail. He never disclosed the distress from that 2017 Champions Dinner, but now there was an anecdote out there.

So I mentioned the Faldo interview and wondered if Tiger really said those things at the dinner. Tiger was clearly annoyed, and he could have easily shut it down. But to his credit, despite obviously not wanting to go there, he answered the question with shocking honestly while avoiding the topic of who leaked the info from the dinner.

"At that time, I *was* done," Woods said as we walked one of the fairways at Ridgewood Country Club along with USA Today's Steve Dimeglio, whose ears also suddenly perked up.

"I didn't know what I was going to be doing. I had no golf in my future at that time," Woods said. "I couldn't walk. I couldn't sit. I left from there to go see a specialist about what are my options."

Woods disclosed that upon the advice of Jack Nicklaus, he first visited with a physical therapist in South Florida named Pete Egoscue, but ultimately decided on surgery. And once that decision was made, Woods didn't waste much time. The surgery by Dr. Richard Guyer of the Center for Disc Replacement at the Texas Back Institute was performed on April 19, 2017.

"I wasn't confident; I was having a fusion," he said that day in New Jersey. "At the time, I needed to try and get rid of the pain. It wasn't so much about golf. I tried everything. I tried stem cell; I tried lidocaine; I tried Marcaine, nerve block. Nothing took the pain away."

There were a lot of medical terms and medications I needed to look up.

Woods was told he would need six months for the fusion to take hold and wasn't permitted to swing a golf club during that time. At September's Presidents Cup, where Woods made one of his first public appearances since the surgery and a rehab stint to deal with prescription pain medication issues, he said, "I don't know what my future holds."

"It was not a fun time," Woods said. "Tough couple of years there. But I was able to start to walk again. I was able to participate in life. I was able to be around my kids again, be at their games and their practices. Got to take them to school again. These were all things I couldn't do for a very long time. Golf was not in my future or even in my distant future. Playing the game again, I couldn't even do that with my son Charlie. I couldn't do that in my backyard. After the surgery, I started to feel a lot better."

But a few weeks later, Woods actually felt worse. The affairs that led to divorce, the subsequent shame, the difficult comeback, the injuries, the back surgeries, the spinal fusion—all of it perhaps led to what occurred on May 29, 2017.

Woods was asleep at the wheel of his car in the early-morning hours on Memorial Day. Driving a black 2015 Mercedes-Benz AMG S65, Woods came to rest on the side of a road called Military Trail, some nine miles from his Jupiter, Florida, home. How he ended up there has never been disclosed. There were no reports of him being out that night. A good bit of speculation suggested that Woods was doing the equivalent of sleepwalking—except in a car, driving.

The driver's side and front and rear tires were flat, the rims damaged. So was the front bumper, which had scrape marks, according to the police report. No other vehicles were involved.

The first instinct was to believe that Woods was intoxicated, but lab reports would later show there was no alcohol in his system. He did, however, have enough prescription medication to cause him to fall asleep at the wheel and possibly do further damage if he were not so fortunate.

Woods struggled to get out of his car, and he first told the officer who questioned him that he was in Los Angeles, on his way to Orange County. His speech was slurred, and he nearly fell.

There was a 12-page police report. And there was police video that made its way onto YouTube. It was not pretty. A toxicology report released nearly three months later reported he had painkillers, sleep drugs, and an ingredient active in marijuana in his body.

The five different drugs that were traced in his system were hydrocodone, an opioid pain medication; hydromorphone, another type of painkiller; alprazolam, an anxiety drug sold under the brand name Xanax; zolpidem, a sleep drug sold under the brand name Ambien; and delta-9-tetrahydrocannabinol (THC), which is found in marijuana.

Weeks before the report was released, Woods announced he would take part in a rehabilitation program.

"I'm not at liberty to say where he is, but he is receiving in-patient treatment," Steinberg, his agent, said when this sensitive subject was broached. "Tiger has been dealing with so much pain physically. And that leads to insomnia and sleep issues. This has been going on for a long time."

On May 24, in Woods' first extensive comments since the fusion surgery, his fourth back surgery in just more than three years, he explained in a website post that he had been dealing with nerve pain that caused quality of life issues.

"It is hard to express how much better I feel," Woods wrote. "It was instant nerve relief. I haven't felt this good in years."

Five days later, Woods was arrested and failed multiple field sobriety tests but blew a 0.00 on a breathalyzer after being taken into custody.

"Was the night in question a tipping point?" Steinberg said. "He's now gone and checked himself into a facility . . . He's been in pain for so long. He's had to handle the pain, which then potentially leads to the lack of sleep because you're in so much pain."

Woods agreed to enter a diversion program that allowed his driving under the influence charge to be dropped later in the year; he also pleaded guilty to a lesser charge of reckless driving.

Eventually, Woods got back to the business of getting healthy. After the Presidents Cup in September, he began slowly posting photos or video on Twitter of him swinging a club or hitting a shot. He sparked interest in his golf again.

Woods said when Guyer gave him permission to finally hit driver shots six months after his spine was fused, the first ones he hit carried barely 90 yards. "I was a little bit apprehensive," Woods said.

His tee shot on the first hole during the first round of the 2019 Masters went 317 yards into the fairway.

And so began one of the most remarkable tournaments ever.

WOODS MADE AN ASTONISHING COMEBACK IN 2018. IN JUST HIS fourth tournament, at the Valspar Championship, he finished second, missing a playoff by a shot. He contended at both the Open (tied for sixth) and the PGA Championship (second). And later that year, with a throng of spectators swarming behind him as he played the 18th hole at East Lake Golf Club in Atlanta, Woods won the Tour Championship for his 80th PGA Tour victory.

He could have retired right there, and his legacy was more than secure with 80 PGA Tour wins, 14 majors, a comeback for the ages.

But there was more to come. And nobody could have predicted the magical week that unfolded at Augusta National over those four days in 2019.

What stood out to Tiger was the noise. He knows it well. The various stages now routine, from a loud whisper to thunderous applause, from the echoes that cascade down a fairway when his name is announced on the first tee to the ear-splitting decibels it reaches when a fist-pumping iron shot lands close to the hole.

Augusta National noise is on yet another level, a polite but cascading rumble through the tall pines, a rolling thunder of clatter from Amen Corner escalating all the way up to the stately clubhouse.

Then there's *the* sound.

The raucous, partying sound that was unmistakable as he put the finishing touches on the most improbable of major championship wins, of his five Masters Tournament victories, of any triumph for that matter.

His 15th major might have been sweetest of all.

The sound can, with the slightest imagination, still be heard on Magnolia Lane and outside the club gates onto Washington Road and throughout Georgia and down to Florida where Woods resides. And certainly the sound can never leave Woods' own mind; it was the memory of a lifetime.

"I had never, ever in all my years of going there and all my years of watching the Masters . . . I had never heard chanting at Augusta National," Woods said in an interview several months later of the continuous "Tiger, Tiger" bellowing that followed him from the 18th green all the way to the clubhouse and beyond. "I get goose bumps talking about it still. The chanting. The amount of support I had. So many people that wanted to see me do it.

"It was special to have that kind of support, that kind of backing. I was going up against the best players in the world. I was trying to come from behind for the first time [to win a major]. And that support was so important."

Woods' Masters win in 2019 resonated in so many ways. It was his first major triumph in 11 years, since his epic U.S. Open playoff victory over Rocco Mediate in 2008 that seemed just another step along the way to Jack Nicklaus' record of 18. It was his first Masters win since 2005, when Woods was not yet 30 years old.

Perhaps most important to him, it was his first with children Sam and Charlie in attendance. They visited Augusta National just once prior, for the 2015 Par-3 Contest.

This was the first glimpse of Dad doing his thing in Sunday red.

Just a day earlier, it was unclear if they would be able to witness the drama that unfolded at one of the most storied places in golf. Had Sam's soccer team won its semifinal tournament game that day in Florida, there would be no trip to Augusta. And Charlie wouldn't be making the journey, either. Alas, the team lost, and Tiger gained a familial audience.

Due to the early Sunday fourth-round start because of the threat of inclement weather, they were unable to make it to the course before Woods teed off in the final round alongside 54-hole leader Francesco Molinari and Tony Finau at 9:20 A.M. Woods struck his opening tee shot into the first fairway unsure when and if they arrived.

"I didn't know until I got to [No.] 7 and I had that little tap in for birdie, and I see Charlie is jumping up and down," Woods said. "And I thought, 'Good, they made it; they made it.' And I didn't see them the rest of the day until 18."

Of course, that's when it all happened, right? When Woods made that birdie at the seventh hole, he was struggling to stay in the tournament. Molinari was a rock to that point, going 49 holes without a bogey. Just like the previous summer at Carnoustie, where Woods could not shake the Italian golfer in their final-round pairing, as "Frankie" went on to win the Claret Jug.

And the likes of Finau, Brooks Koepka, Dustin Johnson, Xander Schauffele, Bubba Watson, and Patrick Cantlay were all in pursuit, further sucking up all the oxygen, Woods' comeback story none of their concern.

Woods made another birdie at the 8th hole and remained just a stroke behind Molinari. He made a miraculous par save at the 9th, bogeyed the 10th, was fortunate to have a shot through the trees at the 11th, and then saw everything change: Koepka, a group in front, then Molinari and Finau beside him, could not avoid Rae's Creek at the par-3 12th.

The splash by Molinari, especially, left more than a ripple in the creek; try ground-shaking madness. And when Woods two-putted from 50 feet for par, he was tied for the lead. Birdies at the 13th and 15th gave him a one-shot advantage, with three heart-pounding holes to play.

And then came that tee shot to the 16th, the 8-iron that landed softly, perfectly on a right-side ridge of the green, then trundled slowly toward the pin, the murmurs growing louder as the ball got closer, stopping just a few feet away. (A highlight reel moment of interest: Olympic swimmer Michael Phelps behind the tee eyeing the tee shot as Tiger hits it and then stares it down.) The birdie putt was but a few feet, so close that when Woods asked caddie Joe LaCava for a read, in the heat of the moment, he said, "Are you kidding me? Knock it in!"

Noise? It was madness, spectators scurrying for position, players on others tees trying to take in the scene, a sporting scene to be cherished and chiseled in the brain.

"The roars were obviously loud, but ironically enough, I've heard that before when I chipped in there," Woods said, referencing his birdie chip from behind the green in 2005 that saw him hit away from the pin and watch the ball trickle . . . ever . . . so . . . slowly . . . into . . . the . . . cup.

"That place was rocking," he said.

Back then, Woods' birdie at the 16th gave him a two-shot lead. But he would bogey the last two holes before prevailing in a sudden-death playoff over Chris DiMarco.

This time, Woods striped his drive on the 17th, then played safely at the 18th, setting up a bogey that would win the tournament by a stroke.

All the while, Woods' mother, Tida, was inside the Augusta National clubhouse, nervous energy and anticipation consuming the room while her son was attempting to finish off the most improbable of major championship victories.

This was far different from that first Masters she witnessed with Tiger's late father, Earl, in 1997 when the final day was a coronation walk to a record-setting win.

By now, her grandchildren had made their way behind the 18th green along with Tiger's girlfriend, Erica Herman; his agent, Steinberg; publicist Glenn Greenspan; and good friend and confidant Rob McNamara.

"After I hit my pitch, I was walking up onto the green, and I could see them in the walkway," Woods said. "I know the tournament's pretty much over, but I remember thinking, 'Let's get it together here.' I saw my mom there . . . and started to get a little weepy."

Woods two-putted, and after knocking in the short putt for victory, he let out a primal yell, pumped his arms and held them aloft as the waft of cheering continued to thwart out all reasonable thought. Among those there to congratulate on the green was LaCava, who was along the way for some of Woods' darkest physical days as he endured the effects of four back surgeries.

And then came the long embrace with Charlie, wearing a backward ball cap, evoking memories of when Woods hugged his own father after winning in 1997, before greeting all of his friends and family and then taking the long, boisterous walk with spectators crammed along the ropes, yelling, screaming, crying.

When Woods finally arrived at the scoring area, he was met by all the players he had just beaten as well as several others who were there to congratulate him and soak in the incredible vibe. Among them were several past Masters champions, all wearing their green jackets, including Trevor Immelman, Bubba Watson, and Bernhard Langer.

The victory produced some of the same emotion Jack Nicklaus provided 33 years prior when he won the Masters at age 46. Woods, at 43, became the second-oldest champion.

"I think this is one of the best sports stories we've ever seen," said Immelman, who won the 2008 Masters—when Woods finished second, the closest he had been to victory at Augusta National since his last win in 2005.

"When I was coming through the ranks, and he was at the height of his game, you always got the feeling that he knew he was the best, you knew he was the best, and that's just the way it is.

"But a couple of years ago, after surgeries and everything else that happened, it was the first time I had ever seen him uncertain. It's a word that I would have never used for Tiger Woods is *uncertain*. To dig himself back from that moment to here is something that is just so special. Special for our game. This is awesome. For my mind, this goes down in the same vein as Jack in '86."

McNamara never doubted. A vice president with Woods' TGR Ventures, McNamara has worked for Woods since 2000 and has become a trusted advisor as the golfer played without a coach.

"I've always been an eternal optimist," McNamara said. "Even before the surgery, I thought if he's standing on two legs, he's still Tiger Woods. He was the best guy with a different swing and a different body at [age] 5, at 10, at 15, at 20. So why not 43 with a bad back? In my mind, I was always optimistic. I know the reality of getting it done is pretty surreal."

Woods made four bogeys in his final-round 70 and nine for the tournament and led the field in greens in regulation, hitting 58 of 72. He also made 22 birdies but no penalty shots. And despite taking 15 more putts than Molinari, he mostly avoided the issues on the greens that plagued him during his comeback.

And for the first time, Woods rallied to win a major championship, having won each of his previous 14 with at least a share of the 54-hole lead.

Following the traditional green jacket ceremonies in Butler Cabin and on the practice putting green, where 2018 champion Patrick Reed helped him slip into the coat, Woods sat before a packed interview room in the Press Building to recount the victory prior to a series of events that took place at Augusta National as part of a whirlwind day.

First, Woods went to the Champions Locker Room—where he shares a locker with 1956 Masters winner Jackie Burke Jr., the oldest living Masters champion.

And then he had his green jacket tailored on the spot. The one he was wearing for the various ceremonies and post-round interviews did not fit just right, and there was no time during the tournament to get it altered.

It was in the Champions Locker Room that Woods would have noticed a note Phil Mickelson left for him. Written on an Augusta National cocktail napkin and left at Woods' locker, it read: "Tiger, so impressive! What a great tournament you played! So very happy for you! Phil."

(Later in the day, Mickelson sent out congratulations via Twitter: "What a great moment for the game of golf. I'm so impressed by @TigerWoods incredible performance, and I'm so happy for him to capture another Green Jacket. Truly a special day that will go down in history. Congratulations, Tiger! #rematch")

Then it was back to Butler Cabin for a 15-minute interview with CBS's Nantz that aired during the rebroadcast of the final round. A cocktail party in the clubhouse followed and then a reception dinner in the Founders Room of the Augusta National clubhouse that included an emotional speech to the members. Woods later posed for photos with every member and spouse who wanted one.

"The thing that was really remarkable about what Tiger did was really how it affected him," said Fred Ridley, the Masters and Augusta National chairman. "We've all watched him win many, many tournaments, and the impact this one had on him was really noticeable. I don't think I've ever seen him so taken by a win.

"I think, perhaps, in years past, it might have been something he expected. I think this was something he probably didn't expect, honestly. It was refreshing to witness the grace in which he accepted that win and the appreciation he showed for the ability to compete. He was remarking in one of the post-tournament interviews that he really didn't know if he was going to be able to play again, and just to be able to get out on the golf course and compete was something very special."

After a few more media obligations, it was time to take the celebration elsewhere.

But given the early start to the day because of impending bad weather that never came, the sun had not yet completely set on the course as Woods exited the clubhouse. It was a surreal scene, Woods recounted, as on the previous four winning Masters occasions, he walked out into late-night darkness.

"I have never seen the golf course empty like that," Woods said. "I was out there with Sam and Charlie, and I said, 'This is what Augusta National is like.' You see the beauty of it. The rolling hills. The perfect grass. It was immaculate.

"It's so different when nobody is out there. That's when they started to understand how beautiful the place is."

And quiet. Blissfully, peacefully, serenely quiet—but with the noise from earlier still ringing in his ears.

20

KIAWAH

Tiger Woods endured nearly as many injuries as he won major championships. And that is in no way meant to make light of the serious car crash he was in on February 23, 2021, that went far beyond any golf issues he ever encountered. It was life-threatening and somber.

Before the accident, Woods was in the midst of another rehabilitation while recovering from a back procedure, his fifth. He had also undergone five knee surgeries in his career. He endured neck and Achilles issues. He once skipped a tournament due to a sore elbow.

Hitting millions of golf balls takes its toll. Golf is not a contact sport, but it is a sport of contact—with the ground. The club hitting the dirt just as it hits the ball. Walking, miles and miles, day after day. Sore feet, sore ankles, sore knees, sore elbows, sore wrists, sore backs, sore necks. And bad habits as a result of the various compensations made for those injuries.

Injuries robbed Woods of some prime major championship time. He missed two major championships in 2008. Two more in 2011. Two in 2014. All four in 2016. All four in 2017.

Phil Mickelson missed exactly one major championship due to injury: he did not play in the 1994 Masters, because in early March of that year, he suffered a broken leg while skiing. He returned at the U.S. Open that year and missed just two majors through 2021: the 2009 Open, when he stayed home as his wife, Amy, battled breast cancer; and the 2017 U.S.

Open, when he chose to attend his daughter's high school graduation instead.

Unlike Tiger, Phil remained physically fit, which is ironic when you consider how often Woods chided Mickelson over the years for his, well, lack of fitness.

Phil might not have been the workout fiend that Tiger proved himself to be, but he gradually learned to take better care of himself. He worked with a trainer. Into his late forties and fifties, he remained amazingly flexible. A bout with psoriatic arthritis that he announced in 2010 started him on a better path, one that he struggled to remain on at times.

Perhaps some of what Phil did might have been viewed as comical, often due to his own self-deprecation. The 2018 Mizzen and Main commercial, in which he dances, is a great example of his flexibility. A fasting program that he implemented at various times of the year might have been seen as Phil being Phil, but it worked. The Coffee For Wellness brand he founded might have raised eyebrows.

But Mickelson for a good bit of his career played with a long, flowing swing. Yes, at times he tried to shorten it for control. And he wanted to hit the ball far just like the next guy. And yet for various reasons, he never needed to deal with the number of physical ailments others encountered throughout a 30-year career.

"You can play golf for a lifetime and injury-free if you swing the club like Bobby Jones did, where it's a swinging motion rather than a violent movement," Mickelson said.

As Mickelson played into his mid-to-late forties, he never once gave into the idea that age would be a detriment.

"There is nothing I can't do now that I could do when I was in my thirties," Mickelson said in 2016, not long after parting ways with his swing coach of nine years, Butch Harmon. He brought on an Australian instructor, Andrew Getson, who was based in Arizona and got the recommendation of Phil's then-caddie Jim Mackay.

Sure, many things were different. The singular focus that young golfers have was often replaced by other priorities, such as family and, especially in Mickelson's case, business. He didn't practice as long, but experience taught him to get more out of his time hitting balls.

"I'm in better shape than I was years ago," he said. "I eat better. I work out better. I feel better. I wake up and feel better. In my case, I feel like age is just a number."

This clearly contrasted the stories surrounding Woods at the time. Woods' 40th birthday in late 2015 was met with considerable skepticism about his ability to be an effective golfer in the future, numerous surgeries—the most recent being another back procedure—potentially keeping him out indefinitely.

And yet, Mickelson flew through his 40th birthday in 2010 without any such discussion. Two months earlier, he'd won the Masters. At 43, he won the Open. And as Phil approached his 50th birthday in 2020, he was in better shape than he was 15 years earlier.

The results simply did not follow. Yes, Mickelson won a World Golf Championship event in 2018, defeating Justin Thomas in a playoff in Mexico City. That was his 43rd PGA Tour victory and it was his first since the Open in 2013. And he won again in 2019 at Pebble Beach, his 44th PGA Tour title.

Following that victory, he played 20 more times that year, with no top 10s and eight missed cuts.

In 2020, he played 18 times, with one second- and two third-place finishes and eight more missed cuts.

And in the early part of 2021, Mickelson played 10 times, with three missed cuts and no finish better than 21st at the Masters.

Then Kiawah happened.

TO SUGGEST ANYONE COULD HAVE PREDICTED WHAT OCCURRED at the 2021 PGA Championship is the stuff of a wild imagination. Phil Mickelson was on nobody's radar, and even if he was, he was a tiny blip in the distance, a Hall of Famer whose status as a past champion made him eligible despite any fall in form. The Friday before the championship, he received a special invitation from the USGA to play in the U.S. Open in his hometown of San Diego the following month.

It was an invitation Mickelson at one time threatened not to accept. In March, during the week of the Arnold Palmer Invitational, Mickelson fell outside of the top 100 in the world for the first time in 28 years. He had been there for a record 1,425 weeks.

Mickelson first entered the world rankings as an amateur in 1990 when he finished 19th at the Northern Telecom Tucson Open. That put him at 540th in the world. The following year, Mickelson won the same tournament as an amateur while a junior at Arizona State. He entered the top 100 in the summer of 1993 after capturing the International, his second PGA Tour victory.

Although he never reached No. 1 in the world, Mickelson was No. 2 for 270 weeks—all with Woods as No. 1.

Not being exempt for the U.S. Open for the first time in 30 years, Mickelson wanted to earn his way into the tournament where he finished second a record six times.

But Phil thought better of it and wisely accepted the invite. He was deserving. More than deserving. A former U.S. Amateur champion who captured five majors and remained competitive for so long deserved the pass. Nobody would argue it. And it was a nice story.

A bigger one was about to unfold.

Rounds of 70–69 saw Mickelson tied for the 36-hole lead at the wind-swept Ocean Course on Kiawah Island, South Carolina. The venue was the site of an epic U.S. victory over Europe in the 1991 Ryder Cup. It is also where Rory McIlroy won his second major championship in an eight-shot romp at the 2012 PGA.

But Phil in the lead?

Just two weeks earlier, Mickelson complained about focus issues that thwarted many of his opportunities. At the Wells Fargo Championship, he opened the tournament with a 64, only to follow with scores of 75, 76, and 76. In each of those three rounds, Mickelson hit it in the water at the par-3 17th hole. Surely that's not all down to swing mechanics.

With his 51st birthday in sight, Mickelson was keenly aware that men his age don't win majors. He was the first 50-plus golfer to hold the lead at any major since Fred Couples did it at the 2012 Masters and zeroing in on the task at hand could very well be a problem.

Because when you look at other aspects of Mickelson's game, age was hardly a factor.

While he might not have been as sharp as he was as a thirtysomething hotshot, he still was hanging with the best in the game.

Mickelson was averaging over 311 yards on the measured driving holes through two rounds and led the field in strokes gained tee to green, a statistic that combines driving distance, accuracy, and approach shots. He was also third in strokes gained off the tee.

That was impressive for someone who gives up some 20 years to a player such as Justin Thomas. Dustin Johnson, who was No. 1 in the world that week but missed the cut, was 14 years younger. McIlroy was 18 years younger.

So the physical skills remained, certainly enough to be competitive.

And there's this: Mickelson was in the World Golf Hall of Fame for nearly a decade. Until 2019, he did not miss a U.S. Ryder Cup or Presidents Cup since 1993. For some 25 years, he was ranked among the top 50 in the world.

"If he can keep it straight and hit it the way he's been hitting, he's going to be around on Sunday for sure," said Jason Day, who played with Mickelson and Pàdraig Harrington the first two rounds.

It was the mental side that even Phil has questioned, although the Kiawah course and all of its diabolical conditions might actually have been more beneficial than hindering.

"I wouldn't put it past him," said Harrington, the 2021 European Ryder Cup captain and three-time major winner. "In the position he is, I expect him to contend and I wouldn't put it past him being there at the end of the week, for sure.

"He has the bit between his teeth. I think he believes he can do it in these conditions, just like myself. Phil would find it easier to compete on this style of golf course in these conditions in a major tournament all the time. You can be patient on these courses, and obviously you've got to make a few birdies. But it suits somebody who is a player, somebody who is thinking."

Mickelson still loved the banter, loved the competition. That would seemingly be a prerequisite for greatness but is hardly a common trait among the elite. It's why careers fade away, why glory is fleeting.

Lefty never lost that passion, which is why he became the oldest major champion in the game's storied history.

Mickelson still acted like a kid. He took on players half his age and relished beating them, getting into their pockets, and then telling the world about it. And when the calendar kept turning, Mickelson never gave in to the clock on the wall, instead choosing to fight back and stay relevant.

And yet, there was bound to be a Phil-being-Phil moment.

It wasn't quite the same storyline that enveloped another major championship. The issue there was whether or not a beeper in his golf bag would go off at any moment, summoning him home.

But Mickelson requesting that a drone be removed from his line of flight when sizing up his second shot to the fourth hole at the Ocean Course during Saturday's third round put in perspective the longevity of his career.

Mickelson won a PGA Tour event as an amateur 30 years prior, one sponsored by a telecommunications company whose main business at the time was not cell phones, as they were barely a thing yet.

He contended at the 1999 U.S. Open when his wife, Amy, was due any minute, hence the beeper, a product virtually no longer in existence. (Their daughter, Amanda, was now out of college.)

At Kiawah, he was trying to become the game's oldest major champion, surpassing the record set by Julius Boros at the 1968 PGA when he was 48 years old.

And it was a drone that got his attention.

Faced with a 188-yard shot, Mickelson was distracted by the buzzing drone being used for the television broadcast. He backed off, summoned a technician in the fairway, and asked that he radio in help to have it removed.

While Mickelson ended up parring the hole, it was part of a wild scene that saw Kiawah Island tilt on its side as Phil birdied five of his first 10 holes to take a five-shot lead during the round.

And that's where reality seemingly jumped up to remind Mickelson that he was 50 and turned the second major championship of the year into a riveting spectacle, with major stalker Brooks Koepka ready to do bicep curls with another Wanamaker Trophy.

Mickelson made his first bogey in 21 holes after driving his ball into an awkward bunker, which necessitated a pitch out at the 12th. Phil left a long-range par putt on the lip and then watched as Louis Oosthuizen buried his birdie putt. The lead was just two. Then, after watching Oosthuizen rinse his tee shot at the 13th, Mickelson inexplicably hit a worse shot to drown his ball in the same hazard, leading to a double bogey. Game on.

"Even though it slipped a little bit today, and I didn't stay as focused and as sharp on a few swings, it's significantly better than it's been for a long time," said Mickelson, whose 2-under-par 70 was good for a one-shot lead over Koepka and a two-stroke advantage over Oosthuizen. "So I'm making a lot of progress, and I'll continue to work on that, and hopefully I'll be able to eliminate a couple of those loose swings tomorrow.

"Because I'm playing a lot better than the score is showing, and I think if I can just stay sharp tomorrow, I'll post a score that better reflects how I'm actually playing."

Mickelson had not contended in a major championship since the 2016 Open at Royal Troon where he finished second to Henrik Stenson—11 strokes ahead of third place. And he had not won a major in eight years, since he rallied for an all-world 66 in the final round at Muirfield in 2013.

That was seen as the crowning moment on top of his career, a fitting victory at the game's oldest championship, where Lefty never fared very well.

This? It was historic. Winning a major championship at age 50 could not be overstated. He was just the sixth player age 45 or older to win one of golf's biggest tournament and the first in his fifties.

Boros in 1968 was the previous oldest. Boros, who won three majors, felt a guy named Arnold Palmer breathing down his neck that day in San Antonio, trying to win what would be an elusive PGA Championship.

Staring at Phil was Koepka, who was amazingly in contention after playing just four official rounds heading into the PGA since the end of February. March knee surgery saw the four-time major winner doing more rehab than golf work, yet here he was again, with another major in sight, surely not worried about the guy who was 20 years older.

"It just feels good, feels normal," Koepka said. "It's what you're supposed to do, what you practice for. I'm right where I want to be, and we'll see how tomorrow goes. Just be within three of the lead going into the back nine and you've got a chance."

Koepka was going for his fifth major, Mickelson his sixth. Two players had not played in the final group of a major with at least four each since 1981. That would be Jack Nicklaus and Tom Watson at the Masters, where Watson prevailed.

Could Phil find the magic for one final round?

"It's Phil, right? It's theater," said Jordan Spieth. "It's pretty incredible. The guy's got four good rounds on any golf course in him, and no one would bet against that, and what he did in the wind the last two days [Thursday and Friday] with kind of the struggles, I think accuracy off the tee that's been kind of his biggest struggle . . . to carve into these fairways and to be gaining strokes on the field and to shoot those scores consistently in the conditions we had, I mean, that's pretty awesome."

If anything, Mickelson did not lack for confidence. Earlier in the week, he played a practice round with Steve Stricker as his partner against Zach Johnson and Will Zalatoris.

Stricker, the U.S. Ryder Cup team captain, noticed how well Mickelson was hitting the ball, and it became apparent quickly as they got an early lead in the match.

"Just to give you a glimpse of what Phil said, Phil and I were 3-up after 3, and he said it loud enough so everybody could hear: 'You know, Strick, I thought we'd be more up at this point,' and we were 3-up after 3," Stricker said, noting that was the largest lead they could possess. "Typical Phil.

"He came in here very focused, it looked like, and confident in what he was doing, and he drove it well with me and hit some great iron shots. So it's impressive when you've got a 50-year-old leading. But he's a special player. He's one of the greatest players in the game, in the history of the game, and he's kept his health and his flexibility, and he still hits it long enough to compete. It's pretty cool to see him up there at the top."

Cool, for sure.

Confidence? Never lacking with Phil.

None of that has wavered in the 30 years of change that has seen Mickelson go from baby-faced hotshot to elder statesman.

RICKIE FOWLER, 18 YEARS YOUNGER AND A FREQUENT PLAYING companion of Mickelson's, took in the euphoric scene in front of the Ocean Club clubhouse late Sunday as thousands of fans chanted the PGA champion's name. And he marveled at the accomplishment.

"It's the same way I talk about Tiger [Woods]: they're both golf nerds," Fowler said. "I got to spend some time with Phil the week before he went to [the Valspar Championship] and he was just playing a bunch of golf. Because we were in carts, you could play as many holes as you wanted. He just wanted to go play.

"The love is there. He obviously loves the game. And he still has the drive to go and chase. This is a pretty big deal. It's record breaking. Will it ever be done again? Who knows. But this is pretty special."

Jon Rahm, who won the U.S. Open a month later and saw Mickelson as something of a mentor, was another player taking in the scene as Phil finished.

"I love Phil," Rahm said. "And the Mickelson family is very close to me. They mean a lot. I'm not going to lie: with how windy it was out there and toward the end all I could say is, I cannot believe he's going to pull this off. Like I don't know if I told him this, but I will tell him straight up, if I would tell you like the last person I would put money on to win that week, Phil would be one of those. It would be down there. Just because of how long it is, how many drivers you need to hit, and how windy it is.

"Now I played with him on Monday, and he had a new driver that he was hitting really well, it was much more under control. And after Monday I could believe him putting on a good performance. But he hadn't been playing great golf, but that shows you the greatness of a great champion—it doesn't matter. When he got himself in that position after 36 holes, it was good old Phil. He got it going, at one point he had a big lead, and both Saturday and Sunday he was able to create a lead and defend it.

"It's unbelievable. At the age of 50, he's been playing on the PGA Tour for as long or longer than I've been alive. He still has that enthusiasm and that drive to become better and beat the best. And at his age, simply it hadn't happened."

Mickelson surpassed Boros as the oldest major champion. Tom Morris Sr. at 45 was the oldest to win the Open, during Andrew Johnson's presidency. Jack Nicklaus was considered ancient when he won the Masters at 46 in 1986. And Hale Irwin, in the tournament on a special exemption, won the U.S. Open in 1990 at age 45.

Those are outliers. Davis Love III was the last player to win on the PGA Tour past the age of 50, and he did that six years prior.

Nicklaus' victory at Augusta National was long considered the gold standard for out-of-nowhere wins, even though he didn't become the oldest major champion with the victory. He was the oldest Masters winner, however, and he outlasted a Hall of Fame list of players that includes Greg Norman, Tom Kite, Seve Ballesteros, Nick Price, and Tom Watson.

He also shot a back-nine 30 that included an eagle, five birdies, and a bogey for a final-round 65. That he produced that kind of magic on that kind of stage at that age against that field was and will continue to be understandably lauded.

Mickelson's victory, however, is no less epic. He didn't shoot the low final-day score, nor was it as dramatic. He was the 54-hole leader and carried the spotlight all weekend. Much of the world awaited a collapse that never occurred. And the magnitude of winning a major at age 50 in this era cannot be dismissed or ranked among the ordinary.

The game is too deep, the young players too seasoned, the physical skills too demanding for AARP members to remain factors. And yet here was Phil, finishing above them all, including Koepka, a seasoned major winner himself who seemed poised to steal Phil's moment.

"Worked harder is the deal," Mickelson said. "I just had to work harder physically to be able to practice as long as I wanted to, and I've had to work a lot harder to be able to maintain focus throughout a round. That's been the biggest challenge of late.

"My desire to play is the same. I've never been driven by exterior things. I've always been intrinsically motivated because I love to compete, I love playing the game. I love having opportunities to play against the best at the highest level. That's what drives me, and I think the belief that I could still do it inspired me to work harder. I just didn't see why it couldn't be done. It just took a little bit more effort."

Mickelson's 1-over-par 73 on Sunday produced its moments of glory and gory. He holed a sand shot on the fifth for a birdie; he hit a poor approach into the water on the 13th and made bogey. He hit a poor shot on the third hole and made bogey; but he blasted a drive on the seventh to set up a birdie.

He began the day with a one-shot lead over Koepka, seemed doomed after a shaky first hole that saw him lose that advantage, then took it back on the next hole. There were five multi-shot swings between Mickelson, Koepka, and Louis Oosthuizen in the first 10 holes.

But ultimately, Mickelson prevailed, helped by the fact that his closest pursuers were unable to avoid the pitfalls that the Ocean Course presented all week.

He even overcame two equipment malfunctions, one that saw his beloved 2-wood need to be replaced after its face caved in while Mickelson practiced Saturday night. Mickelson's 2-iron suffered the same fate while he warmed up Sunday, so he went to a 4-wood instead, one that he used several times off the tee.

The result was a nervy final round that saw him hit 7 of 14 fairways and 11 of 18 greens while seeing newfound success off the tee and in his iron game. Mickelson hadn't finished among the top 20 going back 17 events to the previous summer. And here he was holding the hardware.

"When you don't expect them, they are one of a kind," said Steve Loy, Mickelson's coach at Arizona State and his longtime agent. "I knew we would win a Masters. I knew he was going to win more than one major. I never dreamed he'd win the [British] Open [which he did in 2013 at Muirfield], and to come back and do this on this course, after we haven't had a great two years, it's heaven-sent.

"This is maybe his greatest win because of the golf course, the venue, the odds against him. It's breathtaking. I told him in a text this morning, I said, ' Phil, I'm getting too old for this, but you aren't. Let's get it done.'"

Given where Mickelson was just a few weeks earlier, this seemed all but a dream. He bogeyed two of the last three holes at Innisbrook to miss the cut at the Valspar Championship and was at a loss for words afterward. He suggested that week he was unsure if he would accept a special exemption to the U.S. Open at Torrey Pines if offered one.

Then he saw those struggles at the Wells Fargo Championship, where he dropped all the way to 69th. Trying to take on Kiawah's Ocean Course, where the wind whipped off the ocean every day, appeared futile.

But while others withered in the wind, Mickelson stood tall, hanging near the lead after the first round and moving to the top after 36 holes.

"He never doubted himself," said Tim Mickelson, Phil's brother and his caddie since 2017. "His will and desire to win is as high as it's ever been in my opinion. He just loves golf. He loves golf. I mean, when he's at home, he's still playing almost every single day, sometimes 36. He's grinding. It never stops for him."

Things did stop for a moment for Phil when he was engulfed by the masses while trying to play the 18th hole. Still with work to be done, Mickelson got caught up in the crowd first as he surveyed his approach to the green, and lost in the madness was Phil at his best, still needing to execute. A mistake there, and he could allow Koepka back into the tournament with a birdie. But Phil hit the perfect shot out of the rough onto the green, from where he would two-putt for the two-shot victory.

It was a rare scene: a champion being celebrated in such a manner. Phil, always a man of the people, was among them for a few harrowing moments, swept up in the adulation. What a cool memory, cool scene, cool ending. "It's a moment I'll always cherish," he said.

Tiger won his sixth major when he won the 2001 Masters, completing the Tiger Slam with Mickelson there in an uncomfortable front-row seat. He was just 25, half the age of Mickelson when he notched his sixth. Their careers were wildly different in that aspect, but Mickelson certainly wasn't lamenting his fate at this point in life. This was a monumental victory, one to be celebrated, cherished.

Now a six-time major winner, joining Lee Trevino and Nick Faldo at that number, Mickelson's legacy was already secure. But we said the same thing eight years prior when he swept out of Muirfield with the Claret Jug.

Phil still clearly loved the chase.

21

A Fascinating Rivalry

On the morning of February 23, 2021, Tiger Woods was in Southern California and on his way to the second day of shooting for a documentary series he was doing as part of an endorsement deal with Discovery/*Golf Digest*. He arrived in the Los Angeles area on the weekend to be present for the final two rounds of the Genesis Invitational, the PGA Tour event his foundation runs. And then he was to stay an extra two days for his filming obligation.

Woods was recovering from a December back procedure and much of the focus on him involved whether or not he'd be fit to play the Masters, which was six weeks away. He couldn't firmly answer the question when CBS's Jim Nantz asked him about his status during the final-round broadcast of the Genesis Invitational. Woods was not yet back to hitting full shots.

Two days later, Woods' golf career lay in shambles, his golf game of little importance.

Something went terribly wrong as he traversed a winding road on his way to Rolling Hills Country Club just after seven in the morning, according to a 22-page report released by the Los Angeles County Sherriff's Department some six weeks after the accident.

The cause was "driving at a speed unsafe for the road conditions and the inability to negotiate the curve of the roadway." According to the report, Woods was traveling at more than 82 in a 45-mile-per-hour zone, and it was unclear whether he attempted to negotiate the curve.

Instead of staying in his lane as the road curved to the right, Woods went straight into a median, struck a curb, knocked down a wooden sign, and drove into opposite lanes before hitting a tree and rolling over in the Genesis GV80 SUV provided to him by the Genesis tournament. The accident occurred in the Rolling Hills Estates south of downtown Los Angeles.

Woods suffered broken bones in his right leg and injuries to his right foot and ankle.

Among some of the findings in the report, Woods mistakenly believed he was in Florida when he was interviewed at a Los Angeles area hospital following the crash.

An empty pharmaceutical bottle with no label or indication of what was inside it was found in a backpack at the scene. Wood's blood pressure was "too low to administer any type of pain medication" shortly after the crash, likely due to shock.

Woods was not issued a citation because there were no independent witnesses and no officers who observed the collision sequence, according to Sheriff Alex Villanueva.

The sheriff also said his department did not try to examine Woods' blood for evidence of medication because there was not strong enough reason for it.

The report was issued on the eve of the 2021 Masters, where Woods' absence was notable. Just two years earlier, he captured an unlikely fifth Masters victory and 15th major title. At the 2020 Masters played in November due to its postponement in the wake of the coronavirus pandemic, Woods was well out of contention, having made a 10 at the par-3 12th hole (his highest score ever at Augusta National) before responding to birdie five of the last six holes—just one more example of his career-long resilience.

Those were the last official, competitive holes of golf Woods has played to date.

In a statement released the day of the police findings, Woods said he was "so grateful to both of the good Samaritans who came to assist me and called 911" following the crash.

"I am also thankful to the LASD deputies and L.A. firefighter/paramedics, especially L.A. Sheriff's Deputy Carlos Gonzalez and LAFD

Engine Co. 106, Fire Paramedics Smith and Gimenez, for helping me so expertly at the scene and getting me safely to the hospital.

"I will continue to focus on my recovery and family, and thank everyone for the overwhelming support and encouragement I've received throughout this very difficult time."

A few weeks later, Woods posted a photo of himself in his backyard, on crutches, wearing a cast and a boot. For months afterward, there were no public updates on his health.

IN THE HOURS AND DAYS AFTER THE CRASH, GOLF UNDERSTANDABLY was not on anyone's mind. Woods' accident was worldwide news, and one of the most famous athletes of his generation saw his well-being as the ultimate concern. If it wasn't evident already from the horrific photos of his smashed car, the release of the final police report made clear how lucky Woods was to have survived. His ability to resume normal activity and achieve quality of life goals seemed far more important than anything to do with a golf career.

Many wondered why Woods was driving at all, why he didn't hire someone to do the task, why someone didn't pick him up, why one of his friends or his agent or any number of other people wasn't behind the wheel that morning.

That simply was not Tiger. As famous as he is, Woods often drove himself, whether it was near his home or to a tournament site with his caddie sitting in the passenger seat. In 2019, when the Golf Writers Association of America was honoring Woods at a dinner on the eve of the Masters, I greeted him outside of the Savannah Rapids Pavilion, a venue just outside of Augusta, Georgia, before he was due inside. Woods drove himself from his rental home, parked, got out of the car, and walked toward the entrance without being bothered.

While I knew this to be his habit, it certainly was striking to see a person of his stature and fame arriving at a public venue alone. I even good-naturedly chided him about it, and he simply smiled. Both his agent, Mark Steinberg, and publicist, Glenn Greenspan, attended. They didn't give him a ride because Woods didn't want one.

That memory was vivid as the news of the crash circulated and details began to emerge. What I viewed as something uniquely neat about Tiger—a celebrity who didn't want a driver—all of a sudden seemed sad. Perhaps things would have been different that day if someone whose job it was to get people from one place to another had been driving.

And yet, as it relates to his golf career, it was a brutal reminder of the fact that an athlete we came to admire and enjoy was not going to go on entertaining us forever. The days of glory were predominantly in the past, and the fleeting moments of greatness would be rare. We didn't want any end to be something so scary and serious, however.

That is why Phil Mickelson's win at the 2021 PGA Championship just a few months after Woods' accident stirred all those memories. It was a remarkable achievement, but likely a lightning bolt that was more of a one-time return to prominence than any sort of resurgence.

At 50, Phil was unlikely to wow us with his greatness for much longer, and the fact that he summoned—perhaps—one last great victory is a tribute to his longevity and perseverance.

Such a win raised hopes that Mickelson might yet make one more U.S. Ryder Cup team, extending a streak that began in 1995 to 13 straight. Several of his potential teammates were not even born when Phil went 3–0 for captain Lanny Wadkins in a losing team effort at Oak Hill Country Club in Rochester, New York. Even Woods was still a year away from turning pro.

But Mickelson could not maintain a level of play worthy of selection, and so for the first time, he joined the U.S. squad as a vice captain, this time at Whistling Straits in Wisconsin, where he assumed the role of elder statesman, regaling the players with his foibles and fables.

"Phil obviously is a great storyteller," said Collin Morikawa, who at age 24 was playing in his first Ryder Cup. "I don't know if he's telling the truth at this point. You get to a certain age and you kind of just make stuff up, and I have a hard time believing some of the stuff I heard, but it is what it is."

That might be a line Tiger would use, and the hope all along in the weeks following his accident was that he could join the other vice captains in the team room at Whistling Straits to lend his voice and expertise to captain Steve Stricker. Woods and Mickelson collaborating behind the scenes as assistants would have been quite the twist.

But when Stricker announced his final vice-captain roster, which included Mickelson, Woods' name was not among them.

"He's just not able to be there at this time," Stricker said in early September of 2021. "He's progressing nicely, but Whistling Straits is a tough place to get around. He's already been helping and will continue to."

And so it became reality that for the first time since the 1993 Ryder Cup—the last won by an American team in Europe—neither Woods nor Mickelson would be competing in a U.S. Cup competition.

MICKELSON WAS A SOPHOMORE IN COLLEGE THE FIRST TIME I HAD the opportunity to interview him. He was already so famous and so accomplished that newspaper reporters who covered golf were calling him for interviews. He was about to embark on the NCAA Championship at the Innisbrook Resort in Palm Harbor, Florida. Not only was his Arizona State team among the favorites to win the team title but he was also among the favorites to win the individual crown.

"I like being considered as one of the contenders," Mickelson said during that phone call. "It's more of a positive. Plus, it's a neat honor to be called the NCAA champ. I'd like to keep it for another year. I enjoy it."

Quintessential Phil. More than 30 years later, those words sum him up perfectly. He was good and he knew it. A year earlier, he became the rare freshman to win an NCAA title, joining Ben Crenshaw (1971), Curtis Strange (1974), and Billy Ray Brown (1982) as the only players to do so.

And despite the lure of professional golf, Mickelson—as he said he would then—stayed through four years of college, despite winning a professional event as an amateur the following year.

Mickelson did win that NCAA title, and Arizona captured the team championship. Those were heady times for Phil, for some perhaps the highlight of a playing career. But he was just getting started. Actually, he had started long prior, winning everything and anything. That summer he won the U.S. Amateur. As a senior, he won the NCAAs again, just a short time before turning pro at the 1992 U.S. Open, beginning a Hall of Fame career.

Predicting pro success seemed easy. But 30-plus years' worth?

For all of Woods' accomplishments, Mickelson might have started and ended (if the end has even occurred) more spectacularly. And that is saying something because Woods came upon the scene with enormous fanfare. The first time I ever saw him in person was at the 1995 Masters. He was 19, a freshman at Stanford, and competing in his first major championship, having earned an invitation because he'd won the U.S. Amateur the previous summer.

Woods was already a star in the making. He conducted a pre-tournament news conference that was packed. He had practice rounds set up with the likes of Nick Faldo and Greg Norman. He played the Par-3 Contest with Gary Player, who afterward said, "Certain players you look at them once and you see something. As soon as I saw Tiger Woods swing today, I thought, 'Man, that young guy has got it.'"

It was difficult not to get caught up in the mania. Woods was amazing to watch, with that willowy, skinny frame that somehow produced high, piercing tee shots that flew incredible distances. Tiger pounded drives effortlessly, and even as an amateur without the skills he would eventually refine, he routinely hit shots that left seasoned pros gasping. His caddie, Augusta veteran Tommy "Burnt Biscuits" Bennett, guided him around, and it was impressive.

In his first Masters, Woods led the field in driving distance at 311.1 yards. He struggled to score, shooting rounds of 72–72–77–72. It was the first time he made a 36-hole cut in a PGA Tour event after missing in his first seven attempts, and he was low amateur.

A year later, Jack Nicklaus and Arnold Palmer played a practice round with Woods. "Both Arnold and I agree that you could take my Masters and his Masters and add them together and this kid should win more than that," Jack said.

Since Nicklaus (six) and Palmer (four) combined to win 10 Masters, it was quite the statement. And while some viewed it as hyperbole, Nicklaus was simply trying to make clear how impressed he and Palmer were at the type of golf they witnessed.

"This kid is the most fundamentally sound golfer I've ever seen at any age," Nicklaus said. "I don't know if he's ready to win or not, but he will be the favorite here for the next 20 years. If he isn't, there's something wrong."

Jack was not a bad prognosticator. Over the next 20 years, Woods had 13 top 6 finishes and four victories. He added the fifth win in 2019. But that same year that Nicklaus heaped his green jacket praise, Woods missed the cut—the last time he did so through 2020. Woods made a career out of chasing the Golden Bear, and it was an incredible journey, with plenty of stops and starts along the way.

ALL OF THIS TENDS TO MAKE US VIEW THE WOODS-MICKELSON rivalry as something from the past. Who knows if it will continue in any form, but to this point it has been a glorious ride through more than two decades of highs and lows.

Claude "Butch" Harmon Jr. already enjoyed a front-row seat to golf history before ever working with Woods or Mickelson. He came from a family of instructors, most notably his father, Claude Harmon, who in 1948 won the Masters and held prestigious club pro jobs at Winged Foot in New York and Seminole in Florida.

Among the many players Harmon worked with, coached, instructed, counseled over the years were Greg Norman, Ernie Els, John Daly, Stewart Cink, Fred Couples, Darren Clarke, Davis Love III, and Lee Westwood.

But topping the list: Woods and Mickelson.

Nobody else could say that.

Harmon was Woods' instructor from 1993 through 2002, a period that saw Woods emerge as an amateur star, turn pro, win the Masters by 12, transform his swing, and go on one of the most unprecedented runs in the game's history, winning seven of 11 major championships and eight overall.

A few years later, Mickelson hired Harmon and almost immediately won the 2007 Players Championship. He won the Masters in 2010 and later the Open at Muirfield when he was 43, considered at the time his crowning achievement. Harmon was with him through 2015—or a total of 17 years between the two players.

What a journey. And there are a million and one stories he undoubtedly has stored away, some of which he cannot tell.

One of his favorites, one that he is fond of sharing, speaks to the unique relationship that Harmon witnessed between this generation's two biggest golf stars.

It occurred at the 2009 Masters, where for one of the rare times, Tiger and Phil were grouped together during the final round of a major championship. Although they were tied for 10th and seven strokes back of the leaders, both players made a charge that day that left the Augusta National pines rattling.

They eventually came up short, but their duel was a big part of the overall picture that day, another example of their allure, the story within the story.

And Harmon was witness to a scene that unfolded prior to the round.

"Phil liked to have two practice sessions at the majors," Harmon said. "So we went out early and worked on the range, and afterward he invited me up to the Champions Locker Room before he was going to go out again. We get up there, and there's only like three tables in there. One of them has a sandwich on it. So we go to another table. And then Phil takes off his pants. Says he doesn't want them to get wrinkled. And in walks Tiger. It's Tiger's sandwich sitting there and Phil's standing there in his underwear.

"Tiger goes, 'Dude, what are you doing?'"

"I don't wear cheap Nike shit like you do. Tom Ford makes my pants," Phil said. "I don't want them to get wrinkled, and plus when I kick your ass today I want to be wearing nice pants."

And Tiger says, "I don't care about your damn pants; cover your shit up. I just want to eat my sandwich."

"It was all in fun," Harmon chuckled. "And they did a good job of needling each other. And they did that a lot. And there was tremendous respect. Phil always said he credits Tiger for motivating him."

Were they truly rivals?

"You bet," Harmon said. "Look at what Phil has done. He's won more than anybody in the Tiger era. Nobody's come close to that. Tiger elevated him and he always said as much. They had some rough times early on and their rivalry was difficult at times. Tiger never said much about Phil, but he knew he was there. He knew how talented he was and how good he could be."

―――――

IT IS CERTAINLY FAIR TO ARGUE THAT TIGER HAD NO RIVAL, THAT perhaps his greatest rival was history. Almost from the day he came upon the scene, certainly from the time he won the 1997 Masters and captured his first major championship, he always seemed destined to be linked with Nicklaus and his 18 major titles rather than Phil, who for years struggled to win any.

Woods turned pro four-plus years after Mickelson. And he won eight major titles before Mickelson won his first. Rivalry? Sure, back then, nobody was on his level.

But as Harmon said, who did better than Phil in Tiger's time? Vijay Singh produced a great run in the early 2000s, winning a total of 34 PGA Tour titles in his career including three major championships. He won nine times in 2004 when Woods won just twice. Ernie Els was a worldwide winner, with 19 PGA Tour titles, dozens more around the globe, and four majors. Both players stood up to Woods as well or better than Mickelson at times.

But neither enjoyed the full arc quite like Phil, who posted nine PGA Tour wins prior to Tiger's arrival, then added 36 more, including all six major championships. In four of Mickelson's major wins—the 2005 PGA, the 2006 Masters, the 2010 Masters, and the 2013 Open—Woods contended, frustrated that he could not overcome Lefty.

"I think Tiger viewed everybody as a rival," said Tom Lehman, the 1996 Open winner—where Woods was low amateur, the catalyst to him turning pro—and also the 2006 U.S. Ryder Cup team captain. "He embraced the rivalry with Phil and was looking for rivals.

"It just so happened that for maybe 10 years there was nobody in the history of the game who played like him. Nobody could compare. He knew it and everybody else knew it. It's hard to have rivalries if nobody is better. Duke and Carolina probably are a 10–10 draw if they play 20 times. That's the essence of a rivalry.

"And as great as Phil is—one of the top 10 players in the history of the game, and I view his game highly—he wasn't as good as Tiger. Tiger knew it and Phil knew it. And that's saying a lot because Phil was better than everybody else. It's just that Tiger was that good.

"I would never diminish Phil Mickelson's skills. I've seen him hit shots and do things on a golf course that I thought were impossible. The courage to hit shots. And he's a larger-than-life character. Immensely successful. And we're comparing him to the best guy who ever lived."

That is what makes Mickelson's record all the more impressive. He began his career with incredible fanfare, saw Woods come on the scene and dominate like no one since Nicklaus, garner every golf headline, and win at unprecedented levels. Phil had to sit by and take it as everyone questioned what was taking him so long.

But Mickelson slowly chipped away. He was never going to match Woods in total victories or majors. He did, however, become more of an adversary, bringing their record in head-to-head group encounters more even—with the help of Harmon, who knew better than anyone how best to deal with the Tiger dynamic inside the ropes. And he needed to overcome some of the disdain that Tiger originally had for him.

Prior to the 2002 Ryder Cup in England, most of the competitors played at the WGC-American Express Invitational in Ireland. It was purposely scheduled then to allow players a big payday in close proximity to the Ryder Cup.

The U.S. players were to take a charter to The Belfry early Monday morning of Ryder Cup week, and they were waiting for a bus to take them to the airport. Mickelson produced a couple of gloves and baseballs and was killing time by playing catch with other players and caddies. Woods could only stand by in wonder. "What the fuck does he think he's doing?" Tiger said to no one in particular, his disdain apparent.

Who else would think to bring a baseball glove and ball? That's Phil. Not Tiger.

And so it went for years and years. Woods took things seriously, Mickelson not always so much. It simply showcased a difference in their personalities.

"They were both in the prime of their careers and both trying to win majors and golf tournaments," said former Tour player Chris Riley, who was a teammate of Woods and Mickelson at the 2004 Ryder Cup. "I never saw anything other than they were super competitive people who were trying to win golf tournaments. You don't expect them to be buddies, right? The better the deal Tiger got, the better the deal Phil got. They were definitely not friends."

That 2004 Ryder Cup might have been their lowest point, and that was not of their own doing. Putting them together as partners during that timeframe was probably a mistake, although as U.S. captain Hal Sutton pointed out, why could the two best players of the era not get along for the good of the Ryder Cup?

And ultimately, winning hammers all—personalities and grievances be damned. Woods and Mickelson's animosity toward one another at that time surely should not have stood in the way of the overall objective, right?

That was a time, however, when their rivalry was at its zenith. Of the 12 major championships played from 2004 through 2006, Woods and Mickelson combined to win seven of them. They traded green jackets in Augusta National's Butler Cabin during that time. They racked up numerous victories.

Off the course issues, injuries, family illnesses—all of it served to temper some of the rancor as time passed. Perspective helped, too. So did the knowledge that as they grew older, appreciation for each other's success only served to highlight their own. And a career-long nemesis for both—the Ryder Cup—served to bring them closer for the greater good.

It is only fitting that both players may have saved their best for last.

When Mickelson won the 2021 PGA Championship at Kiawah, becoming at 50 the oldest major champion in the game's history, it was difficult not to think back to Woods' 2019 win at the Masters, another remarkable and unlikely achievement.

The tournaments were unique in so many ways, from completely different players who played in them to the complications those players overcame, to the venues at which the two triumphed.

And it's fair to wonder: which victory was more astonishing?

Tiger winning the Masters at age 43, just two years removed from spinal fusion surgery and a litany of back problems, capturing a major title for the first time in 11 years and beating back several of the game's up-and-coming stars?

Or Phil winning the PGA Championship at age 50 on a brutish windy course having shown virtually no form over the previous two seasons, again holding off a slew of young stars, including one who was built to win major championships?

No matter how that argument skews, both players can claim an unlikely revival, a resounding victory to—possibly—cap off their careers and only add to their legacies.

Just like they did during their prime, Woods and Mickelson lifted golf from niche to mainstream, from the hard-core golf zealots to the occasional hackers to those who simply appreciate sports at its highest level.

For most of the previous decade, Tiger and Phil were still a huge part of the pre-tournament conversation, regardless of the state of their games. But deep down, who really felt they would—or could—win another major title again? It was certainly possible, but it was far more probable that their best moments, their best memories, were in the past.

Taken on their own, both those major wins were simply too ridiculous to comprehend.

As the Masters dawned in 2019, Woods certainly was trending in the right direction. He won the previous fall at the Tour Championship for his 80th PGA Tour victory. But it was a 30-player field. He was unable to cross the line at the Open and the PGA in 2018 when he had chances, although his high finishes were impressive enough. Heading to Augusta National, Woods played nicely but didn't contend down the stretch in any stroke-play tournaments. And considering where he had been two years prior, you'd never fathom he'd be standing on the first tee at Augusta National, let alone win. "The truth is, I thought I was done," Woods said.

When Woods began his comeback at an unofficial event in December of 2017, he was ranked outside of the top 1,000 in the world. (He made it all the way back to fifth in the world by the summer of 2019.)

Four events later, he was contending at the Valspar Championship and tying for second in March of 2018. Just a week earlier, Mickelson won in Mexico, his first victory since his 2013 Open win.

"I texted him when he was playing at Valspar that it felt like it was a different time continuum because I found myself pulling so hard for him," Mickelson said that spring. "It was unusual. And I find that I want him to play well, and I'm excited to see him play so well."

For all their success, Woods and Mickelson achieved their Hall of Fame status in wildly different ways.

Woods won eight majors before Mickelson won his first and captured 14 by the age of 32. His first major title, the Masters, came in his first start in a major as a pro. Mickelson didn't win his first major, also the Masters, until he was 33 after going 0-for-46.

Tiger endured injury woes, his body breaking down repeatedly, causing him to miss a total of 14 major championships from 2008 through 2017. Phil stayed healthy, missing two majors well into his career due to family obligations.

Both players seemed destined to win late in their careers, Woods because his game remained strong if he could just stay healthy, Mickelson because his free-flowing swing and lack of physical problems allowed him to continue to hit the ball tremendous lengths despite his age.

Mickelson always believed he enjoyed an advantage because the swing he employed over the years was not the violent, body-breaking move that so many young players in the game embraced.

And yet, while he bombed his drives into oblivion, he was unable to deliver with much frequency. His PGA title was just his third since winning the 2013 Open, and he went five years without a victory following that win in Scotland. Along the way, he suffered one of his most difficult defeats, a second-place finish at Royal Troon to Henrik Stenson in 2016, where Mickelson opened with a 63, went nearly shot for shot with the Swede, and beat everyone else by 11 strokes—but still came up three short.

That was the last time he contended in a major championship until Kiawah, where even Phil's mom and dad, Mary and Phil Sr., would have been excused if they did not give him a chance. He was ranked 115th in the world, the lowest since he was climbing the chart in his early days as pro.

Out of nowhere, there was Phil on the leaderboard, tied after 36 holes, leading through 54, playing the final round with the current era's major tough guy, Brooks Koepka, who is 20 years his junior.

After a shaky start, Mickelson put aside his "Phil the Thrill" mantra of his younger days and played smart, efficient golf. He let others make the mistakes. And when he needed it, Mickelson unleashed a 366-yard drive on Kiawah's par-5 16th hole—the longest of the week.

As he played the last hole with a two-shot lead, Mickelson was swarmed by the masses in a momentarily scary scene that reminded one of Woods' Tour Championship victory in 2018 at East Lake.

An aging champion summoning his powers again as the golf world celebrated in unison, chanting his name, Phil all but suffocated amid the humid air and fire-breathing revelers and still had the wherewithal to hit a tricky shot out of the rough and onto the green.

"Truly inspirational to see @PhilMickelson do it again at 50 years of age," Tiger tweeted. "Congrats!!!!!!!"

Woods was still on crutches at the time, a harsh reminder of the injuries he suffered from the horrific car crash he endured three months earlier, the ones for which the entire golf world mourned.

Surely it brought him back to his own unlikely victory, the one celebrated by golfers near and far. The outpouring of support from around the sports world—not just inside the confines of golf—was an endearing and enduring result for both players. If Tiger were capable at the time, it is quite obvious he would have been out beating balls that evening, just so he could enhance his opportunity to beat Phil the next time.

For the time, it was not possible; if only we could wish it to be so in the future. Nothing would be better than a comeback of any sort, with no expectations, simply adulation. There is no question Mickelson would welcome that, too.

Tiger offered a glimmer of hope when he posted a video just prior to Thanksgiving 2021 that lasted three seconds and with the caption: "Making progress." He took one swing, hitting a short iron while wearing a compression sock on his right leg. The Twitter post exploded on social media.

On November 30, Woods conducted his first news conference since the crash. He was at his Hero World Challenge event in the Bahamas, and struck both a positive and somber tone. Positive in that he seemed at peace, that he was walking, thankful to be alive, happy to have a quality of life, suggesting he would attempt some sort of comeback.

But the somberness came when he acknowledged that such a return would be arduous.

"I don't foresee this leg ever being what it used to be," he said. "I'll never have the back what it used to be and the clock's ticking. I'm getting older, I'm not getting any younger. All that combined means a full schedule and a full practice schedule and the recovery that would take to do that . . . no, I don't have any desire to do that."

Woods suggested he could summon the strength to try and prepare for a few tournaments a year, in the manner of another Hall of Famer who was also involved in a serious car crash: Ben Hogan. "There's no reason I can't do that and feel ready," he said.

"It's great to see Tiger swinging a golf club again," Mickelson wrote on Twitter. "I know he can't stand me holding a single record so I'm guessing HE wants to be the oldest to ever win a major. I'll just say this. BRING IT!"

It seemed, after all the tumult, after all the coolness, after all the times that Tiger and Phil could never see eye to eye, they had reached common ground. But it didn't take long for that foundation of fondness to show cracks. And by the end of 2022 it had completely crumbled.

There were no such battles to take place on the course, save for one. Woods and Mickelson played in the same tournament just once, both missing the cut at the Open at St. Andrews. It was remarkable that Woods was even there, having somehow returned to play in three major championships far sooner than anyone could dream following that toll the car crash took.

Mickelson missed the Masters and the PGA Championship, a stunning situation due to his outspoken comments about the PGA Tour and its "greed," his flirtation with the upstart LIV Golf League, and his eventual signing of a guaranteed contract well in excess of $100 million. Mickelson took a four-month hiatus (and during that time was suspended by the PGA Tour), returning for LIV Golf's first event in June outside of London and then playing the U.S. Open—which Woods missed—the following week.

At the Home of Golf in Scotland, Woods made it clear that he was no fan of LIV Golf, that he felt the disruptor was a negative for the game. Mickelson, meanwhile, was touting the new format and its appeal for young people and the fact that top players were being rewarded for their value.

In other words, the rivalry continued to thrive—and it had taken on a fascinating new twist.

ACKNOWLEDGMENTS

· ·

The transcription service ASAP Sports lists approximately 1,654 interviews that Tiger Woods conducted from the time he turned pro in 1996 through 2020, all of them saved for reference. Another service, Tee-Scripts, counts 88 Woods interviews.

During his time as a pro starting in 1992, Phil Mickelson did 1,505 transcribed interviews through 2021, according to ASAP, and another 92 with Tee-Scripts.

Those numbers don't count other companies that were around to transcribe various formal interviews over the years. Nor do they include the random one-on-ones, television sit-downs, radio interviews, podcasts, media scrums, walk-and-talks, and all manner of ways in which two of the game's greatest players dealt with the media.

Mickelson was always viewed as the more media-friendly of the two players, and to a large extent that is true. But Woods did far more interviews, and suffered far more blowback if he skipped. And he rarely did. There are exceptions, but for the most part, Woods stood in front of the microphones and notepads and answered the questions on good days and bad. Perhaps not always to our satisfaction, but he was there nonetheless. Same for Mickelson, although on a bit smaller scale.

I was fortune to develop a good relationship with both players. Sure, there were some tense moments, examples of disagreement. It's inevitable in the media world, and we make our share of double bogeys, too. But for all the scrutiny Tiger and Phil endured over the years, I was lucky to have time with them, get a glimpse into their worlds, listen to their views on various topics, and be afforded some access that they were not always so keen to give. And for that, I am forever thankful.

Thanks, too, goes to Tiger's longtime agent, Mark Steinberg, as well as his former public relations guru, Glenn Greenspan, who resisted the urge to block my number; and same, too, for Phil's longtime agent (and onetime golf coach), Steve Loy, and his former publicist and longtime golf writer, T. R. Reinman.

Golf allows for lengthy careers, and so it is that golf fans—sports fans—have been aware of Woods and Mickelson for the better part of 30 years. They started accumulating trophies as kids, added them through their junior and amateur days, and kept on going into mega-multimillion-dollar success as pros. It doesn't take much for a conversation about either one of them to evolve into whether you were a Tiger guy, a Phil guy, both, or neither; whether you felt they were rivals or not; which major victory was the best; which one got away. There are so many facets to their stories.

And yet had it not been for the encouragement from longtime friends and colleagues Gene Wojciechowski and Ian O'Connor, this project would have never happened—at least not by me. Authors of several books themselves, they pushed and prodded and coached and cajoled and kept telling me I was more than equipped to pull this off. O'Connor's book, *Arnie & Jack: Palmer, Nicklaus, and Golf's Greatest Rivalry,* served as a perfect guide. And when the idea first came about for a book on the Tiger and Phil rivalry, I had no bigger support than what I received from Gene and Ian, and I will likely pay for that forever.

Other authors who provided great counsel and insight were Michael Bamberger, Rick Reilly, and John Strege, whose 1997 book *Tiger* is an excellent read and the source of remarkable information made even more so because it all came before Woods won his first major championship.

ESPN road colleagues Kevin Van Valkenburg, Mark Schlabach, and Michael Collins have been there through numerous Tiger and Phil moments. As were behind-the-scenes TV maestros Malinda Adams, Eric Lundsten, and Jim Witalka, whose roles are invaluable.

And a big shout-out to my man Jason Sobel, ESPN.com's first golf editor who started with no staff, got stuck with me, then became my golf-writing colleague.

Among the many books that provided background and reporting information for this book were biographies of Woods (*Tiger* by John Strege and *Tiger Woods* by Jeff Benedict and Armen Keteyian); Mickelson's book on his 2004 Masters victory (*One Magical Sunday*); the story of Earl Woods, Tiger's father (*His Father's Son* by Tom Callahan); the inside view from one of Tiger's coaches (*The Big Miss* by Hank Haney); the recap of Tiger's time following his 2017 back surgery through his 2019 Masters victory (*The Second Life of Tiger Woods* by Michael Bamberger); the year after Tiger's 2008 knee surgery that culminated with his biggest personal crisis (*Unplayable* by Robert Lusetich); and the story of Tiger's longtime caddie (*Out of the Rough* by Steve Williams).

Colleagues and friends who offered insight and guidance over the years include Jeff Babineau, Tommy Bonk, Mark Cannizzaro, Jay Coffin, James Corrigan, Karen Crouse, Jaime Diaz, Steve DiMeglio, Craig Dolch, Larry Dorman, Steve Elling, Mick Elliott, Doug Ferguson, Hank Gola, Will Gray, Ron Green Jr., Rex Hoggard, John Huggan, Ron Kroichick, Ryan Lavner, Derek Lawrenson, Tod Leonard, Todd Lewis, Robert Lusetich, Jim McCabe, Pete McDaniel, Randy Mell, Alex Miceli, Scott Michaux, Ewan Murray, Tim Rosaforte, Geoff Shackelford, Len Shapiro, Dave Shedloski, Glenn Sheeley, Alan Shipnuck, Mark Soltau, Art Spander, Wright Thompson, Gary Van Sickle, and many more.

A special thanks to editing and fact-checking life-savers Julie Bennett and Ben Everill. And to my photographer friends Scott Halleran, Sam Greenwood, and Al Messerschmidt.

And I can't thank enough all the various players, caddies, tournament officials, friends, family, coaches, and numerous others who gave their time to be interviewed for this book.

Unless otherwise noted, the material in this book is the result of my own interviews, research, and coverage of past golf events, including all 21 of the major championships won by Woods and Mickelson.

Finally, thanks to my editor at St. Martin's Press, Pete Wolverton, who kept steering me in the right direction, as well as his assistant, Lily Cronig, who rescued me from various technology struggles. And my agent, Susan Canavan, who knows a thing or two about sports rivalries and was the perfect person to pitch this project.

INDEX

· · · · · · · ·

ESPN

Sports Illustrated golf writer BOB HARIG, formerly at ESPN and the *Tampa Bay Times*, has covered Tiger and Phil since the very beginning of each of their careers and has had dozens of one-on-one interviews with each of them. He holds degrees in journalism and history from Indiana University and is an active member of the Golf Writers Association of America (GWAA). He lives in Florida.